BANJO ROOTS AND BRANCHES

MUSIC IN AMERICAN LIFE

A list of books in the series appears at the end of this book.

Banjo Roots and Branches

Edited by
ROBERT B. WINANS

UNIVERSITY OF
ILLINOIS PRESS
Urbana, Chicago, and Springfield

Publication of this book was made possible in part through a
donation from the Uncle Shlomo's Brooklyn Kids Fund for Music,
dedicated to ensuring that Shlomo Pestcoe's generous spirit will
continue to enrich us with the music he so loved to share, and by a
grant from the L. J. and Mary C. Skaggs Folklore Fund.

Library of Congress Cataloging-in-Publication Data
Names: Winans, Robert B.
Title: Banjo roots and branches / edited by Robert B. Winans.
Description: Urbana : University of Illinois Press, [2018] | Series: Music
    in American life | Includes bibliographical references and index.
Identifiers: LCCN 2017060726| ISBN 9780252041945 (cloth : alk. paper) |
    ISBN 9780252083600 (pbk. : alk. paper)
Subjects: LCSH: Banjo—History. | Lute—Africa—History. | African
    Americans—Music—History and criticism.
Classification: LCC ML1015.B3 B34 2018 | DDC 787.8/809—dc23
LC record available at https://lccn.loc.gov/2017060726

Ebook ISBN 9780252050640

This book is dedicated to Dena J. Epstein (1916–2013), whose work, as explained in the Editor's Introduction, led to the research informing the chapters included here. It is also dedicated in memoriam to Shlomo Pestcoe, who was a leading force initiating and shaping the creation of this book, whose tireless research as author and co-author account for five of these chapters, and who passed away in September 2015.

CONTENTS

At the Beginning

The genesis of this book was conversations at the 2007 Banjo Collectors' Gathering in Philadelphia. This event attracts collectors and historians of the banjo, as well as instrument builders and musicians, with a lot of overlap among these categories. A number of very capable and knowledgeable attendees were engaged in research building upon the scholarly literature on the banjo, dealing with significant issues not addressed in that literature. We were trying to promote awareness of those communities and traditions we were researching, and trying to find a way to make the content and issues matter to both general readers and special interest groups within and beyond academia. I was asked to spearhead this endeavor and be its editor. I sent invitations to thirty persons whom I felt had something to contribute to this project. For a one-day conference in 2008 devoted to the project, potential contributors submitted drafts of, or detailed proposals for, their essays in advance so that attendees could read and be ready to discuss them and offer suggestions. The number of potential chapters for this book at that point was twenty-five. Over the ensuing years, for a plethora of reasons, some of the invited authors left the project, and a few others were added, arriving at the current anthology of seventeen chapters, from ten contributors.

Goals and Intended Audiences

This anthology owes a debt to Dena J. Epstein's trailblazing journal article "The Folk Banjo: A Documentary History" (*Ethnomusicology* 19, no. 3 [1975]: 347–71), and her groundbreaking book *Sinful Tunes and Spirituals: Black Folk Music to the Civil War* (Urbana: University of Illinois Press, 1977), which have strongly influenced all the contributors. Although the banjo occupies only a portion of her very broad and detailed historical survey of black folk music prior to the Civil War, her work was the first modern step toward reconnecting the banjo with its actual provenance, endeavoring to overcome the generalization (still embraced by many) of the banjo as iconic of American "whiteness." Many of the chapters in this volume focus on the banjo's black heritage, whether in West Africa, the Caribbean, or North America, as a lasting legacy shared by all of us, to keep us

mindful that the banjo always carries with it issues of race and racism. Through
the vehicle of the banjo, the chapters hint of historical connections between musical cultures in those three regions of the world. The goal was to inspire and collect
important new banjo research, especially but not limited to that on early banjo
history. One thing the chapters in this volume share is that all present aspects of
banjo history that previously have not been fully explored. And since this book
does not exhaust banjo history that has not yet been fully explored, another goal
is that it will engender, as did Epstein's works, further banjo history research.

These chapters will be of interest to scholars in a number of fields, including
ethnomusicologists and organologists in general, those who study American
vernacular musics, New World creolization, and the African diaspora, and, more
generally, those in music history, Africa studies, and African American studies.
Beyond academia, in recent years a variety of banjo "revival" interest communities have come into being, complete with their own online listservs: makers and
players of gourd banjos, makers and players of minstrel-era banjos, Civil War
reenactment and living history musicians, players of finger-style and ragtime-
era banjo, and black musicians who are "reclaiming" the banjo as part of their
heritage, in addition to the preexisting legions of old-time banjo enthusiasts. This
book can be seen, in part, as an extension of these developments, and as making
an important contribution to them. We would like the various banjo communities
and those of related traditional instruments that we study, whether in Africa, the
Caribbean, or the United States, to become part of the readership of this book
and of the discourse we hope it generates.

Brief Synopsis of This Book's Contents

That the organization of this book is both geographical and chronological is
indicated by part titles. In part I, the scene is set by Shlomo Pestcoe and Greg C.
Adams's chapter on banjo roots research, which provides a brief framework of
banjo history, from its African roots to the use of various forms of the banjo in
musical cultures around the world today. A number of the issues raised briefly
are treated at much greater depth in other chapters in the book. In that sense,
chapter 1 serves as a partial extension of this introduction.

Part II explores the African roots of the banjo. Due to the paucity of detailed
written records of plucked lutes in Africa prior to the seventeenth century (and
not much better after that), much of the study of the African roots of the banjo
inevitably takes place in the present, looking at continuing traditions. Pestcoe,
however, in his chapter on the banjo's ancestors, looks at plucked lute history
before it reaches West Africa. Pestcoe and Adams go on to catalogue the known
examples of West African plucked spike lutes. Nick Bamber narrates his expedition in search of previously unknown (outside of their localities) plucked spike
lute traditions in Greater Senegambia along West Africa's Upper Guinea coast.
Chuck Levy presents his interviews with two West African bearers of one of those

traditions (the Jola *ekonting*, also transliterated as *akonting*), one of whom now makes the United States his home. Adams and Levy present a detailed comparative musicological study of West African *ekonting* music and American minstrel and old-time five-string banjo music, demonstrating considerable continuity.

Chapters then move to the Caribbean from the seventeenth to the nineteenth centuries (part III), followed by North America in the eighteenth century (part IV), and, finally, a diverse set of banjo topics involving various regions of North America in the nineteenth and twentieth centuries (part V). One of the strengths of the book is that the chapters demonstrate that a variety of source materials and diverse methodologies are essential in studying this history, and that dedicated nonacademic researchers can make valuable contributions to this study.

In respect to Caribbean developments in the New World, Pestcoe analyzes documentary evidence from the seventeenth century of the early gourd banjo's West African roots and circum-Caribbean origins. Saskia Willaert reports on the "rediscovery" of the nineteenth-century Haitian *banza*, and Pete Ross analyzes its structure and its connections to early images we have of the early gourd banjo and to the earliest commercially made banjos in North America.

Moving to North America, Pestcoe and Adams analyze in detail the earliest known reference to the banjo in North America, a 1736 New York City newspaper article. Pestcoe then uses an interdisciplinary approach in his thorough examination of the earliest North American depiction of the early gourd banjo, *The Old Plantation* watercolor. Winans gathers exhaustive data from newspaper advertisements on runaway slave musicians, presenting a picture of black musical culture of the time, followed by a chapter showing the geographical location of all known eighteenth-century and early nineteenth-century references to the banjo.

Inquiries into the banjo in nineteenth- and twentieth-century America begin with George R. Gibson's chapter, which uncovers much new information about black banjo and fiddle players—as well as African American vernacular music and dance in general—in Kentucky, and their influence on white musicians, from the 1780s to the early twentieth century. Jim Dalton presents a rigorous technical analysis of the acoustics of the early five-string banjo in the nineteenth century, using as his data the instructions found in early banjo tutors. Tony Thomas presents Gus Cannon as a professional, rather than a folk, musician, offering a different perspective on African American banjo playing in the late nineteenth and early twentieth centuries. Winans explores a fairly unique style of playing the five-string banjo found in the Piedmont areas of North Carolina and southern Virginia.

Illustrations that are referenced in more than one chapter are gathered in the illustrations section of this volume, along with color illustrations (which may or may not be referenced in more than one chapters). Figures in this section are given alphabetic designations, while figures within individual chapters are given numeric designations.

The Authors

The contributors to this collection come from a variety of backgrounds (see the list of contributors, p. 305). Only a few are academics, although a couple others have advanced degrees. All but one are banjo players, and their playing preceded their devotion to doing banjo history research. Several have gone to Africa to learn firsthand about multiple African traditions whose history may have contributed to the banjo's development; others have done in-depth library research and/or fieldwork to explicate their topics. They have different writing styles, ranging from informal and somewhat colloquial to rigorous scholarly analysis, each appropriate to the author's topic and approach. Degree of documentation also differs, appropriate to each individual chapter's goals. This diversity of style and format among the chapters is another strength of this book. One does not have to speak like a university scholar to say something worthwhile. An editor's headnote before each chapter acquaints the reader more fully with each author, and how the chapter interacts with other chapters and furthers the goals of the book.

I wish to express my deep appreciation to all of the contributors, whom I consider colleagues. They patiently responded to my editorial comments and complied with my sometimes numerous requests for revised drafts, and they patiently awaited the publication of this book. I am grateful to two of these colleagues, Greg C. Adams and Shlomo Pestcoe, for their assistance with some of the wording of this introduction. I must also honor the generous financial support of Marvin and Elizabeth Pestcoe, whose donations covered some of the costs of publishing this book.

PART I

Setting the Scene

Banjo Roots Research
Changing Perspectives on the Banjo's African American Origins and West African Heritage

Shlomo Pestcoe and Greg C. Adams

Editor's Headnote

This chapter began as a response to the historic challenge issued by the late Dena J. Epstein in her 1975 article "The Folk Banjo: A Documentary History" to systematically investigate the historical record for period documentation tracing the banjo's roots, origins, and early history. Shlomo Pestcoe and Greg C. Adams have combined Epstein's research techniques with those of ethno-organology (the scientific study of music instruments and their musical-cultural contexts) to create an innovative scholarly approach, which they term banjo roots research. *Here Pestcoe and Adams explain how this approach works, and share some of the crucial findings of this research that broaden the narrative of the banjo's history. They outline issues that will be dealt with in greater depth in following chapters covering the early history of the instrument, from its roots in West Africa to its origins in the Caribbean and its early history as an African American folk instrument, and then move on to the development of the modern banjo family and the current globalization of the banjo as a popular instrument in vernacular music forms the world over.*

Banjo roots research is the empirical study of the banjo's early history, its origins in the early African diaspora in the Americas, and its deep roots in West Africa, the wellspring of the banjo's African heritage. Our work in this area of banjo studies is based on the trailblazing efforts of Dena J. Epstein (1916–2013), the "mother" of early banjo scholarship.[1] In the 1950s, she first applied systematic research techniques to uncover historical evidence of early African American vernacular music and dance culture, including the banjo, prior to the American Civil War.[2] A music librarian by training and vocation, she described her research approach as being informed by "the application of library techniques."[3] Regarding the banjo in particular, Epstein was interested in uncovering the early African American "folk banjo" through "the raw materials from which can be drawn a sound discussion of the banjo and its role in the development of black folk music in the western hemisphere."[4]

The principal focus of our approach to banjo roots research is the original African American gourd-bodied genus of the banjo—the *early gourd banjo*, our general term for what Epstein called the *folk banjo*. It was the immediate forebear of the wood-rimmed five-string banjo (see figure M), which first emerged in the United States around 1840 in the context of professional blackface performance on the popular stage and in the circus ring.[5] This connection makes the early gourd banjo the ancestor of the modern banjo family we know today.

The scholarly infrastructure of our work is founded on two platforms: Epstein's application of library science principles to historical research; and ethno-organology, the study of music instruments and their musical and cultural contexts. Ethno-organology combines ethnomusicology's key principles, the study of music within any cultural context (or, as Jeff Todd Titon calls it, "the study of people making music"),[6] with organology, the study of the historical development, classification, technology, and use of instruments. The synthesis of these two distinct research approaches facilitates multifaceted investigations of the historical record, combined with explorations of living traditions.

In this context, ethno-organological precepts and methodologies provide support for cross-cultural analysis and field research, on the one hand, and modern organological classification of music instruments, on the other. This approach enables us to identify and trace what we call the *banjo genome*—that is, the sum total of the various design concepts, morphological characteristics, and musicological factors that have defined the banjo family over the course of its historic continuum, stretching back to its African ancestors. At the same time, it also allows us to better study the traditions of the people who created and played these instruments, as well as the historic conditions and sociocultural matrices in which the banjo family, its ancestors, and its extant relatives first emerged.

First Banjos: The Early Gourd Banjo

The historical evidence shows that the banjo first appeared in the seventeenth-century circum-Caribbean, emerging from the harsh crucible of slavery and the transatlantic slave trade. The first banjos were plucked spike lutes, that is, plucked lutes on which the neck goes through or over the wall of the instrument's body. Akin to several traditions of plucked spike lutes still found throughout West Africa, they typically had a drum-like body, made of gourd (*Lagenaria siceraria*, also referred to as *Cucurbita lagenaria* L., which grows on vines)—or, in certain cases, calabash (*Crescentia cujete*, which grows on trees)—topped with a taut animal hide soundtable; a fretless full-spike neck that extended the full length of the body to pass through its tail end; and a floating (moveable) bridge that sat on the instrument's animal hide soundtable (see figures J, K, L, and M for examples). However, recent research indicates that the early gourd banjo, while fundamentally West African in design, was not an exact replica of any known African instrument. Rather, it embodied a synthesis of structural features from one or more West African traditions and several additional features, which were most likely inspired by Spanish and Portuguese plucked lutes encountered in the Caribbean, such as the *vihuela de mano, guitar, tiple,* and *cavaquinho.*[7] Instead of the sliding tuning rings used on all traditional West African plucked spike lutes, the early gourd banjo had tuning pegs. In place of the typical West African round cylindrical fretless stick neck, it had a carved wooden neck with a flat fretless fingerboard (see figures A and K for these contrasting features).

Recognizing these distinctions, it is clear that the early gourd banjo was unique to the African diaspora in the New World. As such, it was the product of creolization (also referred to as interculturation),[8] the same self-determined, internalized process that combined diverse African and European influences and admixtures in a syncretic fusion to create all other forms of early African American culture throughout the Americas.

Toward Greater Clarity

In the past, the banjo and its African forebears and kin were only considered in vague generalized terms as string instruments, without any real sense as to what kind of string instruments they were or where they fit in the greater music instrumentarium—the vast spectrum of all instruments of every description the world over throughout history. This inability to characterize the banjo and its relatives more precisely severely hampered serious analysis and study of these instruments. In order to surmount this obstacle, we use the organological analytical criteria and terminology provided by the system of instrument classification developed by the pioneering musicologists-organologists Erich Moritz von Hornbostel (1877–1935) and Curt Sachs (1881–1959) in 1914.[9] Today the Hornbostel-Sachs (HS) classification system is the standard in the fields of musicology, ethnomusicology, organology, anthropology, museology (museum studies), and other scholarly disciplines.

According to HS categorization, the banjo and related instruments are lutes, that is, chordophones (string instruments) with a distinct neck and body. On most types of lute, various notes are made both by playing open strings and by stopping some or all of the strings at different places along the neck. Lutes are divided into two major categories based on how their strings are sounded: plucked lutes, which are played by plucking and strumming the strings with the fingers and/or plectrums; or bowed lutes (fiddles), which are played by drawing a bow across the strings.[10] The banjo and its kin are, therefore, plucked lutes.

Using the HS classification we can further determine that the early gourd banjo, like its West African forebears and present-day kin as well as its North African cousins, was a spike lute—a lute that has its "handle" (neck) pass through its "resonator" (body), or, as in the case of most West African and North African plucked spike lutes, over the wall of its body. As spike lutes, the roots of the family tree of the banjo and its African relatives can be traced back more than four thousand years to the earliest known lutes: the plucked spike lutes of ancient Mesopotamia[11] and their descendants, the plucked spike lutes of the ancient Near East and Pharonic Egypt.[12]

We can achieve greater specificity and accuracy in our classification of plucked spike lutes by subdividing them into two main categories based on the span of their necks in relationship to their bodies: full-spike, where the neck extends the full length of the body to pass over or through the body's tail end (see figure A); and semi-spike, where the neck extends only about three-quarters of the body's length to end within the body just short of its tail end (see figure B). Recognizing that the early gourd banjo was a full-spike lute helps us to better refine and sharpen our comparative analyses of the vast family of West African plucked spike lutes and any potential relationships with the early gourd banjo.

At this point, we should clarify that another key element of our approach is to increase knowledge of the many plucked spike lutes still found throughout West Africa today. This aspect of banjo roots research first emerged in 2000, when the independent researchers Daniel Laemouahuma Jatta of The Gambia and Ulf Jägfors of Sweden introduced the banjo community to two traditional West African plucked spike lutes that were largely unknown outside the Senegambian region. They are the *ekonting* (also transliterated as *akonting*) of the Jola (also transliterated as Diola in French, though pronounced the same) and the *bunchundo* of the Manyago (also Manjak, Manjaco, etc.).[13] Jatta was, in fact, the first researcher to document substantively these traditions, beginning in the mid-1980s. Nearly identical three-string plucked spike lutes, the *ekonting* and the *bunchundo* are made with a drum-like gourd body, a full-spike fretless neck, a large bipedal floating bridge, and a top short thumb-string, akin to the top short fifth string on the five-string banjo, which is played open (see figures A and E).[14]

Awareness of the Jola and Manyago lutes has spurred banjo roots research on two levels. First, it has reinvigorated early banjo scholarship, inspiring researchers within the banjo community to build on Epstein's pioneering archival and library-based research. Second, it has encouraged a new generation of focused field research in West Africa to seek out more plucked spike lute traditions that have existed under the radar of international researchers. For instance, in 2006 alone, we learned about three gourd-bodied full-spike lutes of the Greater Senegambia that were previously unknown to international researchers:[15] the five-string Wolof *xalam geseré*[16] (Ben Nelson, The Gambia, April 2006); and the Bujogo *ñopata* (see figure F) and the Balanta *kusunde* (Nick Bamber, the Bijago Islands, Guinea-Bissau, August 2006),[17] both of which are three-string gourd-bodied full-spike lutes akin to the Jola *ekonting* and the Manyago *bunchundo*.

Based on available current documentation, we estimate at least eighty culturally distinct traditions of plucked spike lutes are found today throughout West

Africa.[18] The majority of these are instruments with semi-spike necks and bodies made from either carved wood or gourd, depending on the given tradition (e.g., the four-string wooden-bodied Bamana-Maninka *n'goni* [Mali]—see figure B; the two-string gourd-bodied Frafra *koliko* [Ghana]; and the three-string gourd-bodied Gwari *kaburu* [Nigeria]). Within the West African plucked spike lute family, however, there also exists a small but significant subgroup of full-spike lutes, that is, those with full-spike necks and bodies that are not made of wood, but of either gourd or calabash. In addition to the Jola *ekonting*, the Manyago *bunchundo*, and the other Greater Senegambian lutes mentioned above, other examples of full-spike lutes include the two-string gourd-bodied Hausa *gurmi* (Nigeria), the three-string calabash-bodied Kilba *gullum* (Nigeria) (see figure G), and the three-string calabash-bodied Bana *ngùlăn* (Cameroon). These full-spike lutes draw significant interest in our work because they share the most organological similarities with the early gourd banjo.

Surveying Sources and Points of Transmission

Perhaps the earliest evidence linking West African plucked spike lutes to the Americas comes from the Jesuit missionary Alonso de Sandoval (1577–1652)[19] and is framed in the context of slavery in the Americas and the transatlantic slave trade.[20] For most of his life, Sandoval ministered to enslaved Africans and Afro-Creoles in Cartagena de Indias (Cartagena of the Indies), present-day Colombia's port city on the Caribbean Sea, then the hub of Spain's trade in African captives throughout the New World.[21] In his treatise *De instauranda Aethiopum salute* (On Restoring Ethiopian Salvation) (1627), Sandoval described the musical proclivities of "Guineans" from Greater Senegambia, in the region of the Gambia, Casamance, and Cacheu Rivers along West Africa's Upper Guinea Coast:[22] "Their music combines the sounds of sonorous instruments and many voices. . . . Some play guitars similar to our Spanish-style guitars, although they are made of rough sheepskin."[23]

Sandoval's specification that these "guitars" were "made of rough sheepskin" implies that these instruments had drum-like bodies, topped with tightened membrane soundtables made of animal hide. If that was indeed the case, then Sandoval was describing plucked spike lutes, the same type of plucked lute that was the early gourd banjo and its West African ancestors. Unfortunately, his terse observation does not provide us with enough information to determine what these instruments were specifically, whether they were West African plucked spike lutes or Afro-Creole early gourd banjos.

Moving beyond Sandoval's reference, the first documentation and depiction of instruments that researchers can positively identify as early gourd banjos come from Sir Hans Sloane (1660–1753) in his book *A Voyage to the Islands of Madera, Barbados, Nieves, S. Christophers and Jamaica* (1707). During his fifteen-month stay in Jamaica (December 1687–March 1689), Sloane observed that enslaved blacks played "several sorts of Instruments in imitation of Lutes, made of small Gourds fitted with Necks."[24] The book illustration, "plate III," in Sloane's *A Voyage to the Islands* provides us with the earliest known depiction of early gourd banjos, called "Strum Strumps" in the plate's Latin caption (see figure H).[25]

From this point on, throughout the eighteenth and early nineteenth centuries, the early gourd banjo would be found in African American communities throughout the Caribbean; the South American countries of Suriname ("Dutch Guiana") and Guyana; and what would become the United States—specifically, the entire eastern seaboard, from New England to Florida, as well as Louisiana.

It was known by a variety of names, including the following:

- *bangil* (Barbados, 1708; Jamaica, 1739 and 1740)
- *banger* (New York City, 1736, the earliest report of the banjo in North America)
- *banjo* (Pennsylvania, 1749; Maryland and Virginia, 1774; North Carolina, 1787)
- *banshaw* (St. Kitts, 1763)
- *banza* (French Antilles, 1765 and 1810; Louisiana, 1851)
- *creole bania* (Suriname, 1773–77)
- *merry-wang* (Jamaica, 1774)[26]

While a few reports describe three-string banjos, those with four strings are the best-documented, most commonly cited form of the instrument, starting with the four-string *banza* in the French Antilles, first reported in the late 1690s.[27] The four-string early gourd banjo was what Thomas Jefferson famously described in *Notes on the State of Virginia* (1781) as he commented on the African American music of his day: "The instrument proper to them is the Banjar, which they brought hither from Africa, and which is the original of the guitar, its chords [strings] being precisely the four lower chords of the guitar."[28] It is also what John Rose, a slaveholding planter and amateur artist in South Carolina, depicted as being played by a black banjoist for an African American dance gathering in the 1780s in his watercolor sketch, now titled *The Old Plantation* (see figure N).[29]

In addition, at least three eighteenth- and nineteenth-century instruments survive, which further reinforce the four-string form of the banjo with three long strings and one short thumb-string:

1. The calabash-bodied *creole bania*, collected by Captain John Gabriel Stedman (1744–97) "from a slave in Suriname"[30] sometime during his tour of duty in the Dutch colony in northeastern South America, 1773–77; currently on display in the Rijksmuseum voor Volkenkunde, Leiden, The Netherlands (see figure J).[31]

2. The gourd-bodied *banza*, acquired by the French abolitionist writer Victor Schœlcher (1804–93) in Haiti during his 1840–41 journey through the Caribbean, which he described as being an "imitation of an African instrument widely used by the black people of Haiti;"[32] currently in the collection of the Musée de la Musique, Cité de la Musique, Paris, France (see figure K).

3. The calabash-bodied *panja* (*banja*), collected in Suriname around 1850 by Brother Jansa, a Moravian missionary who was stationed at Warappa Creek in the early 1850s; currently in the collections of Ethnologisches Museum, Staatliche Museen zu Berlin.[33] According to the original 1861 catalogue entry on the instrument, it was played in traditional Afro-Surinamese funeral rites to accompany the ritual telling of Anansitori (literally "Spider Stories," featuring Anansi, the spider trickster of West African and Afro-Caribbean folklore).[34]

Beyond the number of strings, these three instruments emphasize an important facet about the early banjo—those made with a calabash versus a gourd. While we use the term *early gourd banjo* to facilitate discourse as a generic descriptor for the type of banjo that preceded the wood-rimmed five-string banjo of the mid-nineteenth century, it is important to acknowledge the scientific distinction between these two related, but different kinds of fruits. In her groundbreaking article "When is a Calabash not a Calabash?" (1982), the Caribbeanist anthropologist Sally Price argues that "with few exceptions, the terms 'calabash' and 'gourd' have been assumed by speakers of European languages to be synonymous and to designate a more or less homogeneous botanical (and cultural) domain. This . . . has led to confusions in the ethnographic literature on African and Afro-American 'calabash' arts and . . . violates distinctions that are important to the people who cultivate, process, and embellish these fruits."[35]

Accounts of the early banjo in the historical record bear out Price's contention that the designations *gourd* and *calabash* have been used interchangeably in European languages to describe the two different fruits. Taking this historic confusion between the gourd and the calabash into consideration when looking at period reports of early banjos, we see that when early banjo bodies were identified as being made of calabash, it is highly probable that the authors were actually referencing the gourd. A case in point is the report by the German physician-naturalist Dr. Johann David Schoepf where he observed black musicians playing a *banjah* aboard the schooner on which he sailed to the Bahamas from St. Augustine, Florida, in 1784. In describing this four-string instrument, he specified that its body was made of a "hollow calabash," yet parenthetically classified the word with the scientific Latin term *Cucurb Lagenaria L.*, which specifically denotes the bottle gourd.[36] Recognizing that the *creole bania* and the *panja* have bodies made of calabash while the body of the *banza* is made of gourd enables us to better discern regional differences in early banjo design and construction. Furthermore, the evidence of the calabash bodies on the two instruments from Suriname—taken together with their other unique features, such as the placement of the thumb-string's peg and the elaborate ornamentation of the peghead—suggest the development of a distinct Afro-Surinamese form of the early banjo that differed in several significant ways from those documented in the West Indies and North America, where gourd bodies predominated.

The Afro-Surinamese *creole bania* and *panja* and the Haitian *banza* do share two crucial commonalities: they were all built to be four-stringed and they were all strung in the same configuration that Stedman described on the *creole bania* in his *Narrative of a Five Years Expedition*, the only period textual description of the early gourd banjo's exact stringing ("This instrument has but four Strings, three Long, and one Short").[37] This stringing configuration was also shown on the *creole bania* illustrated in Stedman's book, as well as on the four-string *banjar* that John Rose depicted in *The Old Plantation*.

The defining characteristic of the four-string version of the early gourd banjo was its top fourth string—a short unstopped string called a thumb-string because it is sounded exclusively by the player's thumb. This feature can be traced back to West Africa, where most plucked spike lutes with three or more strings include at least one short thumb-string. It is also found on the banjo's three-string cousins of West African heritage from Tunisia, which all have as their top third string a short thumb-string: the *gumbri* (*gombri*) with a large wooden body resembling a side drum, the *gambara* with a narrow oblong wooden body, and the *fakrūn* (literally "turtle") with a body made from a large tortoise shell.[38]

In terms of placement, on both the four-string early gourd banjo and its successor, the wood-rimmed five-string banjo, the peg for the top short thumb-string is typically situated on the neck somewhere in the first quarter down from the peghead. Where the three extant gourd- and calabash-bodied banjos diverge is in how the peg is placed on the neck. The thumb-string peg on the Haitian *banza* is inserted dorsally from the back of the neck on through the fingerboard to protrude above it to receive the string. This dorsal back-to-front insertion is also seen on the four-string early gourd banjo depicted in *The Old Plantation* and possibly implied on the two Afro-Jamaican "Strum Strumps" depicted in Sloane's 1707 book. It would later be the most common placement for the thumb-string peg on early wood-rimmed five-string banjos from the 1840s through the 1860s. Conversely, on the *creole bania* (as well as on the illustration of the instrument in Stedman's book) and on the *panja*, the peg is inserted into the upper side of the neck.[39] This side-mounted insertion of the thumb-string peg is one of the distinguishing features of the distinctive Afro-Surinamese style of the instrument. It would also be found on some early five-string banjos, starting in the 1850s. Yet, by 1880, this side-mounted insertion would be the standard placement for the thumb-string peg on the necks of most modern five-string banjos.[40]

Evidence in Playing Styles

Aside from the physical "genetic markers" in early banjo construction, evidence of the banjo's West African heritage may also be seen in the earliest known techniques used to play the instrument. Down-picking[41] (also called down-stroking) was the original playing technique that the first European American players initially learned from African American banjoists in the early nineteenth century.

Referred to as "Banjo Style" in the first published banjo tutors of the 1850s and 1860s (later, "Stroke Style" in the 1880s and "Negro Style" in the 1890s), it was the most prevalent form of playing the five-string banjo until overshadowed by the "Guitar Style" of three-finger up-picking (finger-picking), starting in the late 1860s. Traditions of banjo down-picking are also found throughout the rural South, where they have been commonly referred to by various names, such as frailing, clawhammer, rapping, or thumping.

Recent research indicates that banjo down-picking playing techniques share the same fundamentals with a number of West African plucked spike lute traditions today, including, for example, instruments like the aforementioned Jola *ekonting* and Bujogo *ñopata*, as well as the two-string wooden-bodied *konou*[42] of the Dogon (Mali). Griot lutenists also use down-picking in place of or in addition to the more common griot two-finger and three-finger up-picking techniques. Down-picking is also present with single-string griot lutes, such as the Mande-Tukulor *molo* (Senegambia) and the Songhai *jurkel* (Burkina Faso) and *n'jurkel* (Mali). Additional forms of down-picking are also used to play the banjo's North African cousins of West African heritage: the three-string wooden-bodied semi-spike Gnawa *hajhuj* (also *sintir, guinbri*, and *gnbri*) of Morocco and Algeria and the *gumbri, gambara*, and *fakrūn* of Tunisia.

The diverse styles of two-finger up-picking found in American old-time banjo traditions also share fundamental links with West African traditions. All across West Africa, two-finger up-picking, in various forms, is a common technique for finger-playing plucked lutes, such as the two-string gourd-bodied *gurmi* and the three-string wooden-bodied *molo* (also called *tafashe*) of the Hausa (Nigeria and Niger).[43] Evidence in the historical record suggests that early African American banjoists were employing two-finger up-picking as well as the more prevalent down-picking. Frank B. Converse (1837–1903)—a leading early five-string banjoist whose *New and Complete Method for the Banjo With or Without a Master* (1865) heralded the transition from "Banjo Style" down-picking to "Guitar Style" three-finger up-picking—offers a tantalizing eyewitness account of African American two-finger banjo up-picking prior to 1850. As a boy growing up in the Upstate New York town of Elmira, Converse was first exposed to the banjo by an itinerant black banjoist who frequently "busked" on Elmira's streets. As Converse later recounted, the street performer's playing technique was "limited to the thumb and first finger—pulling or 'picking' the strings with both."[44] Since *pulling* was Converse's term for up-picking, the busking black banjoist of his youth that Converse recalled was most likely playing in a two-finger up-picking style.

The Modern Banjo Family

In the United States, the banjo's narrative continues in the early 1840s with the advent of the five-string banjo. The five-string banjo differed from its gourd- and calabash-bodied predecessors in that it had a frame drum-type wooden hoop body and was strung with four long strings and a short thumb-string (see figure M). The instrument was introduced in professional performances by Joel Walker "Joe" Sweeney (1810–60), the earliest known European American banjoist, probably sometime between December 2, 1836 (his first documented appearance in Richmond, Virginia), and 1840, when the first images of the five-string banjo begin to appear on sheet music and theatrical handbills and posters.[45] The context in which Sweeney, his pupil William "Billy" Whitlock (1813–78), and others first popularized the new type of banjo was that of professional blackface performances in the circus ring and on the popular theater stage, what would eventually be called minstrelsy after the seminal performances of the Virginia Minstrels in February and March 1843.[46] A year earlier, Sweeney had introduced the instrument in Britain. Eventually, the five-string banjo would take its place on the world stage as a major popular instrument.

The late nineteenth and early twentieth centuries saw the development of the modern banjo family, which includes, in addition to the five-string banjo, the four-string tenor banjo, the four-string plectrum banjo, and multiple banjo hybrids (e.g., banjo-guitar, banjo-mandolin, and banjo-ukulele). Today, these instruments are most commonly associated with American genres of music, such as folk, old-time country, bluegrass, modern country, ragtime, blues, and jazz. Yet, the banjo, in all of its various forms, has long been heard in contemporary popular music worldwide. It appears in local regional idioms of traditional and tradition-based vernacular music that range from *mento* (Jamaica), *parang* (Carriacou), *quelbe* (St. Croix and the Virgin Islands), *twoubadou kreyol* (Haiti), and *samba e pagode* (Brazil), to *amarg souss* and *tazenzart* (Morocco), *chaabi* (Algeria), *ceili* (Ireland), *ceilidh* (Scotland), and *faikava* (Pule'anga 'o Tonga [The Kingdom of Tonga], South Pacific).

Conclusion

In her pioneering article Epstein issued a call to scholars to investigate the historical record for documentary evidence about the banjo's early history and its role in the development of early African American music and dance throughout the Americas. Her call has been heard by a growing number of people both inside and outside the academy and is the foundation of the work we present today. As we build on the great endeavor that Epstein initiated, we recognize that developing a viable historiography of the banjo encompasses a complex matrix of changing perspectives about the instrument's African American origins and West African heritage. By working toward greater clarity, new research is delineating how the historic African American early gourd banjo is connected to West African living traditions. Surveying the diversity of sources, points of transmission, and evidence in playing styles allows us to discover how the modern banjo family relates to an ancestry that begins in the seventeenth century amid the horrors of the transatlantic slave trade with the forced displacement of millions of Africans across the Middle Passage.

This chapter is our offering to advance a more practical research methodology for tracing the banjo genome through the theoretical framework of banjo roots research by combining Epstein's "application of library techniques" with ethno-organology. Utilizing systematic research techniques keeps us connected with the ever-widening scope of banjo-related historical references that continue to surface in private collections as well as libraries, archives, and a variety of web-based access points. Drawing on modern ethnomusicological precepts provides further guidance as we carefully consider the many variegated African, European, and American influences, admixtures, and sociocultural contexts that contributed to the development and globalization of the banjo family. Employing modern organological classification makes us better equipped to identify, investigate, and compare the banjo's genetic markers for a fuller, more realistic, and measureable approach to framing key chapters in the banjo's broader history. Ultimately, banjo roots research offers greater accountability for how we study evidence about the past and draw correlations with living traditions. It also allows us to find ways of collaborating with wider groups of researchers, musicians, tradition bearers, and scholars in other fields of study to facilitate an open-ended discourse about the banjo's fascinating history and cultural significance.

Notes

Our thanks and appreciation to Robert B. Winans for his editorial guidance and Ed Britt, Kerry Blech, Tony Thomas, and Laurent Dubois for their feedback in our preparation of the original *Banjo Roots Research Initiatives Mission Statement* (2010), on which this chapter is based.

1. Everyone typically called her "Dena." See Jim Carrier, DVD insert for his documentary film *The Librarian and The Banjo* (2013): "The inspiring true story of music librarian Dena Epstein who labored 25 years to document the musical contributions of African slaves to the New World." http://jimcarrier.com/librarian/, accessed October 17, 2017.

2. For our purposes here, the descriptor *African American* indicates someone or something of either African origin or African descent found anywhere in the Americas, including the Caribbean, rather than just within the confines of the present-day United States. When discussing the history of slavery and the transatlantic slave trade, we use *African Americans* to include African-born survivors of the Middle Passage as well as Afro-Creoles "country-born" anywhere in the Americas.

3. Dena J. Epstein, *Sinful Tunes and Spirituals: Black Folk Music to the Civil War* (Urbana: University of Illinois Press, 1977, 2003), xvii.

4. Dena J. Epstein, "The Folk Banjo: A Documentary History," *Ethnomusicology* 19 (September 1975): 359. Epstein used the descriptor *folk banjo* to distinguish between the "folk" (non-commodified) gourd-bodied instrument of enslaved African Americans and its "commercial" (commodified) successor, the wood-rimmed early five-string banjo (347).

5. For more on the emergence and development of the wood-rimmed five-string banjo in the nineteenth century, see Lowell H. Schreyer, *The Banjo Entertainers, Roots to Ragtime: A*

Banjo History (Mankato: Minnesota Heritage Publishing, 2007); Philip F. Gura and James F. Bollman, *America's Instrument: The Banjo in the Nineteenth Century* (Chapel Hill: University of North Carolina Press, 1999); and Bob Carlin, *The Birth of the Banjo: Joel Walker Sweeney and Early Minstrelsy* (Jefferson, NC: McFarland & Company, 2007).

6. Jeff Todd Titon, *Worlds of Music: An Introduction to the Music of the World's Peoples* (Belmont, CA: Schirmer Cengage Learning, 2009), xviii.

7. The *vihuela* (originally *vihuela de mano* [the "hand" or finger-played *vihuela*]) was a six-course plucked lute, with a figure-8-shaped wooden box body, which first emerged in Spain sometime in the mid-fifteenth century. Despite its guitar-like appearance, however, the *vihuela* was more closely related to the short-necked, bowl-backed western lute than the early guitar. It was the first plucked lute in the New World, introduced by the Spanish in the early 1500s. The four-course renaissance guitar would follow very shortly after. However, by the early seventeenth century, both were superseded by the five-course baroque guitar, which would be popular as the "Spanish" guitar until the end of the eighteenth century. Other historic guitar-family instruments to be considered include the Spanish *tiple* and the Portuguese *cavaquinho*. For more on the *vihuela* and the various types of early guitar, see Tom and Mary Anne Evans, *Guitars: Music, History, Construction and Players from the Renaissance to Rock* (New York: Facts On File, 1977), 16–55, 210–14.

8. Cultural creolization is an anthropological theory that posits the development in the New World during the colonial period of an internalized dynamic and process of socio-cultural adaptation, transformation, and creation through the everyday social interaction and exchange between different groups. See Edward Kamau Brathwaite, *The Development of Creole Society in Jamaica, 1770–1820* (New York: Oxford University Press, 1971), xxv, xxix–xxxii, and Richard Price, "On the Miracle of Creolization," in *Afro-Atlantic Dialogues: Anthropology in the Diaspora*, ed. Kevin A. Yelvington (Santa Fe, NM: School of American Research, 2006), 113–45.

9. Erich Moritz von Hornbostel and Curt Sachs, "Systematik der Musikinstrumente: ein Versuch" (A System for Classifying Musical Instruments: An Open Ended Discussion), *Zeitschrift für Ethnologie* (1914): 553–90; and "Classification of Musical Instruments: Translated from the Original German by Anthony Baines and Klaus P. Wachsmann," *The Galpin Society Journal* 14 (March 1961): 3–29.

10. Curt Sachs, *The History of Musical Instruments* (New York: W. W. Norton & Company, Inc., 1940), 464.

11. See Richard Dumbrill, *The Archaeomusicology of the Ancient Near East* (Victoria, BC: Trafford Publishing, 2005), 321.

12. For more on the links between West African plucked spike lutes and those of the ancient Near East and Pharonic Egypt, see in this volume Pestcoe's chapter "Banjo Ancestors: West African Plucked Spike Lutes."

13. For more on the *ekonting* and *bunchundo*, see Ulf Jägfors, "The African Akonting and the Origin of the Banjo," *The Old-Time Herald* 9, no. 2 (November 2003–January 2004): 26–33; Shlomo Pestcoe and Greg C. Adams, "Ekonting," in *The Grove Dictionary of Musical Instruments: Second Edition*, ed. Laurence Libin, 5 vols. (Oxford: Oxford University Press, 2014), 2:140–41; and Greg C. Adams and Chuck Levy's chapter in this volume.

14. The *ekonting* is further distinguished from the *bunchundo* in that its second and third strings are both played open with the thumb. See the Adams and Levy chapter in this volume about the Jola *ekonting*.

15. Boubacar Barry, *Senegambia and the Atlantic Slave Trade* (Cambridge: Cambridge University Press, 1988), xi. *Greater Senegambia* is the West African historian Boubacar

Barry's designation for the Western Sudan region of West Africa. It includes present-day Senegal, The Gambia, Mauritania, Mali, Guinea-Bissau, and Guinea.

16. For more on the *xalam geseré*, see Pestcoe and Adams's "List of West African Plucked Spike Lutes" in this volume. The word *griot* (pronounced "gree-oh"; originally spelled *guiriot*) made its first appearance in *Relation du voyage du Cap-Verd* (1637) by the French Capuchin missionary Alexis de Saint-Lô (Eric Charry, *Mande Music: Traditional and Modern Music of the Maninka and Mandinka of Western Africa* [Chicago: University of Chicago Press, 2000], 361–62; Thomas A. Hale, *Griots and Griottes: Masters of Words and Music* [Bloomington: Indiana University Press, 1998], 84–85). It refers to hereditary male music-word artisans who belong to the middle artisan caste in the traditional tripartite societies of certain Islamized West African ethnicities, such as the Mandinka, Maninka, Bamana (Bambara), Wolof, Soninke, Songhai, and Fulbe (Fula, Fulani, Peul, etc.). The Wolof *xalam geseré* actually represents an extremely rare type of griot lute (Charry's term for the unique subgroup of West African plucked spike lutes traditionally played exclusively by griot lutenists). Unlike standard griot lutes, the *xalam geseré* is a full-spike lute with a round gourd body and a floating bridge that sits on the soundtable. For more on griot traditions, see Charry, *Mande Music*, and Hale, *Griots and Griottes*.

17. See Nick Bamber's chapter in this volume, "Searching for Gourd Lutes in the Bijago Islands of Guinea-Bissau." (N.B.: A more recent 2012 visit to Guinea-Bissau by another American traveler has revealed more information about one or more instruments identified as *kusunde*, which will hopefully lead to forthcoming clarifications about the tradition.)

18. For more on the West African family of plucked spike lutes, see in this volume Pestcoe's chapter "Banjo Ancestors" and his and Greg C. Adams's "List of West African Plucked Spike Lutes."

19. Nicole von Germeten, ed. and trans., "Introduction" to Alonso de Sandoval, SJ, *Treatise on Slavery: Selections from De instauranda Aethiopum salute* (Indianapolis: Hackett Publishing Company, Inc., 2008), ix–xi; see also Mayra E. Beer, "Alonso de Sandoval: Seventeenth-Century Merchant of the Gospel, Aethiopia praeveniet manus eius Deo," http://www.kislakfoundation.org/prize/199702.html, accessed October 17, 2017.

20. For more on Sandoval's account, see Pestcoe's chapter in this volume, "'Strum Strumps' and 'Sheepskin' Guitars: The Early Gourd Banjo and Clues to its West African Roots in the Seventeenth-Century Circum-Caribbean."

21. Germeten, *Treatise on Slavery*, x–xiii; Hugh Thomas, *The Slave Trade: The Story of the Atlantic Slave Trade, 1440–1870* (New York: Simon & Schuster Paperbacks, 1997), 434–35.

22. Sandoval, *Treatise on Slavery*, 25. The term *Upper Guinea Coast* generally refers to the coastal and riverine lands along West Africa's Atlantic coast stretching down from the Gambia River to Cape Mount in northwestern Liberia. See Walter Rodney, *A History of the Upper Guinea Coast, 1545–1800* (New York: Monthly Review Press, 1970), 1–2.

23. Germeten's translation in Sandoval, *Treatise on Slavery*, 27–28.

24. Hans Sloane, MD, *A Voyage to the Islands of Madera, Barbados, Nieves, S. Christophers and Jamaica*, 2 vols. (London, 1707), 1:xlviii, republished online by BHL Biodiversity Library: http://www.biodiversitylibrary.org/item/11242, accessed October 18, 2017.

25. For more on Sloane's account, see Pestcoe's chapter in this volume, "'Strum Strumps' and 'Sheepskin' Guitars."

26. Epstein, "The Folk Banjo," 359–60, and *Sinful Tunes and Spirituals*, "Appendix II: Table of Sources for the Banjo, Chronologically Arranged," 359–62. All but three of the

various references to the early gourd banjo listed here are cited in both of Epstein's chronological lists. The ones not given in her works include *banger* (*The New-York Weekly Journal*, March 7, 1736); *banjo* (*Pennsylvania Gazette*, July 7, 1749); and *creole bania* (John Gabriel Stedman, *Narrative of a Five Years Expedition against the Revolted Negroes of Surinam: Transcribed for the First Time the Original 1790 Manuscript*, ed. Richard Price and Sally Price [Baltimore: Johns Hopkins University Press, 1988; New York: iUniverse, 2010], 540).

27. Epstein, *Sinful Tunes and Spirituals*, 27–33.

28. Thomas Jefferson, *Notes on the State of Virginia* (Philadelphia, 1781), query XIV, 266. In the second half of eighteenth century, most English-language references to the "guitar" were not to the gut-strung predecessor of the modern guitar—which was typically specified as the "Spanish guitar"—but, rather, to the metal-strung English guitar, a cittern that had ten metal strings arranged in six courses, most commonly tuned C-E-GG-C'C'-E'E'-G'G'. James Tyler and Paul Sparks, *The Guitar and Its Music: From the Renaissance to the Classical Era* (Oxford: Oxford University Press, 2007), 207, and Robert Spencer, Ian Harwood, and Jenny Nex, "English Guitar," in *The Grove Dictionary of Musical Instruments: Second Edition*, ed. Laurence Libin, 5 vols. (Oxford: Oxford University Press, 2014), 2:220–21. Therefore, Jefferson's reference to the banjar's "chords [strings] being precisely the four lower chords of the guitar" probably meant the first four courses of the English guitar. If this was indeed the case, the open notes of each course, ranging from the fourth course to the first course (the one closest to the player's lap), would have been GCEG. Assuming that Jefferson was probably referencing a typical four-string early gourd banjo of the period with three long strings and one short thumb-string, then it is possible that the instrument he observed was tuned in the reentrant tuning of gCEG. Thus the tuning of the early gourd banjo's three long strings would have been CEG, exactly the same as that of the first three strings in the earliest published tuning for the five-string banjo: cFCEG (Elias Howe's *Complete Preceptor For The Banjo* [Boston: Oliver Ditson & Co., 1851], 4). While the actual pitches vary to reflect different keys, these intervals for the banjo's first three strings—an ascending major third and a minor third—would remain the same for most five-string banjo standard tunings through the present.

29. *The Old Plantation* (South Carolina, ca. 1785–90), watercolor on laid paper, 11 11/16 x 17 7/8 inches, Abbey Aldrich Rockefeller Folk Art Museum, Colonial Williamsburg Foundation, Williamsburg, Virginia, gift of Mrs. John D. Rockefeller, 35.301.3. For more on the picture, see Susan P. Shames, *The Old Plantation: The Artist Revealed* (Williamsburg, VA: The Colonial Williamsburg Foundation, 2010), and Pestcoe's chapter in this volume, "The Banjar Pictured: The Depiction of the African American Early Gourd Banjo in *The Old Plantation*, South Carolina, 1780s."

30. Price and Price, introduction to *Narrative of a Five Years Expedition*, xxix.

31. Richard and Sally Price, "John Gabriel Stedman's Collection of 18th Century Artifacts from Suriname," *Nieuwe West-Indische Gids* 53, nos. 3–4 (June 1979): 126, 131, 138. In 1979, the Prices rediscovered Stedman's lost *creole bania*, which had been mislabeled and misplaced in the Leiden museum for years.

32. "Banza imitation d'un instrument africain / d'usage general [sic] parmi les no[irs?] d'Haiti [sic]." For a description of the instrument, see also *Banjo!* ed. Mia Awouters, catalogue of the banjo exhibition, MIM Brussels, October 16, 2003–February 15, 2004, Brussels, 2003. Our thanks to Saskia Willaert, curator, African Collections Museum of Musical Instruments in Brussels, for providing the text of Schœlcher's original label for the *banza* as well as the preceding source citation and general information about the

inclusion of the instrument in the MIM Brussels's exhibition on the banjo and its African precursors. For more on the Haiti *banza*, see the chapters by Willaert and Pete Ross in this volume.

33. Verena Höhn (MA), research associate, Department of Ethnomusicology, Media Technology, and the Berlin Phonogram Archive, Ethnological Museum Berlin, email to S. Pestcoe, April 8, 2014; report from Suriname, *Periodical Accounts Relating to the Missions of the Church of the United Brethren Established Among the Heathen*, 33 vols. (London, 1853), 21:44, 440. Richard Price, one of the foremost authorities on early Afro-Surinamese language and culture, suggests that the designation "Panja" given in the original 1861 curatorial notes may have been an error and was probably Banja, which he explains "was the standard name [for the early banjo] in Sranantongo [literally "the Surinamese tongue"; Sranan, Suriname Creole], the language of the [Afro-Surinamese] slaves in 1850" (Price to S. Pestcoe, email, June 6, 2014). A photo of the *panja* may be accessed online at http://www.mimo-international.com/MIMO/doc/IFD/SPK_BERLIN_DE_EM_OBJID_169626, accessed October 25, 2017.

34. Original entry in the main catalogue of the Königliche Kunstkammer (Berlin, Germany) made in 1861 by the head curator Leopold von Ledebur, Höhn to S. Pestcoe, April 8, 2014. For more on *Anansitori* and other folktales in Afro-Surinamese tradition, see Jan Voorhoeve and Ursy M. Lichtveld, eds., *Creole Drum: An Anthology of Creole Literature in Surinam* (New Haven, CT: Yale University Press, 1975), chapter 3, "Folktales," 76–115.

35. Sally Price, "When is a Calabash not a Calabash?" *Nieuwe West-Indische Gids* 56, nos. 1–2 (1982): 69.

36. Johann David Schoepf, *Travels in the Confederation, 1783–1784*, trans. and ed. Alfred J. Morrison (Philadelphia: W. J. Campbell, 1911; reprint New York: Bergman Publishers, 1968), vol. 2, *Pennsylvania, Maryland, Virginia, the Carolinas, East Florida, the Bahamas*, 261–62.

37. Stedman, *Narrative of a Five Years Expedition*, 540. Stedman's *Narrative* is the only source for *bania* as a designation for an early gourd banjo. The word may have been his transliteration of Sranantongo term *banya*, which refers to a type of traditional Afro-Surinamese song and dance. In his textual list and depiction of eighteen "Musical Instruments of the African Negroes [of Suriname]" (plate 69), Stedman applies the term to two other instruments, which are not chordophones: the "Ansokko-Bania" (no. 3), an unusual instrument similar to a slit drum, and the "Loango-Bania" (no.10), a thumb-piano (538). The prefixal designations "Ansokko" and "Loango" are clearly ethnic-cultural associations: the former may be a reference to a Yoruba subgroup, while the latter indicates the West-Central African Kingdom of Loango, one of the principal sources for Suriname's African-born slaves. That said, "Creole-Bania" (no. 15) reflects the eighteenth-century custom of referring to blacks of African descent country-born in the New World as creoles. By characterizing this instrument as "Creole," Stedman conveys his perception that the early gourd banjo he encountered in Suriname was not an African import, but rather, an instrument unique to Surinamese creoles, and, therefore, a product of the African diaspora in the New World.

38. Richard C. Jankowsky, *Stambeli: Music, Trance, and Alterity in Tunisia* (Chicago: University of Chicago Press, 2010), the *gumbri*, 97–102; the *fakrūn*, 106–7. For the *gambara*, see Jankowsky's liner notes for the CD album *Stambeli, featuring Salah el-Ouergli: The Legacy of the Black Tunisians* (Paris: Les Chemins Productions [PLC101], 2010), 44.

39. As the *panja* was clearly built for left-handed play, the thumb-string peg is placed in reverse of how it is placed on the *creole bania*. See also note 33.

40. Our use of the phrases *back-to-front* and *side-mounted* comes from an unpublished document created by Ed Britt and Peter Szego entitled "Early Banjo Design Elements c. 1800 to 1865" (ca. November 1, 2000). In the context of the Banjo Sightings Database project, Greg C. Adams and George Wunderlich use the word *vertical* as a synonym for *back-to-front* and *horizontal* for *side-mounted*.

41. The term *down-picking* was coined in the 1960s by modern old-time banjoist Art Rosenbaum "in order to avoid ridiculous arguments about where 'frailing' leaves off and 'clawhammering' begins" (Art Rosenbaum, *The Art of the Mountain Banjo* [Mel Bay, 1999], 6). For further discussions of down-picking techniques, see in this volume Pestcoe's chapter "The Banjar Pictured" and Greg C. Adams and Chuck Levy's chapter comparing the West African Jola form of down-picking to nineteenth-century "Banjo Style."

42. Special thanks to Jayme Stone for sharing his findings from his field trip to Mali in 2007 on the previously unreported Dogon *konou* and the technique used to play it.

43. See David W. Ames and Anthony V. King, *Glossary of Hausa Music and Its Social Contexts* (Evanston, IL: Northwestern University Press, 1971) for the technique used to play the *gurmi* (44) and the *molo* (46).

44. Frank Converse, "Banjo Reminiscences," *The Cadenza* 7, no. 11 (July 1901): 4.

45. See Schreyer, *The Banjo Entertainers*, 9–19; Gura and Bollman, *America's Instrument*, plates 1–3, 51.

46. Hans Nathan, *Dan Emmett and the Rise of Early Negro Minstrelsy* (Norman: University of Oklahoma Press, 1962, 1977), 118–22.

PART II

Exploring the African Roots

CHAPTER 2

Banjo Ancestors
West African Plucked Spike Lutes

Shlomo Pestcoe

Editor's Headnote

For "Banjo Ancestors" and its following companion piece, "List of West African Plucked Spike Lutes"

As the starting point for exploring the African roots of the banjo, this chapter traces the banjo's organological "genome" thousands of years back to the world's first plucked spike lutes—those of Mesopotamia and the ancient Near East, including Pharonic Egypt. It then provides an historical and ethno-organological overview of the development of the current extensive family of plucked spike lutes throughout West Africa. The chapter concludes with some thoughts on the West African heritage of the African American early gourd banjo. The chapter that follows ("List of West African Plucked Spike Lutes," co-authored by Pestcoe and Greg C. Adams) presents a classificatory list of the eighty known West African plucked spike lutes that Pestcoe had been compiling since 2009, with full annotations and source citations.

> Negroes are very fond of the discordant notes of the banjar. . . . This instrument is the invention of, and was brought here by the African Negroes, who are most expert in the performance thereof, which are principally their own country tunes, indeed I do not remember ever to have heard any thing like European numbers from its touch.
> —John Luffman, *A Brief Account of the Island of Antigua*[1]

The findings of recent research make it increasingly clear that the African roots of the banjo can be traced to the vast family of approximately eighty known traditions of plucked spike lutes found across West Africa, which encompass a broad diversity of distinctive ethnic forms.[2] However, those same findings have also made it increasingly clear that the banjo is not African in origin, but, rather, African American.

It was once widely assumed that the first banjos were instruments that had come across the Atlantic from Africa in the Middle Passage. More focused investigations of the historical record reveal, however, that the *early gourd banjo* (my descriptor for the original genus of the banjo) was actually a creolized hybrid instrument unique to the early African diaspora. First emerging in the circum-Caribbean during the seventeenth century in the context of slavery and the transatlantic slave trade, it was the product of a synthesis of African and European influences.[3] In other words, the early gourd banjo may best be described as an African American instrument of West African heritage, rather than a West African instrument imported to the New World.

In this chapter I look at the West African roots of the banjo. To begin with, by examining their "genetic markers"—by which I mean the historical fundamental design features that distinguish the instruments in question—I trace the organological "genome"[4] shared by the early gourd banjo and all West African plucked spike lutes thousands of years back to the world's first lutes (i.e., string instruments with necks that are distinct from their bodies), the spike lutes of Mesopotamia and the ancient Near East. I then briefly consider necked lutes, the other major category of lutes. I follow that up with a brief synopsis of what is known of the early history of the West African family of plucked spike lutes and present an overview and a basic typology of the various kinds of traditional West African plucked spike lutes, focusing on key aspects of their traditional design and construction. I also take a brief look at the different types of musicians who traditionally play these lutes and the traditional performance contexts that they are played in. Finally, I conclude with some thoughts on the relationship of the early gourd banjo to the West African plucked spike lute family.

Ancient Connections and Roots

Organologically speaking, the fundamental design feature shared by the early gourd banjo and all traditional West African plucked lutes is that the neck on the instrument passes over or through the wall of its body. This characteristic defines all of these instruments as spike lutes in the Hornbostel-Sachs (HS) classification of instruments, the standard in modern organology.[5] It is also the primary genetic marker that indicates the descent of historical and current spike lutes from the earliest known lutes[6] in the history of humanity: the plucked spike lutes of Mesopotamia—referred to generically by the ancient Sumerian descriptor *pantur*[7]—dating back more than four thousand years.[8]

Following the archaeological trail, the *pantur* appears to have spread northwest from Mesopotamia to ancient Anatolia (present-day Turkey), where it was adopted by the Hittites (ca. 1600–1178 BCE), as well as westward and southward to the various Semitic peoples of Syria and Canaan (present-day Israel and Palestine). The plucked spike lute is then thought to have been introduced into Pharonic Egypt sometime in the late Second Intermediate Period (1640–1540 BCE), when the Hyksos (various nomadic Semitic tribes from Canaan and Syria) dominated the country. It first appears in Egypt's archaeological record after the expulsion of the Hyksos and the establishment of the Eighteenth Dynasty (1543–1292 BCE) of the New Kingdom (the Egyptian Empire) (ca. 1550–1077 BCE).[9]

To return to our organological analysis of West African spike lute genetic markers, all of the traditional plucked spike lutes of West Africa share three fundamental design features:

1. A drum-like body topped with an animal hide soundtable (see figures A, B, E, F, and G for examples). In the great diversity of the West African plucked spike lute family, instrument bodies have been historically made from a variety of materials: either carved wood, gourd (*Lagenaria siceraria*, also referred to as *Cucurbita lagenaria* L., which grows on vines), or calabash (*Crescentia cujete*, which grows on trees). In modern times, metal cans, plastic jugs, and other re-purposed commercially manufactured containers and materials have also been used.

2. A plain round stick neck without frets, which is a spike neck because, depending on the given tradition, it either passes over (most common) or pierces through the wall of the lute's body (see figures A, E, F, and G). In many West African traditions, lute necks have historically been made of papyrus sedge (*Cyperus papyrus*; also referred to as reed, bamboo, or bamboo reed). This plant grows wild in wetland areas throughout West Africa, and is known by a variety of names: for example, in Mandinka, *bang* (also *bangjolo*)[10] (The Gambia), and in Hausa, *gora*[11] (northern Nigeria). The necks on West African plucked spike lutes—as well as on those found across the Sahara in North Africa—fall under one of two fundamental divisions, based on their span in relationship to the instrument's body: full-spike—the neck extends the full length of the instrument's body so that its lower end protrudes over or through the body's tail end (see figure A); or *semi-spike*—it extends only about three-quarters of the instrument's body's length to end within the body just short of its tail end (see figure B).

3. Sliding tuning rings to which the strings are affixed (see figures A and D). Typically made of either leather or cloth strips or a loop of the given string knotted at one end, sliding tuning rings are the means by which the instrument's strings are attached to its neck and tuned. Tuning is done by literally sliding the rings up or down the neck, which are then held in place by the strings' tension.

Judging from period depictions in the archaeological record, all three of these basic design features were also found on ancient Mesopotamian plucked spike lutes, as well as those found throughout the ancient Near East, including ancient Egypt, later during the Bronze Age (3300–1200 BCE).

We see these features on the world's oldest extant complete lute: a three-string wooden-bodied spike lute that was found buried alongside the coffin of the court singer Harmose (Thebes, Egypt, Eighteenth Dynasty, ca. 1490 BCE).[12] The Harmose lute is remarkably similar in many ways to the various ethnic forms of wooden-bodied plucked spike lutes still found throughout West Africa today.

As seen on the Harmose lute—as well as in depictions in ancient Egyptian and Near Eastern art—the plucked spike lutes of Pharonic Egypt and the ancient Near East in general had round stick necks with drum-like bodies of various shapes, topped with a tautly stretched soundtable made of animal hide.[13] The evidence of the Harmose lute and the remains of other ancient Egyptian lutes, as well as period depictions from the Eighteenth Dynasty, show that the shape of the body on lutes of this period indicated the material it was made of. Carved hollowed-out wooden bodies were typically either narrow elliptical or oval, while those made of tortoise shell were round. Late in the Eighteenth Dynasty, some depictions also appear of lutes that have narrow figure-8-shaped bodies with a waist and concave sides, which are also seen in depictions of Hittite plucked spike lutes; these were most likely made of carved wood. Conversely, as evident from the few extant examples in museum collections, lutes of ancient Egypt's Late Period (664–332 BCE) had mostly wooden pear-shaped bodies with a bowlback.

Like ancient Egyptian lutes, the shapes of the bodies on traditional West African plucked spike lutes also indicate the materials of which they are made. Bodies of carved hollowed-out wood tend to be narrow and either elliptical, canoe-shaped, or figure-8-shaped, while those made of gourd or calabash are wide and round or, to a lesser extent, oval or teardrop in shape.

In period depictions of spike lutes throughout the ancient Near East and Pharonic Egypt, the strings were not affixed to their necks with tuning pegs, but, rather, with sliding tuning rings, similar to those still used on all traditional West African plucked spike lutes. In the case of the Harmose lute, its tuning rings are actually several rings of twine tightly coiled together to form a single movable unit for each string, all of which are made of gut. Moreover, on the Harmose lute the tuning rings of the two shorter strings serve as capos[14] to shorten the adjacent longer strings in order to make all three of the lute's strings equal in length. This same capo feature appears on most West African plucked spike lutes with two or more strings.

As on most traditional West African plucked spike lutes, the necks on ancient Egyptian and Near Eastern plucked spike lutes did not pierce the body. Rather, the neck was threaded through slits made in the animal hide soundtable and rested on shallow indentations made in the body's upper rim. This over-the-rim construction is found on the Harmose lute. Another example of over-the-rim neck-on-body placement is clearly seen on the lute being played by a nude female Canaanite lutenist, portrayed in a bronze statuette (IAA M969), unearthed in Beit She'an, Palestine (present-day Israel), in 1931; it is roughly dated to sometime between the Late Bronze Age and Early Hellenistic Period (ca. 322–140 BCE) of ancient Israel-Judea.[15] Furthermore, the neck on the Harmose lute was full-spike, which seems to have been the standard for ancient Egyptian and Near Eastern spike lutes. However, a few examples of Late Period Egyptian lutes with semi-spike necks are extant.

The evident organological similarities between the plucked spike lutes of the ancient Near East and Pharonic Egypt and those of present-day West Africa obviously suggest a likely kinship between these instruments. But the exact nature of that relationship—how they are related historically and what the specific historical routes of transmission and diffusion of the plucked spike lute concept were—will remain an unsolved mystery until pertinent evidence can be found in the archaeological and/or historical records to help us more substantively trace the historical development and dissemination of these instruments.

Necked Lutes: The Other Principal Category of Lutes

In the 330s BCE, depictions of the *pandoura*, the ancient Greek plucked lute, began to appear on terra-cotta figurines and reliefs in the art of ancient Greece.[16] As evident from these representations, the *pandoura* was a new type of lute that differed greatly from the spike lutes of the ancient Near East. Judging from the various depicted forms of the *pandoura*, the instrument's neck was not a spike neck as it did not pass over or through the wall of the instrument's body. On the contrary, the necks on ancient Greek lutes were either carved from the same piece of wood that formed the body or attached to the body. In the HS classification of instruments, the *pandoura* falls under the heading of "Necked Lutes," the other principal category beside "Spike Lutes" in the HS subsection "Handle Lutes" (i.e., string instruments with "handles" [necks]).[17] A necked lute is any type of lute (plucked or bowed) that has its neck attached to or carved from or built up from its instrument's body. Today, necked lutes are the predominant kind of plucked lutes and bowed lutes (fiddles) throughout the world.

The ascendency of the necked lute began during the Hellenistic Period (323–31 BCE) when the *pandoura* spread throughout the ancient Near East, apparently supplanting indigenous local spike lutes. The ancient Greek lute was later adopted into Roman musical material culture, referenced as *pandura* in Latin transliteration. During the Pax Romana (27 BCE–180 CE) and the Late Roman Period (250–450 CE), the Greco-Roman *pandoura-pandura* became a popular vernacular instrument, generally associated with social dancing, carousing in taverns, and other public entertainments.[18] Today, nearly all of the modern traditional plucked lutes of the Near East, Central Asia, and Caucasia (e.g., ʿūd [oud], *tambur* [*tanbur*], *baglama* [*saz*], *dombra, komuz, tobshuur, panduri, chonguri*, etc.) are necked lutes, as are those found the world over of European origin or heritage (e.g., Western lute, guitar, mandolin, *cavaquinho*, ukulele, *tiple, balalaika, tamburitza*, etc.). As such, they all can trace their roots back to the ancient Greco-Roman *pandoura-pandura*.

Necked lutes, similar to the *pandoura-pandura* types depicted in ancient Greek and Roman art, are commonly seen in the Greco-Bactrian Buddhist art of the Kingdom of Gandhāra (situated in the north of modern-day Pakistan and eastern Afghanistan) from the first to the third centuries CE.[19] It is highly probable that the necked lute concept spread from Gandhāra to India and China, as well as to Central Asia. The plucked lutes of South Asia and East Asia, however, include both spike lutes (e.g., *sanxian, shamisen, dàn-tính, ektar*, etc.) and necked lutes (e.g., *pipa, ruan, yuequin, dàn-doán, sgra-snyan, danyen, sitar, dotara, ravaj*, etc.).

To return to sub-Saharan Africa, the few indigenous plucked lutes found along the Swahili coast of Southeast Africa (primarily Kenya's Mombasa and the Zanzibar Archipelago off the coast of Tanzania) and the Indian Ocean islands off the coast of Mozambique-Madagascar and the Comoros Islands—are necked lutes. These include the *kibangala* (Mombasa and the Swahili coast), the *gabbus* (Zanzibar), the *kabozy* (Madagascar), and the *gambusi* (Comoros). They are all descended from the *qanbus* (*turbi*)[20] of San'a, Yemen, classified as a necked lute because its body and neck are carved from a single piece of wood.

West African Plucked Spike Lutes: Beginnings

At present, any study of the origins and early history of the West African family of plucked spike lutes is seriously hampered by the aforementioned dearth of pertinent archaeological evidence and historical documentation. Still, based on what little evidentiary information is available, we can surmise that the plucked lute concept most likely came to West Africa from across the Sahara in the course of early trade with Muslim traders—mainly Berbers from North Africa, the original "Moors"—which began in the ninth century of the Common Era. Moreover, we can further infer that the introduction of the plucked lute was probably contemporaneous with the introduction of Islam into West Africa, the principal agents of transmission for which were, again, Muslim Berbers from North Africa.[21]

In his 1068 work *Kitāb al-Masālik wa'l-Mamālik* (Book of Routes and Realms), the Muslim Andalusian geographer-historian Abu 'Ubayd al-Bakri (1014–94) specified the three major centers of that trade in Bilad al-Sudan (Arabic, literally "The Land of the Black People": West Africa):[22]

1. Ghana,[23] which was how the powerful Soninke Empire of Wagadu (ca. 750–1100) was generally known outside West Africa.[24] It was based in the southern region of present-day Mauritania, northern Senegal, and southwestern Mali.[25] It would be succeeded by the Mande Empire of ancient Mali (ca. 1235–1500).

2. Takrur (ca. 800–1285), located in northern Senegal in the middle of the Senegal River valley. Around 1033, Takrur became the first West African kingdom to formally adopt Islam as its official state religion.

3. Gao, a town located on the banks of the Niger River in eastern Mali, which was not only an important trading center but also a major power. The Gao Empire apparently existed from the ninth century until the late thirteenth century when it was absorbed into the Mali Empire. It would later become the capital of the Songhai Empire (ca.1464–1591), the successor of the Mali Empire.

These hubs of international commerce and cross-cultural exchange were also probably the epicenters for the emergence and development of the many distinctive indigenous forms of the plucked spike lute in this subregion of West Africa, referred to as Greater Senegambia or the Western Sudan.[26] It is generally accepted that *jaliya* (also *jeliya*)—the art and essence of the griots,[27] for which the lute has always been such a crucial traditional instrument—first emerged in the ancient Mali Empire, springing from earlier bardic traditions associated with Wagadu (ancient Ghana).[28] In fact, the earliest documentation of plucked lutes in West Africa occurs in some of the first published reports on the splendor of the royal court of ancient Mali.

The earliest mention of West African plucked lutes appears in 1337, when the Arab historian al-'Umarī (1301–49) in his work *Masālik al absār fī mamālik al amsār* (Pathways of Vision in the Realms of the Metropolises) describes the fabulous wealth and majesty of the Mali Empire, considered then to be one of the richest kingdoms in the known world. Drawing on reports from contemporary Muslim travelers and traders, al-'Umarī wrote: "When the king of this kingdom [Mali] comes in from a journey, a *jitr* [parasol] and a standard are held over his head as he rides, and drums are beaten and *tunbūr* [lutes] and trumpets, well made of horn, are played in front of him."[29] Ibn Battuta (1304–69) of Morocco, the first foreign visitor to Mali to leave us a firsthand account of his visit, wrote in the memoir of his journey to West Africa in 1352 a detailed description of the royal court of Mansa Sulayman, who ruled from 1341 to 1358. According to Ibn Battuta, when the *mansa* (the Mande term for supreme ruler) went into the palace yard for a royal audience, "the sultan is preceded by his musicians, who carry gold and silver *qunburī* [lutes], and behind him come three hundred armed slaves."[30]

Shortly after first contact with the Portuguese in the 1440s,[31] reports began to appear in European literature of West African plucked lutes, most often as instruments of the griots encountered in Senegambia. The earliest such account is that of Luís de Cadamosto (Alvise da Ca' da Mosto) (1432–83), a Venetian explorer and trader in the employ of Portugal's Duke of Viseu, better known to history as Prince Henry "the Navigator" (1394–1460).[32] In his first voyage to West Africa in 1455,[33] Cadamosto visited Cayor (also Kayor; one of the four kingdoms in northern Senegal that comprised the Wolof Empire [1350–1549]) and described a local string instrument that "is somewhat like a fiddle, having only two strings, which they play on with their fingers."[34] While Cadamosto does not identify this plucked lute as being specific to griot musicians, we can surmise that it probably was since lute playing in traditional Wolof society—as in most West African societies with a griot tradition—has always been the exclusive domain of griot lutenists from families with a history of specializing in the instrument. Another Portuguese report, this one from the early sixteenth century, seems to bear out this contention: in describing "the kingdom of Gyloffa" (the Jolof [Wolof] Empire) in northern Senegal, the account describes "Gaul," who "are usually jesters and singers and play on viols and cavacos [plucked lutes]."[35] In this case, the descriptor *Gaul* appears to derive either from *gewel*, the generic term for griot in Wolof, or from *gaulo* (*gawlo*),[36] the generic Fulbe-Tukulóor term for griot, which in the Jolof region of northern Senegal is borrowed by the Wolof to designate a *xalamkat* (Wolof, literally "*xalam* player"; a griot lutenist). Centuries later, in his travels through Senegambia (1795–97), the Scottish explorer Mungo Park (1771–1806) encountered "the *koonting*, a sort of guitar with three strings," played by "the singing-men, called *Jilli kea*."[37] Park's term "*Jilli kea*" seems to be his take on *jeli ke*, which is Mande for "male griot," indicating that players of the *koonting* were probably griot lutenists.

As mentioned earlier, the plucked lute concept most likely came to West Africa around the same time that Islam was introduced. Looking at the early spread of Islam throughout the then known world, we see a pattern whereby the initial agents of transmission of the Muslim faith often brought, along with the Qur'an, music instruments—especially lute family string instruments—from their own lands and cultures. Throughout the Islamic sphere of influence—from Central Asia to Southeast Asia, from North Africa to the Balkans—plucked lutes and bowed lutes of Arab, Persian, and/or Turkish origin were adopted by the various peoples and adapted for incorporation into local traditions.

West Africa, however, is the one notable exception. In terms of lute family instruments, no evidence can be found here of Near Eastern plucked necked lutes such as the short-necked bowlbacked '*ūd* (also *oud*), the long-necked *tanbur* (*tambur*), or the long-necked *buzuq*. Quite to the contrary, as stated above, the many historically traditional plucked lutes of West Africa are all spike lutes. Similarly, the more than eighty forms of fiddle found throughout West Africa[38] (e.g., the Fulbe *nyaanyooru* [Senegambia], the Wolof *riti* [Senegambia], the Dagbamba *gondze* [Ghana], the Hausa *goge* [Nigeria], etc.) are also very different from their Near Eastern counterparts—the various ethnic-regional forms of Arab *rebab*, Persian *kamānche*, or Turkish *kemençe*: they are single-string instruments with round stick spike necks, like their plucked lute kin, and round gourd bodies.[39] Considering the evidence presented by the distinctive spike lute genetic markers of traditional West African plucked lutes and fiddles, clearly Arab, Persian, and Turkish influences were not factors in the organological development of West African lute family instruments.

As stated, the principal agents of transmission of Islam into West Africa were Berber Muslims rather than Arabs, Persians, or Turks. Thus, when we look at the genetic markers of West African lute-family instruments, we see an organological kinship between West African plucked spike lutes and the various kinds of North African plucked spike lutes of Berber heritage, such as the semi-spike lutes of Morocco's Berbers, with drum-like bodies that have animal hide soundtables: the four-stringed Amazighi *loutar* (also *guimbri*) with a pear-shaped carved wooden body and the four-stringed Shilha (Chleuh) *lotar* with a round body typically made from a metal washbasin.[40] We likewise see a similar link between West African spike fiddles and North African Berber fiddles like the single-string Shilha (Berber) *ribāb* of Morocco and the single-string *rabāba* of Libya (also of probable Berber origin).

The transmission of spike lute family instruments would also flow from West Africa to North Africa as a consequence of the trans-Saharan slave trade, which began in the early 800s CE and ended in the early 1900s. Over the centuries, millions of enslaved captives and mercenaries from West Africa would be forcibly brought across the Sahara to North Africa.[41] One result was that North Africa would become the home to the banjo's cousins—plucked spike lutes of West African heritage that originated among the enslaved West Africans and their descendants, probably in the seventeenth or eighteenth century. In Morocco and Algeria, the Gnawa[42] play the three-stringed semi-spike *hajhuj* (also called *gnbri*, *guinbri*, *guembri*, or *sintir*)[43] with a narrow oblong or lozenge-shaped wooden body. Tunisia has three three-stringed full-spike lutes: the *gumbri* (*gombri*) with a large wooden body resembling a side drum; the *gambara* with a narrow oblong wooden body; and the *fakrūn* (literally "turtle") with a body made from a large tortoise shell.[44] The *hajhuj* is traditionally played to accompany the Gnawa *lila*, a nightlong spirit possession and healing ritual that includes ceremonial trance dancing, and to invoke the spirits of their West African ancestors, the *ulad al-Bambara* (literally "the Sons of the Bambara," a reference to the Bamana, modern Mali's predominant ethnic group).[45] Similarly, the Tunisian lutes are primarily played to accompany *stambeli*, which is likewise a spirit possession–healing trance dance ritual of West African derivation.[46]

Classifying and Analyzing West African Plucked Spike Lutes

In his seminal article, "Plucked Lutes in West Africa: An Historical Overview" (1996), the Africanist ethnomusicologist Eric Charry made the first attempt to study and analyze the rich diversity of traditional plucked spike lutes found throughout West Africa.[47] At the time, however, little hard data were available on these instruments. "To this day," Charry noted, "there is no comprehensive overview of West African lutes, nor is there a great wealth of documentation of the specific kinds of lutes that are found in West Africa. Speculation on the history, distribution, diffusion, and use of lutes in West Africa, therefore, has had little documentary support."[48]

In terms of furthering research and documentation of the West African family of plucked spike lutes, Charry provides useful fundamental criteria for classifying and analyzing these instruments by focusing on the "three major features which may be used to distinguish plucked lutes in West Africa from each other: who plays them, the kind of bridge, and the kind of resonator."[49]

Criterion 1: "Who Plays Them"

Charry divided West African plucked spike lutes into two major sections based on the musicians who historically played these instruments in their traditional sociocultural performance contexts: *griot lutes* (a term Charry coined to denote the unique class of lutes exclusive to griot lutenists from families with a history of specializing in the instrument), and *non-griot lutes*. Griot lutes are mainly used vocationally in performances for patrons in exchange for gifts, such as to accompany praise-singing, historically themed recitative songs, and storytelling, as well as to play instrumental listening music. In terms of organology, most griot lutes are what I would call standard griot lutes, that is, various ethnic versions of similar wooden-bodied lutes with semi-spike necks and three or more strings. Examples of standard griot lutes include the five-string *xalam* of the Wolof *xalam-kats*; the four-string *n'goni* of the Bamana and Maninka *jeliw* (singular *jeli*; griot); the four-string *gambaré* of the Soninke *geserun* (singular *geseré*); and the *hoddu* of the Fulbe *wambaabe* (singular *bambaado*), which may have three to five strings.

Since the vast majority of West African traditional lutenists have historically been word-music artisans (i.e., bards, praise-singers, and musicians for whom performing is their traditional vocation, be they griot or non-griot), we can refine Charry's "non-griot lutes" category as "non-griot artisan lutes" in order to specify lutes that are primarily associated with (but not exclusive to) professional bards and musicians in cultures that have no griot traditions. For instance, the Hausa of northern Nigeria and Niger are an Islamized people with traditional social stratification similar to that seen in those Islamized West African ethnic societies with the tripartite caste system that engenders the development of the griot tradition. However, contrary to the popular misconception, the *marok'a* (bards, praise-singers) and *maka'da* (musicians and musical performers) of the Hausa are not griots.[50] While similar in vocation and sociocultural function to griots, Hausa word-music artisans embody a different and highly distinctive tradition. For one thing, unlike in the griot tradition, anyone can be a *marok'i* or *maka'di*. While traditional praise singing and music making are typically inherited vocations in Hausa society, anyone can take up these callings. By the same token, while most Hausa instruments are traditionally associated with vocational music making, they are not exclusive to *marok'a* and *maka'da* in the same way that griot instruments are exclusive to specialists from certain griot families. In terms of the seven Hausa plucked spike lutes—the three-string gourd-bodied full-spike *gurmi*, the two-string calabash-bodied full-spike *gurumi*, the two-string wooden-bodied semi-spike *garaya*, the two-string gourd-bodied semi-spike *komo*, the three-string wooden-bodied semi-spike *molo*, the two-string gourd-bodied semi-spike *kwamsa*, and the diminutive one-string semi-spike *kuntigi* with a small body typically made from a sardine can—while they are all traditionally associated with *marok'a* and *maka'da*, anyone can play them. Other examples of non-griot artisan lutes include the two-string wooden-bodied semi-spike Yoruba *duru* (*molo*) (Nigeria), the two-string gourd-bodied semi-spike Farefare (Frafra) *koliko* (*kologo*) (Ghana), and the massive three-stringed gourd-bodied semi-spike Gwari *kaburu* (Nigeria).

To these two categories I have added a third category, folk lutes,[51] to cover those instruments traditionally played by non-artisan vernacular musicians in non-vocational social contexts, like accompanying informal socializing and social dancing as well as other forms of personal and communal entertainment. Examples of folk lutes include the members of Atlantic-Bak cluster[52] of similar three-string gourd-bodied full-spike lutes from Casamance (southern Senegal), The Gambia, and Guinea-Bissau along the Atlantic coast: the Jola *ekonting* (*akonting*)[53] (see figure A), the Manyago *bunchundo* (see figure E), the Bujogo *ñopata* (see figure F), the Balanta *kusunde*, and the Papel *busunde*.

Criterion 2: "Kind of Bridge"

Charry identified two main categories of bridges that he encountered in his research:[54]

1. Fan-shaped. This type of bridge is unique to griot lutes with semi-spike necks and narrow carved wooden bodies. (Notable exceptions to this rule are the two semi-spike lutes of the Dogon of Mali: the single-string gourd-bodied *kona* and the two-string wooden-bodied *konou*, both of which are non-griot lutes with fan-shaped bridges.)[55] The fan-shaped bridge is typically made of a flat piece of gourd. The upper portion of the bridge, over which the strings pass, is convex and somewhat rounded, much like the shape of the tops seen on European violin-family bridges and fiddle bridges the world over throughout history (see the Malian *n'goni* in figure B). This shaping of the bridge's top allows for the proper spacing between the individual strings and their proper positioning for playing. The lower end of the fan-shaped bridge is inserted into a soundhole made in the tautened animal hide soundtable that tops the instrument's body, right above where the instrument's semi-spike neck ends. The bridge has a hole made in its lower portion that enables it to be slipped onto the neck's narrow "spike" end.

2. Cylindrical. Unlike the fan-shaped bridge, a cylindrical bridge is a floating bridge that sits on the soundtable and is moveable. It is the most common type of bridge found in West Africa's Central Sudan[56] (eastern West Africa) subregion.

One kind of cylindrical bridge is a round cylindrical wooden tube, hollowed out and filled with seeds or gravel to produce a soft rattle. Other examples may be small pieces of wooden stick, twig, or plant stalk. Examples of lutes with cylindrical bridges include the three-string gourd-bodied full-spike Kilba *gullum* (Nigeria; see figure G), the two-string calabash-bodied full-spike Toubou *gurumi* (Niger), the two-string gourd-bodied semi-spike Berom *yomshi* (Nigeria), and all of the aforementioned Hausa lutes (Nigeria and Niger).

Because of our recent knowledge of traditional Senegambian full-spike lutes previously unknown to international researchers, I have added two more categories to the "slip-on" and floating "cylindrical" bridge types specified by Charry: bipedal bridge and block bridge, both of which are floating bridges. The former is a large wooden bridge with two distinct legs that rest on the instrument's soundtable that is only found on instruments in the aforementioned Atlantic-Bak cluster (see figure C). The latter is the floating version of the fan-shaped bridge found on the few known gourd-bodied, full-spike griot lutes: the five-string Wolof *xalam geseré* (The Gambia), the five-string Wolof *geseré* (Senegal), and the four-string Diawara *kôla-lemmé* (Mali).[57] The floating block bridge has a fan-shaped top on a block body with a flat bottom that sits atop of the instrument's animal hide soundtable. It is also seen on the earliest known depiction of a West African plucked spike lute: a line drawing of a four-string, gourd-bodied, full-spike griot lute, shown with various other West African music instruments (most of which appear to be griot), in plate 9, "Musical Instruments," of Major William Gray and Staff Surgeon Dochard's *Travels in Western Africa* (1825).[58]

Criterion 3: "Kind of Resonator"

As stated earlier, historically, West African plucked spike lute resonators (bodies) have been made of either carved hollowed-out wood, gourd, or calabash. In modern times, materials used to make lute bodies have included repurposed commercially manufactured containers like metal cans, washbasins, and even plastic jugs.

The type of neck on a West African lute traditionally is another factor in determining what kind of body it has. Depending on tradition, a non-griot semi-spike lute may have a wooden body or one made of gourd. Calabash, however, does not appear to be used for semi-spike instruments.

The various ethnic forms of standard griot lutes with three or more strings that have semi-spike necks only have carved wooden bodies that are generally narrow and either elliptical, canoe-shaped, or figure-8-shaped. Yet, single-string griot lutes—like the Songhai *n'jurkel* (Mali) and the Soninke-Diawara *molo* (Mali)—while having semi-spike necks, generally have gourd bodies, though they may occasionally be made of carved hollowed-out wood. Quite to the contrary, the relatively few griot lutes with full-spike necks—the aforementioned Wolof *xalam geseré*, Wolof *geseré*, and Diawara *kôla-lemmé*—have round bodies only made of gourd.

In sharp contrast, all West African full-spike lutes have non-wooden bodies. The bodies on the aforementioned Atlantic-Bak cluster lutes from Senegambia are only made of gourd and are generally round, though the gourd bodies on Jola *si'konting* (the plural form of *ekonting*) may also be oval or teardrop-shaped. Conversely, the full-spike lutes of West Africa's eastern Central Sudan subregion may have bodies made of either gourd or calabash, depending on tradition: for example, the three-string gourd-bodied Kilba *gullum* (Nigeria; see figure G), the three-string gourd-bodied Hausa *gurmi* (Nigeria), and the two-string calabash-bodied Toubou *gurumi* (Niger).

The Missing Criterion: Neck Span

In his list of "three major features which may be used to distinguish plucked lutes in West Africa from each other," Charry does not include one other fundamental criterion: the span of a West African plucked spike lute's neck in relationship to its body. The main reason for this omission was Charry's belief at the time that the necks on West African spike lutes were all of the same span: "On West African plucked lutes the neck, a round fretless stick, traverses most, but not all, of the length of the resonator body."[59] As described earlier, this neck span is what I refer to as *semi-spike* (this is actually Charry's term),[60] which is where the neck extends about three-quarters the length of the body to end just short of the body's tail end (figure B). Although Charry was mistaken in assuming that semi-spike is the standard neck span for all West African spike lutes, it is true that the vast majority of them are semi-spike lutes.

However, thanks to the revelations in recent years of previously unknown instruments like the Jola *ekonting* (figure A), Manjak *bunchundo* (figure E), and Toubou *gurumi*, it is now clear that full-spike lutes have historically constituted a small but significant subgroup within the greater family of West African plucked spike lutes. What is more, by incorporating the criterion of neck span—along with the three other criteria specified by Charry—into our ongoing ethno-organological studies of West African lutes, we have a better basis on which to develop more effective, comprehensive cross-cultural analyses comparing these instruments to the early gourd banjo.

Conclusion: The Early Gourd Banjo's Relationship to West African "Living" Traditions

Ever since the early gourd banjo first began to appear in letters, journals, and vernacular literature as an object of curiosity and conversation, it has been generally assumed that this African American instrument either came across the Atlantic as-is from Africa or developed here from a specific African prototype, some sort of African ur-banjo. In the late nineteenth century, Carl Engel (1818–82), one of the earliest pioneers of the scholarly field of music instrument studies that we now call organology, speculated on which known African instrument could possibly be the actual ancestor of the banjo. In 1874, he wrote: "The name *bania*, given in Senegambia to an instrument of the guitar kind, may, perhaps, be identical to the Vei *bana* ["a harp with seven strings"], and also with the *banjo*, which appears to be the Senegambian *bania* imported by negro slaves into America."[61] Engel's supposition that the *bania* of Senegambia was the imported West African instrument that became the banjo was accepted as historical fact and continued to be accepted as such right up to the present. The only problem is that, as of yet, no evidence has been found in the historical record or in the various ethnic traditions of Senegambia of the term *bania* or of it ever being used there as the name of "an instrument of the guitar kind." Quite to the contrary, the only place it was documented was in the South American country of Suriname in the 1770s by Captain John Gabriel Stedman (1744–97) and that was as the local designation for a four-string early gourd banjo.[62]

Fast forward to 1955 and we have two new contenders for the title of African ur-banjo. That year the Africanist anthropologist David W. Ames would cautiously observe that the five-string *xalam* of the Wolof xalamkats "may have been the 'grandfather' of the American banjo."[63] Also that very same year, the eminent African American linguist Lorenzo Dow Turner (1890–1972), when asked for his take on *The Old Plantation*[64] (South Carolina, ca. 1785–90, see figure N), one of the earliest and most detailed depictions of African American music making and dancing, would categorically identify the early gourd banjo portrayed in the painting as being "a stringed instrument . . . called a *molo* . . . found among the Hausa and Yoruba peoples of Northern and Southwestern Nigeria, British West Africa, respectively."[65] Eleven years later, Victor Grauer would explicitly connect the *molo* to the banjo when he wrote: "The *molo*, a small, three stringed Hausa lute, may be the ancestor of the five-string banjo. Its third string . . . like the fifth string of the banjo, is fastened at a point so high on the fingerboard that the left hand cannot reach it. Consequently it plays only one note. The plucking technique used . . . has some resemblance to five-string banjo technique."[66]

All of these assertions were purely speculative, based on little more than cursory observations rather than actual in-depth research. Moreover, they also reflect how little was known at the time about the forms of the banjo that came before the wood-rimmed five-string banjo. For instance, the Wolof *xalam* (the same as all other standard griot lutes) and the Hausa-Yoruba *molo* both have semi-spike necks and narrow bodies made of carved wood. Conversely, early gourd banjos had full-spike necks and wide bodies (typically, round, oval, or teardrop in shape) made of either gourd or calabash.

The quest for a hypothetical African ur-banjo seemed to come to a head in 2000 when the independent researchers Daniel Laemouahuma Jatta of The Gambia and

Ulf Jägfors of Sweden first presented to the banjo community the Jola *ekonting* (figure A) and the Manjak *bunchundo* (figure E), two similar three-string traditional folk lutes that had been virtually unknown outside rural Senegambia. They are both very banjo-like in that they each have a full-spike neck, a gourd body, a large upright bipedal bridge, and a short thumb-string as their top third string. The *ekonting* has especially captured the imagination of banjo players the world over because *oo'teck*, the traditional Jola technique for playing the instrument, is a form of down-picking that is akin to the earliest documented technique for playing the five-string banjo, nineteenth-century "Banjo Style," as well as to the various forms of traditional old-time banjo down-picking (e.g., clawhammer, frailing, thumping, etc.).[67]

These striking similarities between the *ekonting* and the early gourd banjo have encouraged many to view the Jola folk lute as the principal "Ancestor of the Banjo." Yet, here too problems arise when we compare the *ekonting*'s fundamental design to that of the early gourd banjo. First and foremost is the issue of the relationship of the necks on both instruments to their bodies. Whereas on the early gourd banjo its full-spike neck pierced its body diametrically to pass through it, the *ekonting*'s full-spike neck does not go through its body but, rather, passes over the body's upper rim. Quite unlike the early gourd banjo, the *ekonting*'s neck is threaded through slits made in the lute's animal hide soundtable in order to rest on shallow grooves made in the top rim of its body (see figure 9.2 in chapter 9). As stated earlier, the *ekonting*'s over-the-rim construction is found on most other West African plucked spike lutes, including the nearly identical Manyago *bunchundo* and their fellow members of the aforementioned Atlantic-Bak cluster of similar Senegambian three-stringed gourd-bodied folk lutes. Indeed, the only exceptions to the over-the-rim rule are full-spike lutes from West Africa's Central Sudan section (e.g., the Kilba *gullum*, the Hausa *gurmi*, the Toubou *gurumi*, etc.), the only West African plucked spike lutes on which their necks go through the instruments' bodies.

The fact remains that hard evidence has yet to be found in the historical record to show that the banjo is unilineally descended directly from one or more specific members of West Africa's vast family of traditional plucked spike lutes. What the available historical organological evidence does suggest, however, is that the early gourd banjo was a hybrid. As such it was the product of the same process of creolization that informed the creation of early African American music-dance and musical material cultures throughout the New World. It apparently incorporated design elements from several different West African lute traditions, in addition to features inspired by European lute- and guitar-family instruments, such as the banjo's flat fingerboard and tuning pegs.

In all likelihood, the cross-cultural syncretic process that spawned the early gourd banjo happened on this side of the Atlantic. Evidence of the synthesis of African and European instrument design elements and features seen on the early gourd banjo is not found on any known traditional West African plucked spike lute. As a matter of fact, only in more recent years have some West African lute-nists modernized their traditional plucked spike lutes by modifying them with features borrowed from outside their traditions, such as replacing their instruments' traditional sliding tuning rings with tuning pegs and/or modern geared tuners. Conversely, where we do see an African-European fusion is on the *konigai* of Sherbro Island, Sierra Leone, the only known West African plucked lute that is not a spike lute, but, rather, a necked lute. The *konigai* is a three-string box-guitar with a wooden box body, a wooden top (soundboard), a flat fingerboard, and wooden friction tuning pegs, which seems to have developed sometime in the early twentieth century after the introduction of the modern guitar into local vernacular musics all along the western coast of sub-Saharan Africa.[68]

Recognizing these facts, the best way to develop a more realistic perception of the early gourd banjo's West African heritage is to learn everything we can about the entirety of the West African plucked spike lute family, historic and current: the history and development of these instruments; their design and construction; the musicians who traditionally make and play them; how they are traditionally played and the traditional music played on them; and the traditional sociocultural contexts in which they are played. Using actual verifiable documentation (e.g., field notes, photographs, video and audio recordings, etc.) from field studies as well as from reports in the historical record, we can better identify not only the similarities but also the differences between all of these instruments and the early gourd banjo for more comprehensive comparative analyses. In these ways we can more effectively investigate the banjo's past and develop a better sense of its West African roots.

Notes

I would like to express my gratitude and appreciation to Robert B. Winans for his editorial guidance; Ken Moore (the Frederick P. Rose Curator in Charge of the Department of Musical Instruments, Metropolitan Museum of Art, New York), who first encouraged and assisted me in my initial studies of traditional African instruments back in the 1980s and 1990s; Ulf Jägfors of Sweden and Daniel Laemouahuma Jatta of The Gambia for blazing the trail for my own research; Saskia Willaert (African Collections, Musical Instruments Musum, Brussels) for sparking my interest in studying the Hornbostel-Sachs system of instrument classification; Greg C. Adams, my partner in Banjo Roots Research Initiatives; and my many friends and colleagues in the banjo, banjo roots, and organological communities as well as in various fields of study.

1. John Luffman, *A Brief Account of the Island of Antigua . . . In Letters to a Friend. Written in the Years 1786, 1787, 1788* (London: Printed for T. Cadell, 1789; reprint Gale ECCO, Print Editions, 2010), 135–36; quoted in Dena J. Epstein, "The Folk Banjo: A Documentary History," *Ethnomusicology* 19, no. 3 (September 1975): 354, and *Sinful Tunes and Spirituals: Black Folk Music to the Civil War* (Urbana: University of Illinois Press, 1977, 2003), 36.

2. See chapter 3 in this volume, "List of West African Lutes," which I co-authored with Greg C. Adams.

3. For more on the early gourd banjo, see in this volume my chapter co-authored with Greg C. Adams, "Changing Perspectives on the Banjo's African American Origins and West African Heritage."

4. My own approach to banjo roots research—what I like to call "tracing the banjo genome"—is inspired by genetic genealogy, as well as genetics and evolutionary biology in general, hence my use of scientific descriptors like *genome* and *genetic markers*, which are borrowed from those disciplines. In doing so, however, I do not mean to suggest that inanimate cultural objects such as music instruments are somehow organic. I believe that the way genomes are mapped and sequenced in genetics offers some useful ideas, in terms of practical approach and methodology, that are applicable to our own ethno-organological research as we endeavor to trace the roots and origins of the banjo and related instruments. For example, I have found that the descriptor *genome*—a portmanteau fusing the terms *gene* and *chromosome* to indicate the entirety of the genetic material of a given organism—can also serve as an effective umbrella term to indicate the totality of the various design features and musical attributes that have defined the banjo throughout its history and connect it to its kin around the world as well as its ancestors across the Atlantic.

5. Erich Moritz von Hornbostel and Curt Sachs, "Systematik der Musikinstrumente: ein Versuch" (A System for Classifying Musical Instruments: An Open-Ended Discussion), *Zeitschrift für Ethnologie* (1914): 553–90. In this chapter I reference "Classification of Musical Instruments: Translated from the Original German by Anthony Baines and Klaus P. Wachsmann," *The Galpin Society Journal* 14 (March 1961): 3–29; "Spike lutes," 23. See also Klaus P. Wachsmann, "Classification," in *The Grove Dictionary of Musical Instruments: Second Edition*, ed. Laurence Libin, 5 vols. (Oxford: Oxford University Press, 2014), 1:568–82. For more on organology, the Hornbostel-Sachs (HS) classification system, and defining spike lutes, see the "Changing Perspectives on the Banjo's African American Origins and West African Heritage" chapter in this volume.

6. Plucked lutes—that is, lutes whose strings are primarily sounded by plucking and/or strumming—were the original kind of lutes. "Lute," in *The Grove Dictionary of Musical Instruments: Second Edition*, ed. Laurence Libin, 5 vols. (Oxford: Oxford University Press, 2014): Klaus Wachsmann, "Lute. 1. The Generic Term," 3:525; and James W. McKinnon and Robert Anderson, "Lute. 2. Ancient Lutes," 3:325–26. Bowed lutes (better known as fiddles)—lutes whose strings are sounded by drawing a bow across them—are thought to have originated in Central Asia sometime in the ninth century CE. Werner Bachmann, "Bow, §1, 1: History of the Bow, 1. Origins to c. 1650," in *The Grove Dictionary of Musical Instruments: Second Edition*, ed. Laurence Libin, 5 vols. (Oxford: Oxford University Press, 2014), 1:385–86.

7. Curt Sachs, *The History of Musical Instruments* (New York: W. W. Norton & Company, Inc., 1940), 82–83. Scholars have long considered the ancient Sumerian word *pantur* (also *bantur*; literally "little bow") to be the common Mesopotamian designation for the plucked lute. *Pandoura*, the ancient Greek term for the lute, and its Roman Latin cognate, *pandura*, are thought to be derivations of *pantur*. In more recent years, however, new findings suggest that the Sumerian word *ğiš.gù.di* and the Akkadian word *inu* (talking or noise-producing stick or wood) may have also been ancient Mesopotamian designations for the lute. Richard Dumbrill, *The Archaeomusicology of the Ancient Near East* (Victoria, BC: Trafford Publishing, 2005), 316–18.

8. Harvey Turnbull, "The Origin of the Long-Necked Lute," *The Galpin Society Journal* 25 (July 1972): 58–66. This dating is based on the oldest known depictions of people

playing the lute that appear on two cylinder seals from Mesopotamia's Akkadian period (ca. 2350–2150 BCE), currently in the collection of the British Museum: BM 89096 and BM 28806 (ibid., 59–61; Dumbrill, *The Archaeomusicology of the Ancient Near East*, 322–24). In 1996, Dr. Dominique Collon (assistant keeper [emeritus], the British Museum's Department of Western Asiatic Antiquities) acquired for the British Museum a cylinder seal (BM 308035) from ancient Sumer's Uruk period (ca. 4000–3100 BCE), which depicts a woman playing what appears to be a round-bodied long-necked lute in the stern of a long boat (Dumbrill, *The Archaeomusicology of the Ancient Near East*, 321–22). This depiction predates the Akkadian seals by some eight hundred years. However, according to Collon, who is the foremost expert on ancient Near Eastern cylinder seals, the seal has "been extensively reworked and the evidence is ambiguous" (Collon to Pestcoe, email correspondence, March 19, 2009).

9. Lisse Manniche, *Music and Musicians in Ancient Egypt* (London: British Museum Press, 1991), 45–47.

10. Samuel Charters, *The Roots of the Blues: An African Search* (Salem, NH: Da Capo Press, 1981), 49. Historically, papyrus sedge has been valued throughout West Africa, as its long thin stalks are dried to make hard sticks for various purposes and its fibers are used to make instrument strings, rope, and other materials. Banjul—the capital of The Gambia, which is located on Banjul Island (St. Mary's Island) in the mouth of the Gambia River where it meets the Atlantic Ocean—derives its name from the Mandinka words for papyrus reeds, *bang* and *bangjolo*.

11. David W. Ames and Anthony V. King, *Glossary of Hausa Music and Its Social Context* (Evanston, IL: Northwestern University Press, 1971), 45–46.

12. Nora E. Scott, "The Lute of the Singer Ḥar-Mosĕ," *The Metropolitan Museum of Art Bulletin*, New Series, 2, no. 5 (January 1944): 159–63.

13. For the earliest, most detailed museum photos of the Harmose lute, see ibid., 161. The necks depicted on Babylonian and Hittite lutes were often shown to be fretted. The frets may have been made from pieces of rope or leather. More probably, however, they were tied-on pieces of gut cord and were movable rather than fixed, similar to those seen on certain types of traditional fretted plucked lute encountered across the Near East and Central Asia today. The frets on the depicted ancient lutes are laid out in a gapped-scale pattern akin to that of modern traditional Near Eastern-Central Asian fretted plucked lutes like the *tar, tanbur*, and *setar*. As shown in an Eighteenth Dynasty wall painting from Nebamun's tomb (British Museum EA 37981), the necks on ancient Egyptian lutes of the New Kingdom were depicted as being both fretted and unfretted. One common theory hypothesized that these frets were made by twisting a single long cord up and down the length of the neck. This contention, however, seems to be based on a misperception of the cord found twisted along the Harmose lute's neck as being fretting. On the contrary, the purpose of the cord was to secure the wooden plectrum (which is needle-like, long, and thin) used for playing the instrument: the plectrum is tied to the top end of the cord while the cord's tail is tied to the lute's neck right above its body. Again, as seen in Nebamun's tomb painting, the purpose of tying the plectrum to a long cord seems to have been to allow the lutenist to alternate between playing with the plectrum and then dropping it for finger-playing. For the lutes depicted in EA 37981, see Richard Parkinson, *The Painted Tomb-Chapel of Nebamun: Masterpieces of Ancient Egyptian Art in the British Museum* (London: British Museum Press, 2008), illustration 93, 82–85.

14. The term *capo* denotes any device used to shorten the length of a lute's strings. It comes from the Italian *capotasto* (also written as *capo tasto*, literally "the head fret"), and

originally meant the string nut at the top end of a lute's fingerboard, which serves to lift the strings up and facilitate their passage to the peghead. Ian Hardwood, "Capo tasto [capo]," in *The Grove Dictionary of Musical Instruments: Second Edition*, ed. Laurence Libin, 5 vols. (Oxford: Oxford University Press, 2014), 1:456.

15. Joachim Braun, *Music in Ancient Israel/Palestine: Archaeological, Written, and Comparative Sources* (Grand Rapids, MI: Eerdmans, 2002), 83.

16. R. A. Higgins and R. P. Winnington-Ingram, "Lute-Players in Greek Art," *The Journal of Hellenic Studies* 85 (1965): 62–71; Martha Maas and Jane McIntosh Snyder, *Stringed Instruments of Ancient Greece* (New Haven, CT: Yale University Press, 1989), 166.

17. Hornbostel and Sachs, "Classification of Musical Instruments," 22–23. In *The History of Musical Instruments*, Curt Sachs, in effect, proposed replacing the original "Spike Lutes" and "Necked Lutes" categories in the HS subsection "Handle Lutes" with two new ones: "Long Lutes" to denote lutes on which "the neck or stick is longer than the body" and "Short Lutes" for those lutes on which the "neck is, morphologically speaking, an elongation of the body (though of course is added to the body in all recent specimens) and seldom reaches the length of the body" (464). Over the years, Sachs's terms *long lute* and *short lute* have given way to the designations *long neck lute* and *short neck lute* in common usage. As all of these terms are problematic at best as effective descriptors due to their imprecision and ambiguity, I hold to the original 1914 HS classifications of "spike lutes" and "necked lutes," which I believe are more useful for banjo and lute family studies.

18. For more on the *pandoura-pandura* during the Late Roman period, see Charlotte Roueché's notes VIII.3 and VIII. 4, "Section VIII: Christian prayers and invocations," on her website, *Aphrodisias in Late Antiquity: The Late Roman and Byzantine Inscriptions* (revised second edition, 2004), http://insaph.kcl.ac.uk/ala2004/narrative/sec-VIII .html#VIII.3, accessed October 25, 2017.

19. Richard Widdess, "Vīṇā, 3. Lutes," in *The Grove Dictionary of Musical Instruments: Second Edition*, ed. Laurence Libin, 5 vols. (Oxford: Oxford University Press, 2014), 5:186.

20. Christian Poché, "Qanbūs," in *The Grove Dictionary of Musical Instruments: Second Edition*, ed. Laurence Libin, 5 vols. (Oxford: Oxford University Press, 2014), 4:187–88.

21. Basil Davidson, *West Africa Before the Colonial Era: A History to 1850* (London: Addison Wesley Longman Limited, 1998), 26–28.

22. Al-Bakri, "Ghāna and the Customs of its Inhabitants," in *Corpus of Early Arabic Sources for West African History*, ed. Nehemiah Levtzion and John F. P. Hopkins (Princeton, NJ: Marcus Wiener Publishers, 2000, 2011), 62–63.

23. Davidson, *West Africa Before the Colonial Era*, 26–27; Robert O. Collins and James M. Burns, *A History of Sub-Saharan Africa, Second Edition* (New York: Cambridge University Press, 2014), 82–83. Ancient Ghana should not be confused with the modern Republic of Ghana (founded in 1957), which was formerly known as Gold Coast and is located much farther south in West Africa, along its Lower Guinea coast. The term *Ghana* is Soninke for "War Chief" and was actually the hereditary title of the rulers of this West African empire, much like "Caesar" in ancient Rome.

24. Al-Bakri, "Ghāna and the Customs of its Inhabitants," 79–87.

25. Ibid., 80.

26. The terms *Greater Senegambia* and *Western Sudan* refer to the western half of West Africa and include the modern countries of Mauritania, Mali, Senegal, The Gambia, Guinea-Bissau, and Guinea.

27. The word *griot* (pronounced "gree-oh"; originally spelled *guiriot*) made its first appearance in *Relation du voyage du Cap-Verd* (1637) by the French Capuchin missionary Alexis

de Saint-Lô (Eric Charry, *Mande Music: Traditional and Modern Music of the Maninka and Mandinka of Western Africa* [Chicago: University of Chicago Press, 2000], 361–62; Thomas A. Hale, *Griots and Griottes: Masters of Words and Music* [Bloomington: Indiana University Press, 1998], 84–85). It refers to hereditary, endogamous bards in the middle artisan caste of the similar traditional tripartite social systems shared by certain Islamized West African ethnicities, such as the Mandinka, Maninka, Bamana (Bambara), Wolof, Soninke, Songhai, and Fulbe (Fula, Fulani, Peul, etc.). While outside Africa, griots are mostly seen as storytellers, praise-singers, and musicians, they also have always served in many capacities beyond those functions, such as being historian-genealogists, official spokesmen, viziers, diplomats, and even military leaders (Hale, *Griots and Griottes*, 18–58). Each people with a griot tradition has their own descriptors for griots: for example, in Mandinka, it is *jalolu* (singular *jali* or *jalo*), while in Maninka it is *jelilu* (singular *jeli*) (Charry, *Mande Music*, 1). In terms of griot musical tradition and culture, males (griots) are traditionally the instrumentalists as well as singers, while females (griottes; singular griotte) are typically only singers. For more on griot culture and music, as well as the role and status of griots in certain traditional West African cultures and societies, see Charry, *Mande Music*; Hale, *Griots and Griottes*; and Barbara G. Hoffman, *Griots at War: Conflict, Conciliation, and Caste in Mande* (Bloomington: Indiana University Press, 2000).

28. David C. Conrad, "Blind Man Meets Prophet: Oral Tradition, Islam, and *Funé* Identity," in *Status and Identity in West Africa: Nyamakalaw of Mande*, ed. David C. Conrad and Barbara E. Frank (Bloomington: Indiana University Press, 1995), 86–132.

29. Al-'Umarī, *Masālik al absār fī mamālik al amsār* (Pathways of Vision in the Realms of the Metropolises), in *Corpus of Early Arabic Sources for West African History*, ed. Nehemiah Levtzion and John F. P. Hopkins (Princeton, NJ: Marcus Wiener Publishers, 2000, 2011), 266–67. *Tunbūr* (also *tanbūr*) is an Arabic term that refers to a plucked necked lute with a long neck. It was commonly used in the contemporary Arabic literature of al-'Umarī's day to specifically denote various forms of these instruments. Egon Wellesz, *Ancient and Oriental Music* (Oxford: Oxford University Press, 1957, 1999), 446–47.

30. Ibn Battuta, in *Corpus of Early Arabic Sources for West African History*, ed. Nehemiah Levtzion and John F. P. Hopkins (Princeton, NJ: Marcus Wiener Publishers, 2000, 2011), 291. In the 1920s, the British Arabist musicologist Henry George Farmer (1882–1965) recognized Ibn Battuta's descriptor *qunburī* as a reference to plucked lutes, which he characterized generically as "pandores." Indeed, Farmer transliterated Ibn Battuta's term as *gunībrī*, which is another common name for the aforementioned *hajhuj* of the Gnawa in Ibn Battuta's homeland of Morocco. The actual instrument that Farmer clearly had in mind, however, was apparently the *guimbri* (*loutar*), a spike lute of Berber origin traditionally played by Morocco's Amazighi Berber and Jbala Arab vernacular musicians, which is also sometimes called *guinbri*. Henry George Farmer, "Early References to Music in the Western Sūdān," *Journal of the Royal Asiatic Society of Great Britain and Ireland* 4 (October 1939): 572, 575.

31. Davidson, *West Africa Before the Colonial Era*, 95; Collins and Burns, *A History of Sub-Saharan Africa*, 177–78.

32. Luís de Cadamosto (Alvise da Ca' da Mosto), in *The Portuguese in West Africa, 1415–1670: A Documentary History*, ed. Malyn Newitt (Cambridge: Cambridge University Press, 2010), 55.

33. Ibid., 67.

34. Alvise Da Cada Mosto, "Original Journals of the Voyages of Cada Mosto and Piedro de Cintra to the Coast of Africa; The Former in the Years 1455 and 1456, and the Latter

Soon Afterwards," reprinted in English translation in Robert Kerr's *A General History of Voyages and Travels*, 18 vols. (Edinburgh: George Ramsay and Company, 1811), 2:236.

35. Valentim Fernandes's period account excerpted in Newitt's *The Portuguese in West Africa* as Document 18, "The Wolof Kingdom at the End of the Fifteenth Century," 74–78: Fernandes's description of the "Gaul," 77. *Cavaco* is the Portuguese designation for a type of small guitar found in various traditional regional forms throughout Portugal and the Azores. The best known of these instruments is the smallest form of *cavaco*, the four-string *cavaquinho*, which is also popular in former Portuguese colonies like Brazil and Cape Verde. "Cavaco," in *The Grove Dictionary of Musical Instruments: Second Edition*, ed. Laurence Libin, 5 vols. (Oxford: Oxford University Press, 2014), 1:473, and "Cavaquinho," 1:475.

36. Joseph B. Hill, "People of Word, Song, and Money: The Evolution of Senegalese Griots and Their Art" (undergraduate thesis, Brigham Young University, 1999), 15–17; Hill to Pestcoe, email correspondence, December 19 and 20, 2014.

37. Mungo Park, *Travels in the Interior Districts of Africa* (1799) (Ware, Hertfordshire: Wordsworth Classics of World Literature, 2002), 271–72.

38. Jacqueline Cogdell DjeDje, *Fiddling in West Africa: Touching the Spirit in Fulbe, Hausa, and Dagbamba Cultures* (Bloomington: Indiana University Press, 2008), "Appendix: Distribution of the One-Stringed Fiddle (Listed by Country)," 251–55.

39. Ibid., 28.

40. Philip Schuyler, "A Repertory of Ideas: The Music of the Rwais, Berber Professional Musicians from Southwestern Morocco" (PhD diss., University of Washington, 1979), 6.3, "The Lotar," 119–37. In addition to the *loutar* and *lotar*, another Moroccan plucked spike lute is the *swisdi*, a small version of the *loutar* used primarily in instrumental ensembles that accompany *mahlun*, a popular urban style of song based on *qassida* and *zajal*, forms of Darija (Moroccan Arabic) poetry that emerged in the eighteenth and nineteenth centuries. Other North African spike lutes include the *gambre*, a two-string version of the *loutar* with a smaller narrow elongated body, and the *gimimbri* (also *gimbri*), a diminutive two- or three-string lute with a small tortoise shell body. Both instruments seem to have become obsolete by the mid-twentieth century. Thereafter, unplayable, cheaply made versions of these instruments became popular souvenirs of the tourist trade.

41. Ralph A. Austin, *Trans-Saharan Africa in World History* (Oxford: Oxford University Press, 2010), 32: "In contrast to the European Atlantic slave trade, scholars do not have very precise statistics for the various Islamic enslavement systems in Africa. The best estimates are that between 800 and 1900 CE about 4 million people were driven across the Sahara."

42. Deborah Kapchan, *Traveling Spirit Masters: Moroccan Gnawa Trance and Music in the Global Marketplace* (Middletown, CT: Wesleyan University Press, 2007), 17–21. The Gnawa (Gnaoua in French transliteration) are at once a distinct ethnic community and a Muslim religious order consisting mainly of the descendants of enslaved captives and mercenaries brought from West Africa. Today primarily found in Morocco—and, to a lesser extent, Algeria—the Gnawa have a unique language and culture called Soudania or Gnawi. While West African captives had been brought to Morocco (the hub of North Africa's trans-Saharan slave trade) since at least the ninth century, the Gnawa as a group and culture can trace their origins to the thousands of captives transported from present-day Mali, Senegal, Guinea, Niger, and Nigeria after the Moroccan defeat of the Songhai Empire in 1591.

43. Lucy Durán, "Guinbri," in *The Grove Dictionary of Musical Instruments: Second Edition*, ed. Laurence Libin, 5 vols. (Oxford: Oxford University Press, 2014), 2:491–92.

44. Richard C. Jankowsky, *Stambeli: Music, Trance, and Alterity in Tunisia* (Chicago: University of Chicago Press, 2010): the *gumbri*, 97–102; the *fakrūn*, 106–7. For the *gambara*, see Jankowsky's liner notes for the CD album *Stambeli, featuring Salah el-Ouergli: The Legacy of the Black Tunisians* (Paris: Les Chemins Productions [PLC101], 2010), 44. The West African heritage of the Gnawa *hajhuj* and the three Tunisian lutes is reflected on many levels. In terms of design, all of these instruments have sliding tuning rings instead of tuning pegs. They are all also three-string lutes with one short string and two long strings. On all three Tunisian lutes, the short string is the top thumb-string, just like on most West African plucked spike lutes with three or more strings and the African American four-string early gourd banjo and its descendant, the wood-rimmed five-string banjo. However, on the Gnawa *hajhuj* the short string is the second middle string. In terms of playing technique, all four of these instruments are played with forms of down-picking (also referred to as down-stroking), which are most likely West African in origin, as they are similar to that traditionally used to play the Jola *ekonting*, the Bujogo *ñopata*, and other West African lutes. Down-picking was also the technique with which African American banjoists used to play the early gourd banjo and which they taught to the first European American banjoists who introduced the early five-string banjo around 1840.

45. Kapchan, *Traveling Spirit Masters*, 13, 20.

46. Jankowsky, *Stambeli*, 18–19.

47. Eric Charry, "Plucked Lutes in West Africa: An Historical Overview," *The Galpin Society Journal* 49 (March 1996): 3–37.

48. Ibid., 3.

49. Ibid., 4.

50. The Hausa term *makaʾda* (singular *makaʾdi*) literally means "drummers." However, the designation is used generically to mean traditional artisan instrumentalists, regardless of the type of music instrument they play. Those who specialize in specific instruments are referred to by the prefix *masu* (singular *mai*) with the name of the given instrument following as the suffix: for example, *masu garaya*, "players of the *garaya*." See Ames and King, *Glossary of Hausa Music*, 62, 69.

51. In recent years, it is increasingly accepted that the use of the word *folk* as a descriptor for traditional musics and musicians is problematic. Recognizing the very real issues surrounding this ambiguous term, I only use *folk* here as a convenient shorthand to distinguish non-artisan vernacular lute players from griot and non-griot artisan lutenists.

52. My term *Atlantic-Bak cluster* references the fact that all of these peoples' languages belong to the Bak subgroup of West Africa's Atlantic linguistic family, which, in turn, is a subdivision of the greater Niger-Congo family of sub-Saharan African languages.

53. For more on the *ekonting* and *bunchundo*, see Ulf Jägfors, "The African Akonting and the Origin of the Banjo," *The Old-Time Herald* 9, no. 2 (November 2003–January 2004): 26–33; Shlomo Pestcoe and Greg C. Adams, "Ekonting," in *The Grove Dictionary of Musical Instruments: Second Edition*, ed. Laurence Libin, 5 vols. (Oxford: Oxford University Press, 2014), 2:140–41, and Greg C. Adams and Chuck Levy's chapter "The Down-Stroke Connection: Comparing Techniques Between the Jola *Ekonting* and the Five-String Banjo" in this volume.

54. Charry, "Plucked Lutes in West Africa," 4–5.

55. Special thanks to Marc Nerenberg for sharing his memories of encountering the Dogon *kona* in the village of Kané-Kombolé, Mali, in 1981, and to Jayme Stone for sharing his findings on both Dogon lutes, the *kona* and the previously unreported *konou*, during his field trip to Mali in 2007.

56. Burkina Faso, Niger, Chad, Côte d'Ivoire, Sierra Leone, Ghana, Togo, Benin, Nigeria, and Cameroon.

57. Michael T. Coolen, "Xalamkats: The Xalam Tradition of Senegambia" (PhD diss., University of Washington, 1979), *geseré*, 75, 119; and idem, "Senegambian Archetypes for the American Folk Banjo," *Western Folklore* 43, no. 2 (April 1984): *kôla-lemmé*, 123. My special thanks to Ben Nelson for sharing his findings on the *xalam gesere* as introduced to him by the Gambian *xalamkats* Matar Jeng and Manga Jallo in April 2006.

58. Major William Gray and Staff Surgeon Dochard, *Travels in Western Africa in the Years 1818, 19, 20, and 21, from the River Gambia, through Woolli, Bondoo, Galam, Kasson, Kaarta, and Foolidoo, to the River Niger* (London: John Murray, Albemarle Street, 1825), plate 9, "Musical Instruments," 300.

59. Charry, "Plucked Lutes in West Africa," 5.

60. Charry, *Mande Music*, 123. In describing this neck span, Charry argues that West African instruments "are classed as spike, or more precisely semispike, lutes" (123). I believe that this sentence is the first appearance of the term *semi-spike* in a publication. Previous to that, Charry's 1996 article references the two older organological descriptors for the semi-spike neck span that were current in academic literature: *internal spike* (German *Binnenspieß*) (Curt Sachs, *Die Musikinstrumente des Alten Agyptens* [Berlin: K. Curtius, 1921], 55); and *tanged* (Erich von Hornbostel, "The Ethnology of African Sound-Instruments [Continued]," *Africa: Journal of the International African Institute* 6, no. 3 [July 1933]: 300n1, in which Hornbostel cites as his source the work of the pioneering British ethnographer Henry Balfour [1863–1939]). The term *tanged* references the tangs (points) on the tail end of some lutes' semi-spike necks onto which the strings are tied. This same feature is found on the "internal spike" plucked lutes from West Africa's Central Sudan, such as the Frafra *koliko* (also *koloko, kologo*; Ghana), the Gwari *kaburu* (Nigeria), and the Hausa *garaya, komo,* and *molo* (Nigeria). Conversely, nearly all of the semi-spike plucked lutes of the Western Sudan—namely, the various different ethnic traditions of griot lutes, including single-string griot lutes like the Mandinka and Tukulor *molo* (Senegambia) and the Songhai *n'jurkel* (Mali), as well the non-griot two-string *konou* of the Dogon (Mali)—do not have tanged string anchors at the ends of their necks.

61. Carl Engel, *A Descriptive Catalogue of The Musical Instruments in The South Kensington Museum* (1874), 151.

62. John Gabriel Stedman, *Narrative of a Five Years Expedition against the Revolted Negroes of Surinam: Transcribed for the First Time the Original 1790 Manuscript*, ed. Richard Price and Sally Price (Baltimore: Johns Hopkins University Press, 1988; reprint New York: iUniverse, 2010), 540. To the best of my research, Stedman's *Narrative* is the only source for *Bania* as a descriptor for any kind of instrument of African heritage. In it, Stedman presented a textual list and depiction of eighteen "Musical Instruments of the African Negroes [of Suriname]" (plate 69) in which he documented three dissimilar Afro-Surinamese instruments with the word *Bania* in their names: the "Ansokko-Bania" (no. 3), an unusual bench-like wooden plank drum similar to a slit drum; the "Loango-Bania" (no.10), a thumb-piano; and the "Creole-Bania" (no. 15), a four-string early gourd banjo. *Bania* was apparently Stedman's transliteration of *banya*, the Sranantongo (Suriname creole) designation for a type of traditional Afro-Surinamese song and dance. As the word *Bania* appears nowhere else in the historical record, I suspect that Stedman was Engel's source for the term. Moreover, I believe that Engel inferred from Stedman's documentation of the Afro-Surinamese "Creole-Bania" that the instrument must have originated in West Africa's Senegambia subregion. For more on Stedman and the Afro-Surinamese "Creole-Bania,"

see in this volume "Changing Perspectives on the Banjo's African American Origins and West African Heritage.".

63. David W. Ames, liner notes, *Wolof Music of Senegal and The Gambia* (New York: Folkways FE 4462, 1955),3.

64. *The Old Plantation*, watercolor on laid paper, 11 11/16 x 17 7/8 inches, Abbey Aldrich Rockefeller Folk Art Museum, Colonial Williamsburg Foundation, Williamsburg, Virginia, gift of Mrs. John D. Rockefeller, 35.301.3. For more on the picture, see Susan P. Shames, *The Old Plantation: The Artist Revealed* (Williamsburg, VA: The Colonial Williamsburg Foundation, 2010), and my chapter in this volume, "The Banjar Pictured: The Depiction of the African American Early Gourd Banjo in *The Old Plantation*, South Carolina, 1780s."

65. Turner to Nina Fletcher Little, August 15, 1955, Colonial Williamsburg Foundation/ Abby Aldrich Rockefeller Folk Art Museum curatorial file 35-301-3.

66. Victor Grauer, liner notes, *Music of the Jos Plateau and Other Regions of Nigeria: Recorded by Stanley Diamond/Edited, with notes by Victor Grauer* (New York: Folkways Ethnic Library FE 4321, 1966), 4.

67. The term *down-picking* was coined in the 1960s by the modern old-time banjoist Art Rosenbaum "in order to avoid ridiculous arguments about where 'frailing' leaves off and 'clawhammering' begins" (Art Rosenbaum, *The Art of the Mountain Banjo* [Mel Bay, 1999], 6). For further discussions of down-picking techniques, see in this volume my chapter "The Banjar Pictured" and Greg C. Adams and Chuck Levy's chapter "The Down-Stroke Connection," which compares *oo'teck*, the West African Jola form of down-picking, to nineteenth-century "Banjo Style."

68. The *konigai* was first encountered in June 2007 by the American ethnomusicologist Luke Wassermann and documented in his album of field-recordings, *Music of Sierra Leone, Volume 7: Folk Songs of Sherbro Island* (EarthCDs MOSL-CD-7), http://www.earthcds.com/ africa/west/sierra-leone/mosl7.shtml, accessed October 25, 2017; Wassermann to Pestcoe, email correspondence, June 2 and 18, 2008.

CHAPTER 3

List of West African Plucked Spike Lutes

Shlomo Pestcoe and Greg C. Adams

In his seminal article "Plucked Lutes in West Africa: An Historical Overview" (1996), the Africanist ethnomusicologist Eric Charry made the first attempt to study and analyze the rich diversity of traditional plucked spike lutes found throughout West Africa.[1] As part of that effort, he first created a map of West Africa on which he situated the known named lutes.[2] He then followed that up with a list of forty-three different named and unnamed instruments[3] in "Appendix 2: References for Fig. 2."[4] Building on Charry's pioneering efforts by triangulating ongoing field research with library-, archives-, and web-based research, Shlomo Pestcoe's findings present an additional thirty-seven instruments, thereby bringing the number to eighty distinct traditional forms of West African plucked spike lute. However, the total number given here is by no means conclusive or definitive. Further research will most likely yield more traditional instruments, which have existed under the radar of international researchers and were, therefore, previously unknown outside their regions.

West Africa is divided geographically into two major subregions. The first subregion is the Western Sudan (also referred to as Greater Senegambia; western West Africa), which includes Mauritania, Mali, Senegal, The Gambia, Guinea-Bissau, and Guinea. The second is the Central Sudan (eastern West Africa), which includes Burkina Faso, Côte d'Ivoire, Sierra Leone, Ghana, Togo, Benin, Nigeria, Niger, Chad, and Cameroon.[5] In presenting these traditional West African instruments we recognize that the historical division between the Western Sudan and Central Sudan is not only geographical but also cultural, especially in terms of local music material cultures. The Western Sudan–Central Sudan cultural and musical divide is clearly reflected in traditional plucked spike lute design. For instance, only on full-spike lutes from the Central Sudan does the instrument's neck diametrically pierce through the instrument's body. On full-spike lutes from the Western Sudan, like on all other West African plucked spike lutes from both the Western and Central Sudan subregions, the neck is threaded through slits made in the instrument's animal hide soundtable and rests on shallow indentations made in the rim of the body. Accordingly, we broadly classify these various instruments as being of either the Western Sudan or Central Sudan, as well as by the fundamental organological categories of "full-spike lutes" and "semi-spike lutes," which reflects the span of the given instrument's neck in relationship to its body.

We then classify each lute into one of three categories based on its traditional social performance context: "folk," "griot," and "non-griot artisan." However, these categories are based on historic tradition and do not account for the ways in which any of these traditions have changed over time, geographically, or as the result of cross-cultural exchange and/or sociocultural change.

For each entry we give the ethnic group that the lute belongs to, the country of that group, the number of strings each lute has, the type of bridge, and the type of material the body is made from. Those instruments for which we have little or no specific information we list under the final section "Additional Plucked Lutes." For a fuller discussion of the terminology, as well as the classification categories and criteria used here, see Pestcoe's preceding chapter, "Banjo Ancestors: West African Plucked Spike Lutes."

Full-Spike Lutes

These are spike lutes with necks that extend the full length of the instrument's body to protrude over or through the body's tail end.

Folk (Western Sudan): All of the following have gourd bodies with three strings and a large bipedal floating bridge. Like most other West African plucked spike lutes, their necks pass over the rim of the lute's body, resting on shallow indentations in the top of the body's rim and threading through slits made in the instrument's animal hide soundtable (see figure C for both of these features).

bunchundo (Manyago [Manjak, Manjaco, etc.]: Guinea-Bissau; Senegal; and The Gambia)[6] (see figure E)

busunde (Papel: Guinea-Bissau)[7]

ekonting [*akonting*, plural *si'konting*; cognate descriptors: *econtine*, *kotin*, and *entofen*] (Jola [Diola, Joola, Floup, etc.]: Casamance [southern Senegal]; The Gambia; and Guinea-Bissau)[8] (see figure A)

kisinta (Balanta: Guinea-Bissau)[9]

kusunde (Balanta: the Bijago Islands of Guinea-Bissau)[10]

kusunde (Balanta: Guinea-Bissau)[11]

ñopata (Bujogo [Bijago]: the Bijago Islands of Guinea-Bissau)[12] (see figure F)

Folk and Non-Griot Artisan (Central Sudan): All of the following have non-wooden bodies—either gourd or calabash, depending on the tradition—with cylindrical floating bridges. Their necks pierce through the lute's body diametrically. Through-the-body placement of the neck is only found on full-spike lutes from West Africa's Central Sudan subregion (see figure G for all of these features). All other West African plucked spike lutes have the over-the-rim construction described above.

> *gullum* (Kilba [Höba, Hba]: Nigeria) (three strings)[13] (see figure G)
> *gulum* [*gulom*] (Kotoko [Mser, Moria, Bara, and Makari]: Chad; Cameroon) (three strings)[14]
> *gurmi* [*kumbo*] (Hausa: Nigeria) (two or three strings; gourd body)[15]
> *gurumi* (Hausa: Niger) (two strings; calabash body)[16]
> *gurumi* (Toubou: Niger) (two strings; calabash body)[17]
> *ngùlăn* (Bana: Cameroon) (three strings; calabash body)[18]
> *unnamed* (possibly: *molo* or *molooru*) (Fulbe: Niger) (two strings; calabash body)[19]

Griot (Western Sudan): All of the following have gourd bodies with a block floating bridge.

> *geseré* (Wolof: Senegal) (five strings)[20]
> *kôla-lemmé* (Diawara: Mali) (four strings)[21]
> *xalam geseré* (Wolof: The Gambia) (five strings)[22]

Semi-Spike Lutes

These are spike lutes on which the neck extends only about three-quarters of the instrument's body's length to end within the body just short of its tail end. Semi-spike lutes constitute the majority of the West African family of plucked spike lutes.

Griot (Western and Central Sudan): Griot lutes, like the griot tradition itself, apparently originated in the Mande Empire of ancient Mali (ca. 1235–1500). The fact that ancient Mali's successor, the Songhai Empire (ca. 1464–1591), expanded farther east and that, over the centuries, various Western Sudanese peoples with a griot tradition also spread eastward account for the appearance today of griot lutes in West Africa's Central Sudan eastern subregion. Except for the very few gourd-bodied full-spike griot lutes listed above, standard griot lutes with three or more stings are distinguished by having a semi-spike neck; a narrow wooden body (typically elliptical, canoe-shaped, or figure-8-shaped); and a fan-shaped bridge (typically made of thin piece of gourd) that is inserted into a hole made in the body's soundtable to slip onto the pointy end of the semi-spike neck (see figure B for all of these features). Conversely, single-string griot lutes may have bodies made of gourd or wood, though they have a semi-spike neck and a fan-shaped bridge.

bappe [*xalam bappe*] (Wolof: Senegal) (five strings)[23]

diassaré (Wolof-Soninke: Senegal) (five strings)[24]

gambaré (Soninke-Serahuli: Mali; Senegal) (four strings)[25]

hoddu [*hodu, hordu, kerona*] (Fulbe [Fula, Fulani, Peul, etc.]-Tukulor: throughout West Africa) (three to five strings)[26]

jurkel (Songhai: Burkina Faso) (one string; gourd body)[27]

kambre [*kambreh, cambreh*] (Fulbe: Sierra Leone) (three strings)[28]

kerona (Fulbe: Guinea) (four or five strings)[29]

keronaru [*khalam*] (Fulbe: Sierra Leone) (six strings)[30]

koni (Maninka: Mali) (five strings)[31]

koni [*kontin*] (Xasonka: Mali) (five strings)[32]

kontingo [*konting*] (Mandinka: The Gambia; Senegal) (four or five strings)[33]

kook [*xalam*] (Tukulor: Senegal) (five strings)[34]

kubru [*kouco, kurubu*] (Songhai: Mali; Niger) (three strings)[35]

molo [*molooru*] (Songhai: Mali; Niger) (three or four strings)[36]

molo (Soninke-Diawara: Mali) (one string)[37]

n'déré (Wolof: Senegal) (five strings)[38]

n'goni [*n'koni*] (Bamana [Bambara]-Maninka: Mali) (four strings)[39] (see figure B)

n'goni ba [literally "low *n'goni*"; bass *n'goni*] (Bamana: Mali) (four strings)[40]

n'goni micin [literally "high *n'goni*": soprano *n'goni*] (Bamana: Mali) (four strings)[41]

n'jurkel (Songhai: Mali) (one string)[42]

teharden [*tahardent*] (Tuareg [Kel Tamashek]: Mali; Niger) (three strings)[43]

tidinit (Moor: Mauritania) (four strings)[44]

xalam [*khalam, halam*] (Wolof: Senegal; The Gambia) (five strings)[45]

Non-Griot Artisan and Folk (Western Sudan): All of these have fan-shaped bridges.

juru kelenni (Bamana: Mali) (one string; either wood or gourd body)[46]

kona (Dogon: Mali) (one string; gourd body)[47]

konou (Dogon: Mali) (two strings; wood body)[48]

molo (Fulbe: Senegambia) (one string; gourd body)[49]

Non-Griot Artisan and Folk (Central Sudan): All of these have cylindrical floating bridges and, unless otherwise noted, carved wooden bodies.

duru [*molo*] (Yoruba: Nigeria) (two strings)[50]

garaya [plural *garayu*] (Hausa: Nigeria) (two strings)[51]

garaya [*garayaaru, garayaaji*] (Fulani [Fulbe]: Cameroon) (two strings; gourd body)[52]

gurumi (Mauri: Chad) (three strings)[53]

gurumi [*gouroumi*] (Dosso [Zarma]: Niger) (three strings)[54]

gzopoli (Bana: Nigeria; Cameroon) (two strings; gourd body)[55]

jurkel (Fulbe: Burkina Faso) (one string; gourd body)[56]

kaburu (Gwari [Gbari, Gbaygi]: Nigeria) (three strings)[57] *kakanza* (Lamang: Nigeria; Cameroon) (two strings)[58]

keleli (Teda: Chad) (two or three strings; wood, gourd, or enamel metal bowl body)[59]

kologo [*kolgo, koliko, koriko, molo*] (Farefare [Frafra]: Ghana; Burkina Faso) (two strings; gourd body)[60]

komo [*babbar garaya* (literally "big *garaya*")] (Hausa: Nigeria) (two strings; gourd body)[61]

konde [*kondo*] (Bissa: Ghana) (two strings; gourd body)[62]

kuban [*kubangu*] (Bassari: Togo) (two strings; gourd body)[63]

kuntigi [*kuntugi, kwantagi*] (Hausa: Nigeria) (one string; body made of metal sardine can)[64]

kwamsa [*komsa, khamsa*] (Hausa: Nigeria; Niger) (two strings; gourd body)[65]

molo [plural *molaye; tafashe*] (Hausa: Nigeria; Niger) (three strings)[66]

moolooru (Fulani [Fulbe]: Cameroon) (three strings)[67]

yakandi (Bura: Nigeria) (two strings; gourd body)[68]

yomshi (Berom: Nigeria) (two strings; gourd body)[69]

Additional Plucked Lutes

Western and Central Sudan: These are lutes with incomplete specifications due to a lack of more detailed documentation.

biegu (Dagbamba: Ghana) (three strings; gourd body)[70]

chegeni [*chegendi*] (Daza: Chad) (three strings)[71]

chegeni [*chegendi*] (Kanembu: Chad) (two strings)[72]

gambra [*genbra*] (Haratin: Mauritania) (one string; gourd body)[73]

goumbale (Diawara: Mali)[74]

kibewe [*kegbier*] (Konkomba: Togo)[75]

konimesin (Guinea) (four strings; either wood or gourd body)[76]

kono (Kasena: Ghana)[77]

kuntunji (Dagbamba: Ghana) (three strings; body made from a metal sardine can)[78]

lawa (Kotokoli [Tem, Temba]: Togo; Benin; Ghana)[79]

moglo (Dagbamba: Ghana) (three strings; gourd body)[80]

moglo (Gurunsi: Ghana) (three strings; body made from a "one gallon can")[81]

molo (Mama: Nigeria) (number of strings not specified; gourd body)[82]

pomsa (Zarma: Niger) (two strings)[83]

tcheguendi (Toubou: Niger; Chad) (two strings)[84]

wase (Hausa: Nigeria)[85]

Notes

Our special thanks to Ulf Jägfors for reviewing and critiquing this endeavor.

1. Eric Charry, "Plucked Lutes in West Africa: An Historical Overview," *The Galpin Society Journal* 49 (March 1996): 3–37.

2. Ibid., 8.

3. Charry actually lists forty-four lutes. However, the third lute listed under the heading "LUTES WITH CYLINDER-SHAPED BRIDGES" is the *gimbri* (Gnawa) (ibid., 24), which is not a West African lute, but rather a North African lute of West African heritage.

4. Ibid., 22–26.

5. Scholars have historically considered the modern-day countries of Chad and Cameroon to be part of West Africa, though Chad and Cameroon are currently identified as being part of Central Africa, especially in terms of African subregional political and economic associations. However, the UN global geoscheme, developed by the United Nations Statistics Division in 1999, categorizes these two countries as being part of Middle Africa, a new subregional designation that includes Central Africa and West-Central Africa.

6. Ulf Jägfors, "The African Akonting and the Origin of the Banjo," *The Old-Time Herald* 9, no. 2 (November 2003–January 2004): 26–33. First reported and documented by Daniel Laemouahuma Jatta and Ulf Jägfors in 2000–2004; Greg C. Adams and Chuck Levy in 2008.

7. First reported by Daniel Jatta, 2000–2004.

8. Jägfors, "The African Akonting and the Origin of the Banjo," 26–33; Robert M. Baum, *Shrines of the Slave Trade: Diola Religion and Society in Precolonial Senegambia* (New York: Oxford University Press, 1999), "*econtine*," 171, 249n75; Michel Huet (text by Claude Savary), *The Dances of Africa* (New York: Harry N. Abrams, Inc., Publishers, 1996), "*ekontin*," 114 (photograph of the instrument on p. 112); Michael T. Coolen, "The Wolof Xalam Tradition," *Ethnomusicology* 27, no. 3 (September 1983): "*konting*," 480. First documented extensively by Jatta in the 1980s and reported by Jatta and Jägfors in 2000–2004; additional field research and documentation by Nick Bamber, Paul Sedgwick, Adams, and Levy. Shlomo Pestcoe and Greg C. Adams, "Ekonting," in *The Grove Dictionary of Musical Instruments: Second Edition*, ed. Laurence Libin, 5 vols. (Oxford: Oxford University Press, 2014), 2:140–41.

9. First reported by Jatta, 2000–2004.

10. First encountered and documented by Nick Bamber in 2006.

11. First encountered and documented by Randii Oliver in 2012.

12. First encountered and documented by Nick Bamber in 2006.

13. K. A. Gourlay, "Gurmi," in *The Grove Dictionary of Musical Instruments: Second Edition*, ed. Laurence Libin, 5 vols. (Oxford: Oxford University Press, 2014), 2:514–15.

14. Brandily, "Gulom," 513.

15. Gourlay, "Gurmi," 515; David W. Ames and Anthony V. King, *Glossary of Hausa Music and Its Social Context* (Evanston, IL: Northwestern University Press, 1971), 43–44.

16. P. G. Harris, "Notes on Drums and Musical Instruments Seen in Sokoto Province, Nigeria," *The Journal of the Royal Anthropological Institute of Great Britain and Ireland* 62 (January–June 1932): 105–25: *gurumi*, 124–25; Foundation for Hausa Performing Arts (Nigeria), video on YouTube: "Salamatu Mai Gurmi [Female Hausa Gurmi Player]," http://youtu.be/sztELbeZAng, accessed October 25, 2017. In Hausa, the designations *gurmi* and *gurumi* seem to be interchangeable in everyday usage as the lute Harris described and illustrated as a *gurumi* appears to be a three-stringed *gurmi* while the one Hajiya Salamatu plays in the YouTube video looks more like a *gurumi* than a *gurmi*.

17. Nathaniel Berndt, "Malam Maman Barka: The Man and the Name," http://www.beautysaloonmusic.com/press-group-13.html, accessed June 2, 2008.

18. Renate Wente-Lukas, *Die materielle Kultur der nicht-islamischen Ethnien von Nordkamerun und Nordostnigeria* (Wiesbaden: Franz Steiner Verlag GMBH, 1977), 256–57 (figure 340).

19. D. W. Arnott, "FulBe Music," *Grove Music Online* (*Oxford Music Online*, Oxford University Press), http://www.oxfordmusiconline.com/subscriber/article/grove/music/10365, accessed December 26, 2014.

20. Michael T. Coolen, "Xalamkats: The Xalam Tradition of Senegambia" (PhD diss., University of Washington, 1979), 75, 119. *Geseré* (plural *geserun*) is the Soninke term for griot; see Thomas A. Hale, *Griots and Griottes: Masters of Words and Music* (Bloomington: Indiana University Press, 1998), 10. "Among Wolof musicians," Coolen explains, "this term is most often used to describe a type of xalam [with a gourd body] which is played in the Salum [Saloum] region of Senegal" (Coolen, "Xalamkats," 75). Coolen suggests that the four-string *gambaré* (the standard griot lute of the Soninke *geserun*) may offer a possible clue as to why Wolof lutenists might have named the full-spike, gourd-bodied version of the *xalam* after their Soninke counterparts. According to Coolen, the descriptor *gambaré* "apparently comes from the Soninké word *gamba*, which means a certain gourd. Although most [Soninké *gambaré* players] now use a wood resonator, the instrument traditionally had a gourd resonator" (116).

21. Michael T. Coolen, "Senegambian Archetypes for the American Folk Banjo," *Western Folklore* 43, no. 2 (April 1984): 123.

22. Documented by Ben Nelson on April 21 and 22, 2006, in Serekunda, The Gambia. The *xalam geseré* player in question was Manga Jallo, a *xalamkat* (Wolof, literally "*xalam* player"; griot lutenist) who was introduced to Nelson by Matar Jeng, the *xalamkat* who was teaching him the five-string *xalam* with a semi-spike neck and a narrow wooden "trough" body. Nelson described the *xalam gesere* as being strung and tuned in the same way that the wooden-bodied *xalam* on which he was learning "but [it] was a full-spike, gourd-bodied lute with no soundhole [in the vellum soundtable] and an independent wooden bridge that rested on the vellum, held by the tension of the strings" (Ben Nelson's field notes, The Gambia, April 21, 2006). Our special thanks to Nelson for sharing his original field notes and the findings from his field studies in The Gambia in 2006, as well as his insights on the *xalam geseré* and the wooden-bodied *xalam*.

23. Tolia Nikiprowetzky, "The Griots of Senegal and Their Instruments," *Journal of the International Folk Music Council* 15 (1963): 80.

24. Ibid.

25. Coolen, "Xalamkats," 116–17.

26. "Hoddu," in *The Grove Dictionary of Musical Instruments: Second Edition*, ed. Laurence Libin, 5 vols. (Oxford: Oxford University Press, 2014), 2:680.

27. Stephen Davies, blog article, "Meet the Griots," *Voice in the Desert: Stephen Davies*, Burkina Faso, www.voiceinthedesert.org.uk, accessed October 23, 2005.

28. Betty Warner Dietz and Michael Babatunde Olatunji, *Musical Instruments of Africa* (New York: The John Day Company, 1965), 84–85.

29. Coolen, "The Wolof Xalam Tradition," 481.

30. Sibyl Marcuse, *Musical Instruments: A Comprehensive Dictionary* (Garden City, NY: Doubleday & Company, Inc., 1964), 280–81.

31. Eric Charry, *Mande Music: Traditional and Modern Music of the Maninka and Mandinka of Western Africa* (Chicago: University of Chicago Press, 2000), 123.

32. Ibid.

33. Lucy Duran, "Konting," in *The Grove Dictionary of Musical Instruments: Second Edition*, ed. Laurence Libin, 5 vols. (Oxford: Oxford University Press, 2014), 3:200. Duran references the report by the Scottish explorer Mungo Park (1771–1806) of "the *koonting*, a sort of guitar with three strings," played by "the *singing-men*, called *Jilli kea* [*jeli ke*, Mande

for 'male griot']" in his book recounting his travels in Senegambia, 1795–97, *Travels in the Interior Districts of Africa* (1799), 271–72. Samuel Charters, *The Roots of the Blues: An African Search* (Cambridge, MA: Da Capo Press, 1981), photo, 57.

34. Coolen, "Xalamkats," 111; Charry, "Plucked Lutes in West Africa," 124.

35. "Kubru," in *The Grove Dictionary of Musical Instruments: Second Edition*, ed. Laurence Libin, 5 vols. (Oxford: Oxford University Press, 2014), 3:220.

36. Hale, *Griots and Griottes, molo*, 240, 275–76, 280.

37. Nikiprowetzky, "The Griots of Senegal and Their Instruments," 80.

38. Ibid.

39. Lucy Duran and Aurelia W. Hartenberger, "Nkoni [n'goni]," in *The Grove Dictionary of Musical Instruments: Second Edition*, ed. Laurence Libin, 5 vols. (Oxford: Oxford University Press, 2014), 3:601–2.

40. Ibid., 602.

41. Ibid.

42. Elijah Wald, "ALI FARKA TOURE INTERVIEW" (written for *Acoustic Guitar* in 1993), http://www.elijahwald.com/longarch.html#alifar, accessed October 25, 2017.

43. Caroline Carol Wendt, "Tuareg Music," in *The Garland Handbook of African Music*, ed. Ruth M. Stone (New York: Garland Publishing, 2000), the *tahardent*, 219–22.

44. K. A. Gourlay, "Tidinit," in *The Grove Dictionary of Musical Instruments: Second Edition*, ed. Laurence Libin, 5 vols. (Oxford: Oxford University Press, 2014), 5:3.

45. Coolen, "Xalamkats," 1–288, and "The Wolof Xalam Tradition," 477–98.

46. First encountered and documented by Jayme Stone, April 2007.

47. First encountered by Marc Nerenberg in the village of Kané-Kombolé, Mali, August 7, 1981.

48. First encountered and documented by Jayme Stone, April 2007.

49. Jacqueline Cogdell DjeDje, *Fiddling in West Africa: Touching the Spirit in Fulbe, Hausa, and Dagbamba Cultures* (Bloomington: Indiana University Press, 2008), 64, 131, 141, 284n44.

50. Ulrich Wegner, *Afrikanische Saiteninstrumnete* (Berlin: Museum für Volkerkunde, 1984), 142.

51. Ames and King, *Glossary of Hausa Music*, 40–41.

52. Veit Erlmann, "Notes on Musical Instruments among the Fulani of Diamare (North Cameroon)," *African Music* 6, no. 3 (1983): 16–41; *garaya* (illustration, figure 8), 24.

53. K. A. Gourlay, "Gurmi," in *The Grove Dictionary of Musical Instruments: Second Edition*, ed. Laurence Libin, 5 vols. (Oxford: Oxford University Press, 2014), 2:515.

54. Ibid., 111.

55. Wente-Lukas, *Die materielle Kultur*, 258 (figure 342), 360.

56. Sandrine Loncke, liner notes, *Burkina Faso: La voix des peuls* [Burkina Faso: Voice of the Fulbe] (CHANT DU MONDE CNR 274 1079) (Paris: CNRS and the Musée de l'Homme, 1997), 13 (English translation, 36). Among the Fulbe, the *jurkel* is played by word-music artisans of the Fulbe social caste known as *riinraaybe* (literally "captives"). *Riinraaybe* constitute the lowest rung of traditional Fulbe society, being descendants of those who have been "dispossessed of their cultural origins after being captured during wars or raids, or purchased from neighboring powers by the Fulbe" (25–26).

57. Siegfried Nadel's fieldwork diaries (Nigeria, 1935–36), 120–22 http://www.rogerblench.info/Anthropology/Africa/Nigeria/Nadel/Nadel%20composite.pdf, accessed October 25, 2017; "Kaburu," in *The Grove Dictionary of Musical Instruments: Second Edition*, ed. Laurence Libin, 5 vols. (Oxford: Oxford University Press, 2014), 3:94.

58. Wente-Lukas, *Die materielle Kultur*, 257 (figure 341), 360.

59. Monique Brandily, "Keleli," in *The Grove Dictionary of Musical Instruments: Second Edition*, ed. Laurence Libin, 5 vols. (Oxford: Oxford University Press, 2014), 3:128.

60. Gavin Webb, "Kologo," in *The Grove Dictionary of Musical Instruments: Second Edition*, ed. Laurence Libin, 5 vols. (Oxford: Oxford University Press, 2014), 3:194–95.

61. Ames and King, *Glossary of Hausa Music*, 40; Wegner, *Afrikanische Saiteninstrumente*, 258.

62. Francis Bebey, *African Music: A People's Art* (Brooklyn: Lawrence Hill & Co, Publishers, Inc., 1975), 45.

63. Wegner, *Afrikanische Saiteninstrumente*, 258.

64. Ames and King, *Glossary of Hausa Music*, 45–46; Wegner, *Afrikanische Saiteninstrumente*, 139–40, 258–59.

65. Harris, "Notes on Drums and Musical Instruments," 124.

66. Ames and King, *Glossary of Hausa Music*, 46–47; Wegner, *Afrikanische Saiteninstrumente*, 258; illustration, figure 87, 136–37.

67. Erlmann, "Notes on Musical Instruments among the Fulani of Diamare (North Cameroon)," *moolooru* (illustration, figure 7, 24), 18, 20, 23, 28, 30, 35.

68. Paul Newman and Eric H. Davidson, liner notes, *Music from the Villages of Northeastern Nigeria: Recorded in the Field by Paul Newman and Eric and Lyn Davidson [in 1969]* (New York City: Asch Records, Asch Mankind Series, AHM 4532, 1971; Smithsonian Folkways, FW 04532, 2004), 4, 10.

69. Roger Blench, "The Traditional Music of the Jos Plateau in Central Nigeria: An Overview," paper presented in 2004, published online in 2005, 7; Wegner, *Afrikanische Saiteninstrumente*, 140.

70. DjeDje, *Fiddling in West Africa*, 185.

71. Monique Brandily, "Chegeni," in *The New Grove Dictionary of Musical Instruments, edited by Stanley Sadie in three volumes* (London: Macmillan Reference Limited; New York: Grove's Dictionaries of Music Inc., 1997, 1984), 1:342.

72. Ibid.

73. "Genbra," in *The Grove Dictionary of Musical Instruments: Second Edition*, ed. Laurence Libin, 5 vols. (Oxford: Oxford University Press, 2014), 2:408.

74. Gaston Boyer, *Un peuple de l'Ouest Soudanias: Les Diawara* (Memoires de l'Institut Francias d' Afrique Noire, no 29. Dakar: IFAN, 1953), cited in Charry, *Mande Music*, "Table 8. Chronological Lute References for Map 5," 124.

75. "Kibewe," in *The Grove Dictionary of Musical Instruments: Second Edition*, ed. Laurence Libin, 5 vols. (Oxford: Oxford University Press, 2014), 3:159.

76. "Konimesin," in *The Grove Dictionary of Musical Instruments: Second Edition*, ed. Laurence Libin, 5 vols. (Oxford: Oxford University Press, 2014), 3:199.

77. Vema Gillis, *Ghana: Music of the Northern Tribes* (Lyrichord LYRCD 7321).

78. DjeDje, *Fiddling in West Africa*, 185.

79. Gerhard Kubik, *Musikgeschichte in Bildern 1(11): Westafrika* (Leipzig: VEB Deutscher Verlag für Musik Leipzig, 1989), cited in Charry, *Mande Music*, "Table 8. Chronological Lute References for Map 5," 125.

80. DjeDje, *Fiddling in West Africa*, 185.

81. John Miller Chernoff, *African Rhythm and African Sensibility: Aesthetics and Social Action in African Musical Idioms* (Chicago: University of Chicago Press, 1979), 128.

82. O. Temple and C. L. Temple, *Notes on the Tribes, Provinces, Emirates and States of the Northern Provinces of Nigeria* (London: F. Cass and Co. Ltd., 1925), 52, cited by Ken A. Gourlay in his "Letter to the Editor," *Ethnomusicology* 20, no. 2 (May 1976): 328.

83. Curt Sachs, "Pomsa," in *Real-Lexikon der Musikinstrumente* (Berlin: Julius Bard, 1913; reprint New York: Dover, 1964), 303–4; "Pomsa," in *The Grove Dictionary of Musical Instruments: Second Edition*, ed. Laurence Libin, 5 vols. (Oxford: Oxford University Press, 2014), 4:147.

84. Berndt, "Malam Maman Barka: The Man and the Name."

85. In the collection of the Musical Instruments Museum, Brussels, Belgium.

CHAPTER 4

Searching for Gourd Lutes in the Bijago Islands of Guinea-Bissau

Nick Bamber

Editor's Headnote

A number of researchers, from the United States and other nations, interested in the history of the banjo and, particularly, its African predecessors, have gone to Africa to do fieldwork regarding West African plucked spike lutes. Nick Bamber, an Englishman, a trained musician, and an accomplished banjo player, is one of those, having made six trips to West Africa in order to make extensive field recordings of folk musicians playing gourd lutes. Bamber's ethnographic narrative of his trip to the Bijago Islands employs a more informal style than many of the other chapters in this book, which is appropriate to conveying some sense of what it is like to search for plucked spike lutes in West Africa. And his search was successful, uncovering two plucked spike lutes previously unknown to outsiders. His chapter is a logical companion to the preceding two chapters, indicating the kind of fieldwork that was important in the discovery of the many plucked spike lutes enumerated there and is necessary for the expansion of that list in the future. This chapter is also an example, common elsewhere in this book, of serious and valuable research into banjo history being done by non-academic researchers.

Inspired by an article on the African *akonting* by Ulf Jägfors,[1] I had spent two months in Senegal in 2005 and a further month in Casamance immediately prior to this trip in 2006. I had been looking forward to visiting a different area so that I could compare and contrast what I might find with the various aspects of Jola culture I had encountered in Senegal. Moreover, I was interested in discovering whether other ethnic groups in the region had gourd lutes similar to the Jola *ekonting*. The Jägfors article also described a trip he had made to Guinea-Bissau the same year, during which he documented a *bunchundo* gourd lute played by both Manjago and Balante musicians. My travel guide, the Rough Guide to West Africa, noted that the indigenous ethnic group of the Bijago Islands, the

Bujogo, had to a great extent maintained their traditional beliefs and customs in the same way that the Jola have. Thus, the Bujogo are not Muslims and only a small minority are Christian. Like the Jola of Casamance, they maintain a system of fetishes (spirit shrines), and perform animal sacrifices on suitable occasions. These similarities enhanced the possibility that the Bujogo had a musical culture similar to that of the Jola, including some kind of spike plucked lute.

Armed with this information and my existing knowledge of the Jola and their *ekonting*, I set off for the Bijago Islands with my Jola travel companion Tako Diedhiou. A complex, two-day journey by boat and public land transport brought us to Bissau, the capital of Guinea-Bissau and the port we would embark from to reach the Bijago Islands. The Bijago Islands form an archipelago of more than forty islands and islets in the Atlantic a few hours' boat ride from Bissau. The island of Bubaque is the main tourist center and almost the only island with visitor accommodations. Due to incorrect information about the time of departure, we missed the village boat to Bubaque and decided to travel in a considerably smaller fishing boat, despite rough waters, arriving in Bubaque six hours later.

The Bijago Islands are heavily forested, with various palms predominating. The two main ethnic groups are the Bujogo and the Balante. They live from subsistence agriculture, fishing, and hunting. Their communities consist of small villages scattered across the various islands. Their dwellings are not dissimilar to those of the Jola—square or oblong thatched mud huts containing a varying number of rooms. Also like the Jola, they make much use of oil palms, which grow extensively on the islands, harvesting both the clear red oil and the milky white sap that they drink as palm wine. Their other favorite form of alcohol is cashew wine.

Portuguese is commonly spoken; French and English are little understood. The lingua franca is Kriolu, a little of which Tako claimed to understand. We were glad to find a Senegalese hostel owner named Titi who spoke French, Wolof, Jola, and even some English. Chez Titi is a rather run-down building with two rooms for guests and a leaking roof. However, Titi was always eager to please and full of useful information with contacts on the various other islands.

The *Nõpata*

Our first excursion was to the neighboring island of Soga. We set off in a small fishing boat, arriving at the wrong place in our first attempt to land, where we waded ashore only to confront impenetrable mangrove. The second landing was more favorable, and we marched inland for a mile or two through palm forest until we reached the Bujogo village of Eticoba. The village consisted of about twenty mud houses with straw roofs. The houses were closer together than in the Jola villages I had seen in Casamance, and there was a sense of poverty here.

While waiting for the musician Titi had brought us here to meet, I was able to examine the instrument that he was about to play for us. The *ñopata* is a three-string gourd lute similar in construction to the Jola *ekonting* and the Manjak *bunchundo* (see figures F, A, and E). This exemplar, the only one I was to find during my visit, consisted of large round calabash, perhaps 14 inches in diameter, with a portion cut away and an animal skin stretched over the opening and fixed around the rim with metal pins. The lightweight neck was well over 39 inches in length and was made from some kind of large reed. It extended as a pole under the skin resting on opposite sides of the rim of the calabash. The three strings were attached at the bottom of the calabash around the protruding piece of the pole. The strings were made from fishing line, though presumably in days gone by they would have been made from some natural material such as palm root fiber, as is the case with the Jola *ekonting*. The massive two-footed wooden bridge stood freely on the animal skin. The calabash had a large circular hole, about 4 inches in diameter, cut into the back of the calabash. The placement of holes in calabashes is also found in other gourd lutes such as the *ekonting* and is intended to improve the acoustic properties of the instrument. The skin of this instrument was decorated with bold black text and some small red designs.

The stringing of this *ñopata* was as follows. Each string was attached to the neck pole at different positions. They were simply tied in loops around the neck and knotted. The top string was the shortest. The middle string was the longest but was capoed by the loop of the bottom string so that its speaking length was the same as that of the bottom string. The initial tuning I found was as follows:

top (short) string	G
middle string	C♯ (diminished 5th below the top string)
bottom string	E (minor 3rd above the middle string)

The three strings thus formed a diminished triad.

For the musical entertainment we proceeded to the adjoining village of En-camigno, where Titi had arranged for the local *ñopata* player, Joaquim Cabritan, to play at our request. Joaquim was from another nearby village named Ebegé and was the main practitioner of the *ñopata* on the island. On reaching Encamigno, we found most of the men well plied with the lethal cashew wine. Soon Joaquim appeared and Titi explained that I was interested in hearing Bujogo lute music. I offered Joaquim the gifts I had been advised to buy for him, rum and tobacco. Joaquim then began tuning his *ñopata* and broke the short string. This was soon repaired and the newly tuned short string was raised a semitone higher than its previous pitch. This new tuning therefore made a perfect 5th between the top string and the middle string. Thus the new tuning was:

top (short) string	G♯
middle string	C♯ (perfect 5th below the top string)
bottom string	E (minor 3rd above the middle string),

the open strings now forming a chord of a minor triad. Now ready to play, he attached metal bells to his right-hand middle and ring fingers. These tinkled away throughout his performance (see figure F).

From what I could make out the playing technique was a form of stroke style, with the middle finger striking down on the middle and bottom strings. The thumb seemed restricted to the short drone string. The left hand stopped the longer two strings at a single position that corresponded to the second fret of a banjo and therefore produced tones each a major 2nd higher than the respective open strings. Thus the five notes played on the instrument were as follows:

top string open	G♯
middle string open	C♯
middle string stopped	D♯
bottom string open	E
bottom string stopped	F♯

These tones form the initial five notes of the scale in C♯ minor, that is, C♯ D♯ E F♯ G♯.

What Joaquim actually began to play was a four-note ostinato figure. This accompanied his singing, which consisted of long descending diatonic phrases that tended toward E major. I sensed immediately the influence of Portuguese music. The right-hand finger seemed sometimes to strike both middle and bottom strings together, both on the open strings (C♯ E) and the stopped strings (D♯ F♯). The ostinato figure varied occasionally but never included more than five notes and could not be compared with the melodic *ekonting* picking practiced by the Jola.

As Joaquim played, one or two of the men sang along and some of the women began dancing. Not being an expert in West African dance, I can only comment that it mostly looked quite familiar, though not of course identical to the Jola dancing I had already seen. Some of the dance moves, however, seemed to remind me more of flamenco. Some of the women wore the traditional short grass skirts over their other clothing. The remaining villagers looked on and continued to enjoy their cashew wine.

After presenting rum and tobacco to the village elder, I asked Joaquim about the viability of the *ñopata*-playing tradition on the island. He told me that he was the only player, although some boys were learning the instrument. At this point the village elder took the opportunity to explain the impoverished state of the village. They had no medical center and islanders relied on people bringing donations of medical supplies from the clinic on the main island of Bubaque. They had a school but it had virtually no equipment for its students. I replied that the best I could do was to make the village of Encamigno and the island of Soga known to the banjo roots community. I consider the writing of this chapter to be a significant part of my response to this obligation. After my being presented with a grass skirt, we took our leave and returned to Bubaque under a full moon.

The *Kusunde*

The following day on Bubaque I met a Balante named San Sau Mbale. He owned a gourd lute that he called *kusunde*. Unfortunately, owing to a working accident several years before, San Sau was no longer able to use his right-hand fingers to play his *kusunde*. I asked him nevertheless if he would show me the instrument and demonstrate the basics of the playing technique. The instrument on first appearance was a three-string gourd lute almost identical in its basic features to the *ñopata*. The stringing, however, was most remarkable in that it was exactly a mirror image of the *ñopata* stringing: the short string was at the bottom rather than at the top, the top string was of middle length, and the middle string was the longest although, as with the *ñopata*, it was capoed by the middle-length string (in this case, the top string) and its open sounding length was therefore the same as that string. The tuning I found was a perfect 4th from the top string down to the middle string and then something between a major 6th and a minor 7th back up from the middle string to the short string at the bottom. The actual pitches of the open strings were as follows:

top string	F♯
middle string	C♯ (perfect 4th below the top string)
bottom (short) string	A♯/B (major 6th-minor 7th above the middle string)

When San Sau attempted to play for me he used his right-hand thumb, plucking in an upward direction on all three strings. The first and second fingers also picked up but were confined to the short drone string at the bottom. The top and middle strings were both stopped at a single position, making approximately a major 2nd above the open string pitches. Thus, the tones used on the instrument were:

top string open	F♯
top string stopped	G♯
middle string open	C♯
middle string stopped	D♯
bottom string open	A♯/B

This tuning and the method of picking this *kusunde* raise several questions. As all the lutes I had hitherto heard of and seen had short strings at the top, I of course wondered whether this particular *kusunde* had been strung incorrectly. Perhaps the player had restrung his instrument the opposite way round in order to manage some notes with his crippled right hand. Would this also explain the fact that he up-picked with both his fingers and his thumb? It is clearly dangerous to generalize on the basis of a single exemplar, and this appears to be a case in point. However, since my visit to the Bijago Islands in 2006, the Swiss banjo player Martin Brügger visited northern Guinea-Bissau in December 2007. There, in the town of Sao Domingos, he found and made video recordings of a Balante musician playing a *kusunde* (although Brügger is unable to verify the name of this particular exemplar). His recordings confirm that the *kusunde* is indeed strung in the manner I have described and that the exemplar belonging to San Sau was not an exception. Finding additional Balante *kusundes* would, of course, help to verify this conclusion.

The notes that San Sau picked on his *kusunde* were interesting in that, as with those generally used on the Jola *ekonting*, they formed a pentatonic scale. Especially remarkable is that the commonly found ambiguity in the tuning of the *ekonting* short string is repeated here with exactly analogous consequences. Thus, if we treat the tuning of the short string here as an A♯ we have a pentatonic scale rooted on F♯, that is, C♯ D♯ F♯ G♯ A♯. If, however, we interpret the drone string tuning as being B, then we have a pentatonic scale rooted on B, that is, C♯ D♯ F♯ G♯ B. Such ambiguity of pitch is often found with the *ekonting*.

The notes that San Sau played formed simple four- or five-note ostinato figures that accompanied his singing. This practice is therefore more akin to the *ñopata* playing of the Bujogo musician than to the melodic picking of the Jola *ekonting*. As to San Sau's singing, this contained scale notes not present in either of the pentatonic scales that the notes he plucked could be said to occupy. All in all, the encounter with San Sau raised many more questions than it answered. What was clear was that whatever the structural similarities between the Bujogo *ñopata* and the Balante *kusunde*, the music played on the two instruments differs significantly. Nevertheless, the *ñopata* and the *kusunde* both share and lack features that place them closer to each other than either is to the Jola *ekonting*.

Further Excursion and Return to Casamance

The second major excursion during our stay in the Bijagos was to the larger island, Cagnabaque, hoping to find more *ñopata* players living there. During our one-day visit, however, we failed to find any. Instead, on our request the young men of the village entertained us with traditional Bujogo music and dance. Three instruments were played as accompaniment to the singing and dance. A long narrow drum was used, which consisted of what seemed to be a length of drainpipe with an animal skin stretched over one end. Another of the participants blew a cow's horn, while one of the dancers had bells attached to some part of his costume.

We also got to witness a traditional divination, in which the village elder decapitated a chicken and "read" its innards to answer a particular question about the future. We then made our return trip through Bissau and on to Casamance, a journey as eventful as the one on the way out to the Bijagos.

Conclusion

The trip to the Bijago Islands confirmed my suspicion that gourd lutes similar to the Jola *ekonting* might be found in areas of the West African coast to the south of Casamance where traditional beliefs are still practiced and the influence of Islamic culture is less strong. The instruments I found shared structural similarities with the Jola *ekonting* and especially with the Manjak *bunchundo*. Thus, all of them are three-string gourd lutes with long poles, strings of unequal length, and two-footed bridges standing free on animal skins. As might be expected, each of these instruments has its own unique tuning system. Perhaps less obvious, each is played with its own proper finger technique. In the case of the *kusunde* this actually involves a complete reversal of the plucking action. The music played on each instrument is characteristic of the ethnic group to which it belongs; their musical cultures show marked differences.

There is much scope for further research. Further exemplars of the *ñopata* and *kusunde* should be sought and more detailed documentation of playing techniques and the music played should be investigated. This effort should accompany an in-depth study of the culture of each respective ethnic group. Comparison of the respective musical and general cultures of each ethnic group will help us to better understand how these gourd lutes are related to one another. At the same time, the possibility of finding more gourd lutes in the region should inspire future field trips.

Note

1. Ulf Jägfors, "The African Akonting and the Origin of the Banjo," *The Old-Time Herald* 9, no. 2 (Winter 2003).

CHAPTER 5

Interviews with Ekona Diatta and Sana Ndiaye, Master Musicians Playing within Traditional and Contemporary Commercial Contexts

Chuck Levy

Editor's Headnote

If one wants to learn more about West African plucked spike lutes as precursors to the banjo, going to West Africa would be a good plan. Chuck Levy is one of several contributors to this book who have gone there more than once with this in mind. Once there, he met with and interviewed Ekona Diatta, a middle-aged rice farmer and akonting *(ekonting) player. Upon his return, he then met with and interviewed Sana Ndiaye, an* akonting *player now residing and performing in the United States who performs in a rap band. In the absence of historical documentation with any details of the tradition of* akonting *playing, the only way to study it and consider its relation to the modern banjo is to interact with living players, knowing that local knowledge speaks of a tradition going back several hundred years. Levy's verbatim transcripts of his interviews with Ekona Diatta and Sana Ndiaye offer rare and personal accounts of African* akonting *players in their own voices. These accounts give us a glimpse of the impact and place of this banjo ancestor in the lives of contemporary Africans, relatively unfiltered and fully contextualizing the playing of this instrument both in its home culture and in another culture.*

In the course of my study of the banjo and its history, I have often found myself at unexpected destinations in the company of remarkable individuals. Two such individuals are the Jola *akonting* master musicians Ekona Diatta and Sana Ndiaye. Ekona, a 46-year-old rice farmer in the village of Mlomp in Southern Senegal at the time of my interview, carries on the traditions of music making, mostly at informal gatherings in his home village. In contrast, Sana is a professional musician who has taken the *akonting* far from his home village of Djembering (also Diembéring) in Southern Senegal, to Dakar and ultimately to the United States and beyond. In contrast to the other chapters, the interviews here give first-person accounts from living West African musicians who play the *akonting*, the African instrument that most closely resembles the early gourd banjo when considering both its construction and musical attack.[1]

Like many students of the old-time music, I felt called to learn my craft from my fellow players, as well as an older generation of tradition bearers, which led me from private music lessons, festivals, and workshops to the homes of older rural musicians in West Virginia, Virginia, North Carolina, and Ohio. This path eventually drew me to the written record of the minstrel banjo as documented in the banjo tutors, sheet music, playbills, and photographs from the 1850s and 1860s. Although the minstrel sources pointed clearly to an African banjo heritage, it did not occur to me that there might be a way to find it until 2006, when I stumbled across Ulf Jägfors and Daniel Laemouahuma Jatta's discovery and documentation of the Jola *akonting*, a significant banjo ancestor.

Besides being a banjoist, I am a physician. My practice includes involvement with the University of Florida's Center for Arts in Medicine program (AIM). In 2007, with help from a State of Florida Artists Enhancement grant, I visited The Gambia's Royal Victorian Teaching Hospital (RVTH) to lay the groundwork for an arts-in-medicine collaboration between the RVTH and the University of Florida, and to follow my banjo muse across the Atlantic, where Daniel agreed to be my host and guide to learn about the Jola *akonting*[2] and to introduce me to the Jola (Diola) culture. I returned in 2008 to further my exploration.

As a native Jola, Daniel Laemouahuma Jatta grew up in The Gambia hearing his father play the *akonting*, but did not take up the instrument himself. After graduation from high school, he managed to secure an academic scholarship in the United States, residing there for eleven years, ultimately earning his MBA. While in the United States, he encountered the clawhammer banjo and was struck by its resemblance to the *akonting* of his childhood. Through Daniel's fine scholarship and detective work in partnership with Ulf we have come to appreciate the similarities between the two instruments.[3]

Daniel arranged that I meet with two Jola musicians to teach me *akonting*, Ekona Diatta and his nephew Remi Diatta (figure 5.1). Since I am conversant only in English, which neither Ekona nor Remi could speak, our verbal interactions were limited. Nonetheless, by demonstration, imitation, and gesture, Ekona and Remi managed to instruct me well enough that I was able to learn the fundamentals of playing the *akonting*.

Some might view the music of the Jola *akonting* as simple. The songs are typically constructed of one short part, usually less than twelve bars in length, that repeats over and over. Every other time through, a verse is sung. In most instances, the verses do not progress; the same verse is repeated over and over. Traditionally, only five tones are produced by the *akonting* (a pentatonic scale).[4] Of the three strings on the *akonting*, the shorter top and middle strings are played exclusively

Figure 5.1. Remi Diatta and Ekona Diatta; photo courtesy of author.

by the thumb and are never stopped (fretted). The bottom string (the longest string) is always played with the fingernail of the index or middle finger, using a down-stroke motion of the wrist and hand, with fingers half closed as if grasping a hammer. The bottom string is either played open, stopped by the index finger for the 3rd degree of the scale, or stopped by the ring finger for the 4th degree.

Despite the limited number of tones and the seemingly simple repetitive structure of most of the material, I always found Ekona's music riveting. He sings with conviction, seeming to channel an extraordinary, almost devotional joy. His voice is strong and certain, his playing dynamic, filled with subtle rhythmic and melodic variation. His music at one point might serve as the anchor for a group of Jola men relaxing after work. They would pass around a dipper from a plastic bucket filled with palm wine, sharing laughter and good cheer, joining Ekona in song. In another setting, Ekona's music would propel the traditional dance being learned by Jola youth, a transmission of Jola culture. When Ekona performed, his eyes would often drift upward and to the left, as he looked inward. His face would fill with a broad smile, as he would swell with contentment and pride, singing the songs of his people. Toward the end of my stay, Ekona agreed to an interview, with Daniel acting as a translator.[5]

In 2008, I visited The Gambia again to study under Ekona and Remi, and again was hosted by Daniel. My visit overlapped with that of Greg C. Adams, who was also visiting and studying with Remi, Ekona, and others. I joined Greg, Daniel, Remi, and Ekona for a visit to Remi and Ekona's home village of Mlomp, on the Casamance River in Southern Senegal, which appeared to have a population of between five hundred and one thousand inhabitants. Ekona's primary occupation, like that of most of the community, was that of a rice farmer; other common occupations were growing groundnuts, fishing, and raising animals such as goats, sheep, and chickens. On the occasion of our visit, a celebration took place at Remi's dwelling. The celebration included food and drink, good cheer and laughter. Many of the men took turns singing and playing the *akonting*, passing it from one to another. However, it was clear that Ekona was the most respected player and the one who was the prime interpreter of the musical traditions of his people. Although the *akonting* was played, it appeared that this was not a usual occurrence for most of the men. My impression was that the *akonting* was viewed as frivolous and old-fashioned and as a distraction from the necessary industry of farm life, and that Ekona's dedication to it was not viewed entirely positively. This might be in part because alcohol was imbibed freely on many of the occasions that included the *akonting*. My sense was that the *akonting* traditions were disappearing in the face of increased access to outside musics. There was a boom box in the village that played reggae music. We were told that Remi organized a group of youth to learn to play the *akonting*, but that the effort had flagged and that the group was no longer meeting.

Ekona Diatta Interview

This interview took place at the Bakadaji Hotel in Kotu, The Gambia. I started by asking about biographic details and learned that Ekona was 46 years old; he started playing when he was 3 years old in the village of Etedimy Mlomp.

CHUCK: What got you started?

EKONA: I saw my fathers playing.

DANIEL: In Casamance, you don't have one father. In Jola culture, every relative at the age group of your father is your father, so he saw it from his fathers.

CHUCK: What were the common occupations? Mostly fishers and rice farmers?

EKONA: Fishing, rice, groundnuts, raising animals like goats, sheep, chickens.

CHUCK: How many people played? Was it common to see people playing the *akonting*?

EKONA: There are still a large number of people playing but there used to be more.

CHUCK: Do you know thirty people who play?

EKONA: More than thirty people.

CHUCK: More than one hundred?

EKONA: In the larger community, more than one hundred.

CHUCK: What was the first tune you learned to play?

EKONA: The name of the song is "Eliba."

CHUCK: Are there young people who are still learning the *akonting*?

EKONA: There are still a reasonable amount of youths who are interested in learning from their parents.

CHUCK: Are they all learning the *o'teck*[6] style?

EKONA: Nobody that is young that I know is playing any other style than the *o'teck* style.

CHUCK: What kind of events call for the playing of the *akonting*?

EKONA: The *akonting* is played for different purposes. One of the main purposes is *wholel*,[7] which I will show you tomorrow in the program. Mainly when you have someone that is engaged who wants to marry, the *akonting* is the main instrument that Jolas use for the wedding ceremony.

CHUCK: Are there regular events other than weddings where people get together to play music?

EKONA: You know Jolas tap palm wine. Normally when we work all day, in the evening we like to relax and go home.

CHUCK: So after a hard day's work, you relax, drink, and play music. Do you do this all year-round? Every night, or just during a certain time of the year?

EKONA: We play the *akonting* in the way I have described mostly during the harvest time of the rice, between November and January. That is when we play the *akonting* most.

CHUCK: In a typical evening, in the harvest season, how many *akontings* play together?

EKONA: In some occasions there are people who when somebody plays, the rest of the *akontings* will play the same thing like how I did with you, from time to time. But in some cases we can let each and everyone play, [one] at a time. There are occasions that people just feel like "Oh we can play together," and they play two or three at the same things at a time.

CHUCK: If you are playing with other players, does it change how you play? Do you play differently when you are playing with someone else to complement them better?

EKONA: I can follow you, I can play the same thing, but time to time I will also add in some things to make the sound more complicated.

CHUCK: Where does an *akonting* player learn the tunes he or she plays? Is it mostly from your fathers? From other players?

EKONA: There is no specific person. Anyone who plays the *akonting* is willing to teach, is always happy to see that young generations are interested in learning the art and anytime that we have the time we will show you, even if we are not your father.

CHUCK: Does anyone make up new songs, or is all the music something passed on?

EKONA: There are traditional songs that you can play if you are an *akonting* player, but there is also no rule or law that says you cannot make your own songs. After learning and playing a lot of traditional songs that have been played by our ancestors, at a certain period I started making up my own songs, and now I have made up a lot of songs.

CHUCK: Have other people learned your songs? Have your songs become part of the tradition?

EKONA: Most *akonting* players love and play my songs.

CHUCK: Do you play other *akonting* players' songs?

EKONA: Yes.

CHUCK: So people are still making the music and still sharing. Are there other instruments that are played with the *akonting*? Are drums played with the *akonting*?

EKONA: Drumming has never been common in the *akonting* culture in the old generation. But the new generation, after knowing how to play the drum and *akonting* at the same time started combining the two instruments. But originally the *akonting* has not been subordinated by any instrument.

CHUCK: All the instruments I have seen use fishing line for the strings. How long has fishing line been used?

EKONA: I don't know when nylon strings were introduced.

CHUCK: Do you know of any *akonting* that does not have fishing line as the string?

EKONA: Now it is very difficult to find someone using the old traditional string from the palm tree.

CHUCK: The old string was from the palm tree?

EKONA: The roots of the palm tree.

DANIEL: I remember my father, until the time I went to the United States, was still using the palm tree.

CHUCK: So that was in the 1970s. Did they sound different?

DANIEL: Yes, they sounded more natural. They sounded better to me.

CHUCK: You don't know of any of those instruments, do you?

DANIEL: No, it is very difficult to find them now because the strings are very fragile. When they dry they have to be changed. We used to have to change them every six months.

CHUCK: *Akontings* are made with natural materials and have a lot of string tension. How long does an *akonting* last? Five years? Ten years? Fifty years?

EKONA: An *akonting* will never get spoiled unless if by accident the calabash is crushed.

DANIEL: If you know how to protect it, it can last one hundred years. The only thing that can stop it from functioning is when you crush the calabash. By accident, somebody walks on it, or it falls down and breaks.

CHUCK: Do all *akonting* players build their own instruments? Or are there a few people who build them for other people?

EKONA: Every *akonting* player must have built their own instrument.

CHUCK: Does the *akonting* provide music for people to dance and mix?

EKONA: The music of the *akonting* is communal. Anyone who hears it whether you are from Lun or from another community, it is always a social thing.

CHUCK: Not dance in particular, but share good times?

DANIEL: Exactly!

CHUCK: Does anyone ever get paid for playing? For example, if you play for a wedding, do the musicians get paid?

EKONA-DANIEL: Monetary values have never been attached to the Jola culture of the *akonting*, even though maybe the new generation now, because of some economic problems, people are working for money now in everything. In those days, when the *akonting* culture existed in the Jola community, people will contribute in many forms, some will get palm wine, some will bring animals, some will bring many other things to offer to the occasion. The person marrying will be given this gift; so everyone will share with all these gifts like they donate a cow, they will kill it and cook it and everyone will eat. Someone will donate palm wine, and everyone will drink; someone will donate rice, and everyone will eat the rice. There is no money value attached to any of the musicians because they are not paid to play.

CHUCK: Are there acknowledged *akonting* masters that people look up to and want to learn from?

EKONA: Yes, they have those who appreciate their styles, their different styles or their way of playing the *akonting*. Not in the play style [alone], but the songs they sing, and also the notes they produce. You will find somebody, a young guy who will say, "I want to play like Remi," or "I want to play like Ekona," or somebody who will say, "I want to play like Chuck," so something like that. They have people who see them as idols, as models.

CHUCK: So there are some people who are considered the best players in the community.

DANIEL: And youths identify with them.

CHUCK: You model yourself after someone you think is great. Are you and Remi considered great in your community?

EKONA: I exclude my fathers and grandfathers; at the moment, the highest among the community are me and Remi. We are now next to the elderly people who are really disappearing every day. There are not many. At the moment, in our generation, we are the top.

CHUCK: It would be nice to hear some of these elders before they are gone.

EKONA: There are still very old people within the community. There are very few now. If we had gotten the chance we could have seen them.

CHUCK: Do you know hundreds of tunes?

EKONA: Combining my songs with traditional songs, I know more than five hundred.

CHUCK: What is your favorite tune?

EKONA: I have some favorites, but they are many, not just one. Sometimes I can say this song is better than that one, but then I play another one, I have appreciation of many of them.

CHUCK: Who is the *akonting* player that you like to listen to the most?

EKONA: There are different groups, and some of them play equally well, and I appreciate the way they play.

CHUCK: What do you make of the banjo?

EKONA: Let me see your banjo again. (Starts to play and grins. Daniel asks for the banjo to demonstrate how it is played. Daniel plays a melody reminiscent of "Shortnin' Bread" or "Cripple Creek." He plays with enthusiasm if somewhat lacking in finesse, hooting and laughing while he plays. Ekona plays some more, noodling repetitive patterns. Ekona literally picks and grins. We all laugh.)

DANIEL: Now he is beginning to understand. (Daniel and Ekona converse. Chuck tunes the instrument. Ekona resumes playing. Daniel sings and intermittently yells, "O'teck.")

DANIEL (TO EKONA): Now you play the banjo!

EKONA: The bridge is the same. The banjo is very close to the *akonting*. The only difference is that the banjo has five strings and the *akonting* has three strings.

CHUCK: Do you like the sound of it?

EKONA: I love it. It is a beautiful instrument.

CHUCK: What are the most important things for Westerners to know about the *akonting*? Or the Jola? What can Westerners learn from studying the *akonting*?

EKONA: For the Jola, the *akonting* is part of daily activity, both work and social activity. So Jolas, especially Jolas of Casa,[8] this is the only instrument that they can identify as the unique social instrument within the Jola Casa community. The Jola Fonyi[9] also appreciate the Jola Casa *akonting*. But they have their own unique instrument called the *bugata*, which the Jola Casa cannot play, but the Jola Casa love to listen to it when the Jola Fonyi play. It is the four drums that they play, one man plays it. The *akonting* is a social instrument for the Jola community; its importance cannot be underrated. Because it is the instrument that, when they have a native function, it is one of the instruments that must apply [be played] to have their gathering together.

CHUCK: When we were at Mandinary a couple of days ago the *akonting* was played in memory of Daniel's father. Is the *akonting* played at funerals?

EKONA: The very day the person dies, you can sing some *akonting* songs to just compliment the person, but you do not play the *akonting*, but then there are certain occasions when this select group remembers a person. If they ask, you can play the *akonting*.

CHUCK: So for remembrance, but not at the funeral.

DANIEL: Yeah.

CHUCK: Is there any religious association with the *akonting*? Do you consider yourself a religious person?

EKONA: Even though you have within the community, most of them go to church now, but the strongest belief is the traditional method of belief.

CHUCK: Does the *akonting* have any role in the traditional method of belief? So for instance, at your house we saw chanting to help cure a boy of illness. Is the *akonting* used in any religious ceremonies of spiritual belief?

EKONA: To heal somebody with *akonting* music, you don't play the *akonting*, but you sing the songs and at the same time, you sing them within a shrine or a praying area. You go there, but you don't play the *akonting*.

CHUCK: The ill person doesn't go to the shrine, just the people singing.

EKONA: The ill person does not go to the shrine. He stays at home and they go to the shrine, sing there, and then come home, where he is, and also sing the same songs to him.

CHUCK: It looks to me like everyone in the community has a spiritual role. For instance, Ekona, you are an *akonting* player, but when a child is sick, you have tribal lore as to how to help that child. Does everyone in the community know some of the lore? Would everyone know what to do to help someone who is ill? Is this something that everyone does?

EKONA: The healing process, not everyone can do it, but the majority can do it. It is not difficult to find a healer. Most of the people can do something. If they cannot do this, they can do another thing.

CHUCK: Thank you very much for answering so many of my questions.

The Sana Ndiaye Interview

In March 2008, I organized the Akonting Banjo Collaborative with the help of a grant from the Florida Department of State, Division of Cultural Affairs. My original intent was to invite Ekona Diatta to represent the *akonting*, but because of problems obtaining a travel visa he was not able to attend. Fortunately, Paul Sedgwick, another banjo scholar, introduced me to Sana Ndiaye, a Jola *ekonting* player born in Djembering, Senegal, who was living in Massachusetts. Sana agreed to attend the collaborative, and to be an artist in residence as part of the University of Florida's AIM program. When I first met Sana, he was dressed in a white tank top and baggy pants, with a gold necklace adorning his neck, smoking while leaning against a car. He was lean and handsome, cool and aloof, and looked as I imagined a rapper would. Over time, as we got to know each other, Sana came forward as a serious and thoughtful person and artist, and friendly and personable too.

Sana's history is quite different from Ekona's. Because of health problems, Sana left the village of Djembering in Southern Senegal at age 3 to move to Dakar, where more modern medical services were available. He did not return to Djembering until age 9; his family then moved again to Dakar when Sana was 12. In contrast to Ekona, who appears to be grounded in village life as a musician-rice farmer, Sana spent a great deal of his youth growing up in a more multicultural urban setting. Sana has intentionally pursued a career in music, emigrating to the United States in 1999 with a goal of reaching a large audience to tell the stories of those living in poverty through the contemporary form of rap music.

Sana's story is intriguing because it is so easy to imagine how it might parallel the development of the banjo from the *akonting*. Sana first learned the *akonting* in a traditional setting, from his grandfather. Three years later, he found himself in an urban environment where different cultural standards took precedence. Driven to be a success, Sana adapted his playing to meet new musical demands. In traditional *akonting* playing, only the first (bottom) string is stopped. The middle and top string are always played open. Sana decided he needed more range, so he sometimes stops the second string, adding a 6th tone to the scale. Second, he made important changes to the instrument itself, undoubtedly influenced by his exposure to modern guitars. Sana added Western-style mechanical geared tuners to his instrument. This allows him to precisely tune and easily change strings. He also had an instrument built with a wooden top including F-holes as opposed to the traditional skin head. Perhaps more interesting is what did not change. He employs the traditional right-hand down-stroke technique, nearly identical to stroke-style-clawhammer. Might a similar process of adaptation have occurred when the African banjo ancestors first arrived in the New World? Did the left-hand techniques and the instrument itself evolve to meet the needs of a new cultural environment, while the right-hand technique survived intact? Sana agreed to sit for an interview near the end of his stay in Gainesville.

CHUCK: You told me before that you started to play *akonting* around age 9. How did it happen that you started to play?

SANA: My name is Sana and I am from Senegal, West Africa; I am based in the south in a village called Djembering. Djembering is where I am from, and the region is called Casamance. Casamance is where the Jola people live. So I was born there and at 3 years old I was really sick, and my parents had to take me to the city to take care of me because at the time there was no hospital. So they took me to the city [Dakar]. When everything was okay, they bought a house and stayed there. I went back to the village for school and at 9 years old I found what we call *akonting*. *Akonting* is a very old instrument probably close to the 1500s or 1600s. I don't know exactly when, but it is an instrument that my people, the Jola people, invented, and it is made with a monkey skin, a gourd, a stick, and in the past people used palm fiber to make string. And so I remember when I was coming from school, I heard a sound that wasn't really familiar, 'cause I can tell when I heard a guitar sound or any other instrument I can tell, but when I heard that sound I didn't know what instrument was it. So I kept following the sound, and I could realize that the sound was coming from my house. So when I get to the house, I just saw my granddad playing the *akonting*. And I was so attracted to that beautiful instrument. It just seemed to me, that me and that instrument, we were very related. So I just dropped my stuff and stand there watching him playing. After he played some beautiful songs I asked him, I told him, that I wanted to learn how to play this instrument. He didn't want me to because he just wanted me to finish school. And at the end of school, I just came back and tell him the same thing and he just start teaching me the *akonting*, and it took me a while before I exactly be able to play right, and after that I came back to the city, my parents stayed and I lived in a neighborhood called Ginna Ry, Ginna Ry, which means "at the side of the track." Ginna Ry is our neighborhood's name and is in our national language. Ginna Ry means "neighborhood." And so where I was living, it is a very tough neighborhood, where a lot of people struggle to survive and there was a lot of kids that didn't have the opportunity to go to school, so many of them ended up on the street, and some of them die at the very early age at the ocean because of the lack of surveillance [supervision]. So I met these guys, that we almost grow up together in the same neighborhood, and then, because of the toughness of our neighborhood, we just had the idea of creating a band that we will name our neighborhood, which is Gohk Bi System. So Gohk Bi System is the neighborhood system. The philosophy we are living in our neighborhood, it's a very poor neighborhood, but still people live in community, people live in peace, people live in love. And so when we create the band, we decided to do rap music but rap that would be very very different from what we heard every day from the United States or any other countries 'cause we wanted to be more positive and before anything I just told them that this instrument has to be in something that is very positive because the reason why it is invented, it is intended to be peaceful, to bring people to peace, because there was many time of unrest where people fought for lands and stuff like that. So we all agreed that, you know, anyway that the neighborhood that we live in is very tough so I think it is a very good idea for us to talk about it and represent people that wanted to say something but never have the opportunity. So we wanted to express ourselves, to [play] music, to the rap that we do, and our style is called "Ancient meet Urban" which is a confrontation of two generations. We wanted just to build [bridge] the gap that there is between these generations. And so we started working in it but it was very tough for us because when our parents also knew we wanted to do rap, they didn't want us to do that because, you know, rap had a bad position in my country because people always think that when you do rap, you just want to be bad, you know, you just want to be negative. And which is why, because you know a lot of people make it seem like, you know, it's a bad thing, but that wasn't the way we were taking [it], so we have a different way of expression.

So in 1998 there is this guy named Tony Vacca, he is from the United States. He has a band called World Rhythm. He came to Senegal to visit Massamba Diop. Massamba Diop is a superstar that is in Baaba Mal's band. I think a lot of people know Baaba Mal, he's a superstar. He traveled to the United States a lot. So when Tony Vacca come and visit Massamba Diop in Senegal, we heard about it and then we wanted to go there and show our style, show him what we do. But Massamba Diop didn't let us do that because he just assumed that, you know, we are just going to bother them; anyway those people are busy, they don't want to hear that, so we just were very embarrassed because we were thinking that he's going to do something for us. But we just did come home, you know, and talk about it, say, "You know what, just let's go and pop into his house. Either he want it or not. We are just going to go in there and do our thing." So that's what we ended up doing. One day around 8:00 p.m. we just pop into his house; it was a time exactly when they was having dinner. So Massamba Diop was surprised to see us in his house and he wanted us to go out. But, you know, when we just get into the house we just start playing and Tony Vacca, he tell 'em, "Let 'em play because this is very interesting." Then he just like admired the instrument that I was playing and then he started asking me questions about it. So I told him the story and after the song he told us, "What is the name of the song?" So we told him this song is about real life. We call it "Real Life." We got this inspiration from our neighborhood. So we told him how hard it is to live in a tough neighborhood, and how many people are struggling for their life. And that is not just for our neighborhood, but is just representing everywhere in the world where people are suffering. 'Cause like we know ghettos always look the same everywhere. So he like the song, and he wanted to buy it, but we didn't want to sell the song. We just wanted to be promoted. And finally what he did is that he just took the song and he came back to the United States. So when he came to the United States, he was putting out a CD. Our song is one of his songs in the CD and our song just sold the CD. And before he really liked it and they started questioning, "Who are these people?" And then he just told them we are from Senegal, West Africa, and that's how we got a chance to come here [the United States] in October 1999. That is how we got to the United States.

CHUCK: How old were you when you left Djembering?

SANA: Three when I left Djembering. I went back to Dakar when I was 12 years old.

CHUCK: So you were back in the village for three years [between the ages of 9 and 12]. Your grandfather, did he play an *akonting* with fishing line, or did it have the old fiber strings?

SANA: No, it had the old fiber, the old style. With monkey skin, fiber to represent strings, the gourd, always the gourd because the gourd is something that is in Senegal for years. But with me, I try to innovate things to change it in my way, to make it easier for me. So I decided to put wood on top instead of a skin, and instead of using those fibers, I use fishing lines, and add some tuners, make it easy for me when I am performing, because I remember one day I was performing with the band I have, [with] an old *ekonting* but not as old as the way an *akonting* used to be old. I wasn't using tuners. So I was performing and then in the middle of the concert one of the strings broke. So I did not have a back-up *ekonting* so I had to make it to tie again which took me a long time. That show almost didn't work for us because everything got messed up. So that's when I got the idea of doing the tuners.

CHUCK: How many people beside your grandfather did you see playing the *akonting* when you were growing up?

SANA: I've seen some of his friends that played the *akonting*. Some of them are still there. When I went last November I saw one of them. And we just start talking about *akonting*. He asked me, "How am I doing in playing this?" and just realizing the instrument is everywhere now, a lot of people know it. So they were very happy. And they wanted me to do a concert over there, but it was unfortunate because I didn't have time plus I didn't bring my *ekonting* with me. Because I don't want it broke on the plane. One time when I was going to Senegal they broke my *ekonting* and they didn't pay me. But I found a small *akonting*, but I am so used to the professional one, that one just didn't look professional to me. I just play some, have fun with the family sitting around. And that was really fun.

CHUCK: I am curious as to what things were like. You saw your grandfather and his friends playing. Were there five people playing? Were there one hundred people playing *akonting*? How many people were playing?

SANA: No, it was just four people that was playing the *akonting*. There was this kid who had an *akonting*. He was learning. He was doing pretty good. And when he just saw me it was a big thing for him. I play a song for him so he can see. 'Cause they always think that, you know, because I am coming here in this country so I might be like on top of anybody that plays the *akonting*. So they just consider me as a superstar, so when I am playing, everybody had to come and see me. "Does he play in a different way that makes him good in the United States?" You know I have very good fingers, I have my own scales so that when I play the *ekonting* it is just very interesting. Even, if they tell me that there is the best *akonting* player in the world, he is not Sana, and if that guy just play a song that I know. He plays a song that I know and after he play, I play the same song, I guess you will like it better the way I play it because not only am I trying to innovate, I can play the same way that he does without pressing the second string. I am just going to play regular but sometimes it's the fingers, some people they just have . . . you know, it's just like a god's sign. When they play it is very interesting, the song is even more exciting to hear. So I know that I have that.

CHUCK: The songs that your grandfather played. Did he ever write any songs, or did he just learn songs that other people played? Did he ever make up his own melodies?

SANA: Yeah, they make up their own melodies. Most of the songs they play, it's from tradition songs, like songs that's already have been written by someone, and they use it in traditional ceremonies or like circumcision ceremonies, so they play those songs but some of them, you know, they create some love songs for their girls and think it is kind of neat.

CHUCK: So you said that they play them for ceremonies. They play them for circumcisions, which you said happen about every thirty years.[10]

SANA: Yes.

CHUCK: They play them at weddings?

SANA: Yes, they play them at weddings and sometimes they use the *akonting* in a way when some people got some sort of sickness, they use them to make, sort of kind of, heal, but it's not any kind of sickness. It is certain sickness that they have to take you to what we call "fetish." "Fetish" is some sort of stuff that they put power in it. And so they play *akonting* while they are doing that stuff to heal you.

CHUCK: Are they ever played at funerals?

SANA: Funerals, funerals, no. The funerals I don't know but I have never heard, I never ask but it is possible because when someone dies in my village, but you have to be old. If you are not old, for example I die, no one going to play sounds. That's the way it is because for them, they just consider that, you know, it's just happiness. But a lot of them they don't know that you can play songs just to heal people. So in my village when an old person die, like 80 to 90, when you die they have a celebration, they do dancing, playing drums, and drinking, everybody have fun. In my village they just consider that at 80 years and 90 years old, you just did what you got to do, and if you go, it's okay. For a kid like me, if I die, it would be total, it would be . . .

CHUCK: Tragic.

SANA: It would be very tragic.

CHUCK: So you wouldn't play *akonting* at a tragic . . .

SANA: No, no, they don't do that.

CHUCK: So traditional *akonting* songs have to do with courting, love songs. So it sounds like they also sometimes tell stories?

SANA: Yeah, you can play some songs that you don't sing, but you just tell stories. You just talk about stuff. Talk about the old stuff. Like for us that never heard of it. It is just very interesting sometime when someone play and then we listen to those kind of stories.

CHUCK: Are there songs about animals, songs about chickens, songs about goats, songs about fish?

SANA: Possible, it is possible. There's a song about plants, I think it is possible. In the past people . . . I don't know how they say it in . . . When you tell a story it could be a true story. Sometimes it is not a true story, just to have fun. Something that you just make up.

CHUCK: A tall tale.

SANA: Yeah, like stuff like that. You know sometimes there is, like I remember when I was young, there was this girl that was staying at my father's house and then every night that is what we do. Everyone talk about stuff like that. There was this girl talking about this interesting story I like and I still like it. And even tell it to people. Like this girl living with her parents so they were trying to get her married. She never wanted to get married. So nobody knows, but she fell in love with a fish that she named "Kaybah." So when they tell her "you need to get married," but she never wanted; so her friends were so curious; they wanted to know what was going on with her. They just see her every day that they could. She took a small boat with some rice and then go. So one day her father follow her and she went to the beach, and then she stand there and then said, "Kaybah, Kaybah." She was calling the fish. And the fish swam, she fed him, and the fish swam back. So one day her father just went at the beach when the girl wasn't there. And he said, "Kaybah," and the fish came out and then he shoot the fish and then grabbed the fish and come with it home and then make a nice dinner. So when the girl comes in, they serve and then they open the plate. And the girl look at the fish and say, "Daddy where did you get this fish?" And he said, "Trust me, this is a good fish I just kill in the market." And she said, "No. I recognize this fish." Her father knows that that is the fish, but he didn't want to tell her. To verify, the girl went back to the beach, call "Kaybah, Kaybah, Kaybah" many times. So there is no fish coming out and that is when she realized that the fish, her boyfriend, got killed. So she came home, get really mad and she said that she is just going to commit suicide. So she just go to the ocean and kill herself. So what happened, the father was upset, he shoot himself.

CHUCK: So the father killed himself?

SANA: Yeah! Because the girl killed herself.

CHUCK: She killed herself in the ocean and then he killed himself.

SANA: So a story like that, it is not a true story, but it is a very interesting story that, you know, I was a little kid and I can still remember that story.

CHUCK: Does that kind of story ever end up in a song?

SANA: I just forget the singing of that story. But it might be when they are talking about stories, every story has singing. Every story! We end up with singing. So, with your *akonting*, you can be playing and telling story, at the end of the story that is when you sing, which is very beautiful.

CHUCK: That is a great story! Great tragic story.

SANA: (satisfied smile and easy laughter)

CHUCK: So the *ekonting* that you have is large, and the *akonting* that I have is small. Did you say that they were pronounced differently?

SANA: Yes, they were pronounced differently according to, because Jola has at least three or four different dialects. They speak different dialects, but everything is Jola, for example, us with . . . understand all the Jola, the way they speak we understand them, but a lot of them they don't understand when we speak. So I don't know why, because maybe Jola the way we speak is very tricky. When I was at school, in my class, when I speak, my class they used to make fun of it and they say we [were] Spanish. And I cannot believe it, because the way I speak, my Jola is fast and with the *r*, you roll the *r*. So in my village, *aykonting* is big *akonting*, *uhkonting* is a small *akonting*.

CHUCK: Would you spell the small one with an *a* or an *e*?

SANA: The same writing but only the beginning just change . . .

CHUCK: You spell them both with an *e* but you pronounce them differently.

SANA: No. The *aykonting* start with an *e*, the *uhkonting* start with an *a*. In my village everything that you start with an *ay*, with an *e* is big. Everything that you start with an *uh*, *a* is small.

CHUCK: Very interesting.

SANA: Yeah.

CHUCK: Tell me again, there's Jola Fonyi, Jola Casa. Which Jola are you?

SANA: Jola Djembering.

CHUCK: Like your village.

SANA: Yeah. All the other what they speak, that is what we call in my language, my dialect, that is what we call "Koudiolouwaye." And what we speak, that is what we call "Kouwataya." So this is the problem right here. Then they even when they speak they say "Koudiolouwaye." But when we speak they say" kadjemberingwaye," but we say "Kouwataya." And, for example, what we have some similarities. If you really pay attention, there are some similarities. Sometime, when they want to say "come," some of them say "obill." But us, we say "Ahbime." They have the end with an *il*.

But we have the end of the word with *ime*. But when they say "Ohbah,"
some people say "Ohbah," but we say "Arrrrigo." This is totally different.
And if you heard me speaking with someone who is Jola from Djembering, everything is like fast. Sometimes even almost if I speak, the band,
they laugh. They say, "What the hell are you talking about?" It sounds
funny to them. But it is very interesting.

CHUCK: So when you were growing up, or when you returned to Djembering, were *akontings* being played with drums, or was it just *akontings* with
other *akontings*?

SANA: Usually it was just played with women together clapping their hands.

CHUCK: I heard that the younger generation is playing drums with *akontings*,
but not the older generation.

SANA: No, no, no. The older generation, they have this deep singing. It is like
the circumcision song that I play which is like very interesting and that
is what they like to hear. They don't want to hear something that is more
danceable with a lot of animation in it. They are not into that stuff. What
they like to listen is something complicated that tells a story. You know
that is what they like. After that, they could play something for their girlfriend 'cause they believe in their girlfriend so much. You know so they
have some love songs. But as this generation right now, we are kind of
more fun. We just love to play with a lot of animation, drumming, singing. And that's what a lot of people from this generation right now can't
do. Like play those deep stuff [they can't play the "deep stuff"]. Because it
is complicated. Because it is basically a story that you transform a little bit
in singing. A lot of this generation they can't play it.

CHUCK: So when you were around 12 you moved back to Dakar. Why did you
move back?

SANA: Well, I moved back because I had to continue my education. So that's
the reason why I moved. Because at the time we didn't have college or
high school. There was just primary school. So you have to move to the
city.

CHUCK: Was it when you got back to the city that you started to play the
ekonting differently than you had learned it? When did you start to take
your own license with it?

SANA: First of all, I am someone that is into innovating stuff. I always believe
in, like creating something that people don't do. You know, in anything. I
used to be this kid that, you know, tried to do anything, like fixing radio,
fixing computers, everything. I used to do that. And never learned that
but I just go with my own instincts, and I know a lot about that stuff. So
with the *akonting* I always wanted to play something different. Even if I
am playing right now a song, I can just . . . suddenly something just come
up in my head and I just play it! Risky! Just play it. But I become more,
like into creating my own identity in the *akonting* thing when I am with

the band. Because it just demand a lot of work. They have to be creative all the time because it is about creating the song. And most of the time I create the songs. Most of the Gohk Bi System, the songs come from my idea, like the way the sounds should be. Then I create the chorus and teach them which part they should sing. And the lyrics, each one create the lyrics. Sometimes when we create the lyrics we just sit and then say, "Okay, we want to talk about peace," or everyone, it's like a topic. "Everyone, bring everything you know about peace, and then we do the arrangement." Sometime, everyone create his own lyrics.

CHUCK: In the band there are drums.

SANA: There is *ekonting* first of all, a drum that has all these type of drums from Senegal, like *sabar* and *djun-djun*, and *bougarabou*, which came from my people, the Jola. And we have Djembe. Djembe, everyone knows Djembe. And that's what he does and then we have two MCs that have different style of rapping. Sometime this guy rap in English, the other one rap in Wolof, French. So we mix the languages. And we have a dancer and a bass guitar player and someone who plays a drum set.

CHUCK: A couple of days ago was the first time you saw a banjo. We were in the studio [at a radio station] together. I guess I played first [clawhammer style]. What was your impression?

SANA: My first impression was that the sound was almost the same. The only difference, that makes it a little different, is the stuff, the metal stuff added to the banjo. So it makes the sound a little bit different with the *ekonting*, but like there was a song that you were playing on the radio, the second song, I don't know which, it just sounded like *ekonting*. I was thinking that someone was playing the *ekonting* inside because it's very similar. You know that was my first impression, and I was just like "this is the *ekonting*," you know? This has got modernized, and then add strings, it is just like different, but it is the same.

CHUCK: What was it like being up at camp [Suwannee Banjo Camp, 2008]?

SANA: You know it was a big experience, you know, meeting all these banjo players and having some exchange. You know, I know a lot about the banjo. I was so happy to teach people. I didn't know that the people would be interested. But many of them was interested because the relation that the *akonting* has with the banjo, so some of them learned, and then they did very good. I was so impressed that some people . . . I shouldn't be impressed because the style of playing it is kind of the same, so when we give it to someone that play the banjo, it's just like picking up really quick. So some people bought many *akontings*, which is a good step. Hopefully in the future it will be very, very, very, very well known.

CHUCK: Is there something that Americans should know about the *akonting* that they don't, or about the Jola that they don't? Is there something we should be learning here?

SANA: I just think . . . I don't know how to answer this question . . . They should know about the *akonting* because the *akonting* is the source . . . if I say it right, source, source for me means, source in French means "where it come from," so that I believe that the banjo came from this instrument. The inspiration, I don't know who ever created, but he got the inspiration from that instrument and you know innovated and make it a little bit different but it is the same instrument. And people should know about that. They should approach the instrument, and take a look at it and do the comparison and see what they think about what I just said, that these two instruments are the same.

CHUCK: What do you think the biggest difference between the instruments is?

SANA: Which instruments?

CHUCK: Between the *akonting* and the clawhammer-style banjo.

SANA: The difference? I don't think there is a big difference. I don't think so. It is just that they added more strings. I don't think there is a difference. You know, one thing that I notice, if you tune the banjo to sound exactly like the *akonting*, like I did that with Paul [Sedgwick]. We tuned his banjo to an *akonting* thing, and if you take a guitar and you tune it to sound like an *akonting*, the banjo sound exactly like the *akonting*. But the guitar won't sound exactly like . . . the sound of it is the same. So that is why when you tune this instrument to that one, the sound gets the same. But with the guitar you can tell the difference. It's going to have the same note but it's not going to sound exactly like that.

CHUCK: Do you want a banjo?

SANA: I really want a banjo and I want to learn it. I was just thinking about it. A lot of people say it is good for me to learn, so I thought about it before they even said it, so I should have one. It's right.

CHUCK: That's great. Now we should figure out how to get you one.

SANA: Yeah, I really want one. And maybe one day in a camp like this, I can just have two instruments. This one, and play the other one.

CHUCK: What was it like meeting Cheick [Hamala Diabate]?[11]

SANA: Yeah, Cheick is a nice guy. I saw him. I'm always a little bit spacey the first time I meet someone. He approaches me; he act like an elder. That is what elder guys, they just approach kids to let them know everything is okay. Because it's not the same like if I meet someone from here. In Senegal, elders, you know, we just like take your time 'cause you don't know what kind of person he is and stuff like that. But he just come to me and we just start talking; he told me about his nomination for the Grammy and stuff like that. He told me about Daniel [Laemouahuma Jatta]. But he was so impressed about me. He was so impressed because, I can tell. When I'm talking he's like, you know, "I want to work with you, blah blah

blah." Because you know I have my own style, you know. I play it in a way that everyone will like it so. We kept talking; he gave me all his contact because he want to work with me. I said, "Well, I'd be glad to work with you, you know." Who knows? He is a nice guy and he's talented too. He is very talented with his instrument that he plays. It's beautiful. When we were performing together, I was playing the songs and he said, "You should invite me in this song so we can do something." I plan something already but when you just told me that, I don't know, that we had two minutes left, so I decided to quit that song and invite him. And then it came out very beautiful, and plus we didn't rehearse. He just heard me playing and I think that he can tell that he can play in it.

CHUCK: Well, thank you so much, this has been terrific.

SANA: No problem.

Notes

1. See Greg C. Adams and Chuck Levy, "The Down-Stroke Connection: Comparing Techniques Between the Jola *Ekonting* and the Five-String Banjo," in this volume for a full discussion of this issue.

2. I spell the instrument *akonting* because this is the spelling offered to me by Daniel. In my interview with Sana Ndiaye, he distinguished between the smaller, traditional instruments that I played and that I saw in common use, from the instruments using much larger gourds that he played. He spelled the smaller instruments *akonting* and the larger instruments *ekonting*. I use the same convention.

3. To learn more about Jatta and his discovery and exposition of the akonting, see "An Interview with Daniel Laemouahuma Jatta," *The Old-Time Herald* 13, no. 2 (2012). The full interview, including portions edited out of the article in *The Old-Time Herald*, is available online at http://banjourneys.com/jatta_interview_transcript/, accessed October 15, 2017.

4. For a full discussion of akonting tuning and scales, see the Adams-Levy chapter referred to in note 1 above.

5. There are numerous Jola dialects: Daniel and Ekona did not speak the same dialect, and Daniel is not a translator by profession, which meant that, at least some of the time, Daniel did not understand exactly what Ekona said the first time. I believe that Daniel intended to translate faithfully, but since my questions and Ekona's answers were both being translated, I cannot exclude the possibility that some of our meanings may have been lost.

6. The term *o'teck* (*oo'teck*) has been translated as "to strike" and refers to the down-stroke style of right-hand attack that so closely resembles stroke and clawhammer banjo technique.

7. The following day, I was treated to an informal presentation of Jola singing and dancing by members of the Jola performing group Si Jam Bukan De Saful, which has been translated into "We play even if people think we are nothing." This group is led by Ekona Diatta and includes Remi Diatta. I assume this is "wholel." My impression is that the group is assembled for occasions to present at local gatherings and festivals.

8. The Jola Casa (Cassa, Kasa) are one of the many subgroups within the Jola people. Ekona is a member of the Jola Casa. "Of all the sub groups of the Jola people today, it is

the Jola Cassas that still maintain 99 percent of all the old Jola traditional ways of doing things, still reject Islam and Christianity, and only a few of them go to church" (http://lege.net/web.comhem.se/abzu/akonting/jola.html, accessed October 15, 2017).

9. The Jola Fonyi are another ethnic subgroup within the Jola people.

10. Apparently, circumcisions happen only every twenty-five to thirty years. Men from adolescence to young adulthood take part in circumcision as part of an initiation rite (http://itssunnyingambia.blogspot.com/2011/07/burning-man-of-gambia.html, accessed October 15, 2017; http://caseyacrosstheatlantic.blogspot.com/2011/07/c-is-for-circumcision.html, accessed October 15, 2017.

11. Cheick Hamala Diabate is a West African historian in the griot tradition of Mali and a world-recognized master of the *n'goni*, another instrument that has characteristics similar to that of the banjo. Sana met Cheick at the Akonting-Banjo Collaborative in 2008.

CHAPTER 6

The Down-Stroke Connection
Comparing Techniques Between the Jola Ekonting *and the Five-String Banjo*

Greg C. Adams and Chuck Levy

Editor's Headnote

One way of assessing similarities between African plucked spike lutes and American banjos is to compare their structures, which other chapters in this volume do. Another approach is to compare the playing techniques associated with these instruments. Greg C. Adams and Chuck Levy have undertaken the latter approach in considerable detail. Their discussion of playing techniques associated with the Jola ekonting *is based on observing and recording local players of that instrument encountered on their trips to Gambia and transcribing what they heard into musical notation. These notations they then compare to American banjo tunes found in the earliest notated sources, minstrel-era banjo tutors, and transcriptions of tunes from American "old-time" banjo players reflecting early traditions of banjo playing. The similarities are striking, but are not intended to assert that the* ekonting *is the sole precursor to the banjo. It is a useful instrument to focus on because banjo researchers have acquired more information about the* ekonting *than about other individual African plucked spike lutes.*

The Jola *ekonting* (also *akonting*)[1] is one of West Africa's many culturally distinct plucked spike lute traditions.[2] (For images of the *ekonting*, see figures A and C and figure 5.1 in chapter 5.) In 2000, Daniel Laemouahuma Jatta (The Gambia, Sweden) and Ulf Jägfors (Sweden) presented research on the *ekonting* and another plucked lute, the Manjak *bunchundo*, at the Third Annual Five-String Banjo Collectors' Gathering in Concord, Massachusetts.[3] Jatta and Jägfors's presentation revealed new comparisons with the banjo previously unexplored by non-African researchers, especially as applied to the five-string banjo. The significance of Jatta's research and subsequent collaboration with Jägfors is that no in-depth work focuses on the *ekonting* tradition before Jatta began his own personal research in the 1980s and 1990s and began delivering public presentations in Sweden and the United States by 2000.[4] Before Jatta's involvement, previous references to the Jola *ekonting* and other similarly constructed plucked lutes were on the periphery of scholarly works focusing on other aspects of West African music and culture.[5]

Since 2000, new research into the *ekonting* tradition continues to build on Jatta and Jägfors's ongoing initiatives. For some members of the banjo community involved in this work, the research includes multiple visits to the Senegambian region to study with Jola musicians, often through Jatta's connections, learning about related peoples and instruments, collecting oral histories, and sharing information back in the United States. Other aspects of this new scholarship include intensive desk research and reporting. Together, these collective efforts generated new access points through published articles, museum exhibits, websites, documentary and instructional videos, and at least one dramatic play.[6] The *ekonting* has also been featured in several banjo camps.[7] Even in The Gambia, an *ekonting* has been added to the exhibit space at the National Museum in Banjul, acknowledging its importance in Senegambian culture.

One of the first things that banjoists and other careful observers will notice about the *ekonting* (as was the case for us) is how it is played using a down-stroke technique where a lead finger and thumb work in tandem to sound the strings. This way of playing the *ekonting* (explained below) shares the same fundamentals with banjo-playing techniques found in traditions associated with old-time music of the twentieth century, as well as nineteenth-century banjo tutors. In particular, these similarities are most apparent when comparing the *ekonting* with the five-string banjo—a banjo with four long strings and one short thumb-string.

The purpose of this chapter is to outline our perspective in explaining why these shared fundamentals between the banjo and the *ekonting* are so significant. This significance, however, is not part of an effort to prove that the *ekonting* is "the living antecedent" of the banjo. Rather, it is to acknowledge and appreciate the tradition, moving beyond anecdotal observations that oversimplify the many complexities behind the banjo's West African heritage.[8] We propose an approach that allows us to speak more concretely about why these similarities in playing technique are so striking. First, we provide a summary about the nature of recent *ekonting*-focused field research, which allows us to make such comparisons. Second, we present specific information about the *ekonting* tradition, including instrument construction, playing technique, tuning and scale, the music-making process, and some of the contexts in which the *ekonting* is used. Third, we examine some of the musical similarities and differences between the Jola *ekonting* and the banjo. Finally, we discuss why it is important for banjo-focused researchers to clarify their intent when searching for meaningful and equitable ways of comparing traditions across multiple cultures.

The Nature of Recent *Ekonting*-Focused Field Research

For non-African researchers, evidence about the *ekonting* tradition begins, in part, with several unpublished recordings made by the linguist J. David Sapir while conducting fieldwork in 1961, 1966, and 1970.[9] Sapir documented several Senegalese Jola *ekonting* players from the villages of Diembering and Ziguinchor. As we are now learning, a preliminary analysis of these audio recordings shows that the tuning system, perceived performance contexts, and playing technique are consistent with those documented during recent trips to The Gambia and Senegal beginning in 2002. Typical data collected during these trips include audio and video recordings of formal and informal performances, tutorials, and interviews. This recent study of the *ekonting* also includes preliminary examinations of corresponding musical participants such as singers, dancers, and percussionists.

The type of knowledge, relationships, and access gained in recent years has been built on the work initiated by Daniel Laemouahuma Jatta, Ulf Jägfors, and a local network of colleagues with a genuine interest in perpetuating local traditions and who are willing to act as intermediaries for non-African learners.[10] Yet, even with the influx of new information since 2000, this recent surge of fieldwork does have its limitations. The first of these are language barriers, where most of the American researchers possess limited language skills outside English and most *ekonting* players are conversant in multiple local or regional languages; yet, both are dependent on nonprofessional translators whose dialects may be different from that of the Jola musicians. Second, most of this fieldwork has also been confined to two- to four-week durations, leaving researchers with fragmented views of broader cultural experiences. Third, because professional ethnographers are not actively involved in this new generation of fieldwork, little assistance is available in interpreting content and using it to update scholarly literature. Fourth, and most notably, limited infrastructure prevents African tradition bearers and African researchers from participating actively (or in real time) with the conversations now taking place outside the communities that maintain the tradition. We believe that acknowledging these limitations in our own work provides transparency in reporting what we are learning as part of a larger process shaping the ways in which outsiders represent West African tradition.[11]

Examining the *Ekonting* Tradition

Within this widening view of the *ekonting* tradition, as of 2008, researchers have collectively engaged with more than thirty ekonting players who live throughout the Senegambian region.[12] Those musicians most frequently visited and featured in this chapter, however, come from the village of Mlomp on the southern shore of the Casamance River. The descriptive information we present here is largely based on documentation from Remi Diatta and Ekona Diatta, two of the more-frequently consulted musicians from Mlomp.

Instrument Construction

The *ekonting* consists of half of a gourd, a cylindrical stick neck, an animal hide soundtable stretched and tacked onto the open side of the gourd, and a two-legged bridge, which sits on the middle of the animal hide and is held in place with three strings made from fishing line. The three strings are first attached to the small portion of the neck protruding from the tail end of the gourd body. The highest-pitched third string (located closest to the player's chest) is applied first, measured precisely using the length of the forearm beginning at the edge of the rim. The middle, intermediate pitched string is tied one hand span farther, and the bottom, lowest-pitched first string (located closest to the player's lap) is tied an additional hand span beyond the middle string. The bridge is fixed under the strings at about the midpoint of the head, straddling the neck, which rests just under the animal hide soundtable.[13]

Playing Technique, Tuning, and Scale

The *ekonting* is played using a down-stroke technique. With this technique, the player rests the gourd body of the instrument on or in front of the abdomen. Either sitting or standing, he reaches around the gourd with the playing hand suspended over the bridge and above the strings. Tone is produced with the fingernail of the index or middle finger in a downward motion to the first, lowest-pitched string. The lead finger does not play on the second and third strings of the *ekonting*. These two strings are exclusively reserved for the thumb, which, in turn, plucks the strings as part of a larger hand motion. During any given performance, listeners and other participants might be moved to proclaim, "oo'tek, oo'tek," which, for the Jola Casa (also Kasa; the Jola people from the region south of the Casamance River), literally means, "to hit" or "to strike." This statement is in recognition of how tone production occurs with an almost fist-like action of the right hand.

Ekonting players produce only five pitches with the instrument. They include the three open strings and two additional pitches stopped (fingered) on the first string at the equivalent of the fifth and seventh semi-tone positions. On a fretted instrument, these positions would roughly be equivalent to the fifth and seventh fret positions. To date, field researchers have most often documented the tuning as an ascending major second between the first and second strings followed by an ascending minor sixth between the second and third strings (M2m6). When combined with the two stopped notes on the first string, all five pitches in ascending order, from lowest to highest, can be represented as A, B, D, E, G, as illustrated in musical example 6.1.[14] Using computer spectral analysis software (*Spear*) in 2008, Joanne Davies, then a student at the University of Birmingham, United Kingdom, was able to confirm the fundamental and frequency of the

A B D E G

Musical Example 6.1. Treble clef with representation of the five pitches created on the *ekonting*, consisting of three open strings and two stopped notes on the first string.

tones played by Ekona Diatta as closest to F♯ (longest string), G♯ (middle), and E (short), and the two additional stopped pitches as B and C♯ on the first string, yielding an anhemitonic (without semitones) pentatonic scale.[15]

Field researchers have also documented two other instances where *ekonting* players in the Esulalu region had their instruments pitched in something other than the predominant M2m6 tuning. These tunings include a major second–perfect fifth (M2P5) and a minor third–perfect fifth (m3P5).[16] Yet, any perceived variations by American and European researchers from the M2m6 tuning should not necessarily be interpreted, at this time, as distinct culturally designated alternate tunings, as none of our teachers have ever explicitly designated any other tunings. Small changes in pitch can be remedied by simple adjustments of the bridge's position; larger changes call for a greater effort involving collapsing the bridge, placing the gourd body at the player's feet, and pulling the wound knot up the stick neck. Perhaps it is because of the time and effort involved that a wide range of pitch variation is acceptable (i.e., string slippage) before the instrument is deemed "out of tune" and the *ekonting* is retuned to the M2m6 designation. Additional research is required before researchers can validly suggest that *ekonting* players use a series of predefined tunings beyond the M2m6 tuning, such as those commonly found within banjo traditions.

Relationship Between the Ekonting *and the Human Voice*

During a 2006 visit to The Gambia, Daniel Laemouahuma Jatta emphasized the importance of call-and-response in the relationship between the human voice and the *akonting*.[17] Jatta's observation is foundational to understanding how the music of the *ekonting* is firmly rooted in echoing and reinforcing the melodic content of the vocal line. For example, the vocal melody for the song "Mamba Suditan," as performed by both Remi and Ekona Diatta, moves within a pentatonic scale.[18] For the purposes of this chapter, this scale is represented with Western scale pitch names G, A, B, D, E.[19] Using elements of standard music notation, musical example 6.2 represents one way of looking at a vocal melody.[20]

When applied to the *ekonting*, the linear quality and register of the vocal melody is often displaced against the five unvarying pitches of the instrument during a performance. This means that while the *ekonting* player generally re-creates the

Musical Example 6.2. "Mamba Suditan" (vocal melody). The structure of this transcription and those that follow are adaptations of standard music notation. Bar lines are used to mark specific phrases. We have not used key and time signatures so as to avoid imposing a type of order that does not necessarily exist within the culture. The eighth note or quarter note representations of each song generally signify a beat as part of a walking rhythm. "Mamba Suditan" as performed by Ekona and Remi Diatta, July 2008. Transcribed by Greg C. Adams.

vocal melody with the same pitch order as the human voice, those pitches are not necessarily in the same register on the *ekonting*. Further to this point, due to the static nature of *ekonting*'s pentatonic note structure, one or more melody notes (depending on the song) may be displaced an octave, resulting in interval shifts between one melody note and the next. Again, with "Mamba Suditan," this relationship can be more fully realized with the triplet (A-G-G) in the first phrase (musical example 6.3). Here, the vocalist sings the A-G-G sequence in a descending motion (a major second) while the *ekonting* can only realize the pitches of this same triplet as an inversion (a minor seventh).

    Beyond re-creating the linear melody of the human voice, *ekonting* players use a variety of musical devices to accompany a performance. These include the compres-

Musical Example 6.3. "Mamba Suditan" (part 1), excerpt as performed by Ekona and Remi Diatta, July 2008. Line 1, vocal melody; line 2, representative pitches on the *ekonting*; line 3, tablature realization on the *ekonting*. Transcription and tablature by Greg C. Adams.

sion of lyrics within a musical phrase, representing long vocal notes with repeated pitches, pattern-based figures, ostinato-based figures, right-hand double strikes, implied vocal counterpoint, call-and-response phrase structures, and other unique attributes. The compression of lyrics is noteworthy in that not all of the lyrics necessarily line up syllabically with each note produced on the *ekonting*. Looking once again at the previously highlighted triplet (A-G-G) in musical example 6.3, the lyrics "oo'teck cor a" align with the triplet as part of the overall phrase "Mamba Suditan oo'teck cor a san de jo ee." Yet, the four syllables of "oo'teck cor a" are compressed against the three notes of the triplet, demonstrating the complex interplay between the vocal and instrumental representation of the melody.

Ekonting players also use repeated pitches and alternating hand motions to fill in the space of longer vocal notes since the human voice is capable of sustaining a pitch over a longer period than a plucked string. Some *ekonting* players use multiple finger strikes to accompany the duration of a single pitch. For example, in the first phrase of "Mamba Suditan" (musical example 6.3), the vocalist sings the words "Mamba Suditan," the equivalent of four eighth notes and a single quarter note. For both Remi and Ekona Diatta, the sung quarter note is matched with two eighth notes on the *ekonting*. An even more dramatic example is in the first phrase of the song "Gambia" (musical example 6.4), as performed by both Remi and Ekona Diatta, where the *ekonting* plays the equivalent of three quarter notes to the dotted half note in the vocal melody.

Depending on the length of the song's musical phrases and its melodic direction, a number of songs have short, recurring right-hand patterns. On occasion,

Musical Example 6.4. "Gambia," excerpt as performed by Remi and Ekona Diatta, July 2008. Transcription and tablature by Greg C. Adams.

some of the notes in these patterns do not necessarily align with the longer tones found in the vocal melody. In the song "Gambia" (musical example 6.4) the vocal melody consists of two phrases: "Gambia, oo-ay" and "Senegal es oo may nay ndaysan." On the *ekonting*, both phrases begin with a syncopated rhythm (a beat followed by an amphibrach rhythm—short-long-short) between the first and second strings followed by a finger-lead alternating-motion on the subsequent beat. The first phrase concludes with two repeated pitches and a dactylic attack (long-short-short), while the second phrase ends with two dactylic attacks. The last pitch created in both the first and second phrases is not part of the vocal melody, but maintains the rhythm while the vocal line rests. In the second phrase, however, this additional pitch also creates a brief point of tension with a major second interval (or, depending on the register, a minor seventh) before returning to the beginning of the song. Though it is just a single pitch that deviates from the vocal melody, this type of structure shows up again with another version of the same song as performed by Ekona Diatta where the tones are played in a compound meter where the pulse might be felt in eighth note groupings as triplets (musical example 6.5).

"Batima Sijul," as performed by Remi Diatta, serves to illustrate additional techniques beyond the melodic model outlined above (musical example 6.6). First, the bulk of the performance includes Diatta playing what might be described as an ostinato figure, a short repeated figure of eight beats that forms the foundation of the song (each eight-beat grouping is marked with a square bracket; the first and fifth beats are accented on the *ekonting*, but not necessarily in accord with the vocal line). Within this figure comes the second feature where the first and fifth

Musical Example 6.5. "Gambia" (triplet version), excerpt as performed by Ekona Diatta, July 2008. Transcription and tablature by Greg C. Adams.

Musical Example 6.6. "Batima Sijul," excerpt as performed by Remi Diatta, July 2008. Transcription and tablature by Greg C. Adams.

beats are played simultaneously as stacked pitches. Here, the lead finger strikes the first string while the thumb strikes simultaneously the third string as part of a single down-stroke motion. Third, Diatta's performance of the sung melody is unconstrained by the instrumental line and moves freely above it, harmonically linked in counterpoint with the *ekonting*.

With other songs, call-and-response sequencing is characteristic of *ekonting* music, which is layered between the singer and the *ekonting*, between the soloist and the group, or between an ensemble and other participants such as dancers or other singers. Musical example 6.7 ("Mamba Suditan") exemplifies how the song's phrases are generally parsed during a performance between the vocalist and the instrument. Even though the *ekonting* plays continuously, the vocalist sings

Musical Example 6.7. "Mamba Suditan," as performed by Ekona and Remi Diatta, July 2008. Example of phrase-based alternation between voice and instrument. Transcription and tablature by Greg C. Adams.

specific phrases at key points in the song. Truncation of a portion of the melody within the same call-and-response is also common. Both Remi and Ekona Diatta include this device often midway or near the conclusion of the performance as a type of musical coda.

Some *ekonting* players' performances include other unique attributes. During our 2008 trip to Casamance, we met left-handed ekonting player Paul Sambou, from the Esulalu village of Haer, who provided an entirely different performance. Sambou held the *ekonting* in reverse of the usual right-hand posture where the instrument was rotated and the shortest string was placed toward the ground. Sambou stopped pitches on the long string with his right hand while striking the strings with his left. Despite this, Sambou's performance still followed the down-stroke convention with his striking left hand, only now with the lead finger playing the shortest string and his thumb playing the other two strings using the same pentatonic scale common to right-handed players. His song appeared to be a spontaneous narrative delivered in a "talking blues" style (somewhere between speech and song) sung against an ostinato figure played on the *ekonting*.

Other performance practices include those of Jesus Jarju, who incorporates left-hand pizzicatos on the first string and right-hand tapping on the instrument's animal hide soundtable during his performance.[21] Sana Ndiaye, of Djembering, Senegal and now of the United States, has not only altered the physical construction of his instrument to meet personal and professional musical necessity, but also now produces an additional note on the *ekonting* by stopping a note on the mid-length second string, creating a hexatonic scale.[22] Other instances include vocalists who sing at least one note beyond the vocalized pentatonic scale while maintaining the pentatonic pitches on the *ekonting*.[23]

Contextualizing the Ekonting

Recent interactions with *ekonting* players from in and around Mlomp reveal several contexts for use. The most common appears to be in relaxed social settings. Participants sit together, sharing palm wine (or any other beverage), and converse, joke, and sing individually and communally. Within the Esulalu village of Mlomp, on special occasions, Ekona and Remi Diatta lead the performance ensemble Si Jamboukan, made up of adults and children from Mlomp. A single performance by the ensemble might include Ekona on the *ekonting*, Remi, Frederic, and Joseph Diatta playing percussion, and the dance leader Nazaire Sambou facilitating various dances with community members.[24] The dancers may add percussion by way of hand-held clappers that are crafted of wood from a palm tree, and which appear to be most often played by women.[25]

Looking at a longer view of the tradition, Robert Baum reports an *ekonting* being used in relation to specific Jola social events. Discussing the nature of wrestling matches and social dances, Baum states:

> Both boys and girls wrestled and observed the others' skills in wrestling, while providing support through songs and dances of encouragement. Afterward, an *acconkone* social dance was held in which boys and girls danced in separate circles facing one another. Girls of a particular quarter would occasionally hold *heleo* dances, which were attended by boys from within Esulalu. They would bring a two-stringed guitar called an *econtine* and sing about the girls who interested them.[26]

In a footnote, Baum goes on to state that "this type of dance is no longer held, though a few men still play the econtine."[27] While his description of Jola wrestling and dance provides important information about Jola social practices, Baum's report that the *ekonting* had two strings is at odds with more recent field research where every encounter was with a three-string instrument. This suggests that Baum did not observe a third string or that he witnessed a modified form of the instrument.

Recent field research also suggests that the *ekonting* is available to anyone who wishes to play it. While it appears that Jola males are the primary players, we did not learn of any specific prohibition against women playing the *ekonting*, though this seems to occur rarely. The *ekonting* tradition also does not appear to necessarily be attached to any type of strictly regulated social hierarchy or religious function, two categories that might preclude researchers from gaining more of an insider's perspective.[28] Overall, these contexts set the stage for comparisons between the *ekonting* and the banjo, in particular, as relates to playing with a down-stroke technique.

Comparing Techniques Between the *Ekonting* and the Banjo

Down-stroke playing techniques have been perpetuated, documented, and maintained by a diverse multitude of tradition-bearers, scholars, professional musicians, and enthusiasts since the mid-nineteenth century. The first definitive descriptions of banjo playing with a down-stroke technique are found in *Briggs' Banjo Instructor* (1855) and *Phil. Rice's Correct Method for the Banjo* (1858).[29] These two books—and others of the period[30]—essentially represent a type of musical ground zero in the documented evolution of banjo-playing technique,[31] as they share the same fundamentals with other forms of banjo playing commonly identified today by such names as clawhammer, frailing, thumping, and others.[32]

In order to illustrate some of the technical similarities between the banjo and the *ekonting*, we have chosen sources that offer definitive examples of each tradition using a down-stroke technique. While we cannot capture every aspect of playing, we believe it allows for comparisons that would not otherwise be possible. To represent the *ekonting*, we have selected the *ekonting* players Remi and Ekona Diatta (see figure 5.1 in chapter 5).[33] For the banjo, we are using the Briggs (1855) and Rice (1858) banjo tutors, and select transcriptions of tunes played by the clawhammer banjoists Tommy Jarrell, Wade Ward, Giles Lephew, and Calvin Cole.[34] In order to analyze these three source groups, we first define down-stroke, then present our controlled vocabulary to describe specific patterns of motion, and, finally, apply these to musical examples.

Defining Down-Stroke

Broadly speaking, we define down-stroke as the yoking together of a lead finger (usually the index or middle finger) and the thumb to sound a string instrument

Table 6.1   Tone Production on the *Ekonting*

Ekonting	Briggs and Rice	Twentieth-Century Examples
String 1: I	String 1: I	String 1: I
String 2: X	String 2: I X	String 2: I X
String 3: X	String 3: I X	String 3: I X
	String 4: I X	String 4: I X
	String 5: X	String 5: X

Briggs (1855) and Rice (1858) and twentieth-century samples of Tommy Jarrell, Wade Ward, Giles Lephew, and Calvin Cole. String 1 is located closest to the player's lap; the ascending numbered strings are located closer to the player's chest. I = lead finger; X = thumb.

with a downward motion of the hand. With this technique, the fingers are held in a relatively static, curled position, and the thumb is positioned away from the fingers (in palmar abduction and opposition) as if one was grasping the core of a roll of paper towels. The strings are struck either by a single fingernail as a result of a downward movement of the wrist (ulnar deviation) or by the palm of the thumb. The thumb comes to rest on and deflect a string with the downward motion of the wrist. However, the string is actually sounded when the thumb is released with an upward-outward rotational movement (radial deviation) of the wrist. Thus, each time the wrist is propelled downward, it creates an opportunity to sound the string with the finger. Each time it returns upward, it creates the opportunity to sound the string with the release of the thumb.

With this yoking between the lead finger and the thumb, a series of right-hand attack patterns emerge where the finger and thumb are yoked together when they strike the strings in a downward motion or they are unyoked (or uncoupled) when either the finger or thumb sounds the strings with consecutive strikes. All of the *ekonting* players we met strike the first string with a downward stroke of the lead finger while the thumb strikes the shorter second and third strings. This is similar but not identical to what we see in the early banjo tutors and with clawhammer banjo players, where strings two, three, and four may be played by either the thumb or the fingers (table 6.1).[35] Building on a practical use of this definition, we can expand the scope of this study using a controlled vocabulary for right-hand patterns to measure the degree to which the lead finger and thumb are yoked together.

Controlled Vocabulary for Right-Hand Patterns

Our purpose for using a controlled vocabulary is to provide support in discussing what are often ephemeral and intangible forms of expression embedded in the physicality of music performance. Using technical terms based on classical

Table 6.2   Rhythm Names and Examples of Their Duration

Pattern	Duration	Notation
Dactylic	Long-short-short	♫ or ♫
Anapestic	Short-short-long	♫ or ♫
Trochaic	Long-short	♩ or ♩
Iambic	Short-long	♩ or ♩
Amphibrach	Short-long-short	♫ or ♫

rhythmic designations—such as dactylic, anapestic, trochaic, iambic, and amphibrach—serves as an aid in the classification of right-hand attack patterns for both the *ekonting* and the banjo. Table 6.2 outlines these basic terms, their general duration, and some of the ways they are expressed in written notation.

These rhythmic designations as well as triplets (not included in table 6.2) facilitate analysis of the right-hand down-stroke patterns. For example, the 1855 arrangement of "Old Dan Tucker," found in *Briggs' Banjo Instructor*, consists of at least nine instances where a dactylic attack outlines fingerings where the lead finger plays the first two notes of the dactylic rhythm and the thumb plays the final note. The basic framework of any down-stroke arrangement may be characterized with six right-hand attack patterns of tone production and at least two supporting figures: individual consecutive attack, alternating motion attack, dactylic attack, anapestic attack, amphibrach attack, triplet attack, slur-based figure, and chord-based figure.

The first form of attack, individual consecutive attack, exclusively uses the lead finger or exclusively uses the thumb to sound a series of pitches. Here, the musician can essentially play any melodic musical figure or any combination of rhythms at the tempo of his or her choosing. These rhythms generally include stand alone or on-the-beat pitches, dactylic, anapestic, amphibrach, triplet, iambic, or trochaic rhythms, or the even division of any given beat. However, each consecutive tone demands a new downward (strike) and upward wrist motion to reset the hand. This procedure can be laborious and difficult to sustain at faster tempos, especially with demanding passages.

A second category, alternating motion, gives the musician greater facility and flexibility to attack the strings by yoking the lead finger and the thumb together in an alternating form of tone production. These can include even divisions of a beat (e.g., two eighth notes for a single quarter-note value) or dotted rhythms such as iambic (short-long) or trochaic (long-short). Either the lead finger or the thumb can initiate this type of motion, which can occur on a single string (rarely) or between two or more strings. The advantage of yoking is that each motion of the wrist generates a tone. The downward motion (ulnar deviation-wrist flexion) produces a tone when the finger strikes and the upward motion (radial deviation-wrist extension) produces a tone when the thumb releases the deflected string. When combining a single strike from an individual consecutive attack with an alternating motion attack, the player can effectively produce the remaining four categories of attack with a greater economy of motion—dactylic attack (*long*-short-short), anapestic attack (short-short-*long*), amphibrach attack (short-*long*-short), and triplet attack.

All six of these initial components of down-stroke playing technique are further supplemented by additional figures beyond the performance of a melodic line. They include a seventh category that covers slurs and an eighth category that includes chords. Both of these categories can include any of the rhythmic values outlined above. Slur-based figures consist of passages articulated by the lead finger and thumb (as described above) and include the use of ascending slurs ("hammer-ons"), descending slurs ("pull-offs"), left-hand pizzicatos (open-string pull-offs), and glissandi (left-hand slides). Slur-based figures also create additional interest beyond the tones produced by the lead finger and thumb in that they aurally create additional rhythms. For example, if the right hand is creating a dactylic rhythm (long-short-short, i.e., one quarter note and two eighth notes), a left-hand pizzicato or ascending slur (hammer-on) can aurally create an even division of the long note resulting in four eighth notes.

The final category, chord-based figures, includes any figure that uses two or more stacked pitches. For example, chords are only used as a form of musical emphasis in early banjo repertoire and can be grouped together as part of a dactylic, amphibrach, anapestic, triplet, or alternating rhythm. For the clawhammer banjo player, the upbeat part of a dactylic "bum-ditty" rhythm can include a chord on the first short part of the long-short-short rhythm. Each of these categories of the controlled vocabulary can be systematically organized and expanded to begin tabulations for both the *ekonting* and the banjo.

Applying Vocabulary to Musical Examples

Applying this controlled vocabulary to different forms of down-stroke playing allows the researcher's work to be flexible and inductive. Such a vocabulary makes it possible to collect information from a variety of sources (such as a musician's live performance, a piece of sheet music, or a transcription) and build a broader understanding about the similarities and differences between each source. As a preliminary offering in applying this vocabulary to our sample groups, our tabulations highlight several areas of interest (table 6.3).

In table 6.3 the **Y** designations show where each sample group exhibited specific techniques and where commonalities may occur. The center column, Briggs

Table 6.3 Preliminary Worksheet Format

			Ekona and Remi Diatta	Briggs 1855 and Rice 1858	Jarrell, Ward, Lephew, and Cole
Individual Consecutive Attack	Finger	stand-alone or on-the-beat pitches	Y	Y	Y
		dactylic	Y	Y	Y
		anapestic			
		amphibrach		Y	
		triplet		Y	Y
		iambic	Y	Y	
		trochaic	Y	Y	
		even division	Y	Y	
	Thumb	stand-alone or on-the-beat pitches	Y	Y	Y
		dactylic		Y	
		anapestic		Y	
		amphibrach		Y	
		triplet		Y	
		iambic			
		trochaic		Y	
		even division	Y	Y	
Alternating Motion Attack	Finger Leading Phrase	even division	Y	Y	Y
		iambic		Y	
		trochaic		Y	
	Thumb Leading Phrase	even division	Y	Y	
		iambic			
		trochaic		Y	
Dactylic Attack	Finger Leading Phrase	I-I-X	Y	Y	Y
		I-X-X		Y	
		I-X-I	Y	Y	
	Thumb Leading Phrase	X-X-I			
		X-I-I	Y		
		X-I-X	Y	Y	Y
Anapestic Attack	Finger Leading Phrase	I-I-X		Y	
		I-X-X		Y	
		I-X-I		Y	Y
	Thumb Leading Phrase	X-X-I		Y	
		X-I-I			
		X-I-X		Y	
Amphibrach Attack	Finger Leading Phrase	I-I-X			
		I-X-X	Y	Y	
		I-X-I		Y	
	Thumb Leading Phrase	X-X-I			
		X-I-I			
		X-I-X			
Triplet Attack	Finger Leading Phrase	I-I-X	Y	Y	
		I-X-X	Y		
		I-X-I		Y	
	Thumb Leading Phrase	X-X-I			
		X-I-I			
		X-I-X	Y	Y	

Each **Y** highlights where a source's right-hand attack met the basic criteria and requires additional discussion and clarification. I = lead finger; X = thumb.

1855 and Rice 1858, illustrates a disproportionate number of fields marked with a **Y** when compared to the *ekonting* and old-time banjo sample groups (which are surely more robust than what is depicted here). The tabulations for Briggs and Rice collectively account for 135 pieces plus exercises. However, to date, few authoritative transcriptions of *ekonting* music have been produced and it has also been challenging to identify authoritative descriptive transcriptions of old-time banjo music that were not based on another musician's personal synthesis and stylizing of notable tradition bearers. We will continue to work to identify additional sources for ongoing research.

For the purposes of this chapter, we are focusing on those points where the *ekonting* right-hand attacks were noted alongside either one or both of the other sample groups (Rice-Briggs and/or Jarrell-Ward-Lephew-Cole). Each field that contains a **Y** only represents a single instance in which a particular attack occurs. It does not measure the frequency with which an attack occurs within the sample group, which is beyond the scope of what can reasonably be included here.

With the individual consecutive attack for the finger and individual consecutive attack for the thumb, both banjo-based sample groups, together or individually, show some similarity with the *ekonting* in that each rhythm is often sounded with a single physical gesture that produces an individual primary tone. These include the stand-alone or on-the-beat-pitches, iambic, trochaic, and even division rhythms.[36] They generate a sense of melodic direction, establish a rhythmic foundation, or come to a cadence. While all three sample groups also achieve a dactylic rhythm (or a dactylic-based rhythm)[37] with the individual consecutive attack, a significant difference arises in how these rhythms are achieved on the *ekonting* versus the banjo (musical example 6.8). While Ekona Diatta is achieving the dactylic-based rhythm on a single string with three individual strikes (on the second beat of the song excerpt for "Edjoul"), the dactylic rhythms found within the banjo players' repertoire are being achieved with two motions—the first striking the long note followed by

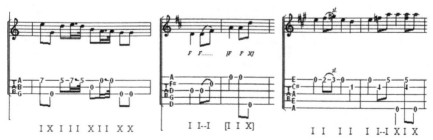

Musical Example 6.8. Lead finger individual consecutive attack (dactylic rhythm). *Left*: "Edjoul" excerpt, as performed by Ekona Diatta, July 2006; transcription and tablature by Greg C. Adams. *Center*: "Rosa Lee" excerpt, from Briggs; tablature by Greg C. Adams. *Right*: "Old Bunch of Keys" excerpt, as played by Tommy Jarrell; transcription and tablature by Paul Brown, right-hand structural reduction on m2 by Greg C. Adams.

the two short notes with a controlled single motion through two adjacent strings. In measure 1 of "Rosa Lee" (Briggs, p. 15), the lead finger initiates the dactylic rhythm by striking the third string (the long note), then re-striking the third string into the second string as part of a single gliding motion that leads to measure 2, where the right hand resumes a more typical dactylic motion; basically, the lead finger glides through three strings as part of a single motion. In the first half of measure 2 of Tommy Jarrell's version of "Old Bunch of Keys," the basic right-hand attack includes a dactylic rhythm that is also sounded by the lead finger gliding through the second and first strings.[38]

With the alternating motion attack covering both the finger lead and thumb lead phrases, the *ekonting* and the banjo groups share an apparent similarity in terms of even divisions of a beat. The second grouping of the excerpt of "Remi's Tune" (musical example 6.9) includes a finger lead alternation between the first and second and first and third strings. Alternately, the song "Alinaume" (the instrumental component) includes a thumb lead alternating motion beginning on the upbeat of the third beat. This type of alternation demonstrates a fundamental yoking between the lead finger and thumb that also exists in banjo repertoire.

Musical Example 6.9. Excerpts of "Remi's Tune" (*top*; as performed by Remi Diatta, 2006) and "Alinaume" (*bottom*; as performed by Ekona and Remi Diatta, 2006). Transcribed by Paul Sedgwick and Greg C. Adams; tablature by Greg C. Adams.

One of the most recognizable figures within banjo repertoire is the dactylic attack. Often referred to in the vernacular as "bum-ditty," this long-short-short figure surfaces in a variety of ways on the banjo and also appears on the *ekonting*. Within the realms of the banjo, musical example 6.10 outlines several banjo-based dactylic attacks that also appear on the *ekonting*. The two dactylic attacks found toward the end of the second phrase in Remi and Ekona Diatta's "Gambia" (musical example 6.4) are not unlike the dactylic attack found in the musical example 6.10 instance (1), which is found in tunes such as "Jim Crow Polka" on measure 10, beat 1 (Briggs, p. 12). Instance (2) is somewhat anomalous where occurrences of this type of attack are present in Briggs ("Who's Dat Knockin' at de Door," measure 15, beat 1), which is probably a typographical error, and another in measure 6, beat 1 of Rice's "That's So and You'd Better Believe It." This type of motion is present in the penultimate beat of Ekona Diatta's "Edjoul" (musical example 6.11). Dactylic attacks (3) and (4), which begin with a thumb-lead on the downbeat, share a structural kinship with measure 1, beat 1 of Phil. Rice's "Excelsior Jig" (Rice, p. 54), measure 2 of Tommy Jarrell's "Old Bunch of Keys" (musical example 6.8), and the second beat of Ekona Diatta's "Edjoul." Yet, dactylic attacks on the *ekonting* do diverge in some ways from the banjo, as found, for example, on beat 8 of "Mamba Suditan" (musical example 6.7), where the attack begins with the thumb (X) on the long note and the lead finger (I) sounding the two short notes.

Although anapestic attacks are common in the Briggs and Rice books as well as with the Jarrell-Ward-Lephew-Cole sample group, at this point no obvious anapestic attack on the *ekonting* became apparent when reviewing field materials. However, just as the *ekonting* generally parallels the human voice and *ekonting* players will often fill in the sound of a long vocal note with additional strikes to the instrument, it would make sense to look at vocal lines to see likely places where anapestic rhythms could be played on the instrument. For example, the first three beats of "Mamba Suditan" (musical example 6.3) include an anapestic (short-short-long) statement in the vocal line. It would depend on the player's initiative in the moment as to whether or not to maintain the long note or represent it with, for example, an even division.

The amphibrach attack (short-long-short) is certainly alluded to in *ekonting* music. The opening four beats of Ekona and Remi Diatta's "Gambia" offer one

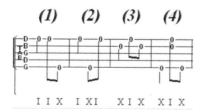

Musical Example 6.10. Examples of dactylic attacks on the banjo.

Musical Example 6.11. "Edjoul," as performed by Ekona Diatta, July 2006. Transcribed by Greg C. Adams and Paul Sedgwick; tablature by Greg C. Adams.

type of amphibrach example, with the rhythm bridging the second and third beats (musical example 6.4, beginning with the second and third syllables of the lyrics "Gam-bi-a"). Here the lead finger (I) sounds the first of three pitches of the amphibrach followed by two strikes of the thumb (X). On the banjo at least one amphibrach attack occurs with an I-X-X configuration between the first and fifth strings in measure 2, beat 2 of the Briggs's version of "O! Lud Gals" (p. 14) (musical example 6.12).

In the final attack pattern, triplet attack, both the *ekonting* and early banjo sample groups share a finger-leading phrase and a thumb-leading phrase designation. With the finger lead, Ekona Diatta's triplet version of "Gambia" (musical example 6.5) executes an I-I-X triplet with three strikes, between the first and second or first and third strings. Alternately, the triplets in the "finale" of "Yankee Doodle with Variations" found on page 30 of Briggs (measure 34, third triplet and fourth triplet groupings) are sounded with the two motions (musical example 6.13). With the third triplet, the I-I is sounded with a controlled glide through the second and first strings followed by the thumb on the fifth string, while the

Musical Example 6.12. "O! Lud Gals" (excerpt, mm 1–2). Tablature by Greg C. Adams.

Musical Example 6.13. "Yankee Doodle with Variations" (excerpt, mm 3–4). Tablature by Greg C. Adams.

fourth triplet (somewhat peculiarly) is meant to be played with a single motion by the lead finger that begins with the open third string, followed by a gymnastic leap over the second string without sounding it, landing on and striking the open first string, and terminating with the thumb on the fifth string. Ekona Diatta's use of another finger-leading phrase for a triplet, I-X-X, is found on the fourth beat in "Mamba Suditan" (musical example 6.7). While this type of configuration for a triplet does not necessarily appear in Briggs or Rice, it does appear in subsequent banjo tutors such as, for example, Frank Converse's 1865 *New and Complete Method for the Banjo With or Without a Master* in the tune "Bully for All," measure 1.

The final triplet example that is sounded with a thumb lead, in this case, X-I-X, is also present with Ekona Diatta's "triplet" version of "Gambia" (musical example 6.5, second triplet grouping). This type of configuration is also present in Briggs's "Walk into de Parlor Jig" (musical example 6.14, measure 1, second beat).[39]

Musical Example 6.14. "Walk into De Parlor Jig" (excerpt, m1). Tablature by Greg C. Adams.

The final two areas for consideration are slur-based figures and chord-based figures. While neither the Briggs nor the Rice book incorporates glissandi (slides), both early and old-time banjo do feature ascending and descending slurs as well as left-hand pizzicatos-open string pull-offs. For examples of slides, hammer-ons, and pull-offs, see musical example 6.15, "Old Bunch of Keys." See musical example 6.16 for examples of open-string pull-offs as found in *Phil. Rice's Correct Method for the Banjo: With or Without a Master* (p. 13) and Tommy Jarrell's "Poor Ellen Smith."

Chords within early banjo music are presented mostly as points of musical emphasis,[40] where in certain sectors of old-time banjo music, chords might be used for both musical emphasis as well as part of the rhythmic underpinning at the center point of the dactylic attack. See musical example 6.15, measure 4, of "Old Bunch of Keys" for an example of a chord centralized within a dactylic attack and musical example 6.17, "Mary Blane" (Briggs, p. 11), for an example of chords as musical emphasis.[41]

The role of slurs or chords is difficult to characterize as a feature of *ekonting* technique. Both Remi and Ekona Diatta do use a type of left-hand slurring gesture, but it appears to be most often part of a percussive muting effect for one of the

Musical Example 6.15. "Old Bunch of Keys," excerpt, in A major a-E-A-C♯-E, as performed by Tommy Jarrell. Transcribed by Paul Brown, edited by Greg C. Adams; tablature by Greg C. Adams. Examples of glissando (slides), ascending slurs (hammer-ons), descending slurs (pull-offs), and centralized use of chords in, for example, a dactylic attack.

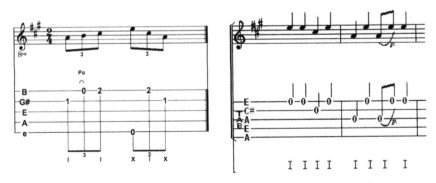

Musical Example 6.16. Left-hand pizzicato in Phil. Rice exercise (p. 13) (*left*) and measure 2 of Tommy Jarrell's "Poor Ellen Smith" (*right*, transcription by Paul Brown).

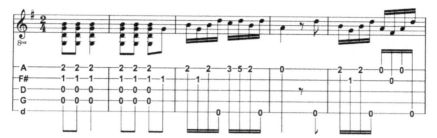

Musical Example 6.17. Chords as musical emphasis in Briggs's "Mary Blane" (1855).

two notes found in double strike attacks in such pieces as "Batima Sijul" (musical example 6.6). While the musical function of this double strike with the finger and thumb is not entirely clear, other than as an additional point of musical emphasis, it occurs in at least three ways: played simultaneously; played simultaneously where the tone produced on the first string appears to be quickly muted and the pitch produced by the thumb continues ringing (when the left-hand fingers quickly come down on the string in either the fifth or seventh semitone positions; this action is reminiscent of an ascending slur, or hammer-on, but results in no sound of the string meeting the fingerboard); or played almost simultaneously where one tone is slightly displaced from the next, sounding like a grace note or ornamentation. Regarding the use of chords in *ekonting* music, Greg C. Adams and Paul Sedgwick originally reported that *ekonting* music did not use chords.[42] However, subsequent research and ongoing review of field recordings show that some players do, in fact, initiate this double strike in a way that, as stacked pitches, may imply a vertical (or chord-like) point of emphasis.

Overall, examining playing techniques using a controlled vocabulary provides important structure when describing similarities and differences between the *ekonting* and the banjo and the ways in which the lead finger and thumb are yoked together. This approach enhances our ability to identify and appreciate the intersection between musicians from multiple locations, traditions, and different points in time. But making such comparisons also challenges us to clarify our intent when exploring the links between any living tradition and the historical record.

The Importance of Clarifying Intent in the Twenty-First Century

While the exact age of the *ekonting* tradition has yet to be independently verified, it is clear that the *ekonting* is important to those who maintain it within Jola communities, for those visitors who wish to study it, and for those exploring potential relationships with the early history of the banjo. Here, we elected to use a structural approach to make cross-cultural comparisons using precise terminology to explore playing technique, tuning and scale, and the music-making process. Yet, as the musicologist Kofi Agawu states when writing about structural analysis versus cultural analysis, "culture insists on context."[43] Just because we can demonstrate compelling structural similarities between how the *ekonting* and the banjo are played does not mean the case is closed culturally.

Ideally, the findings we present here should be expanded and adapted to further examinations of any plucked lute tradition that utilizes a down-stroke technique, acknowledging the subtleties of performance, the nuances of cultural context, and the need to better understand the oral and written histories of these traditions. Ultimately, we view this chapter as our opportunity to dispel any urges to state that the *ekonting* is the "original of the banjo" in the same misaligned way that Thomas Jefferson tried to suggest that the banjo is the "original of the guitar."[44] The historical record is too incomplete to draw such conclusions and the vastness of West African plucked spike lute traditions is too compelling to overlook.

Notes

1. Issues of transliteration, phonetics, and the textual representation of oral tradition affect the way researchers represent the *ekonting* tradition. Of the multiple documented ways of writing the name of the instrument, the spelling *akonting* is preferred by some scholars, including Daniel Lamouahuma Jatta, while other scholars prefer *ekonting* to reflect the pronunciation believed to be more accurate to the Jolas of Casamance, Senegal. Both spellings are used in this chapter, depending on the sources of subject material.

2. See Shlomo Pestcoe's chapter in this volume, "Banjo Ancestors: West African Plucked Spike Lutes," for more background about these many traditions.

3. The *bunchundo* is a related plucked lute played by the Manjak (Manjago, Manyago) people of southern Senegal and Guinea-Bissau. See figure E in the central illustrations section.

4. See Chuck Levy, "An Interview with Daniel Laemouahuma Jatta," *The Old-Time Herald* 13, no. 2 (2012): 22–33. A full transcription of the interview with Daniel Laemouahuma Jatta is also available at www.banjourneys.com, accessed October 20, 2017.

5. Some of these references include unpublished field recordings from 1961, 1966, and 1970 by J. David Sapir, and the following journal articles and books: Michael T. Coolen, "The Wolof Xalam Tradition of the Senegambia," *Ethnomusicology* 27, no. 3 (September 1983): 477–98; idem, "Senegambian Archetypes for the American Folk Banjo," *Western Folklore* 43, no. 2 (April 1984): 117–32; Eric Charry, "Plucked Lutes in West Africa: An Historical Overview," *The Galpin Society Journal* 49 (March 1996): 3–37; idem, *Mande Music: Traditional and Modern Music of the Maninka and Mandinka of Western Africa* (Chicago: University of Chicago Press, 2000); Michel Huet, *The Dances of Africa* (London: Harry N. Abrams, Inc., 1996); Robert Baum, *Shrines of the Slave Trade: Diola Religion and Society in Precolonial Senegambia* (New York: Oxford University Press, 1999).

6. Ulf Jägfors, "The African Akonting and the Origin of the Banjo," *The Old-Time Herald* 9, no. 2 (Winter 2003–4): 26–33; Greg C. Adams and Shlomo Pestcoe, "The Jola Akonting: Reconnecting the Banjo to its West African Roots," *Sing Out Magazine* 1, no. 1 (Spring 2007): 43–51; Greg C. Adams and Paul Sedgwick, "'O'Teck!' An Introduction to the Akonting," *Banjo Newsletter: America's Premiere 5 String Banjo Magazine* 34, no. 401

(March 2007): 12–18; and Greg C. Adams and Paul Sedgwick, "Encountering the Akonting: A Cultural Exchange," *The Old-Time Herald* 10, no. 9 (April 2007): 36–41. Museum exhibits include the November 2003–February 2004 Katonah Museum exhibit *The Birth of the Banjo* and the University of Tennessee, Knoxville's 2006 *The Banjo: From Africa to America and Beyond*. Several personal, institutional, and social networking websites provide users with access to videos and related information about the *ekonting*. Documentary projects such as Marc Fields's *The Banjo Project* and Bela Fleck's *Throw Down Your Heart* also captured important footage covering the *ekonting* tradition. Instructional videos include those produced by The Ships of the Sea Museum with Sana Ndiaye, Greg C. Adams, Chuck Levy, and Paul Sedgwick discussing the *ekonting* tradition (http://shipsofthesea.org/museum-videos, accessed October 20, 2017). At least one dramatic performance includes the banjo—Paul Sedgwick's 2010 "The Banjo Lesson." The UCLA ethnomusicology doctoral candidate Scott Linford has published an *ekonting*-focused essay with *Ethnomusicology Review* (http://ethnmusicologyreview.ucla.edu/content/akonting-history, accessed September 23, 2015) and will include new historical content and more recent fieldwork in his 2016 dissertation, "Interweaving Worlds: Jola Music and Relational Identity in Senegambia and Beyond."

7. Paul Sedgwick offered classes at Banjo Camp North (2007) and Midwest Banjo Camp (2007). Chuck Levy and Ken Perlman's Suwannee Banjo Camp (2008–10) offered *ekonting* classes taught by the Senegalese *ekonting* player Sana Ndiaye with assistance by Paul Sedgwick and Greg C. Adams. Chuck Levy also organized a symposium at the University of Florida (March 20, 08) entitled The Akonting/Banjo Symposium, Digital Worlds Institute, which featured many notable banjoists from the traditional music community as well as the Malian *n'goni* player Cheick Hamala Diabate and the Senegalese *ekonting* player Sana Ndiaye.

8. See Shlomo Pestcoe and Greg C. Adams's chapter "Changing Perspectives on the Banjo's African American Origins and West African Heritage" in this volume.

9. Through direct correspondence with Sapir, Adams received copies of the 1961, 1966, and 1970 *ekonting* recordings. From the 1960s, 1970s, and 1980s, Sapir's work was primarily with the Kujamaat Jóola (Diola Fogny). For more information on Sapir and his work, see http://anthropology.virginia.edu/faculty/emeriti/profile/ds8s, accessed March 28, 2009.

10. As part of Jatta's initiative to establish the Akonting Center for Senegambian Folk Music, he has enlisted the help of a committee headed up by Gambians Paul Correa and Therese Senghor, residents of the village of Lamin, both of whom have worked selflessly as hosts, guides, contacts, and intermediaries for a number of American and European researchers. More recently, as of 2014, Momodou Bah of Child Fund International has been working to build stronger local infrastructure for Jatta's work with Senegambian traditions through the nonprofit Akonting Center Foundation (AFC), established in December 2014.

11. See Kofi Agawu, *Representing African Music: Postcolonial Notes, Queries, and Positions* (New York: Routledge, 2003).

12. Compiled from Ulf Jägfors, Daniel Jatta, Nick Bamber, Chuck Levy, Ben Nelson, and Paul Sedgwick in October 2008.

13. For additional information about the process of constructing an *ekonting*, see Adams and Sedgwick, "'O'Teck!'" 12–18.

14. This assignment of pitch names is meant to convey the interval relationships, not the absolute pitches. While the interval relationships between the strings are relatively constant, the actual pitches vary.

15. Joanne Davies, "Final Dissertation" (BA thesis, University of Birmingham, 2009), 35.

16. The field researchers Greg C. Adams, Paul Sedgwick, and Nick Bamber each documented the different instances of the M2P5 tuning. Bamber noted the m3P5 tuning during his 2006 field research: Nick Bamber, "Ekontings and Feasting on Boa Constrictor: More Cultural Experiences in Casamance, July–August 2007," MySpace.com, entry posted September 8, 2007, http://blog.myspace.com/index.cfm?fuseaction=blog.view&friendID= 76763197&blogID=308070072, accessed October 30, 2008. Ben Nelson also reports varied tunings from his studies with *ekonting* players in 2006.

17. Personal conversation between Greg C. Adams and Daniel Laemouahuma Jatta in 2006. See also Adams and Sedgwick, "Encountering the Akonting," 36–41.

18. All representations of the Jola language are based on phonetic interpretations as experienced by field researchers. Ongoing consultation with the Jola people as well as knowledgeable scholars will help to clarify texts collected by current field researchers.

19. The pitch range for any given *ekonting* is affected by the gauge of the fishing line that is used as well as the preference of the musician or builder.

20. For more on transcribing music from West Africa, see Kofi Agawu, *Representing African Music: Postcolonial Notes, Queries, and Positions* (New York: Routledge, 2003), and Jacqueline Cogdell DjeDje, *Fiddling in West Africa: Touching the Spirit in Fulbe, Hausa, and Dagbamba Cultures* (Bloomington: Indiana University Press, 2008).

21. In 2004 and 2006, Ulf Jägfors and Paul Sedgwick documented Jesus Jarju using a tapping technique as well as a left-handed pizzicato as part of his performance. This is perhaps influenced by observations of *xalam* or *n'goni* players who commonly use some type of tapping on the soundtable. At least one *bunchundo* player (Lawrence Abukwach) also taps on the *soundtable*.

22. Some of the innovations Ndiaye developed include the use of geared tuning pegs, an applied wooden soundtable, and the use of a pick-up for amplification.

23. See Nick Bamber's chapter "Searching for Gourd Lutes in the Bijago Islands of Guinea-Bissau" in this volume.

24. For additional information about how the *ekonting* is used in Jola communities, see Adams and Sedgwick, "Encountering the Akonting." Videos of a spontaneous performance given on the occasion of a visit to Mlomp by the authors are available at www.youtube .com/banjochuck, accessed October 25, 2017. An extensive collection of video clips from Chuck Levy's visit in 2007 is posted at a University of Florida–supported website (http:// www.arts.ufl.edu/CAHRE/senegambia_videos.asp, accessed August 6, 2009).

25. According to Daniel Jatta, these "clappers" are called "Ku Nuk Kata Oh Oahai," which Jatta translates into "sticks from the Run Palm tree."

26. Baum, *Shrines of the Slave Trade*, 171.

27. Ibid., 249.

28. For additional information previously reported about the links between the Jola *ekonting* and the banjo, see Adams and Pestcoe, "The Jola Akonting," 43–51.

29. Thomas F. Briggs, *Briggs' Banjo Instructor* (Boston: Oliver Ditson and Co., 1855); Phil. Rice, *Phil. Rice's Correct Method for the Banjo: With or Without a Master* (Boston: Oliver Ditson and Co., 1858).

30. The banjo scholar Elias Kaufman maintains a comprehensive chronological bibliography of banjo method books beginning with the earliest nineteenth-century references.

31. While the early banjo tutors focus primarily on a down-stroke playing technique (e.g., Briggs, *Briggs' Banjo Instructor*; Rice, *Phil. Rice's Correct Method for the Banjo: With*

or Without a Master; James Buckley, *Buckley's New Banjo Guide* [New York: C. H. Ditson and Co., 1868]; Frank B. Converse, *Frank B. Converse's Banjo Instructor, Without a Master: Containing a Choice Collection of Banjo Solos, Jigs, Songs, Reels, Walk Arounds, etc., Progressively Arranged, and Plainly Explained; Enabling the Learner to Become a Proficient Banjoist without the Aid of a Teacher* [New York: Dick & Fitzgerald, 1865]; Frank B. Converse, *Frank B. Converse's New and Complete Method for the Banjo With or Without a Master* [New York: S. T. Gordon, 1865]), they also document in varying and increasing degrees a guitar-style up-stroke technique. Although it is certainly possible that banjos and banjo-like instruments were played with other techniques such as two-finger styles (thumb and finger) with the thumb pulling down and the finger pulling up, or styles where the fingers pluck the strings with both up and down picking movements, these styles are not clearly documented in the early minstrel era, and, thus, are not a focus of this chapter.

32. For one of the earliest modern analyses comparing these techniques, see Robert B. Winans, "The Folk, the Stage, and the Five-String Banjo in the Nineteenth Century," *The Journal of American Folklore* 89, no. 354 (October–December 1976): 407–37.

33. The primary tunes referenced for the comparative playing technique component are based on transcriptions created by Greg C. Adams and Paul Sedgwick of Remi and/or Ekona Diatta. They include "Batima Sijul," "Mampeu," "Si Jan Jan Si Jamboukan," "Gambia" (two versions), "Edjoul," "Mamba Suditan," "Alinaume," "Mamba Sambo," "Remi's Tune," and "Remi's Exercises 1&2."

34. Special thanks to Paul Brown, who provided the ten transcriptions for our use in this chapter. Brown also studied banjo intensively with Tommy Jarrell under an NEA Folk Arts Apprenticeship Grant. He has observed and made recordings of numerous other banjo players in the Blue Ridge area, including Calvin Cole and Giles Lephew. He has played banjo since childhood, in both clawhammer and finger-picking styles. He is well known in the old-time banjo community as a collector, interpreter, performer, and teacher of traditional styles.

35. The "String 1" entry in the Briggs and Rice column of this table needs elaboration. *Briggs' Banjo Instructor* includes at least twelve occurrences where the notation appears to prescribe the thumb playing on the first string in an alternating motion with the finger: "Ephraim's Lament" (3), "Injun Rubber Overcoat" (4), "Pitch Burgundy Plaster" (3), and "Jordan is a Hard Road to Travel" (2). Although it is not expressed explicitly in these books, other mid-nineteenth-century tutors suggest that double stops (playing the same note on adjacent strings) are actually what is being implied with tunes like these. For example, see "Luke West's Walk Around" in Converse, *Frank B. Converse's New and Complete Method for the Banjo With or Without a Master*, 61.

36. Some examples of these rhythms-fingerings can be seen above in the section covering how the *ekonting* is played.

37. In the song "Edjoul," Ekona Diatta plays a dactylic-based rhythm with his lead finger where the two short notes of the dactylic rhythm often come out sounding trochaic. This effect is possibly due to how the rhythm figures into the overall pulse of the song.

38. This excerpt is a reduction from the original transcriptions conceived by Paul Brown, which includes a hammer-on with the long note and an ornamental hammer-on and slide from the first and second positions to the fourth and fifth positions. See a larger excerpt of the original transcription in musical example 6.15.

39. What further distinguishes this type of triplet in the Briggs book (as well as Rice and other early banjo tutors) is that many triplets are closely related to one or more beats of adjacent material. For example, as is the case in "Walk into De Parlor Jig," early banjo

music commonly uses a dotted rhythm, often trochaic (long-short) (and sometimes an even division of a beat), to precede a triplet (see musical example 6.14).

40. The Rice book does not heavily emphasize use of chords. Other than the "Eighth Lesson" on page 18 where the chord is on the downbeat, "Picayune Butler's Come to Town" on page 32, and "De Ole Grey Goose" on page 45 where chords are used at cadences, Rice includes one chord-like anomaly on page 43 with "So Glad Dinah Left Me" that leaves the banjo part, at times, in a state of ambiguity.

41. Thanks to Marc Smith for his assistance in setting the "Phil. Rice exercise" in musical example 6.16 and "Mary Blane" in musical example 6.17.

42. See Adams and Sedgwick, "'O'Teck!'" 12–18; and idem., "Encountering the Akonting," 36–41.

43. Kofi Agawu, "Structural Analysis or Cultural Analysis? Competing Perspectives on the 'Standard Pattern' of West African Rhythm," *Journal of the American Musicological Society* 59, no. 1 (2006): 1–46 (6–7).

44. Thomas Jefferson, *Notes on the State of Virginia* (Philadelphia, 1781), query XIV, 266.

PART III

Into the New World— Caribbean Developments

CHAPTER 7

"Strum Strumps" and "Sheepskin" Guitars
The Early Gourd Banjo and Clues to its West African Roots in the Seventeenth-Century Circum-Caribbean

Shlomo Pestcoe

Editor's Headnote

The historical record indicates that the banjo first emerged in the African diaspora of the Caribbean Basin during the seventeenth century as the product of a creolization process that combined traditional West African plucked spike lute designs with European-inspired innovations. Enlarging on the discussion of this process begun in banjo roots research, Shlomo Pestcoe analyzes the intriguing period reports of Hans Sloane from Jamaica in the 1680s and Alonzo de Sandoval from Cartagena de Indias (Cartagena, Colombia) in the 1620s, which offer us the earliest known documentary evidence of the early gourd banjo's West African roots and Afro-Caribbean origins. Sloane provided the earliest known textual description and visual image of early gourd banjos. In recent times, however, certain erroneous modern interpretations of Sloane's documentation and illustration of what he termed "Strum Strumps" have been generally accepted as historic fact. Pestcoe offers new research findings that will hopefully correct these misperceptions and lead to a new appreciation of Sloane's Afro-Jamaican "Strum Strumps" as early forms of the banjo.

In this chapter, I examine two period accounts from the historical record that offer us tantalizing leads as we endeavor to trace and document the banjo's African American origins in the circum-Caribbean during the seventeenth century and its West African heritage. The first is the best known: that of British physician-naturalist Sir Hans Sloane (1660–1753), which provides us with the earliest documentation of the *early gourd banjo*—my descriptor for the Afro-Creole forebear of the wood-rimmed five-string banjo. During his fifteen-month stay in Jamaica in the late 1680s, Sloane observed enslaved blacks playing "several sorts of Instruments in imitation of Lutes, made of small Gourds fitted with Necks."[1] His report and an illustration of these instruments—which he referred to as "Strum Strumps" in the illustration's Latin caption—were published some twenty years later in his book *A Voyage to the Islands of Madera Barbados, Nieves, S. Christophers and Jamaica* (1707). Unfortunately, since the early 1990s, certain misconceptions about these Afro-Jamaican instruments have gained wide currency. I present here new findings that, hopefully, will clarify Sloane's documentary evidence and correct the current misapprehensions surrounding it.

The second, though chronologically earlier, comes from Padre Alonso de Sandoval (1577–1652) of Cartagena de Indias (literally "Cartagena of the Indies"), present-day Colombia's port city of Cartagena on the Caribbean Sea. In his 1627 treatise *De instauranda Aethiopum salute* (On Restoring Ethiopian Salvation), Sandoval describes "Guineans" (West Africans from Greater Senegambia)—the kind of captive Africans he characterized as being the most desirable to the Spanish for slaves—as playing "guitars" "made of rough sheepskin."[2] Although Sandoval's mention of the Guineans' "guitars" is limited to a passing reference with few specifics, it is important nonetheless as it is the earliest report found thus far of West African plucked lute playing in the context of slavery in the New World and the transatlantic slave trade. Moreover, it is also significant because it associates that lute playing with a specific section of West Africa: Greater Senegambia.[3] This subregion was the location of the earliest references to plucked lutes in sub-Saharan Africa: fourteenth-century Arabic accounts of the Mali Empire (ca. 1230–1600), the birthplace of *jaliya* (also *jeliya*; "the art of the griot") and griot lute traditions.[4] Today Greater Senegambia is home to a significant portion of the West African family of some eighty traditional plucked spike lutes.[5]

Sir Hans Sloane and the "Strum Strumps" of Jamaica

As a young man, Sloane went to Jamaica in 1687 to be the personal physician to the newly appointed lieutenant governor of the island, Christopher Monck (1653–88), the 2nd Duke of Albemarle.[6] A year after his arrival in Jamaica, the young duke's notorious "intemperate habits" led to his premature demise: he literally drank himself to death toasting the birth of the new Prince of Wales.[7] Sloane stayed on to attend the late duke's family and serve as a general practitioner. His light duties gave Sloane ample time to indulge his passions as a naturalist and botanist and search out that which is "extraordinary in nature in those places."[8] When Sloane returned to England on May 29, 1689, he brought with him not only the copious notes and drawings that would eventually constitute his *Natural History of Jamaica* (Sloane's original title for what would become his 1707 book *A Voyage to the Islands*), but also a collection of eight hundred botanical specimens and a much smaller number of cultural artifacts.[9]

During his stay in Jamaica, Sloane observed that

> The Negroes are much given to Venery, and although hard wrought, will at nights, or on Feast days Dance and Sing; Their songs are all bawdy, and leading

that way. They have several sorts of Instruments in imitation of Lutes, made of small Gourds fitted with Necks, strung with Horse hairs, or the peeled stalks of climbing Plants or Withs. These Instruments are sometimes made of hollow'd Timber covered with Parchment or other Skin wetted, having a Bow for its Neck, the Strings ty'd longer or shorter, as they would alter their sounds. The Figures of some of these Instruments are hereafter graved.[10]

Sloane went on to describe the use of rattles ("ty'd to their Legs and Wrists, and in their Hands") during dancing, as well as the practice of "keeping time with one who makes a sound answering it on the mouth of an empty Gourd or Jar with his Hand." Sloane likewise described how Afro-Jamaicans adorned themselves for dances by tying "Cows Tails to their Rumps" and adding "such other things to their Bodies as gives them a very extraordinary appearance."[11] As with the instruments and dancing he described, this type of costuming was evidently a manifestation of African heritage, one that was carried on in the Afro-Jamaican masquerading traditions in the succeeding centuries, especially in the context of annual festivals such as Jonkonnu (also Jankunu or John Canoe), which traditionally takes place during Christmastime.[12]

Sloane concluded his brief description of Afro-Jamaican music instruments, music-making, and dancing with transcriptions of three melodies that were performed at "one of their Festivals," which he had asked a "Mr. Baptiste" ("the best Musician there") to transcribe. They were entitled: "Angola" (an apparent reference to the West-Central African country that was a principal source of enslaved captives); "Papa" ("Popo," captives from Dahomey[13] [today, the Republic of Benin] on West Africa's Lower Guinea coast); and "Koromanti" ("Coromanti," captives from the Gold Coast [present-day Ghana] on the Lower Guinea coast).[14] Sloane did not provide any background information on these tunes other than to offer the instructions "You must clap Hands when the Base is plaid, and cry, *Alla, Alla.*"[15] Nor did he indicate if these tunes were played on the string instruments he described.

When Sloane published his account twenty years later as *A Voyage to the Islands of Madera, Barbados, Nieves, S. Christophers and Jamaica*, he included an illustration of three Afro-Jamaican string instruments ("Plate III") with a caption in Latin that identified them as

1.1.2.2. *Fidiculæ Indorum & Nigritarum, e cucurbitis inter se diversis, excavatis, pellibus tectis, confectæ, Strum Strumps.*

3.3. *Fidicula, e ligno excavato; oblong, pelle tecto, confecta* (1.1.2.2. 'Strum Strumps', lutes of the Indians & Blacks, made of different hollowed-out gourds covered with animal hides)

(3.3. Lute, [with] an oblong [body] made of hollowed-out wood covered with an animal hide)

Shown below these three instruments is a coiled pile of plant fiber (4444), described as being used to make the instruments' strings, and a tree branch, whittled down to a stick for cleaning teeth (5.5.).

The "Strum Strumps" are the two plucked lutes depicted in the illustration's foreground. SS 1.1., on the right, has an oval-shaped gourd body, while its companion on the left, SS 2.2., has a round gourd body (see figure H).

The string instrument (3.3.) behind them is a harp-lute (also known as a bridge-harp), a form of harp unique to West Africa. Harp-lutes share certain similarities in construction with West African plucked spike lutes, such as a drum-like body (made of either a large gourd or a wooden box, depending on the given tradition), topped with an animal hide soundtable, and a stick neck to which the strings are affixed with sliding tuning rings. The type of harp-lute depicted in plate III, with a narrow wooden box body and a bent stick neck, is found primarily in present-day Sierra Leone, Liberia, Côte d'Ivoire, and Ghana. The one seen here closely resembles the eight-string Ashanti-Ewe *sanku* and the Ashanti-Ewe *seperewa* with six to seven strings (Ghana).[16] No doubt the depicted harp-lute was what Sloane was referring to when he wrote: "These Instruments are sometimes made of hollow'd Timber covered with Parchment or other Skin wetted, having a Bow for its Neck, the Strings ty'd longer or shorter, as they would alter their sounds."[17]

A veil of mystery has long shrouded plate III: Was the image created in Jamaica or England? Were these three instruments part of Sloane's many vast and varied collections that he bequeathed to his sovereign and country, which formed the basis for the establishment of the British Museum in 1753?

There is evidence that Sloane did indeed bring the instruments back to England and that the original depiction for plate III was probably done there several years before his book's publication. First, in folio 28 of Sloane's catalogue of "Miscellanies" (currently in the collections of the British Museum's Department of Ethnography) with annotations mostly written in his own hand, some of which date to 1730–38,[18] there are three entries:

> 28a/56. "Jamaica *strum strum* or musicall instrument, made of an oblong—hollowed piece of wood with a cross in the side, strings of a scendent herbs caulis [?]"
> 28a/57. "The *same* made of cucurbita lagenaria [bottle gourd] covered w^t. skin—holed in the side"
> 28a/58. "*One* of another form w^t. a bell in it"[19]

The first entry clearly describes the harp-lute (3.3.) depicted in the book illustration, while the second could certainly describe either one of the two "Strum Strump" plucked spike lutes. The third entry also seems to indicate one of the lutes, though it is not clear what is meant by "[with] a bell in it."

An intriguing detail mentioned in entry 28a/57 is the comment that the instrument is "holed in the side." This reference is most likely to one or more soundholes carved into the side of the lute's gourd body. Soundholes placed in the body's side(s) or bottom are typical of West African plucked full-spike lutes and harp-lutes with bodies made of gourd. They are also found on the three historic four-string early gourd banjos currently known: the calabash-bodied *creole bania* (Suriname, ca. 1773–77; Rijksmuseum voor Volkenkunde, Leiden, The Netherlands—see figure J); the gourd-bodied *banza* (Haiti, ca. 1840–41; Musée de la Musique, Cité de la Musique, Paris, France—see figure K); and the calabash-bodied *panja* (*banja*) (Suriname, ca. 1850; Ethnologisches Museum, Staatliche Museen zu Berlin, Germany; photo online at http://www.mimo-international .com/MIMO/doc/IFD/SPK_BERLIN_DE_EM_OBJID_169626, accessed October 25, 2017).[20] Small soundholes, decoratively carved in various shapes, are also shown all around the circumference of the gourd body on the four-string early gourd banjo depicted by John Rose in his watercolor *The Old Plantation* (South Carolina, ca. 1785–90—see figure N).[21]

The second piece of evidence is the illustration that the British Arabist musicologist-organologist Henry George Farmer (1882–1965) used for his article "Early References to Music in the Western Sūdān" (1939): "Plate XI," a print he entitled "Musical Instruments of the Western Sūdān" (West Africa).[22] "The plate given herewith," Farmer wrote, "is taken from a manuscript in the British Museum, dated 1701 (Add. 5324, fol. 75). It shows excellent delineations of three African string instruments (see figure I), a harp and two pandores,[23] all of which, I believe, belong to the Western Sudan."[24] Farmer, however, was incorrect in his assessment that these three string instruments "belong" to West Africa. They were, in fact, the ones that Sloane had brought back from Jamaica when he returned to England in 1689. As I will show, the two depicted "Strum Strumps," while evincing West African derivation in their fundamental design and construction, are clearly African American early gourd banjos made in the New World rather than traditional plucked spike lutes imported from West Africa. It is possible, however, that the depicted harp-lute may have been built in West Africa and brought to Jamaica, where Sloane acquired it.

The image itself is a hand-drawn sketch of the very instruments depicted in plate III in Sloane's 1707 book. All three are shown positioned in the exact same configuration that appears in the book's engraved illustration, except that the "Strum Strumps" are reversed: the oval-bodied lute (SS 1.1. in plate III) is placed on the left while the round-bodied one (SS 2.2.) is on the right.

In the sketch, handwritten annotations by each instrument give their dimensions. The total length given for the depicted harp-lute is 36 inches, with its narrow wooden soundbox being 10 inches in length, 3 3/4 inches in width, and 4 1/2 inches in depth, and its bridge 3 inches tall. As for the two "Strum Strumps," SS 1.1. is 23 1/2 inches long and its oval gourd body is 5 1/2 inches wide, while the SS 2.2. is 21 1/2 inches long and its round gourd body is 5 inches wide.[25]

These annotations, taken together with the sketch's inscribed "1701" date, suggest that the image was, in all likelihood, the original master sketch for the engraving of plate III. As such, it would have been drawn by Everhardus Kickius (Kychious), the Dutch artist Sloane personally commissioned in 1700 through 1701 to create all of the master sketches for his book's engraved illustrations. Most of these were copies of the on-the-spot drawings of Jamaica's fauna and flora made by the Reverend Mr. Garret Moore, who accompanied Sloane as he explored the island in 1688. Kickius's sketches were subsequently engraved unto metal plates by the engravers Michael van der Gucht and John Savage for printing.[26]

Sloane's "Strum Strumps": The First Documented Early Gourd Banjos

Sloane's textual description of Afro-Jamaican string instruments and his book illustration of the two "Strum Strumps" offer the earliest known period documentation of the African American early gourd banjo. In this illustration, we can clearly see that they are plucked spike lutes with the same design features common to all other instruments that we now recognize as early gourd banjos:

1. A drum-like body—in the cases of the two "Strum Strumps," they are both made of bottle gourd (*Lagenaria siceraria*, also referred to as *Cucurbita lagenaria* L.), evident by the wide open-mouth stubs on the bodies (the remnants of the gourds' removed bottlenecks) through which the instrument's neck is inserted.

2. A full-spike neck, evident on both instruments in the visible protrusion of the stub of the neck's sawed-off spike through the gourd body's tail end. Like all known early gourd banjos, the necks on both "Strum Strumps" go diametrically through their bodies, the same as full-spike lutes with gourd or calabash bodies from the eastern Central Sudan section of West Africa, such as the two-string gourd-bodied Hausa *gurmi* (Nigeria), the three-stringed gourd-bodied Kilba *gullum* (Nigeria—see figure G), and the two-string calabash-bodied Toubou *gurumi* (Niger). Yet, the type of through-the-stub neck insertion described above is not seen on any West African full-spike lutes. It is, however, a unique characteristic of those early gourd banjos made of bottle gourd, as evinced on the one depicted in *The Old Plantation* and the Afro-Haitian *banza* (see figures O and K).

3. A flat fretless fingerboard.

4. Wooden friction pegs.

Neither instrument is set up for playing as they are both missing their bridges. However, these were, no doubt, movable floating bridges that sat on the body's animal hide soundtable, the same as on all other early gourd banjos, as well as on all West African full-spike lutes with gourd or calabash bodies. Evidence for this contention can be found in the 1701 sketch: on the soundtables of both instruments are clearly indicated stains where the bridges sat.

In both images the two "Strum Strumps" are shown strung with only two strings. Yet, in the 1707 plate III, each instrument appears to have two additional holes, situated immediately adjacent to each other on the upper portions of their fingerboards. As these holes are positioned a few inches down from the peghead, they might have been holes to receive the tuning pegs for top short thumb-strings. The feature of a short thumb-string (so-called because it is only sounded by the player's thumb) is a unique characteristic of the four-string early gourd banjo and its successor, the wood-rimmed five-string banjo (see figure M), which can be traced back to West Africa.

In early banjo construction, the peg hole for the thumb-string peg was often drilled into the instrument's fingerboard—or, as seen on early wood-rimmed five-string banjos (ca. 1840–70), into a bump, a small rise carved above the fingerboard—a little ways down from the peghead for the dorsal insertion of the thumb-string peg from the back of the neck on through the fingerboard. We see this back-to-front thumb-string peg insertion on the necks of the four-string early gourd banjo depicted in *The Old Plantation* and the Afro-Haitian *banza*, as well as on most early five-string banjos.

That being said, the "Strum Strumps" might have been originally built as three-string instruments. In the 1707 plate III, the round-bodied SS 2.2. is shown with two probable adjacent thumb-string peg holes drilled into the upper part of its fingerboard, which appears to be built specifically for left-handed playing. In the 1701 sketch, however, the round-bodied instrument is depicted with only one peg hole on its fingerboard. If that was indeed meant to be for a thumb-string peg, then it is the earliest period depiction of the elusive, oft-hypothesized three-string early gourd banjo—that is, one with a three-string configuration of two long strings topped with a short third thumb-string.[27] This configuration is found on most West African three-string plucked spike lutes (e.g., the Jola *ekonting* [Senegambia]; the Kel Tamashek [Tuareg] *terharden* [Mali]; and the Hausa *molo* [Nigeria]).

Conversely, the oval-bodied instrument in the 1701 sketch and both lutes in the 1707 plate III are shown with two adjacent peg holes in the fingerboard. The banjo historian Ed Britt has proposed that the reason for the two adjacent holes might have been to allow the player to move the thumb-string peg from one hole to the other when tuning for different keys to avoid placing too much tension on the thumb-string and, thereby, prevent breakage. In the 1701 sketch the tuning pegs on both lutes appear to be inserted from the front, which certainly would have made the transfer of a thumb-string peg from hole to hole feasible. Britt's hypothesis also seems to be supported by the evidence of one of the extant historic four-string early gourd banjos, the Afro-Surinamese *panja*. On this instrument (which was purposely built for left-handed playing), the wooden peg for the top fourth short thumb-string is inserted into what would be the topside of the neck's side. But there are two adjacent holes of the same diameter for the thumb-string peg drilled into the neck's topside, about a couple of inches apart from each other.

"Indian & Negro Lutes"

In recent years, Sloane's Latin reference to the "Strum Strumps" being "Indian & Negro Lutes" has been misinterpreted as an attribution of possible East Indian heritage for these instruments. More specifically, an unfounded modern supposition posited that the oval-bodied SS 1.1. is an East Indian–South Asian type of drone lute called *tanpura*,[28] allegedly placed in the illustration for the sake of comparison to the round-bodied SS 2.2., which, according to this assertion, is "a central African lute."[29] These identifications—which are not found or implied in any of Sloane's writings or annotations—have been mistakenly perceived as given historic fact and are now the most widely accepted interpretation of the image.

The "Indians" that Sloane cited were, in fact, Amerindians. Sloane makes this clear when he reports that "the Indians are not Natives of the Island, they being all destroy'd by the Spaniards . . . but are usually brought by surprise from the Musquitos [of Central America] or Florida, or such as were Slaves to the Spaniards, and taken from them by the English."[30]

In portraying the daily life of the English colony, Sloane made several allusions to Jamaica's "Indians and Negroes" sharing certain traits in common, such as wearing "a little Canvas Jacket and Breeches, given to them at Christmas," or eating "snakes or serpents and cossi (a Sort of Worms)."[31] He also noted that "the Negros and Indians use[d] to Bath themselves in fair water every day, as often as conveniently they can."[32]

At one point Sloane does refer to black captives coming from the East Indies. As he described these "Negroes" as being "those from the East Indies or Madagascins," however, Sloane certainly meant the Indian Ocean islands of Madagascar and the Comoros off the coast of the southeastern Africa country of Mozambique, rather than India or South Asia.[33]

Sloane clearly documented a cross-cultural dynamic between Amerindian Jamaicans and African Jamaicans. Taking into consideration Sloane's other cited examples of this phenomenon, that cross-cultural exchange could have conceivably included Jamaica's Amerindians borrowing the plucked lute of their Afro-Jamaican neighbors.

A final bit of evidence that might indicate Amerindian adoption of the Afro-Jamaican "Strum Strump" is the intricately incised ornamentation on SS 1.1's neck and oval gourd body. Sloane alluded to this type of personalizing decoration when he wrote that the "figures of some of these Instruments are hereafter graved."[34] The various Amerindian peoples who were either native to Jamaica (the Taino) or brought to the island (e.g., the Mesoamerican "Musquitos" Sloane cited) all had rich traditions of ornamenting objects for personal and votive use with intricate designs similar to those seen on SS 1.1. In fact, its elaborate fingerboard and body decorative designs are very reminiscent of those seen on Taino stone collars, pottery, and other artifacts, as well as that of other Amerindian peoples found throughout the circum-Caribbean.[35]

In striking contrast, SS 2.2. is rather plain, decorated only with mostly simple line patterns of *X*s sandwiched between horizontal lines etched up and down the fingerboard, similar to crosshatching. This type of fingerboard decoration might, perhaps, indicate the West-Central African heritage of the person who made and/or played this lute, as the "*X*s-and-lines" pattern is a common form of ornamentation there and often used to decorate instruments. Yet, this traditional decorative pattern is also widespread in West Africa. While most West African music instrument traditions tend toward the plain and unadorned, certain examples of ornamented instruments, including those with "*X*s-and-lines" pattern designs, are known.[36]

Despite this difference in decorative neck and body engravings—as well as in the shapes of their gourd bodies—both "Strum Strumps" are early gourd banjos of nearly identical design and construction, though one was evidently built for left-handed playing. The depicted diversity in neck and body art in plate III apparently reflects a creolized tradition of instrument personalization, which almost certainly drew on African and Amerindian influences.

Let us now consider the issue of the Afro-Creole early gourd banjo's West African roots by examining the clues provided by Padre Sandoval's writings from Cartagena de Indias in the early seventeenth century.

First Hints: Padre Sandoval in Cartagena de Indias

In 1605, 28-year-old Alonso de Sandoval of Lima, Peru, was sent north to Cartagena de Indias on his first major assignment as a Jesuit priest. He was to help build up the city's newly founded mission and college of la Compañía de Jesús.[37] A year after his arrival, the Spanish-born *padre* would embark on his life's calling: ministering to the enslaved Afro-Cartagenans—especially, the *negros bozales* (literally "muzzled blacks"; newly arrived African captives).[38]

In Sandoval's day, Cartagena de Indias was the hub of Spain's share of the transatlantic slave trade.[39] It served as the center for the disembarkation of the captive Africans and their distribution to other colonies throughout the Americas—an estimated 135,000 between 1595 and 1640, at a rate of about 3,000 per year. As a result of this traffic, by the dawn of the seventeenth century, a sizable black majority had developed in the city: approximately 7,000 compared to some 3,000 whites.[40]

Working with *ladinos* (acculturated Spanish-speaking Africans) who served as translators, Sandoval is said to have personally baptized and ministered to more than three thousand *negros bozales* over the course of forty-five years.[41] This was often done while the survivors of the horrific Middle Passage were still chained together in the dank holds of the slave ships that had brought them across the Atlantic. Throughout his ministry, Sandoval kept a notebook in which he meticulously recorded information on the ethnic origins of the Africans he worked with and attended to, as well the different languages they spoke.[42] In this way he had come to learn a great deal about the immense diversity of African ethnicities and cultures.

The "Guineans" and Their "Guitars"

In 1617, Sandoval began to write *De instauranda Aethiopum salute* as a manual on how to baptize and minister to "Ethiopians, who, because of their color, are commonly called blacks."[43] It would be published ten years later as a single volume composed of three distinct sections termed *libros* (books), with a fourth *libro* added as the final section in his revised 1647 edition. Book One of *De instauranda Aethiopum salute* presents Sandoval's discourse on the many different peoples and lands of "Ethiopia" (sub-Saharan black Africa). In addition to his own field notes and conversations with European "eyewitnesses to what happens there," Sandoval cited "scholarly books" on Africa and "the writings of the Jesuit fathers who went to Ethiopia as missionaries" as his sources.[44]

Chapter 11 of Book One is devoted to the "Ethiopians in Guinea and their land, rivers, and ports." Here Sandoval uses the early Portuguese-Spanish designation "Guinea" ("Guiné" in Portuguese) to refer specifically to West Africa's Upper Guinea Coast, from Senegal down to Sierra Leone.[45] In discussing the enslaved captives who came from these lands, however, Sandoval states that "all the Ethiopian Guineans are shipped from ports on the Guinean rivers," and specifies just four rivers: the Gambia, the Senegal, the Casamance (in Southern Senegal), and the Cacheu (in northwestern Guinea-Bissau).[46] Actually, the area that Sandoval referenced may be narrowed down even farther to the riverine lands along the Atlantic coast that comprise the Gambia-Casamance-Cacheu region.[47]

Sandoval starts with "the Guineans" because he characterizes them as the "black slaves who have the most value to the Spanish" as they "work the hardest; they cost the most and have the best dispositions."[48] He goes on to extol their virtues, chief among them the love of music and dance as well as musical skills:

> They are attractive with a keen wit, glad hearts; and a joyful spirit. They never pass up the chance to drum, sing, and dance, even while they are doing the most difficult work imaginable. . . . Their music combines the sounds of sonorous instruments and many voices, and they celebrate without sleeping, day or night. The energy that they put into shouting and dancing is amazing. *Some play guitars similar to our Spanish-style guitars, although they are made of rough sheepskin* (my emphasis).[49]

Sandoval's description of the "guitars" of the Guineans being "similar to our Spanish-style guitars,"[50] would seem to indicate that the described instruments were plucked lutes. Moreover, his observation that these instruments were "made of rough sheepskin" would only make sense if they were plucked spike lutes that had drum-like bodies, topped with tightened membrane soundtables made of sheepskin—in other words, the very kinds of lutes that are still principal traditional string instruments in the Gambia-Casamance-Cacheu region that Sandoval had specified.

Later in his book, Sandoval mentions enslaved captives from other parts of Africa playing "guitars"—namely, those from the West-Central African country of Angola: "[The Angolans] have naturally happy hearts and play little guitars called *banzas*, played by placing the head of the guitar on the breast in a very delicate and graceful way."[51] Here Sandoval provides what was perhaps the earliest published use of the West-Central African term *banza* as a descriptor for string instruments.[52] *Banza* would later become the designation for the early gourd banjo favored in the French Caribbean and Louisiana, as first documented in the eighteenth century.[53]

In this particular instance, however, Sandoval seems to have used the word *guitar* as a broad generic designation for a plucked string instrument, rather than limiting it to a plucked lute. From the sixteenth century on, this usage of *guitar* as a general descriptor of common reference is found throughout the historical record as European commentators endeavored to describe unfamiliar African chordophones to their readers. In this case, Sandoval's description of the *banza* as being played "by placing the head of the guitar on the breast" certainly does not reflect a practical method for playing a plucked lute. Assuming that Sandoval's reference to "the head of the guitar" is to the top or upper section of its neck, holding a plucked lute in such a fashion would make playing it difficult or awkward at best. The playing position Sandoval describes would be more in keeping with the techniques used to play some ethnic types of West-Central African *pluriarc* (an instrument composed of several single-string musical bows mounted in single resonator),[54] such as the *akam* of the Fan of Gabon, a pluriarc with three or four strings.[55]

A period example that connects the word *banza* specifically to pluriarcs is a watercolor illustration of the first king of the Kingdom of Ndongo (located just below the Kingdom of Kongo in northern Angola) and his royal entourage by the Italian Capuchin missionary Giovanni Antonio Cavazzi da Montecuccolo (1621–78) in his *Istorica Descrizione de tre regni Congo, Matamba ed Angola* (1687). Cavazzi depicts two attending court musicians playing pluriarcs (in this case, held and played horizontally) labeled in the picture's handwritten caption as "4. *Manibanza.*"[56]

The fact remains that to date no evidence of historically indigenous plucked lutes of any kind has been found in either the historical record or extant traditional musical material cultures of Angola, a principal source of captives for the transatlantic slave trade. This despite the fact that this land has historically had a rich diversity of other types of string instruments in addition to pluriarcs, such as mouth bows, musical bows, zithers, harps, and fiddles (bowed lutes).

To return to Sandoval's reference to the Guineans' "guitars," the implication of his description is that these instruments would have been akin to the plucked spike lutes that are still important traditional instruments to many of the peoples in the Gambia-Casamance-Cacheu region of Greater Senegambia along the Upper Guinea coast. To substantiate this contention, we need to consider just who exactly the "Guineans" that Sandoval references were.

One of the first *castas* (singular *casta*, literally "castes"; Sandoval's term for distinct peoples-ethnic groups) he identifies are the "Fulopos [who] live along the Gambia River from the Santa Maria Cape to the port of Cacheu."[57] "Fulupo" (Floup; also Felupe, Feloop, Floop, etc.) is the Portuguese exonym for the ancestors of the Jola (Diola in French transliteration, though pronounced the same), dating back to first contact with them in the mid-fifteenth century.[58] Sandoval goes on to cite, among others, the "Balanta" and the "Papel" of Guinea-Bissau, as well as the "Bijogoes" (Bujogo) of Guinea-Bissau's Bijago Islands off its Atlantic coast. Sandoval does not specifically mention these peoples' neighbor, the Manjak (also Manjaco, Manjago, Manyago, etc.). Like the ethnonym *Jola*, the term *Manjak* or any of its variants does not appear until the nineteenth century. Still, the forebears of the Manjak (who were closely related to the Brames and the Papel) were, no doubt, included in Sandoval's reference "Bran," the early Portuguese-Spanish designation for the cluster of these and other associated ethnicities in Guinea-Bissau.[59]

Just like their ancestors back in Sandoval's time, today's Jola, Manjak, Balanta, and Papel are neighboring rice-farming peoples, while the Bujogo are mostly fisherfolk. All of these peoples of the Atlantic-Bak cluster[60] share related traditional languages, religions, and cultures, as well as village-centric societies that are not socially stratified. Each has a banjo-like three-string full-spike lute: the Jola *ekonting* (see figure A), the Manjak *bunchundo* (see figure E), the Balanta *kusunde*, the Bujogo *ñopata* (see figure F), and the Papel *busunde*. These nearly identical instruments all have drum-like gourd bodies, topped with soundtables made of "rough" animal hides—though more typically goatskin rather than sheepskin. As music-making in these societies is not a traditional vocation nor is it the exclusive domain of endogamous specialist music artisans like griots, I characterize the lutes of these peoples as folk lutes.

Sandoval also mentions some of Greater Senegambia-Upper Guinea's largest preeminent ethnic groups: the Wolof, the "Mandingas" (Mandinka), the "Soniquies" (Soninke), and the "Fulos" (Fulbe; also Fula, Fulani, Peul, etc.). They also have plucked spike lutes with animal skin-topped, drum-like bodies. These lutes, however, as well as the contexts in which they are played, differ greatly from those of their Atlantic-Bak neighbors. The traditionally stratified societies of these Islamized peoples share similar tripartite caste systems in which music-making is generally considered to be the hereditary purview of griots who belong to the middle artisan caste. In this social context, lute playing is the exclusive domain of griot lutenists, who come from specific families that specialize in the lute. Most griot lutenists play standard griot lutes with semi-spike necks and carved-out narrow wooden bodies (e.g., the Wolof *xalam*, the Mandinka *konting*, the Soninke *geseré*, and the Fulbe *hoddu*).[61]

In reading Sandoval's account of the Guineans playing "guitars," making music, and dancing, the natural assumption would be that, like much of the rest of his discourse on the diversity of African peoples and cultures, Sandoval was relaying data garnered through his desk research since he himself never set foot on the African continent. The vibrant wording of this passage, however, seems to suggest that Sandoval might have been reporting something that he possibly witnessed in Cartagena, rather than merely reiterating secondhand information from Africa. Sandoval's various descriptions of the Africans' great love of music and dance throughout his treatise provide us with a sense of the vital sociocultural and musical milieu throughout the circum-Caribbean in the seventeenth century that fostered and nurtured the birth of the early gourd banjo. We see this in the fact that black Cartagena during this period had a rich cultural life that embodied both transplanted traditions from Africa and new traditions that were emerging through creolization.

At the center of Cartagena's nascent Afro-Creole culture were the *cofradias de negros* (Church-approved Catholic lay confraternities organized by local blacks) and *cabildos* (black mutual-aid societies established to reflect different African ethnicities and/or regions such as Angola, Mandinga, Mina, Carabalí, and Lucumí).[62] As in other Spanish colonies, the city's *cofradias de negros* and *cabildos* featured music and dance of African heritage in their street processions and festivals. African instruments, especially drums, were essential elements in the celebrations and functions of these organizations.[63] In addition, enslaved blacks held social dance gatherings at which were danced the *currulao*[64] or *bunde*. A report from Cartagena in 1770 portrayed the *bunde* as a "very old" dance. It went on to describe the dancers forming a circle in the center of which couples took turns dancing to the accompaniment of drums and singing.[65] The 1770 account from Cartagena is remarkably similar to later descriptions of African American slaves dancing the *calinda* in the French Antilles and similar dances in other colonies, as well as those still danced by their descendants throughout Latin America and the Caribbean. Likewise, it could just as easily be a description of traditional social dancing anywhere in West Africa today.

If Sandoval did indeed observe traditional Senegambian plucked spike lutes being played in Cartagena—either brought directly from West Africa or made in traditional Senegambian style on this side of the Atlantic—it would have been a crucial first as an extremely rare sighting of such instruments in the New World. To date, there has been only one report found in the historical record of an identifiable traditional West African plucked lute sighted in the Americas. In her *Journal of a Voyage to Brazil, and Residence There During Part of the Years 1821, 1822, 1823*

(1824), Maria Graham (1785–1842) reported a plucked lute called a "*Gourmi*" being played at a slave dance gathering in Rio de Janeiro, Brazil, on Sunday, March 3, 1822. She described it as having "more the appearance of a guitar: the hollow gourd is covered with skin; it has a bridge, and there are two strings; it is played with the finger."[66] From her description, it seems that Graham may have observed the calabash-bodied two-string full-spike *gurumi* played by the Hausa, Toubou, and other peoples of Niger and northern Nigeria, which is strummed by flicking the index finger up and down across its strings. This instrument could have also been a similar two-string gourd-bodied full-spike lute of the Hausa called the *gurmi* (also known as the *kumbo*; Nigeria), which is traditionally played with the thumb and index finger in a form of two-finger up-picking.[67]

Yet, in weighing the different possibilities presented by the probability of Sandoval's report being a firsthand account, one stands out: perhaps the cited "guitars" were in actuality early gourd banjos. Unfortunately, we may never know one way or the other on that score as Sandoval simply did not provide us with enough information.

Conclusion

As Dena J. Epstein (1916–2013), whom I call the "mother" of banjo roots research, first stressed: period documents from the historical record, like those of Sloane and Sandoval examined here, are the paper-trail we need follow to piece together a viable narrative of the banjo's origins and historic continuum. In terms of banjo roots research, the account and depiction in Sloane's 1707 book of the Afro-Jamaican "Strum Strumps" he had first observed twenty years earlier stands out as the earliest and one of the best documentations found thus far of instruments that we can recognize as early gourd banjos. Determining the significance of Sandoval's 1627 report, however, requires a bit more effort as its connection to banjo history is not as readily apparent.

Compared to the fuller textual description and remarkably detailed depiction of gourd-bodied Afro-Jamaican plucked lutes in Sloane's *A Voyage to the Islands of Madera, Barbados, Nieves, S. Christophers and Jamaica*, Sandoval's frustratingly brief passing reference to the Senegambians' "guitars" seems far too inadequate and vague to be helpful or useful. The importance of Sandoval's report, however, rests in its value as a lead and springboard for greater contextualization on many levels. First, it is the earliest reference to West African plucked lute playing framed in the context of the transatlantic slave trade. Second, by triangulating Sandoval's observation with his specification of the Gambia-Casamance-Cacheu region of Greater Senegambia along West Africa's Upper Guinea coast as the source of the enslaved captives he references and what we now know of the various ethnic traditions of plucked spike lutes in that area, we can get a better sense of just who "the

Guineans" Sandoval describes were and just what their "guitars" might have been in actuality. Third, the fact that Sandoval was based in Cartagena—Colombia's port city on the Caribbean Sea and the center of the Spanish slave trade during the early seventeenth century—links his observation of the Guineans' "guitars" to the earliest reports of African Americans making and playing early gourd banjos throughout the Caribbean, starting with Sloane's account from Jamaica in the late 1680s. Finally, beyond its importance as a contextualizer, Sandoval's report highlights the need for more investigations of the historical records of South America—and, for that matter, the Spanish Caribbean as well as the New World colonies of Portugal, The Netherlands, and other European countries—in the hope of finding previously unknown evidence of the origins, development, and dissemination of the early gourd banjo.

Notes

1. Sir Hans Sloane, MD, *A Voyage to the Islands of Madera, Barbados, Nieves, S. Christopher and Jamaica*, 2 vols. (London, 1707), 1:xlviii. Republished online by BHL Biodiversity Library, http://www.biodiversitylibrary.org/item/11242, accessed February 27, 2012; Arthur MacGregor, "The Life, Character and Career of Sir Hans Sloane," in his anthology *Sir Hans Sloane: Collector, Scientist, Antiquary* (London: British Museum Press, 1994), 13.

2. Alonso de Sandoval, SJ, *Treatise on Slavery: Selections from De instauranda Aethiopum salute*, ed. and trans. Nicole von Germeten (Indianapolis: Hackett Publishing Company, Inc., 2008), 27–28.

3. "Greater Senegambia" is the West African historian Boubacar Barry's designation for the Western Sudan region of West Africa. It includes present-day Senegal, The Gambia, Mauritania, Mali, Guinea-Bissau, and Guinea. Boubacar Barry, *Senegambia and the Atlantic Slave Trade* (Cambridge: Cambridge University Press, 1988).

4. Henry George Farmer, "Early References to Music in the Western Sūdān," *Journal of the Royal Asiatic Society of Great Britain and Ireland* 4 (October 1939): 569–79; Eric Charry, *Mande Music: Traditional and Modern Music of the Maninka and Mandinka of Western Africa* (Chicago: University of Chicago Press, 2000), 122, 356–58. The word *griot* (pronounced "gree-oh"; originally spelled *guiriot*) made its first appearance in *Relation du voyage du Cap-Verd* (1637) by the French Capuchin missionary Alexis de Saint-Lô (Charry, *Mande Music*, 361–62; Thomas A. Hale, *Griots and Griottes: Masters of Words and Music* [Bloomington: Indiana University Press, 1998], 84–85). It refers to hereditary male music-word artisans who belong to the middle artisan caste in the traditional tripartite societies of certain Islamized West African ethnicities, such as the Mandinka, Maninka, Bamana (Bambara), Wolof, Soninke, Songhai, and Fulbe (Fula, Fulani, Peul, etc.). *Griot lute* is Eric Charry's descriptor for the unique subgroup of West African plucked spike lutes traditionally played exclusively by griot lutenists. Examples include the Wolof *xalam*, the Bamana-Maninka *n'goni*, the Soninke *gambaré*, the Mandinka *kontingo*, the Fulbe *hoddu*, and the Songhai *molo* (also *molooru*).

5. For more on the West African plucked lute family, see in this volume my chapter "Banjo Ancestors: West African Plucked Spike Lutes" and "A List of West African Pluck Spike Lutes," which I co-authored with Greg C. Adams.

6. Sloane to John Ray (1627–1705), November 11, 1684. In this letter to his mentor, Sloane sought Ray's advice on the offer he had just received to accompany the duke and his family to Jamaica as the duke's personal physician. MacGregor, *Sir Hans Sloane*, 12.

7. E. St. John Brooks, *Sir Hans Sloane: The Great Collector and His Circle* (London: The Batchworth Press, 1954), 76: Richard S. Dunn, *Sugar and Slaves: The Rise of the Planter Class in the English West Indies, 1624–1713* (Chapel Hill: University of North Carolina Press, 1972, 2000), 161.

8. Brooks, *Sir Hans Sloane*, 48–49.

9. MacGregor, *Sir Hans Sloane*, 13.

10. Sloane, *A Voyage to the Islands of Madera, Barbados, Nieves, S. Christophers and Jamaica*, xlviii.

11. Ibid., xlix. In her autobiography, *Incidents in the Life of a Slave Girl* (Boston, 1861), the escaped slave Harriet Ann Jacobs (1813–97) described the African American Christmas festivities of her youth in North Carolina. These included the appearance of the "Johnkannaus," which were "companies of slaves from the plantations" that featured "two athletic men, in calico wrappers, [who] have a net thrown over them, covered with all manner of bright-colored stripes. Cows' tails are fastened to their backs, and their heads are decorated with horns" (179–80).

12. For more on Jamaica's Jonkonnu and other masquerading and festival traditions, see E. A. Clarke, "The John Canoe Festival in Jamaica," *Folklore* 38, no. 1 (March 31, 1927): 72–75; see also Robert Farris Thompson's "Charters for the Spirit: Afro-Jamaican Music and Art," 89–101; Barbaro Martinez-Ruiz's "Sketches of Memory: Visual Encounters with Africa in Jamaican Culture," 102–19; and Kenneth Bilby's "More Than Met the Eye: African-Jamaican Festivities in the Time of Belisario," 120–35, in *Art and Emancipation in Jamaica: Isaac Mendes Belisario and His Worlds*, ed. Tim Barringer, Gillian Forrester, and Barbaro Martinez-Ruiz (New Haven, CT: Yale Center for British Art in association with Yale University Press, 2007).

13. Present-day Benin (Dahomey) should not be confused with the Benin Empire (Bini [Edo], Igodomigodo; 1440–1897), which was actually located in southern Nigeria. Jacob U. Egharevba, *A Short History of Benin* (Ibadan, Nigeria: Ibadan University Press. 1960).

14. During the transatlantic slave trade, Dahomey and its neighbors along the Bight of Benin—the southern coastal region of present-day Togo to Dahomey's west and to its east, Yorubaland in southwestern Nigeria—constituted what was then known as the Slave Coast. For one of the most comprehensive, up-to-date discussions of the ethnic origins of the millions of African captives transported to the New World during the transatlantic slave trade, see Gwendolyn Midlo Hall, *Slavery and African Ethnicities in the Americas: Restoring the Links* (Chapel Hill: University of North Carolina Press, 2005).

15. Sloane, *A Voyage to the Islands of Madera, Barbados, Nieves, S. Christophers and Jamaica*, l.

16. Charry, *Mande Music*, 72.

17. Sloane, *A Voyage to the Islands of Madera, Barbados, Nieves, S. Christophers and Jamaica*, xlviii–xlix.

18. MacGregor, *Sir Hans Sloane*, 294.

19. J. C. H. King, "Ethnographic Collections: Collecting in the Context of Sloane's Catalogue of 'Miscellanies,'" in MacGregor, *Sir Hans Sloane*, 241n68.

20. For more on these instruments, see in this volume my chapter co-authored with Greg C. Adams, "Changing Perspectives on the Banjo's African American Origins and West African Heritage."

21. Abby Aldrich Rockefeller Folk Art Center, Colonial Williamsburg Foundation, 35.301.3. For more on *The Old Plantation*, see in this volume my chapter "The Banjar Pictured: The Depiction of the African American Early Gourd Banjo in *The Old Plantation*, South Carolina, 1780s."

22. Farmer, "Early References to Music in the Western Sūdān," 569–79. My thanks to Ulf Jägfors for first making me aware of this print in 2004. It was Jägfors who first recognized that it was a hand-drawn sketch of plate III. Farmer's descriptor "Western Sūdān" was the then current European designation for West Africa and not a reference to the East African country of Sudan. The term *Sudan* comes from the expression, *Bilad al-Sudan* (literally "The Land of the Blacks"), the original Arabic descriptor for West Africa. The western regions of West Africa—in particular, Greater Senegambia—began to be called the Western Sudan in the late nineteenth century. In 1920, Western Sudan became the official designation for French West Africa (1895–1960), which included France's colonial possessions throughout the region: present-day Mauritania, Mali, Senegal, Guinea, Côte d'Ivoire, Burkina Faso, Benin, and Niger. Today the term *Western Sudan* is used to refer to the western half of West Africa, Greater Senegambia: Mauritania, Mali, Senegal, The Gambia, Guinea-Bissau, and Guinea. Alice L. Conklin, *A Mission to Civilize: The Republican Idea of Empire in France and West Africa, 1895–1930* (Stanford, CA: Stanford University Press, 1997), xiii.

23. *Pandore* is actually a French designation for the *bandora* or *pandora*, a cittern-like, metal-strung plucked lute, with a distinctive scalloped outline body design, the invention of which is attributed to John Rose of London in 1562. Ian Harwood and Lyle Nordstrom, "Bandora," in *The Grove Dictionary of Musical Instruments: Second Edition*, ed. Laurence Libin, 5 vols. (Oxford: Oxford University Press 2014), 1:218–19. It is not clear why Farmer latched onto *pandore* as a designation for West African plucked spike lutes since there is no discernable resemblance or historical connection between these instruments and the *bandora*. One possible source for Farmer's usage of the term is *The Golden Trade or A Discovery of the River Gambra and the Golden Trade of the Aethiopians* (1623), the English explorer Richard Jobson's account of his 1620–21 expedition down the Gambia River in Greater Senegambia. In describing the string instruments played by the griots he encountered, Jobson stated that they resembled "in some sort, our Bandora" (Richard Jobson, *The Golden Trade* [London: The Penguin Press, 1932], 144).

24. Farmer, "Early References to Music in the Western Sūdān," 579.

25. Ibid.

26. MacGregor, *Sir Hans Sloane*, 16.

27. Another period image that might also depict a possible three-string early gourd banjo is that of Benjamin Latrobe (1764–1820), the architect famed for designing the United States Capitol. In his journal account of an "assembly of negroes" he observed during his stay in New Orleans in 1819, Latrobe included a drawing he made of a "stringed instrument, which no doubt was imported from Africa." It had a "calabash" body and "on top of the finger board was a rude figure of a man in a sitting posture, and two pegs behind him to which the strings were fastened" (Benjamin Latrobe, *The Journal of Latrobe: The Notes and Sketches of an Architect, Naturalist and Traveler in the United States from 1796 to 1820* [New York: D. Appleton and Company, 1905; reprint Carlisle, MA: Applewood Books, 2007], 179–80). Latrobe's textual reference to the two pegs would seem to imply that this lute must have been two-stringed. However, in his hand-drawn sketch of "the most curious instrument," we see three strings. Latrobe depicts all three strings as being long and of the same length, yet he only shows the two pegs to receive the strings. One

possible explanation for this puzzling paradox could be that the top third string might have actually been a short thumb-string. Latrobe might not have perceived it as such if the string had been attached to a third peg that had been inserted into the back of the neck, as in the early banjo back-to-front thumb-string insertion I describe above.

28. A *tanpura* (also *tanpuri, tambura, tamburi*, etc.) is a type of drone lute with a large gourd body found in many variations throughout South Asia. These are plucked lutes used primarily for accompaniment, on which the instrument's strings are played open and unstopped to produce a constant drone. Alastair Dick, "Tambūrā," in *The Grove Dictionary of Musical Instruments: Second Edition*, ed. Laurence Libin, 5 vols. (Oxford: Oxford University Press, 2014), 4:701–3.

In comparing traditional South Asian *tanpuras* to the oval-bodied "Strum Strump" (SS 1.1.) in Sloane's book illustration, they look nothing alike. While *tanpuras* and SS 1.1. both have bodies made from oval bottleneck gourds, the gourds typically used to make *tanpuras* are much larger and shaped differently from the one used for SS 1.1.'s body. The gourds most often used to make the bodies of *tanpuras* are very wide on the horizontal axis, so that the instrument can rest on the gourd's wide bottom for the *tanpura*'s most common playing position: the player seated on the floor to play the instrument upright. Accordingly, on these gourds the stub of the fruit's severed bottleneck points upward from the center of the gourd, which enables the *tanpura*'s neck, built on the stub, to be positioned upright. Conversely, the gourd of SS 1.1. is much narrower and smaller. Furthermore, SS 1.1.'s gourd's bottleneck stub—like that of SS 2.2.'s gourd—is aligned horizontally for the more typical plucked lute playing position. Also, whereas a *tanpura*'s neck is built on its gourd's bottleneck stub so the joint appears seamless, on both "Strum Strumps" the bottleneck's stub serves as a discernable wide sleeve for the instrument's narrower wooden neck.

29. Richard C. Rath, "African Music in Seventeenth-Century Jamaica: Cultural Transit and Transition," *The William and Mary Quarterly*, 3rd Ser., 50, no. 4 (October 1993): figure II, 704. Rath's identifications of the two "Strum Strumps" was entirely conjectural. He based them on his own speculative analysis of the 1707 plate III illustration and interpretation of its Latin caption, as well as, in the case of SS 2.2., his musical analysis of the melody entitled "Angola," one of Sloane's three musical examples (Rath to Pestcoe, email, July 19, 2010).

30. Sloane, *A Voyage to the Islands of Madera, Barbados, Nieves, S. Christophers and Jamaica*, xlvi. By 1515, Jamaica's indigenous Taino population was all but wiped out. Consequently, the island's Spanish colonists imported Amerindian slaves to work their *encomiendas* (estates) from all around the circum-Caribbean. British colonists continued this practice after 1655, when Jamaica was seized by England. Irving Rouse, *The Tainos: Rise and Decline of the People Who Greeted Columbus* (New Haven, CT: Yale University Press, 1992), 156–57.

31. Sloane, *A Voyage to the Islands of Madera, Barbados, Nieves, S. Christophers and Jamaica*, xlvii, xx.

32. Ibid., liv.

33. Ibid., xlvii.

34. Ibid., xlix.

35. For examples of Taino decorative designs, see Rouse, *The Tainos*.

36. For examples of the "*X*s and lines" pattern ornamentation on West African instruments, see Jacqueline Cogdell DjeDje, ed., *Turn Up The Volume! A Celebration of African Music* (Los Angeles: UCLA Fowler Museum of Culture, 1999), "Part Three: Catalog," 254–55, 257, 259, 273, 328, 331.

37. Germeten, "Introduction," in *Treatise on Slavery*, ix–xi; see also Mayra E. Beer, "Alonso de Sandoval: Seventeenth-Century Merchant of the Gospel, Aethiopia praeveniet manus eius Deo," http://www.kislakfoundation.org/prize/199702.html, accessed October 25, 2017.

38. Enriqueta Vila Vilar, "Introduction," in Alonso de Sandoval, *Un tratado sobre la esclavitud* (Madrid: Alianza Editorial, 1987), 31, cited in Beer, "Alonso de Sandoval."

39. Hugh Thomas, *The Slave Trade: The Story of the Atlantic Slave Trade, 1440–1870* (New York: Simon & Schuster Paperbacks, 1997), 434–35.

40. Vila Vilar, "Introduction," in *Un tratado sobre la esclavitud*, 18, 27–31. Quoted in Germeten's introduction in *Treatise on Slavery*, x.

41. Vincent P. Franklin, "Alonso De Sandoval and the Jesuit Conception of the Negro," *The Journal of Negro History* 58, no. 3 (July 1973): 351.

42. Beer, "Alonso de Sandoval."

43. Sandoval, *Treatise on Slavery*, 8.

44. Ibid., 11.

45. Hall, *Slavery and African Ethnicities*, 80–82; Walter Rodney, *A History of the Upper Guinea Coast, 1545–1800* (New York: Monthly Review Press, 1970).

46. Sandoval, *Treatise on Slavery*, 25.

47. Peter Mark, *"Portuguese" Style and Luso-African Identity: Precolonial Senegambia, Sixteenth-Nineteenth Centuries* (Bloomington: Indiana University Press, 2002), 2, 34.

48. Sandoval, *Treatise on Slavery*, 27.

49. Ibid., 27–28.

50. In Sandoval's time, the designation *Spanish guitar* referred specifically to the guitar with five courses (pairs of strings) of gut strings, which first emerged in Spain in the 1550s and quickly spread to the rest of Western Europe. It was preceded by the four-course *guitarra* of the Renaissance (ca. fourteenth to the seventeenth centuries), which was contemporaneous with another popular Spanish plucked lute, the figure-8-shaped six-course *vihuela* (the guitar-like counterpart of the bowl-backed, short-necked Western lute). By the end of the sixteenth century, however, both instruments were overshadowed by the five-course guitar, which would become the guitar of the baroque period (ca. 1600–1750) throughout Europe. The five-course guitar was referenced as the "Spanish guitar" until the end of the eighteenth century, though in Spain itself the favored guitar from the 1780s on through the early 1800s was a new type with six courses. Starting in the 1770s, the earliest forms of the modern guitar with six individual strings began to appear in France and Italy. The six-string guitar came to Spain around 1820, leading to the birth of the modern classical and flamenco guitars. From the early twentieth century on, as the diversity of the emerging modern guitar family expanded exponentially, the term *Spanish guitar* came to refer to six-string instruments with conventional guitar necks. For more on the history and development of the guitar, see Tom and Mary Evans, *Guitars: Music, History, Construction and Players from the Renaissance to Rock* (New York: Facts On File, 1977).

51. Sandoval, *Treatise on Slavery*, 42.

52. In Congo and Angola, the terms *banza* and *m'banza* have also been used historically to indicate a village, town, or city.

53. Dena J. Epstein, *Sinful Tunes and Spirituals: Black Folk Music to the Civil War* (Urbana: University of Illinois Press, 1977, 2003), 24, 30–38.

54. Also referred to as *bow-lute* (not to be confused with *bowed lute*, which is another term for *fiddle*), pluriarcs are found in West Africa, West-Central Africa, and southwestern Africa. For more on pluriarcs, see Gerhard Kubik, "Pluriarc," in *The Grove Dictionary of*

Musical Instruments: Second Edition, ed. Laurence Libin, 5 vols. (Oxford: Oxford University Press, 2014), 4:142–43, and the chapter "Die Bogenlauten" (The Bow-Lute) in Ulrich Wegner's *Afrikanische Saiteninstrumente* (Berlin: Staatliche Museen Preußischer Kulturbesitz, 1984), 82–92.

55. For more on the *akam*, see *The Metropolitan Museum of Art, Hand-Book No. 13: Preliminary Catalogue of the Crosby-Brown Collection of Musical Instruments of All Nations, 111, Part I. Africa, Gallery 37* (New York: The Metropolitan Museum of Art, 1907), 12–13.

56. Cavazzi, published as plate 20 in Ezio Bassani's *Un Cappuccino nell'Africa nera del seicento: I disegni dei Manoscritti Araldi del Padre Giovanni Antonio Cavazzi da Montecuccolo* (Milan: Quaderni Poro, no. 4, 1987); republished online as *Iron Working, Kingdom of Kongo, 1670s*, Image Reference Bassani-20, www.slaveryimages.org, accessed October 25, 2017, compiled by Jerome Handler and Michael Tuite, sponsored by the Virginia Foundation for the Humanities and the University of Virginia. For more on Cavazzi and the Araldi Manuscript, see John K. Thornton's blog site *Central African History*, "Introduction to the Araldi Manuscript" (August 19, 2008), http://centralafricanhistory.blogspot .com/2008/08/giovanni-antonio-cavazzi-da.html, accessed October 25, 2017.

57. Sandoval, *Treatise on Slavery*, 13. Gambia's Cabo de Santa Maria (known today as Cape Point) is situated at the mouth of the Gambia River. Cacheu is a port town on the southern banks of the Cacheu River in northwestern Guinea-Bissau. Founded in the 1580s, it was an important Luso-African trading center and embarkation point for enslaved captives bound for the New World (Mark, *"Portuguese" Style and Luso-African Identity*, 42).

58. Robert M. Baum, *Shrines of the Slave Trade: Diola Religion and Society in Precolonial Senegambia* (New York: Oxford University Press, 1999), 62–107, 253; James S. Olson, *The Peoples of Africa: An Ethnohistorical Dictionary* (Westport, CT: Greenwood Press, 1996), 255–56. See also Walter Hawthorne, *Planting Rice and Harvesting Slaves: Transformations along the Guinea-Bissau Coast, 1400–1900* (Portsmouth, NH: Heinemann, 2003), and idem, *From Africa to Brazil: Culture, Identity, and an Atlantic Slave Trade, 1600–1830* (Cambridge: Cambridge University Press, 2010). Mark points out that the earliest appearance in print of the ethnonym *Jola-Diola* was as "Guiola" in Geoffroy de Villeneuve's *L'Afrique* (1814) (Mark, *"Portuguese" Style and Luso-African Identity*, 109). Sandoval also cites "Fulupo called Boote" (Hall, *Slavery and African Ethnicities*, 80) These were the *Baiotes* (also *Bayots*; Crioulo, "men of the rice nursery"), a Floup subgroup in the Ziguinchor region of Casamance especially noted for their skills as rice farmers (Hawthorne, *Planting Rice and Harvesting Slaves*, 156; Olson, *The Peoples of Africa*, 83).

59. Walter Hawthorne to Pestcoe, email, February 24, 2012.

60. My term *Atlantic-Bak cluster* references the fact that all of these peoples' languages belong to the Bak subgroup of West Africa's Atlantic linguistic family, which, in turn, is a subdivision of the greater Niger-Congo family of sub-Saharan African languages.

61. For more on griot culture and music, as well as the traditional role and status of griots in certain traditional West African cultures and societies, see Charry's *Mande Music* and Hale's *Griots and Griottes*.

62. For more on these designations for African ethnicities, see Hall, *Slavery and African Ethnicities in the Americas*. The Mina were a people from the Slave Coast (present-day Togo and Benin) on West Africa's Lower Guinea coast along the Bight of Benin, sandwiched between the Gold Coast (present-day Ghana) and Yorubaland (southwestern Nigeria) (Hall, *Slavery and African Ethnicities in the Americas*, 112–25). "Carabalí" refers to Afri-

cans from the eighteenth-century Kingdom of Calabar, which was based in southeastern Nigeria and extended to western Cameroon and the island of Fernando Pó (Bioko) in the Bight of Biafara (116). "Lucumí" denotes Yoruba slaves, primarily from southwestern Nigeria; the term apparently comes from the Yoruba expression *O luku mi* meaning "my friend."

63. Peter Wade, *Blackness and Race Mixture: The Dynamics of Racial Identity in Colombia* (Baltimore: Johns Hopkins University Press, 1995), 88–89.

64. Ibid., 275. In Cartagena de Indias during the seventeenth century, the term *currulao* referred specifically to a dance of enslaved blacks. Today it denotes a genre of Afro-Colombian dance found on Colombia's Pacific coast that features the *marimba* (xylophone), *cununos* (conical drums), *bombos* (double-headed drums), and *quasás* (bamboo tube rattles), all of which are of African heritage.

65. Ibid. Whereas *bunde* was also once a term for a black dance, now it specifically refers to traditional funeral songs found in Colombia's Pacific coastal region.

66. Maria Graham, *Journal of a Voyage to Brazil, and Residence There During Part of the Years 1821, 1822, 1823* (London, 1824; reprint BiblioBazar: Charleston, SC, 2007), 190.

67. For more on the *gurumi*, see Nathaniel Berndt's web article, "Malam Maman Barka," http://www.beautysaloonmusic.com/, accessed February 27, 12. For the *gurmi*, see David W. Ames and Anthony V. King, *Glossary of Hausa Music and Its Social Context* (Evanston, IL: Northwestern University Press, 1971), 43–44.

CHAPTER 8

"Finding" the Haitian *Banza*

Saskia Willaert

Editor's Headnote

For both "'Finding' the Haitian Banza*" and "The Haitian* Banza *and the American Banjo Lineage"*

Extant early gourd banjos are extremely rare, so finding one that had been previously "unknown" (it had, in fact, been in a Parisian museum, but in two pieces that were stored separately) was a major event to those interested in the history of the banjo. With the Haitian banza*, we now had a second actual example of the early gourd banjo to study, helping us to better understand the development of the early gourd banjo in the Caribbean—a physical embodiment of the kind of instrument that is discussed in several other chapters in this book. Just as the Haitian* banza *was found in two pieces, the discussion of it here has two segments, by two different authors. Saskia Willaert, a curator at the Musical Instruments Museum in Brussels who was asked to prepare a showcase presenting the African precursors of the banjo as part of a larger banjo exhibit, tells the story of how the Haitian* banza *was "rediscovered" to become part of that exhibit. Pete Ross, banjo historian and banjo maker, then tells us in his chapter of his trip to Brussels to measure, photograph, and draw the physical instrument, and to describe in technical detail how it compares to the few early images we have of the early gourd banjo and to the earliest commercially made banjos in North America.*

At the beginning of 2003, the Musical Instruments Museum in Brussels made preparations to mount a banjo exhibition.[1] Part of the exhibition was to be devoted to the African precursors of the American banjo. West African lutes have a number of features that link them specifically to American banjos. They have a body over which a skin is stretched and into which a neck is fixed, and many have a short string—an open string that is plucked with the right-hand thumb, thus allowing for a continuous drone note, pitched higher than the other strings.[2]

We searched for material that would illustrate the existence of African lute-like instruments in the Caribbean region, to the shores of which black slaves arrived from the seventeenth century on. We made a request to our colleagues at the Musée de la Musique to lend a *banza* (see figure K), mentioned in their online inventory. The name of the instrument and its origin in Haiti sounded promising.[3] Its construction (a gourd, with a flat neck protruding the body) resembled that in the earliest known illustration of the banjo: an engraving of two "Strum Strumps" and a bridge harp (see figure H) from Sir Hans Sloane's *A Voyage to the Islands of Madera, Barbados, Nieves, S. Christophers and Jamaica*, written in 1688 and published in London in 1707.[4]

Not much was known about this Haitian lute. The *banza* is part of the Fonds Victor Schœlcher and entered the Paris museum in November 1872, together with twenty-two other African, Asian, and American instruments.[5] Philippe Bruguière, curator of the ethnic instruments in the Paris museum, remembered well having put together neck and body, which were preserved in two different boxes.[6] He relates that, when in 1990 the Paris museum moved from rue de Madrid to Parc de la Villette, it was discovered that the *banza* had deteriorated over the course of time. Consequently, the neck and the gourd were put in separate boxes (the gourd being put apart with other fragile and/or soft items) and were wrapped up in silk paper. An inventory list, dated November 1993, mentions the *banza* being taken from its boxes to be treated against insects and moisture. The neck and gourd were then put back in their respective boxes until 1997, when Bruguière gave the instrument its current place in the non-Western collection.

When its inclusion in the Brussels banjo exhibition was announced in September 2003, the *banza* caused quite a stir within the American banjo world, slightly to the amazement of the Brussels and Paris curators. Dr. Allen Feldman, cultural anthropologist, professor at New York University, and banjo aficionado, replied to the news: "Before we all get lost in technical discussion, can we just take a minute and recognize that this is a bloody beautiful instrument, a work of art; I was very moved to see the pictures [from the Paris online catalogue]."[7] Banjo researchers such as Ulf Jägfors, Bob Carlin, and Pete Ross stressed the importance of the "discovery" of the *banza*. The instrument was said to be a missing link in the history and evolution of the plucked lute from the *qunburi* at the Malinese court in the fourteenth century, spotted by Ibn Battuta during his stay there in 1352, to current North American banjos.[8]

The *banza* is the second eldest dateable banjo artifact found so far. The oldest known banjo was made in the early 1770s in "Netherlands Guiana" (Suriname). This *creole bania* (see figure J) was taken by the British-Dutch captain John Gabriel Stedman to Holland and entered the Leyden National Museum of Ethnology collection in 1777.[9] The instrument, now listed in the Leyden collection as the "Creole Bania," might have been made at Stedman's request to be taken to Europe as a decorative souvenir from the black inhabitants of Suriname amid whom the captain had been living.[10] Small S-shaped soundholes meticulously cut in the sides of the gourd and a decorative pegbox scroll cut out in the tradition of a Western violin along with the absence of finger wear suggest that this instrument was made to be looked at and never played.

The Haitian *banza*, on the other hand, has clearly been played; traces of finger wear are evident in the lower registers of the neck. On the skin head of the *banza* is written in black ink, maybe by Victor Schœlcher himself, who brought the instrument from Haiti to France: "Banza, imitation of an African instrument widely used by the black people of Haiti."[11]

Victor Schœlcher (1804–93) was a French politician, writer, traveler, and collector. Smitten with the French Revolution ideas of liberty and equality, he became a tireless champion for the slaves of the French territories. As undersecretary of state in 1848, he wrote, and succeeded in passing, the law abolishing slavery in the French colonies.[12] Apart from being a republican idealist, Schœlcher was a music lover as well. Living in exile in London in the 1850s—he had been banned from France in 1851 by King Louis Napoléon Bonaparte—he published in 1857 his *Life of Handel*, a landmark in the history of Handel studies, being the first biography of the composer to be based on solid documentary research.[13]

In 1840–41, Schœlcher traveled to the Caribbean to report on life conditions of black people. After having visited Guadeloupe, Martinique, Jamaica, and Dominique, he traveled to Haiti and then proceeded to Puerto Rico. He was back in Europe by the end of 1841, loaded with boxes filled with objects bought in the Caribbean from planters, in small villages and in local markets. Schœlcher carefully classified these witnesses of Caribbean daily life before handing them over to libraries and museums. On November 11, 1872, he donated his ethnic instruments to the Conservatoire de Musique.[14] According to Félix Raugel in the *Musik in Geschichte und Gegenwart* edition of 1965, "every sample of musical life as practiced by the black race is represented in [Schœlcher's] collection, including the favourite instruments of the American Negro."[15] Today these instruments are housed in the Musée de la Musique in Paris and are still central to the historical section of the non-European collections there.

Notes

I would like to thank Gérard De Smaele, who instigated the banjo exhibition at the Musical Instruments Museum; Pete Ross and Simon Egan for revising my text; and Ulf Jägfors, Philippe Bruguière, and Shlomo Pestcoe for their banjo expertise.

1. The exhibition *Banjo!* was prepared by Gérard De Smaele, an external contributor to the Musical Instruments Museum, a Belgian banjoist, and the author of two monographs on the five-string banjo. His extensive contacts in the American banjo community enhanced the narrative of the exhibition as a whole and the interpretation of the Haitian *banza*. His recent *Banjo Attitudes* (Paris: L'Harmattan, 2015) is an extension of that exhibition.

2. These links are especially clear in the *ekonting* from Senegambia, the West African plucked lute most thoroughly researched to date, which is considered to be one of the direct forerunners of the banjo. In addition to the round body over which a skin is stretched and the short string, the *ekonting* has a neck that runs right through the body and protrudes from its lower part and a bridge with feet that sits on the surface of the vellum. Additionally, the neck of the *ekonting* is made from a type of papyrus called *bangoe* in the local Mandinka language. See also Ulf Jägfors, "The African Akonting and the Origin of the Banjo," *The Old-Time Herald* 9 (November 2003–2004): 26–33 as well as Shlomo Pestcoe and Greg C. Adams, "Changing Perspectives on the Banjo's African American Origins and West African Heritage," and Greg C. Adams and Chuck Levy, "The Down-Stroke Connection: Comparing Techniques Between the Jola *Ekonting* and the Five-String Banjo," in this volume.

3. As Shlomo Pestcoe points out in "'Strum Strumps' and 'Sheepskin' Guitars: The Early Gourd Banjo and Clues to its West African Roots in the Seventeenth-Century Circum-Caribbean" in this volume, *banza* was the most common appellation for the early gourd banjo in the French colonies in the Caribbean. See also, for example, Jean-Benjamin de la Borde, who in 1780 writes in his *Essai sur la musique ancienne et moderne* (1:291): "Banzas. Instrument des Nègres d'Amérique, est une espece de Guittare à quatre cordes."

4. For images of the Haiti *banza* and the engraving from the Sloane book, see figures K and H. The Jamaican bridge harp on this engraving is very similar to the *seperewa*, a bridge harp from the Akan people in present-day Ghana, and to the *aloko*, a bridge harp from the Baule people in Côte d'Ivoire (see, for example, the online catalogue of the Brussels Musical Instruments Museum, inv. 1984.040). I would like to thank Ulf Jägfors for suggesting the *seperewa* link.

5. See the online catalogue of the Musée de la Musique, Paris, http://mediatheque .cite-musique.fr/masc/?url=/clientbooklineCIMU/toolkit/p_requests/default-collection -musee.htm, accessed November 12, 2017.

6. I would like to thank Philippe Bruguière for his collaboration in the finding of the *banza*.

7. Allen Feldman, email message to me and two dozen mostly American banjo experts, September 28, 2003.

8. See Ibn Battuta, *Voyages. III. Inde, Extrême-Orient, Espagne et Soudan* (1858), trans. C. Defremery and B. R. Sanguinetti (Paris: La Découverte, 1997), 417. For more on the Ibn Battuta citation, see Shlomo Pestcoe, "Banjo Ancestors: West African Plucked Spike Lutes" in this volume.

9. Stedman had arrived in Suriname in 1772, taking part in a military expedition made up of foreign volunteers, to suppress upheavals from local slaves in the Dutch colony. For a full account on John Stedman, see Richard and Sally Price, *Stedman's Surinam: Life in an Eighteenth-Century Slave Society. An Abridged, Modernized Edition of "Narrative of a Five Years Expedition against the Revolted Negroes of Surinam" by John Gabriel Stedman* (Baltimore: Johns Hopkins University Press, 1992).

10. See John G. Stedman, *Narrative of a Five Years Expedition against the Revolted Negroes of Surinam from the year 1772 to 1777* (London: J. Johnson and T. Payne, 1796). According to Price and Price, the instrument was "collected by Stedman from a slave in Suriname" (see Price and Price, *Stedman's Surinam*, xxiv). The Stedman *creole bania* is also discussed in Pete Ross, "The Haiti *Banza* and the American Banjo Lineage," and in Pestcoe and Adams, "Changing Perspectives on the Banjo's African American Origins

and West African Heritage," both in this volume. For an image of the *creole bania*, see figure J.

11. "Banza imitation d'un instrument africain / d'usage general parmi les no[irs?] d'Haiti." For a detailed description of the instrument, see the following chapter by Pete Ross. See also Mia Awouters, ed., *Banjo !* (catalogue of the banjo exhibition, Muziekinstrumentenmuseum Brussels, October 16, 2003–February 15, 2004), Brussels, 27.

12. See Richard G. King, "Schoelcher, Victor," in *The New Grove Dictionary of Music and Musicians*, ed. Stanley Sadie, 29 vols. (London: Macmillan, 2001), 22:576–77.

13. See Nelly Schmidt, *Victor Schœlcher en son temps. Images et Témoignages* (Paris: Maisonneuve Et Larose, 1998), 84.

14. See King, "Schoelcher, Victor," 22:576–77, and Schmidt, *Victor Schœlcher en son temps*, 33. Apart from the *banza*, his gift to the Conservatoire included two other Haitian instruments: a rattle and a *sanza*. See the online catalogue of the Paris Musée de la Musique, E.432 and E.429.

15. Félix Raugel, "Victor Schœlcher," in *Musik in Geschichte und Gegenwart*, ed. Friedrich Blume, 17 vols. (Kassel-Basel: Bärenreiter Metzler, 1965), 12:17: "jede Art von Musikausübung der schwarzen Rasse ist in dieser S[amm]l[un]g vertreten, die auch die Lieblingsinstr[umenten] der amer[ikanischen] Neger enthält."

CHAPTER 9

The Haitian *Banza* and the American Banjo Lineage

Pete Ross

One morning in January 2004, Saskia Willaert opened the door for Ulf Jägfors and me to the restoration laboratories of the Musical Instruments Museum, Brussels, Belgium. We were to begin our examination of the Holy Grail of early banjo research, an actual example of a 165-year-old African American–made gourd banjo. Jägfors is a banjo researcher who traveled from Sweden to document this rare musical instrument. I am a researcher and builder of gourd banjos, and I had flown into Brussels the evening before from my home in Baltimore, Maryland. This instrument is so important and rare that the two of us had been eager to travel great distances for a chance to examine it.

We paused for a moment to savor our first view of the instrument (see figure K). It sat on a plain laboratory table. Well-loved and long-played before having been collected in 1840, it was musty, dusty, damaged, and a great contrast to its sterile, fluorescent white and brushed steel laboratory surroundings.

As unprepossessing as this nearly lost instrument may be to many, my examinations revealed an instrument not only connected to the banjo's African roots, but to a longstanding gourd banjo tradition in the Americas. As I examined the banjo, it became evident that this particular gourd banjo tradition was the one that gave birth to the well-known banjo of the present-day United States.

The fact that the banjo's origins lay in Africa is becoming well known. Dozens of written accounts, along with several illustrations, describe the instrument as being made and played by enslaved African Americans. Typical of these accounts is this one given by Johann David Schoepf in 1784: "Another musical instrument of the true negro is the Banjah. Over a hollow calabash (Cucurb lagenaria L.) is stretched a sheepskin, lengthened with a neck, strung with 4 strings, and made accordant. . . . In America and on the islands they make use of this instrument greatly for the dance."[1] The great number of similar accounts suggests that the banjo was very common in the Americas from colonial times onward.[2]

However, despite more than twenty years of research between us, this was the first chance we had had to examine one of these once-common early gourd

Figure 9.1. Gourd banjo; William Esperance Boucher Jr., courtesy of the Metropolitan Museum of Art, www.metmuseum.org, accessed January 26, 2016.

banjos. In 1993, I made a detailed examination of a gourd banjo in the collection of the Metropolitan Museum of Art in New York City (figure 9.1).

Although the prime inspiration to many now building gourd banjos, the instrument turned out to be a sort of Frankenstein creation that did not begin life as an authentic gourd banjo. This instrument was a commercially made banjo with a wooden drum body, built around 1845 in the Baltimore shop of William Boucher Jr. The original wooden drum shell body had been crudely replaced with a gourd. From this instrument, we can draw no certain conclusions about the typical gourd banjo as made by enslaved people in the antebellum United States.

While at the Musical Instruments Museum, Jägfors and I also had an opportunity to view the *creole bania* (see figure J), which was on loan for the same exhibit that contained the Haitian *banza*. This instrument is held in the collections of the Rijksmuseum voor Volkenkunde, Leiden, Holland, and was collected in Suriname ca. 1770 by John Gabriel Stedman. Unlike the instrument at the Met, the *creole bania* began life as an actual gourd banjo. With a calabash body, a skin soundboard, and four strings, it fits the description of the instrument in Schoepf's account.[3] Unfortunately, a close comparison of this South American banjo with early images from the United States shows that Stedman's banjo resembles North American banjos in only the most general sense. The *bania* is a wonderful example of an early banjo, but we cannot reliably say how similar it is to the ancestors of the modern banjo as they existed in the eighteenth-century North American colonies.

Jägfors and I have both also spent time examining the African cousins of the banjo, which are still played today. Jägfors has made repeated trips to West Africa to examine current instruments in the regions and among the ethnic groups from which many of the enslaved in the New World were taken. This research has been illuminating, but as with the case of the Stedman banjo it has not provided us with a clear lineage leading to the early North American banjo. Though early American gourd banjos retain significant elements from the African instruments, early images portray American instruments that depart considerably from their African cousins.

In fact, two early images indicate a longstanding gourd banjo tradition unique to the Americas. In *Sinful Tunes and Spirituals*, Dena J. Epstein suggests a kinship between the Jamaican "Strum Strumps" illustrated in Sir Hans Sloane's 1707 book *A Voyage to the Islands of Madera, Barbados, Nieves, S. Christophers and Jamaica* (see figure H) and the banjo-like instrument in the late eighteenth-century South Carolina folk painting *The Old Plantation* (see figure P). Both instruments have gourd bodies and skin soundboards, similar to those of known West African instruments.[4]

However, many of the features shared by the two instruments in these two images are also what distinguishes them from known African instruments. Instead of the roughly rounded dowel neck of African instruments, both instruments have broad flat necks. Both of the illustrated instruments have wooden, friction tuning pegs instead of the leather thong tuners of West African instruments (see figure D for the leather thong tuners). In African instruments, the neck generally sits in a notch in the top edge of the gourd body, or on the top edge without a notch, and is bound there by the skin that also forms the instrument's soundboard (figure 9.2).

However, in both of the illustrated New World instruments, the neck enters the gourd body in a way not seen in any African instruments, and the soundboard skin is not integral to the neck-to-body joint. The geographical distance, as well as that of time, between the two illustrated instruments suggests a firmly ingrained, longstanding banjo-building tradition among Africans transplanted to the New World that differs significantly from the tradition as it is known in Africa.

The instrument we had traveled to examine, the Haitian *banza*, adds another forty years to that uniquely American tradition. Collected in Haiti in 1840, the *banza*'s resemblance to Sloane's "Strum Strumps" and the banjo in *The Old Plantation* painting is remarkable, placing the Haitian *banza* within this particular banjo lineage.

The body of the Haitian *banza* is made from a gourd and is about 10 1/2 inches long and 7 inches wide. The instrument has been roughly worked. Scraps of the gourd's outer skin, which usually get moldy and are scraped off, are still in

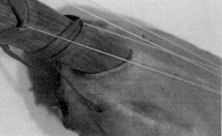

Figure 9.2. Neck-body joint in Gambian *ekonting* and Malian *n'goni* close-ups; photos courtesy of Greg C. Adams.

Figure 9.3. Haitian *banza* neck-to-gourd joint details. All Haitian *banza* photos herein were taken by the author and are used with the permission of the Musée de la Musique, Paris; this combination will hereafter be represented merely by the phrase "courtesy of author."

place. The opening for the drumhead-soundboard is oblong, 7 inches long by 6 1/2 inches wide, and cut so as to create an unusual concave (rather than flat) soundboard. The skin was originally attached with coarse, cut tacks that were later covered over with a ribbon and round-headed upholstery tacks. The side of the gourd has been cut away for the drumhead, rather than the stemmed top. The neck at the top of the gourd, where it originally attached to the parent plant's vine, is still in place. Only the end of this nub has been removed, leaving a short tube of sorts at one end of the gourd. It is from this tube that the instrument's wooden neck emerges (figure 9.3). Although no West African string instruments are configured this way, this is exactly the way both Sloane's 1707 "Strum Strumps" and *The Old Plantation* banjo are depicted (figure 9.4).

When the instrument is made this way, it almost ends up resembling Indian lutes, like the sitar. Two early written references, again cited by Epstein, describe banjos as being made with this neck to body assemblage. Fr. Richard de Tussac, writing on the New World French colonies in 1810, describes the making of a *banza*: "they cut lengthwise through the middle of a calabash."[5] John Allen Wyeth gives his impression of a slave-made banjo from 1850s Alabama: "made from a

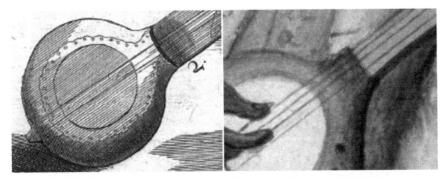

Figure 9.4. Neck-to-gourd joint of Sloane "Strum Strump" and *The Old Plantation* banjo; photos courtesy of Smithsonian Institution and The Colonial Williamsburg Foundation. Gift of Abby Aldrich Rockefeller.

large gourd with a long straight neck . . . The bowl of the gourd was cut away on a plane level with the surface of the neck."[6] Both writers are also accurately describing the configuration one finds in the Sloane, *The Old Plantation*, and Haitian instruments.

The Haitian *banza* has five soundholes in the gourd: two cross-shaped holes on more or less each side of the gourd and a triangular hole on the underside of the gourd. This latter hole is associated with some cracks in the gourd; they may be the result of damage or the hole was put in place to stop cracks from spreading. Although seemingly more randomly placed, these soundholes are remarkably similar, in form and relative size, to the markings around the gourd body of *The Old Plantation* banjo (figure 9.5). We can now safely assume the markings on *The Old Plantation* banjo are in fact soundholes. Although not visible in the engraving, the acquisition notes for Sloane's "Strum Strump" describe it as being "holed in side."[7]

Although soundholes are common in West African string instruments, they seem most often to be in the form of a single large round hole. Although examples are also found with a single large cross, square, or diamond shape, I have seen no examples with the five or more cross or floral hole configuration of the Haitian *banza* and *The Old Plantation* banjo. Multiple, smaller holes of this design are apparently a strictly New World tradition or one that has not survived in Africa. The holes in the side of Sloane's "Strum Strump" might have taken a form similar to that of the other two New World banjos.

Although generally similar in all three instruments, the neck-to-gourd joint is different between the illustrated instruments and the Haitian *banza*. In *The Old Plantation* and Sloane images, the end of the fingerboard is the same width as the cut-off end of the gourd's neck. The wooden neck simply disappears into the gourd. In the Haitian *banza*, however, the end of the fingerboard is actually wider than the gourd's neck. Instead of disappearing into the opening, it is wedged into a slot and visible where it protrudes outside either side of the gourd's neck (figure 9.6). The neck now fits loosely into the slot, but a light spot on the back of the wooden neck

Figure 9.5. Gourd holes in Haitian *banza* and *The Old Plantation* banjo; photos courtesy of author and The Colonial Williamsburg Foundation. Gift of Abby Aldrich Rockefeller.

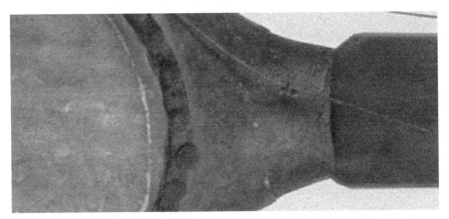

Figure 9.6. Detailed views of Haitian *banza* neck-to-gourd joint; courtesy of author.

reveals where a now missing wedge originally held it tightly in place. This joint is in fact a clever way to quickly make a solid neck-to-gourd connection. The necks of *The Old Plantation* and Sloane instruments might have been wed to the gourd in a similar way, but the width of the wooden neck was tailored to the width of the gourd neck and not visible from the top once it entered the gourd.

The roughly worked, mahogany neck of the Haitian *banza* is cut from a single board and is 34 7/8 inches long. About 14 inches of this length is the "rim stick," extending through the body of the gourd; 2 5/8 inches comes out the gourd's far end, forming a sort of endpin to which each string, or a now-missing tailpiece, was anchored. The neck is 5/8 of an inch thick and entirely flat along its face. It has no tilt at the peg head or where the neck meets the gourd. Again, this is much as Tussac described his *banza* in 1810: " a piece of lath or flat wood makes the handle."[8] The lower edge of the neck, that is, the edge of the neck facing the ground when the instrument is being played, is fairly regular, suggesting that this is where the sawn edge of the original board was. The upper edge is more irregular and looks like the original builder's spoke shave or draw-knife chattered along this edge while trimming the neck narrower (figure 9.7). The back of the neck has been slightly rounded across its width. The marks left by a spoke shave taking off long, thin shavings are very clear.

The fingerboard, between where it enters the gourd and the peg for the short string farther up the neck, is 2 1/4 inches to 2 3/8 inches wide, with several symmetrical cutaways in the neck. Between the peg for the short string and the peg head, the neck is only 1 1/2 inches wide, presumably so the player's fingers can more easily get around it. Below the short string peg are two mirrored pairs of triangular notches in the neck before the wide section finally steps down to the 1 inch width that extends through the body of the gourd. The end of this narrow section butts up against the inside of the gourd except for the rounded 1/2 inch wide, 2 1/2 inch long endpin that pokes through the bottom end of the gourd. Only the narrow section of the fingerboard closest to the peg head shows wear from being played.

Figure 9.7. Tool chatter on edge of *banza* neck; courtesy of author.

In fact, when the entire banjo is assembled, the fingerboard is roughly parallel to the drumhead on which a bridge rested, but 2 inches below the level of the head. Beyond the section showing finger wear, the strings would have been very high off the fingerboard, making them almost impossible to press down to the neck.

Interestingly, the *banza* has no nut or slot for a missing nut at the top of the fingerboard (figure 9.8). Grooves on the outside edges of the neck at the base of the peg head suggest instead that string or gut was once tied around the neck at this point, holding the strings against the fingerboard. Finger wear also abruptly ends where the hypothetical string-nut would have been, suggesting the presence of the string must have kept fingers from burnishing the fingerboard. Despite the presence of tuning pegs on this instrument, the string nut suggests a connection

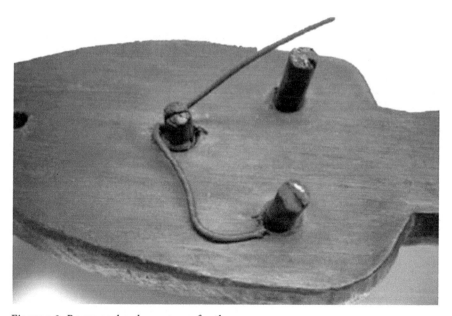

Figure 9.8. *Banza* peghead; courtesy of author.

to the leather thong tuners of West African string instruments, which are also used at times as de facto nuts.

The fingerboard itself features an incised design between the two sets of cuts into the edge of the neck (figure 9.9). It was made by multiple passes of a compass, over which the builder then used a gimlet to drill rows of shallow holes. The compass incisions now seem to connect the drilled "dots," though it is clear that the compass work preceded the holes left by the gimlet.[9] Somewhat similar incised designs are implied in the illustration of one of Hans Sloane's "Strum Strumps" (see figure H).

Through various lines scribed into the back of the neck, one can see how the *banza's* builder laid out all of his cuts before he began working. Some of these lines seem to be made with a compass, perhaps the same one that inscribed the fingerboard design. The builder also left marks showing that the rim stick was planed to be longer, allowing the neck to go farther into the gourd. Most interesting is a long incised line that suggests that a planned cut would have removed the bottom edge of the wide section of the neck (figure 9.10).

If this cut had been made, the bottom edge of the neck would have been one straight line from the nut to where it meets the gourd, making the now symmetrical neck asymmetrical. The neck would then have looked remarkably like those of the early minstrel-era banjos made by William Boucher (figure 9.11). In these banjos, the lower edge is flat, but the upper edge is widened to accommodate the short string, with several decorative cuts into that edge. Perhaps a folk banjo where this cut was completed influenced Boucher's work.

The presence of the narrower rim stick in the Haitian *banza* is in itself a strong connection to the banjos made by European Americans like Boucher. In African banjo-like instruments, the neck keeps the same general dimensions throughout

Figure 9.9. Incised pattern on *banza* fingerboard; courtesy of author.

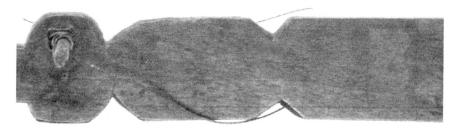

Figure 9.10. Back of *banza* neck, showing (very lightly) the long incised line along the bottom edge; courtesy of author.

its length; it does not change shape or size where it enters the gourd. The narrower rim stick of the Haitian *banza* has the same structural purpose as the rim sticks of later wooden-rimmed banjos. The shoulder at the end of the wide portion of the neck becomes a stop pressing against the edge of the gourd in the Haitian *banza*, or against the side of the drum shell of later banjos. The far end of the rim stick stabilized the neck's attachment to the banjo body (figure 9.12). The joinery of instruments like the Haitian *banza*, *The Old Plantation* banjo, and the "Strum Strump" seems to simply have been carried over to wooden-rimmed banjos as the instrument evolved.[10]

Figure 9.11. Back of neck of Boucher banjo; courtesy of Bernunzio Uptown Music, Rochester, New York.

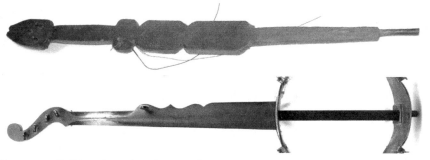

Figure 9.12. Full-length neck and rim stick; *top*, Haitian *banza* (courtesy of author); *bottom*, Boucher banjo (courtesy of editor).

Finally worth noting are the instrument's tuning pegs and string set-up. Like the banjo in *The Old Plantation* painting, this banjo has three long and one short string. Schoepf's account and many of the descriptions unearthed by Epstein tell of four-string instruments. African instruments have varying numbers and arrangements of short and long strings, but based on early accounts, the strongest trend in the New World seems to be for four-string instruments. The earlier mentioned Stedman banjo has three long strings with tuning-pegs entering a fiddle-style peg box from the side and one short string with a tuning-peg directly entering the side of the neck. In the Haitian *banza*, as well as in the "Strum Strump" and *The Old Plantation* banjos, the pegs are perpendicular to the fingerboard, entering through the back of the neck and emerging through the front of the peg head, or in the case of the short string, through the fingerboard. This again is a feature not only shared by Sloane, *The Old Plantation*, and Haitian banjos, but also by the earliest minstrel-era banjos.

So many details of the Haitian *banza* are also found in early minstrel-era banjos that it seems clear that similar gourd banjos influenced the work of European Americans. Instead of the pronounced heel at the bottom end of the neck of European guitars, violins, and lutes, Joe Sweeney, William Boucher, and others influenced by the gourd banjo tradition opted for a heel-less neck, cut from a board. As mentioned above, if the *banza*'s maker had carried out a planned cut, the instrument would resemble a crude copy of Boucher's work. It is easy to imagine a craftsman like Boucher, coming from a European tradition, applying the ogee, a Western architectural form, in place of the simple decorative cuts seen in the neck of the *banza*. Even as it is, the *banza*'s neck resembles 1840s banjos made by Henry Stichter and early images of banjos played by Sweeney. In these banjos the swelling of the width of the neck below the short string is symmetrical, like that of the *banza*. The *banza*'s flat, narrow rim stick, its rounded end protruding through the gourd to become an end pin, perfectly mirrors what is found in early minstrel banjos. Early makers of wood-bodied banjos made only the slightest alteration to the clever neck-to-gourd joinery seen in the Haitian *banza* in order to substitute a wooden rim for the gourd body. All of these similarities are so strong that if the *banza*'s connection to eighteenth-century instruments was not so clear and its own date of origin was not so firm, we would almost suspect that the Haitian *banza*'s neck design was influenced by mainland banjos of the 1840s and 1850s.

African American–built banjos were once a common sight in the colonized Americas, played in city streets and countryside alike. Until the discovery of the Haitian *banza*, our impression of these instruments was cloudy at best. In my work trying to re-create a banjo from this period, I was forced to cobble together information from various sources. Unfortunately, the written accounts from those early times are generally sketchy and incomplete, and even the best images made during the period have many ambiguities.

With the discovery of the Haitian *banza* we finally have a physical example of an early gourd banjo to study, which is clearly akin to two of the instruments illustrated early in the history of the Americas. The great similarity between these instruments suggests a long-lasting banjo lineage culturally connecting the American South to the Caribbean. The existence of such a longstanding tradition suggests that many of the banjos, mentioned in early accounts of the Americas but less clearly described, might have in fact resembled these instruments. All three banjos differ enough from African instruments while sharing some details specific to later banjos played and made by European Americans to place them at a point in the banjo's history where it was no longer simply a relocated African instrument, but on its way to attaining the structure of the well-known antebellum nineteenth-century banjo.

In Brussels, it took me two days, hundreds of photographs, and pages of notes to fully examine the Haitian *banza*. I stood back to take one final look at the instrument I had waited for so long to materialize. Seeing this nearly two-century-old banjo sitting disassembled, surrounded by modern measuring devices and photographic equipment, I had the keen sense that another portion of the long history of the banjo in America had become clear. This examination had been a unique experience. I thought about all the opportunities there should have been to study this widely played, highly popular instrument. As many times as the instrument had been written about early in the history of the American colonies, it is startling that there are not dozens of early banjos in museums throughout the United States. How ironic that this key link in America's cultural history had been preserved instead in a single museum in Europe. After all, in the story of the banjo, we can see a blueprint for the sort of cultural exchange that has happened time and again, throughout America's history.

Unfortunately, those in a position to preserve examples of the instrument in the eighteenth and early nineteenth centuries were unable to recognize the cultural significance of the banjo. Perhaps being commonplace as well as disdained because of its association with enslaved people of African ancestry, no one thought any special effort was worth making to preserve an example of the instrument. Those who did value the banjo then, African Americans, free and enslaved alike, were seldom able to hold on to any nonessential possessions as their lives were cast about by slave trade and wage slave economics.

Notes

1. Dena J. Epstein, *Sinful Tunes and Spirituals: Black Folk Music to the Civil War* (Urbana: University of Illinois Press, 1977), 36.

2. Ibid.; Robert B. Winans, "Black Musicians in Eighteenth-Century America: Evidence from Runaway Slave Advertisements," in this volume.

3. The terms *calabash* and *gourd* are used interchangeably and indiscriminately in early accounts of the banjo. These are common, not scientific, names but they are generally

considered to be the seedpods of two different plants. The calabash is the product of a tree (*Crescentia cujete*) that only grows in the tropics. The gourd (*Lagenaria siceraria*) grows on an annual vine and is closely related to the cucumber. It grows in warm and cool regions, so we may assume that most of the gourd banjos described in North America were in fact made from *Largenaria* gourds. The *creole bania*, collected in Suriname, South America, is made using a tree-born *Crescentia* calabash.

4. According to acquisition notes at the British Museum, these instruments were originally collected by Sloane and made part of the collection of the British Museum but are now lost. Email correspondence between Pete Ross and the British Museum.

5. Epstein, *Sinful Tunes*, 36.

6. Ibid., 146.

7. Email correspondence with the British Museum.

8. Epstein, *Sinful Tunes*, 36.

9. In an email in December 2004 to Sule Greg Wilson, the art historian Robert Thompson explains the meaning of the incising: "You have got a missing mate to the famous Rabeca do Escravo [captive's violin] that I saw once in Brazil and it comes from the 18th c. black community of Itanhaem. This violin is surmounted by a spirit-head, referring to the spirit that arises in true black music. With the Haiti Banza we have another mask of the spirit, eyes and nose clearly rendered, and head coming to a decisive point. If the artist knew Yoruba culture we would automatically recognize a reference to Ashe and Nago influence that was and is very strong in Haiti."

10. Although it is commonly held that Joel Walker Sweeney exchanged gourd for wooden hoop independent of the influence of others, it remains possible and is even suggested in a couple early accounts (see Epstein) that the wooden body was introduced to the banjo by African Americans prior to Sweeney.

PART IV

Into North America—Early Banjo Sightings

CHAPTER 10

Zenger's "Banger"
Contextualizing the Banjo in Early New York City, 1736

Shlomo Pestcoe and Greg C. Adams

Editor's Headnote

The newspaper article Shlomo Pestcoe and Greg C. Adams present and analyze here is important because it is the earliest known North American reference to the banjo, being played at a New York City fair, in the hands of a black man. They analyze what the article tells us about African American culture of the time, and its music, and the extent to which it reveals Afro-Caribbean cultural influence in early New York, partly by bringing in from other source reports of blacks playing the early gourd banjo. Pestcoe and Adams compare the article's description of a fair with a famous scene from one of James Fenimore Cooper's novels and with other fairs and festivals of the period. And they make a convincing effort to identify the real author of the pseudonymous article.

On Monday, March 7, 1736, John Peter Zenger (1697–1746) published an anonymous letter as the lead article in his newspaper *The New-York Weekly Journal: Containing the freshest Advices, Foreign, and Domestick.* The dateline on the piece was "*UTOPIA*, April 10" and it was signed "*The SPY.*" This piece was the first of a series of three letters by *The SPY* lampooning the social mores, proclivities, and foibles of the author's peers—European Americans in eighteenth-century British colonial Mid-Atlantic America, in particular, New York City. The other two letters were printed, also as front-page articles, in the two subsequent editions of the paper: that of March 14 and March 21, 1736.

In this first letter, *The SPY* vividly described blacks playing the "Banger" at a fair held in a "Field, little Way out a Town" to mark an unspecified holiday. This description is the earliest known reference to the banjo in North America found thus far. Moreover, some modern historians like Graham Russell Hodges and Shane White have posited this account as possibly the only actual period evidence for an annual fair in eighteenth-century Manhattan "devoted to Pinkster, the great Saturnalia of the New York blacks," as described by James Fenimore Cooper (1789–1851) in his novel *Satanstoe* (1845).[1]

This early newspaper report provides readers with a rare candid glimpse into the daily life and culture of what was arguably colonial Mid-Atlantic America's most culturally diverse city. The 1736 report, though conveyed through the limited lens of European American gentry, offers an unprecedented wealth of detail about African diasporic musical and cultural expressions in colonial Mid-Atlantic America. And chief among them is the early gourd banjo, seen here as a vital African American instrument making its very first appearance in the historical record of North America.[2]

Below we provide, for the first time, a full text transcription of this important piece of historic documentation. As a preface to this text, we share some of what we have learned about the apparent African American musical and cultural references found in this 1736 "letter," including music instruments and cultural implements, potential commonalities with other historical and geographical references, and the event's definition as a type of holiday or community event. Then we briefly review some of what is known about Zenger's *New-York Weekly Journal* and inferences about the actual identity of the article's author, *The SPY*. We conclude by suggesting how this type of banjo-focused research substantively contributes to a deeper conversation about American history.

Similarities Between the 1736 Account and Cooper's in *Satanstoe*

Several similarities exist between the 1736 *New-York Weekly Journal* account and that of Cooper in his 1845 novel *Satanstoe*. The 1736 narrative begins one morning when *The SPY* hears "my Landlord's black Fellow very busy at tuning of his Banger, as he call'd it, and playing some of his Tunes." In response to the writer's inquiry as to the reason for his merry-making, the black servant explains, "Massa, today Holiday; Backerah[3] no work; Ningar no work; me no savy play Banger; go yonder, you see Ningar play Banger for true, dance too; you see Sport today for true. . . . Massa, you savy the Field, little Way out a Town, no Ho[u]ses there, grandy Room for dance there." Upon reaching "the Field, little Way out a Town" where the fair was taking place, *The SPY* observed:

> The Plain partly covered with Booths, and well crouded with Whites, the Negroes divided into Companies, I suppose according to their different Nations, some dancing to the hollow Sound of a Drum, made of the Trunk of a hollow Tree, othersome to the grating rattling Noise of Pebles or Shells in a small Basket, others plied the Banger, and some knew how to joyn the Voice [to] it.

This portrayal is remarkably similar to Cooper's description in *Satanstoe* of the Pinkster fair in Lower Manhattan that his principal characters attend in 1757:

We went out of town, taking the direction of a large common that the king's officers had long used for a parade ground. . . . On this common, then, was the Pinkster ground, which was now quite full of people, as well as of animation.

By this time, nine-tenths of the blacks of the city, and of the whole country within thirty or forty miles, indeed, were collected in thousands in those fields, beating banjoes, singing African songs, drinking, and worst of all, laughing in a way that seemed to set their very hearts rattling within their ribs. . . . The features that distinguish a Pinkster frolic from the usual scenes at fairs, and other merry-makings, however, were of African origin. It is true, there are not now, nor were there then, many blacks among us of African birth; but the traditions and usages of their original country were so far preserved as to produce a marked difference between this festival, and one of European origin. Among other things, some were making music, by beating on skins drawn over the ends of hollow logs, while others were dancing to it, in a manner to show that they felt infinite delight. This, in particular, was said to be a usage of their African progenitors.

Hundreds of whites were walking through the fields, amused spectators.[4]

Aside from *The SPY*'s 1736 report, the only other known reference to a holiday fair in eighteenth-century Lower Manhattan is that of the "Pinkster frolic" in Cooper's *Satanstoe*. Scholars have long debated whether or not Cooper based his account on an actual historic event as no evidence has ever been found in the historical record to indicate that such a Pinkster fair ever took place in Manhattan. Communal celebrations of Pinkster by African Americans in the form of large annual fairs were documented in Albany and Brooklyn Village (Brooklyn Heights), not early New York City.[5]

Evidence has yet to be found in the historical record of holiday fairs of any type taking place in eighteenth-century New York City. Conversely, holiday fairs did occur in the previous century when the city was Dutch Nieuw-Amsterdam. Two large annual *kermises* (market fairs) were instituted in New Amsterdam in 1641: one on October 15 for the sale of cattle and the other on November 1 for the sale of pigs. Another was established for the Monday following St. Bartholomew's Day (August 24). In the Dutch tradition, these were great social festivals as well as market days. Like the holiday fair described in the 1736 *New-York Weekly Journal* account, refreshment booths were set up and a variety of entertainments took place at the given *kermis* site.[6] It is not clear, however, how long the Dutch *kermis* tradition continued after the city was seized by the English in 1664 and whether it survived in any form in eighteenth-century Manhattan.

This fact raises the question: could *The SPY*'s 1736 account have served as the inspiration and model for Cooper's 1845 tale of the "Pinkster frolic" held in eighteenth-century Lower Manhattan?

The fair that *The SPY* attended took place in "the Field, little Way out a Town," corresponding with Cooper's description in *Satanstoe* of "the scene of the Pinkster sports," located "out of town" in the fields "up near the head of Broadway, on the common."[7] For much of the eighteenth century, New York City proper was confined to the lower tip of Manhattan Island. At the time, "the head of Broadway" was immediately below what is now Chambers Street and denoted the city's northernmost limits in terms of development. "The Common"—so named because the open field was originally used as common grazing land—was, therefore, considered just "out of town" as it literally sat at "the head of Broadway." The Common was the city's principal open civic space and site for public gatherings until it became City Hall Park in 1812.[8] As such, it is very likely that the Common might have been "the Field, little Way out a Town," that *The Spy* was referencing in the 1736 *New-York Weekly Journal* account.

The second similarity is that *The SPY*'s account and Cooper's *Satanstoe* both prominently feature the banjo and African-style drums in the blacks' celebration of the holiday. In the case of the 1736 "letter," the correspondent mentions the "Banger" (banjo) three times, yet apparently presumed that his readers were familiar enough with the instrument so as to require no explication. Conversely, he felt it necessary to describe the other instruments in addition to "the Banger" played by "the Negroes" to accompany dancing: wooden drums ("made of the Trunk of a hollow Tree") and rattles ("Pebles or Shells in a small Basket"). By the same token, in *Satanstoe*, Cooper describes blacks at the Pinkster fair making music for dancing by "beating banjos" and "beating on skins drawn over the ends of hollow logs."

Interestingly enough, neither account makes any reference to the fiddle (violin), the most popular instrument for vernacular dance music in eighteenth-century America. Many period reports describe African American fiddlers playing for white dances and functions as well as for those within black communities. Yet, prior to 1800, very little documentation shows the fiddle and early gourd banjo being played together. On the contrary, the historical evidence indicates that the early gourd banjo was more typically paired with African-heritage drums and other percussion instruments rather than the fiddle. This dichotomy can probably be traced back to West Africa where plucked lutes and bowed lutes (fiddles) are rarely played together in traditional performance contexts.[9] (One notable exception is the large gourd-bodied *kaburu* lute, with two or three strings, of the Gwari [Gbari] of Nigeria, which is traditionally played as accompaniment to the single-string *goga* fiddle as well as the *mwayi* flute.)[10]

The 1736 *New-York Weekly Journal* and *Satanstoe* accounts are not the only historical references from the North to pair the early gourd banjo with drums. These instruments are also referenced in association with Albany's annual Pinkster fair in Absalom Aimwell's epic poem, *A Pinkster Ode* (1803):

> Now hark! The Banjo, rub a dub,
> Like a washer-woman's tub;
> And hear the drum, 'tis rolling now,
> Row de dow, row de dow.[11]

Similarly, the banjo and drums appear in accounts of Negro Election Day, New England's African American springtime festival that parallels Pinkster in terms of historic timeframe and cultural significance and manifestations.[12] The antiquarian Henry Bull, in his essay "Memoir of Rhode Island," offered a vivid image of Negro Election Day in early Newport that echoed the contemporaneous celebrations on Albany's "Pinkster Hill" and *The SPY*'s 1736 description of the fair in Lower Manhattan. Bull states: "All the various languages of Africa, mixed with broken and ludicrous English, filled the air, accompanied with the music of the fiddle, tambourine, the banjo, drum, etc."[13]

The Early Gourd Banjo
in Eighteenth-Century New York

The early gourd banjo has been reported, beyond the context of these festivals, as an African American instrument in the New York metropolitan area during the eighteenth century. In 1753, a slave named Joe, age 38–40, ran away from Captain Charles Ware of New York City; the newspaper ad stated that he "can play the bangeo."[14] "Billy Banjo" (ca. 1738–1826), a freed former slave native to Long Island, "was a famous banjo player" active around the town of Mamaroneck: 'Not on the fanciful instrument of to-day, handled by cork-faced counterfeits, but the genuine banjo of the negro. He not only *played*, but he *made* banjos, having a large dried gourd for the sounding board."[15]

The early gourd banjo's appearance in the North stands in sharp contrast to the popular misconception of the banjo as being exclusive to the South. Looking specifically at New York City, the most likely explanation for the early gourd banjo's presence here was the size of the city's black population. According to the 1737 census—taken a year after the publication of *The SPY*'s letter—out of a total population of 8,666, "Negroes" accounted for 1,719, or 20 percent.[16] Virtually all of the city's blacks were enslaved, making New York City second only to South Carolina's Charles Towne (Charleston) as the largest "slave city" in colonial America.[17]

Another crucial factor to consider is the very large presence within the city of slaves from the Caribbean, the African diasporic cultural wellspring from which the early gourd banjo first emerged in the seventeenth century. During the 1730s, 65 percent of all enslaved captives imported into New York City came from Jamaica, Barbados, Antigua, and the rest of the British West Indies. Many of these were African-born who were "seasoned" in the Caribbean, usually for a period of three to four years, before being brought to North America.[18] The purpose of "seasoning" was to acclimate those fresh off the boat from the horrific Middle Passage to the harsh conditions of slavery, as well as to acquaint them with the English language and culture of their new masters. It did, however, also serve to enculturate[19] and socialize newly arrived Africans into the Afro-Creole culture of the West Indies.

As evinced by the specific examples noted in the 1736 account, this great influx of slaves from the Caribbean—both West Indian–born Afro-Creoles and
African-born survivors of the Middle Passage enculturated into West Indian
Afro-Creole culture—appears to have heavily influenced the development of
vernacular African American culture in eighteenth-century New York, especially
its music and dance. For instance, *The SPY*'s term *Banger* is clearly a cognate of
bangil—a name for the early gourd banjo recorded in Barbados in 1708 and Jamaica in 1739 and 1740—as well as other related designations for the instrument
(e.g., *bonja, banjar, banjer, banjor, banjo*, etc.) reported in the West Indies and
English-speaking North America, starting in the 1740s.[20]

Afro-Caribbean Cultural Influence
in Early New York

Moving beyond the banjo reference, *The SPY* offers yet another example of Afro-
Caribbean influence when he reports "some dancing to the hollow Sound of a
Drum, made of the Trunk of a hollow Tree, othersome to the grating rattling
Noise of Pebles or Shells in a small Basket." Period reports of social dancing
throughout the Caribbean are replete with observations of African-style drums
made from hollowed-out wood or a piece of a hollowed-out tree trunk. Typically, these wooden drums had a piece of animal skin covering one end to form
a *head* (soundtable), and they were referred to, in Jamaica, as either "Ebo drum"
or "goombay."[21]

"The grating rattling Noise of Pebles or Shells in a small Basket" that *The SPY*
described were most likely small wicker basket rattles made from woven strips
of natural materials (e.g., straw or palm leaves), forming a small closed wicker
basket with seeds or pebbles inside. Wicker basket rattles in various forms are
found throughout sub-Saharan Africa, such as the Baule *segesege* (Côte d'Ivoire)[22]
and the Idoma *ichaka* (Nigeria).[23] In Brazil, the *angóia* and the *caxixi*[24] are wicker
basket rattles of African heritage; the former is used as part of percussion ensembles accompanying *jongo* and *batuque* dances in southern Brazil,[25] while
the latter traditionally accompanies *capoeira*[26] with the *berimbau* musical bow.[27]
Just as the early gourd banjo was often reported as being played with drums to
accompany social dancing throughout the Caribbean, wicker basket and other
kinds of rattles of African heritage were cited as being used along with the banjo
and drums.[28]

Finally, the 1736 account differs significantly from Cooper's in that it offers a
rare report of African American sports not found in *Satanstoe*. *The SPY* observed
"several Companies of the Blacks, some exercising the Cudgel, and some of them
small Sticks in imitation of the short Pike." "Exercising the Cudgel" was a reference to the cudgel (also known as the singlestick or backsword), a sword-like

wooden combat stick used in fencing matches for prizes at fairs all over Britain in the seventeenth and eighteenth centuries.[29] "Playing at cudgels" was a prominent feature of annual militia musters known as "Training Day" in colonial New England, dating as far back at least as the late seventeenth century.[30] "Small Sticks in imitation of the short Pike" most likely refers to the Afro-Creole martial art of stick fighting, first documented in the Caribbean during this period. On some islands, stick fighting was called *calinda* (also *calenda, kalenda, kalinda*), the same term used to denote Afro-Creole social dances that were typically accompanied by African-style drums and the early gourd banjo.[31] These many points illuminate the detail offered by *The SPY*, but his account also provides hints about the event's linkage to known holidays and community gatherings.

"Today Holiday"

Graham Russell Hodges, perhaps the first modern historian to have rediscovered the long forgotten 1736 account, contends that Pinkster was the holiday to which *The SPY* alluded but failed to name.[32] Pinkster was an African American springtime festival unique to New York and eastern New Jersey that was celebrated primarily during the eighteenth and early nineteenth centuries. It evolved from the local Dutch American version of Pinksteren, the traditional Dutch celebration of the three-day Christian festival of Pentecost (Whitsuntide in English), which starts on the seventh Sunday after Easter.[33]

Over the course of the eighteenth century, the distinctive Dutch American culture that had emerged in the region was superseded increasingly by the growing prevalence of British American society. With their gradual assimilation into the Anglo mainstream, succeeding generations of Dutch American "Yorkers" and New Jerseyans eventually abandoned Pinkster. It was adopted and adapted by local African Americans, who transformed Pinkster into a unique regional festival that reflected a syncretic synthesis of African, European, and Amerindian influences. This mixture of cultural traditions was akin to the diversity that informed other creolized European festivals throughout the New World, such as Mardi Gras in Louisiana, Carnival in the Caribbean and Brazil, and the Afro-Cuban celebration of Dia de Reyes (Kings' Day).[34]

Considering the rich legacy of Pinkster and its significance in the multicultural heritage of the region, Hodge's categoric identification of *The SPY*'s 1736 account as a celebration of Pinkster is very compelling, but it is not the only plausible explanation. Shane White suggests the likelihood that "the description is of a General Training Day." Apart from Pinkster, he explains, "the other important holiday for many northern slaves was variously called Negro Training or General Training and usually occurred in June. Blacks would come from miles around, ostensibly to watch the black militia drill."[35]

In trying to identify the mysterious holiday, Hodges's and White's readings of the 1736 account do not take into consideration two additional tantalizing clues found in *The SPY's* "letter": the dateline, "April 10," and his description of the holiday as "being one of those set apart to commemorate the Resurrection of our Blessed Saviour."[36] As *The SPY* is clearly describing a religious holiday that occurred on or before April 10, this precludes White's conjecture that the event in question was a General Training Day, a secular festival that typically took place in June. Yet, it also casts doubts on Hodges's assertion that the described holiday was Pinkster. As stated, Pentecost (Pinkster in Dutch) is observed seven weeks after Easter Sunday. If this had been a commemoration of Pinkster, it would have had to occur no earlier than May 10 and no later than June 13, depending on the civil calendar.

The Christian holiday that does fit the dateline of *The SPY's* "letter" is Easter, its date range being from March 22 to April 25. His description of the holiday "to commemorate the Resurrection of our Blessed Saviour" corresponds with Eastertide (Easter Season), the fifty days between Easter Sunday and Pinkster Sunday. Conversely, Pinkster Sunday is the culmination of Eastertide, being "the day when the Holy Spirit descended on the Apostles" after Jesus was crucified.[37]

However, the fair in question would have been held on the following day, Easter Monday, rather than on Easter Sunday, a Holy Day reserved exclusively for religious observance. And if that was, indeed, the case, then the most probable calendar date that corresponds with the April 10 dateline of *The SPY's* "letter" would have been Easter Monday, April 10, 1730.[38]

Throughout Europe, Easter Monday is a traditional day off from work, celebrated with local customs of social recreation. This practice is certainly true in the Netherlands, where Easter is called Paas and Eastertide, Pasen. Tweede Paasdag (Dutch for Easter Monday) is a day off with many recreational traditions associated with it.[39] Like Pinkster, Paas was celebrated in the Dutch American communities of early New York and New Jersey. And like Pinkster Monday, Paas Monday was also a day off and a day of socializing and recreation for all, including African American slaves and servants.[40] Therefore, the holiday described in the 1736 account might very well have been Paas (Easter) Monday rather than Pinkster Monday.

So far, in the cases of the Mondays after both Easter and Pentecost, we have focused on the Dutch heritage of these observances in America. However, most Christians in colonial New York recognized these holidays as festive days off, regardless of denomination, ethnicity, or race.[41] The marking of holidays with market fairs was also found in British tradition. Throughout England during the eighteenth century, fairs were often held on the Monday day off following a Sunday holiday like Easter or Whitsunday.[42] Yet, as indicated earlier, thus far no period evidence has been found in the historical record to suggest that holiday market fairs were held in either Dutch New Amsterdam or Anglo New York City to celebrate either Easter Monday or Pinkster Monday.

The significance of *The SPY*'s story, however, should not hinge on the question of which holiday he was describing. Rather, what is significant here is the event itself and what it represents as a unique multicultural manifestation of early New York's cultural diversity.

Solving the Mystery of *The SPY*'s Identity

The final missing piece in the intriguing puzzle of the 1736 account is: who was *The SPY*?

As researchers seek to responsibly measure the credibility of *The SPY*'s richly detailed narrative, they are taunted by his anonymity. White speculated that the mysterious author was "a pseudonymous newspaper contributor from an unidentified town, probably in the Hudson Valley."[43] While "*The SPY*" was certainly a pseudonym, the piece itself was not necessarily a report "from an unidentified town." As suggested above, *The SPY*'s reference to "the Field, little Way out a Town," was, in all likelihood, an allusion to "the Common" of early New York City. This premise leads us to investigate potential authors who were probably familiar with the city's environs, and had a close relationship with *The New-York Weekly Journal*. One such candidate is a man who was not only a prominent New Yorker at the time, but also someone intimately connected with the newspaper: James Alexander (1691–1756). At least five reasons suggest that Alexander was *The SPY*.

First, the Scottish-born Alexander was one of New York City's leading citizens as well as one of its most respected attorneys and public figures. From 1721 to 1723, he was the attorney general of the royal colony of New York. Beyond that, Alexander was truly a product of the Age of Enlightenment: "Mathematician, scientist, lawyer and politician, he was one of the most extraordinary men of his generation, a gentleman and a scholar, a charter member of Benjamin Franklin's Philosophical Society, and the trusted confidant of more than one Governor."[44] Alexander's prominence in the political milieu of the period where newspapers were an influential force in shaping local and regional thought, as well as his attainments as a scholarly member of the gentry, all point to the newspaper as being his brainchild:

> Now for all of this James Alexander was more responsible than any other man. Just how much he meant to the newspaper can be gathered from his literary remains. They show that he wrote much of the copy. . . . The reason for his obscurity is clear enough: he left little documentary evidence about himself, while his efforts on behalf of the Journal were anonymous. It is mainly from his unpublished notes and memoranda that we have to piece together the full role he played in the New York of his time. Without these we would know that he was a very eminent man, but we would be unable to appreciate his status as a newspaper editor, the most memorable phase of his memorable career.[45]

Alexander was one of the earliest and most vociferous leaders of the opposition to Sir William Cosby (1690–1736), the ill-famed, ill-fated royal governor of New York from 1732 to 1736. Prior to the establishment of *The New-York Weekly Journal* in 1733, New York City had only one newspaper, the *New-York Weekly Gazette*, founded eight years earlier by William Bradford (1663–1753). As Bradford was the official salaried printer for the royal colony of New York, his newspaper served as the organ of Governor Cosby's administration and, by extension, the governing faction, the Court Party.[46] The idea of creating *The New-York Weekly Journal* as a rival newspaper and the voice of the opposition, Lewis Morris's Popular Party (also referred to as the Country Party), most likely came from Alexander. Furthermore, historians now generally agree that he was the actual editor of the paper as well as its principal writer.[47] Zenger did not write or edit the material published in *The New-York Weekly Journal*; he simply printed it.[48] As the only other printer in town aside from Bradford,[49] Alexander, Morris, and their colleague William Smith Sr. naturally hired him to print their paper.[50]

As the newspaper's editor, Alexander was in a good position to influence the placement of this anonymous "letter" (the first installment of three) on the first page of the March 7, 1736, edition of *The New-York Weekly Journal*. This type of submission would not have likely been accepted from a random writer or from someone unaffiliated with the paper. In the typical four-page format of most eighteenth-century newspapers like *The New-York Weekly Journal*, such letters were usually found on the second, third, and fourth pages, where they were most often filler copied from other papers.

Second, a learned individual must have been at the helm in order to provide readers with a reference to such a fanciful location as "UTOPIA." The word *utopia* was extremely rare as an actual public place name until 1847,[51] when it was used to denote the second "equitable village" (mutualist community) founded by the pioneering individualist anarchist Josiah Warren (1798–1874): Utopia, Ohio.[52] Prior to that, *utopia* was used and understood as originally intended and defined by the man who coined it, Sir Thomas More (1478–1535): as a descriptor for a fictional place and society.[53]

Taking his cue from More, *The SPY*'s location citation of "UTOPIA" in the piece's dateline may be seen as a sly (if not pretentious) "wink of the eye" to his readers. He seems to assume that they are well-read enough to get the classic literary reference and understand that what follows will be a witty critique of contemporary society in the guise of a fictitious anonymous letter.

Third, the writer provides a biting lampoon of the social foibles and hypocrisies of his peers, white Christian males, the principal citizenry of eighteenth-century European and European American societies. This critique is quite evident after the initial four paragraphs of the first letter. In paragraph five, *The SPY* takes aim at the whoring carried on by ostensibly religious, upstanding leaders of the community, which he witnessed in one of the concession tents at the fair. He proceeds in paragraph six with his observations at the fair of drunkenness, profanity, and brawling, along with gambling on cockfights in paragraph seven. The SPY's second letter continued in the same vein, though the focus now shifted to "the Ladies" and their custom of spending the Sabbath by paying visits and drinking "their beloved Tea." The theme of gambling was picked up again in the third and last letter as *The Spy* described "the Pastimes, practiced among that Fraternity called Gamesters."[54]

The December 17, 1733, edition of *The New-York Weekly Journal* defiantly proclaimed that the paper would apply "the Lash of Satyr" to "wicked Ministers [of government]."[55] Indeed, witty, highly literate satire, laced with references to classical literature, would be the hallmark of *The New-York Weekly Journal* until it ceased publication in 1751. This usage is clearly evident in all three of *The SPY's* "letters." Comparing them to similar pieces published on the paper's front page, one can discern common formats, writing styles, topics, and approaches to subject matter.[56] The German-born Zenger could not have been the source of these erudite writings "as his grasp of the English language remained defective," and he had received no education apart from his vocational training under Bradford.[57] In sharp contrast, Alexander had the finest classical English education money could buy and a reputation among his peers as a learned scholar. Furthermore, he also had experience as a journalist as he did on occasion write for Bradford's *New-York Weekly Gazette* prior to his political battles with Cosby.[58]

Fourth, Alexander was one of the richest citizens of New York at the time. In fact, he "ranked as the wealthiest lawyer and second wealthiest taxpayer in the city."[59] Like most other white New Yorkers of any means, Alexander was a small slaveholder. In 1729, he owned six slaves.[60] As was common practice in New York City's slaving-owning households, Alexander's slaves most likely lived with him and his family under the same roof. Typically, the enslaved lived in the cellar, where the kitchen was, or in the garret.[61] Under these circumstances, Alexander may well have become familiar with the local African American music and musical material culture reported in *The SPY's* letter with such specific detail.

Finally, one final clue remains in solving the mystery of *The SPY's* true identity. In the second paragraph of the first letter, *The SPY* identifies himself as a music lover: "I, who am always delighted with Music, be it never so rustic." This description aptly fits Alexander. He and his wife Mary were both avid social dancers, so much so that in 1730 Alexander kept a small notebook in which he transcribed the instructions for twenty-seven country-dances.[62]

Conclusion

The 1736 *New-York Weekly Journal* piece denotes a major milestone in the annals of banjo history as the earliest reference to the instrument in the historical record of North America found thus far. Furthermore, if our premise is correct and the event in question was, indeed, a fair held as part of an Easter Monday celebration, then Easter Monday, April 10, 1730, is the only calendar date that matches the dateline of *The SPY*'s "letter." This date would push back the year of the purported Easter Monday fair in Lower Manhattan—the scene of the first documented sighting of the early gourd banjo in North America—six years earlier to 1730!

Yet, this dating also poses a serious dilemma: did the fair in which the "Banger" was reported actually occur? As we have shown, *The SPY*'s "letter" was a satirical op-ed written in the common literary format of a fictitious anonymous letter. Still, James Alexander, who probably was the author, provides enough specific detail to suggest that he based his account on an actual event that he either had witnessed or had heard about. What is more, Alexander was apparently confident that his readers would recognize the described event and get his use of it as a platform for his satire. Likewise, as stated earlier, he also must have felt that they were familiar enough with the "Banger" that they did not require further explication of the term when he cited it three times in his report.

Taking all of this into consideration, the 1736 narrative challenges us to look beyond prevalent assumptions and dig deeper into the historical record as we try to identify, verify, and analyze the many varied facets of its story. By using a variegated network of primary sources and scholarly works, we can more effectively consider the fair and the music instruments and cultural implements cited. Doing so leads to a greater understanding and appreciation of early African American music and culture in the Northeast. And further study of the fair described by *The SPY* will shed new light on early African American festivals such as Pinkster, General Training Day, and Negro Election Day and their significance as the products of creolization as well as mediums of cross-cultural interaction between the various groups and traditions in the region. Finally, *The SPY*'s account serves as a catalyst for greater explorations of the wide range of issues pertaining to the contextualization of the early gourd banjo as an African American tradition in colonial New York City and northeastern Mid-Atlantic America.

*   *   *

Full Text

Note: As per the literary custom of the eighteenth century, the letter *f* generally replaced *s* in the body of a given word throughout the original article. For the sake of expedience, our transcription follows modern practice in this particular regard, so all words are presented without the *f* replacement of *s*. Square brackets [ ] are also used to add clarifications for letters and words that were not clear as part of the text. Other than that, we have maintained the period spelling and grammar of the original piece.

*   *   *

Mr. Zenger;

By an odd Chance I got a Copy of the following Letter, which I desire you to insert in your Journal, and oblige one of your constant Readers,

F.C.[63]

UTOPIA, April 10

Mr.—It is with Pleasure I send you these few Lines; for as I have been some Weeks in this Place, I have some Measure been able to form a Judgment of it.—You need no Description; for as my natural Temper is known to you, take the following Days Ramble and judge of my liking.

This morning I heard my Landlord's black Fellow very busy at tuning of his Banger, as he call'd it, and playing some of his Tunes; I, who am always delighted with Music, be it never so rustic, under a Pretense of Washing came into the Kitchen, and at last asked, what the Meaning was of his being so merry? He started up and with a blithesome Countenance answered, Massa, today Holiday; Backerah no work; Ningar no work; me no savy play Banger; go yonder, you see Ningar play Banger for true, dance too; you see Sport today for true.—He continued, Massa, you savy the Field, little Way out a Town, no Ho[u]ses there, grandy Room for dance there.—Upon this I dress and went to the Place, for I had several Times diverted myself with walking there.

It was no small Amusement to me, to see the Plain partly covered with Booths, and well crouded with Whites, the Negroes divided into Companies, I suppose according to their different Nations, some dancing to the hollow Sound of a Drum, made of the Trunk of a hollow Tree, othersome to the grating rattling Noise of Pebles or Shells in a small Basket, others plied the Banger, and some knew how to joyn the Voice [to] it.—The Warriors were not idle, for I saw several Companies of the Blacks, some exercising the Cudgel, and some of them small Sticks in imitation of the short Pike; and some who had been unlucky enough to get a Dram too much, as I suppose, were got to Loggerheads; all cursing and swearing, and that in a Christian Dialect, enough to raise one's Hair on end. I leave it to you to judge whether all these confused Noises so to one another didn't make a—cord.

I turn'd away from these, not without some Reflection, whether their Rudeness might not be owing in great Measure to the Want of a better Education.

I shap'd my Course towards one of the Booths not so much out of Curiousity of feeling any Thing new, as to get some refreshment: I found it pretty full, and not very noisy; but before I had sipp'd my Pint of Beer which I had called for, I found myself in a Place little better (if any Thing at all) than a Brothel; here I found a mixt Multitude; some with their Doxies[64] on their Laps, others in close Hugg, and to aggravte the Offence, I saw a grave Person, not unknown to me, slyly hiding himself behind a seeming sanctified Beast, both professing our Religion; think how shocking the Sight was when I considred him as Master and Father of a numerous Family, and yet go astray with a Thing that in my Opinion almost deserved the Name of Hagg.—I would have stay'd longer, but I got in Danger of being pickt up by a Jade [65] who seemed to have a Months Mind for me than I had for her or any of her Kind in her Occupation.

I went from this Booth to another, in Expectation of resting a little longer, but I found my Hopes were vain; for here I found a mixt Company again, the Gentleman with the Mechanic,[66] some Maudlin, and some so far intoxicated that they were past making any Noise but among those that were able, Oaths, Curses and Blasphemies were roar'd out to such a Tune as soon sent me thence; for some of them got together by the Ears, and tore one another's Cloaths (which by the by were hardly so good as some of Country Cobblers were) and among them was so kind as to send a Curse after me, and tell me, I might be glad that my Bones were not broke.

Thus disappointed of Resting myself, I thought of going home, but was once more enticed by the Invitation of one with whom I conversed before, to go with him. He told me—that he would bring me to a Place where I should have the Sight of something more diverting than I had seen before; he was attended by a Slave with something in a Bag, of which he seemed as cautious as if it was all Crackery.—At my first Entrance my Ears were saluted with the clamourous Din of I'll fight you! I'll fight you two to one! accompanied with such horrid Oaths, Imprecations, Curses, etc. as soon caused me to wish myself from among them, for at first I imagined that they were going at it themselves, which very much amazed me, for I saw some among them which seemed to be very indifferently qualified for that sort of Exercises; but I was soon convinced of my error by the Prepara-tions I saw making with two Cocks on a sort of a Scaffold which resembled a large Table.—I took this Opportunity to look about me, and found that the Place was crouded with a mixt Multitude, Gentlemen, Merchants, and Mechanics of differ-ent Occupations, and even Day Labourers, of different Ages, in different Garbs, but they seemed to be all hail Fellow well met.—As soon as the combatants were got ready, Mr. Smallrent roar'd out, Five Pistoles [67] upon the Gray; 'Tis done, says Chip the Carpenter; Two to one, says Snip the Taylor; I'll stand you, says Crispin; Hah! Says Mr. Smallrent, there's a Stroke for you, five to one upon the Gray; I hold you, says Mr. Heurt the Carman, the Dan lives yet.—Among the rest I observed a Gentleman who by his venerable Countenance seemed to indicate that he was pretty far advanced in Studying of the Arts and Sciences, he took up the Bottle and Glass, and drank to a Youth that stood at his Elbow, and seem'd to be somewhat cast down, Come! Says he gravely, never heed it, I don't see so much odds in the Battle as yet; and immediately there was a Huzza! For the Dan had cut down the Gray, Mr. Smallrent lost his ten Pistoles;—a pretty sum;—I thought it might have been bestowed much better.—Tired with the Noise I endeavoured to get out of it, and in my Way home, considering the Day, (being one of those see a part to commemorate the Resurrection of our Blessed Saviour) and the Diversions I had seen, I could not chuse but think the Holidays thus spent could be of very little Service, if they were not pernicious; Religion seems to be made the Pretence of consecrating a Day, but how God is served, judge by what I have related.—You can't imagine how irksom it is to me who have been used to a regular Life, to hear the Impieties, and see the Outrages daily committed in the common Streets, not only by the Blacks, or the poorer Whites, but even by the genteeler Sort; and all this too often with Impunity.—I was with my Shoemaker yesterday to pay off, and saw little else than a parcel of small necessitous Children; today I saw him half drunk, playing for a Piece he had received of me.—In short, we have been used to Holidays in our Country, but such as Observation of them in my Opinion, would hardly go down with our civilized Heathens.

I had almost forgot to tell you that I have been drove out of my Quarters several Times by the confused Noise of a Horne, and the singing (or rather howling) of some half drunk Fellows; I am told that the Noise almost resembles the Indians Kintekaying.[68]

In short Time you may expect more from

Yours, etc.

The SPY

Notes

We would like to thank the staff at the Library of Congress's Newspaper and Current Periodical Room for assisting Greg C. Adams in locating and obtaining a PDF of the March 7, 1736, edition of *The New-York Weekly Journal*, as well as the editions of March 14 and 21, 1736, cited here.

1. James Fenimore Cooper, *Satanstoe; or The Littlepage Manuscripts. A Tale of the Colony* (New York: Burgess, Stringer & Co., 1845; reprint American Book Company, 1937), 55; Graham Russell Hodges, *Roots and Branch: African Americans in New York and East Jersey, 1613–1863* (Chapel Hill: University of North Carolina Press, 1999), 88, 301n74; Shane White, "'It Was a Proud Day': African Americans, Festivals, and Parades in the North, 1741–1834," *The Journal of American History* 81, no. 1 (June 1994): 13–50. Hodges was perhaps the first historian to uncover *The SPY*'s account in the *New-York Weekly Journal*. However, he was incorrect in dating the issues as 1737 rather than 1736.

2. For more on the early gourd banjo, see in this volume the chapter Pestcoe co-authored with Greg C. Adams, "Changing Perspectives on the Banjo's African American Origins and West African Heritage."

3. *Backerah* (*Buckra*): an early Afro-Creole designation for a white male.

4. Cooper, *Satanstoe*, 60.

5. Shane White states that "Pinkster was celebrated at the market at Catharine Slip" ("Proud Day," 21) in Lower Manhattan, citing as his source Thomas F. DeVoe's *The Market Book: A History of the Public Markets of the City of New York* (New York: "Printed for the Author," 1862; reprint New York: Augustus M. Kelley Publishers, 1970), 344–45. However, DeVoe makes it clear that African Americans gathered at the market to earn some "pocket-money" to spend on Pinkster, not to celebrate the holiday there (DeVoe, *The Market Book*, 344). White finishes the same sentence by correctly pointing out that Pinkster festivities took place "across the East River in Brooklyn [Heights], at the old market, until that was torn down in 1814."

6. Esther Singleton, *Dutch New York* (New York: Dodd, Mead and Company, 1909), 315–20.

7. Ibid., 55.

8. In 1803, construction began on the third City Hall, which would be situated on the Common, occupying the spot of the first almshouse (1736–97). With the opening of the new City Hall in 1812, the Common was transformed into City Hall Park, as it is known to this very day. See New York City Department of Parks and Recreation, "City Hall Park," http://www.nycgovparks.org/parks/cityhallpark, accessed October 25, 2017; *New York City Guide*, ed. Lou Gody (New York: The Guilds Committee for Federal Writers' Publications, Inc., 1939; reprinted as *The WPA Guide to New York City: the WPA's Federal Writers' Project Guide to 1930's New York City, with a new Introduction by William H. Whyte*, Pantheon Books, 1982), 96.

9. For more on the respective roles of the banjo and fiddle in early African American vernacular dance music, see Dena J. Epstein, *Sinful Tunes and Spirituals: Black Folk Music to the Civil War* (Urbana: University of Illinois Press, 1977, 2003), 144–60; for the relationship between bowed lutes and plucked lutes in West African traditions, see Jacqueline Cogdell DjeDje, *Fiddling in West Africa: Touching the Spirit in Fulbe, Hausa, and Dagbamba Cultures* (Bloomington: Indiana University Press, 2008).

10. Siegfried Nadel's fieldwork diaries (Nigeria, 1935–36), 120–22; "Kaburu," in *The Grove Dictionary of Musical Instruments: Second Edition*, ed. Laurence Libin, 5 vols. (Oxford: Oxford University Press, 2014), 3:94.

11. "A Pinkster Ode" (Albany: Absalom Aimwell, 1803), reprinted (copied by Geraldine R. Pleat and Agnes N. Underwood) in *New York Folklore Quarterly* 8 (1952): 31–45.

12. Negro Election Days were the annual "elections" of African American "kings" and "governors" held throughout New England, at least as far back as the 1740s. Akin to Pinkster, these secular holidays were observed for several days, typically in May or June, for which black slaves were given the entire time off. The festivities included elaborate fairs, parades, and receptions that featured African and African American vernacular music and dancing. See William D. Piersen, *Black Yankees: The Development of an Afro-American Subculture in Eighteenth-Century New England* (Amherst: University of Massachusetts Press, 1988), 117–28.

13. Henry Bull, "Memoir of Rhode-Island," *Rhode-Island Republican* (Newport), August 19, 1837, 1; quoted in Piersen, *Black Yankees*, 121–22, 216n5, 21.

14. *New York Mercury*, November 5, 1753, p. 3, col. 2, as cited in Robert B. Winans, "Black Musicians in Eighteenth-Century America: Evidence from Runaway Salve Advertisements," in this volume. Our special thanks to Winans for sharing this important finding from his research.

15. Thomas C. Cornell, *Adam and Anne Mott: Their Ancestors and Their Descendants* (Poughkeepsie, NY: A. V. Haight, 1890), 26; cited in Philip F. Gura and James F. Bollman's *America's Instrument: The Banjo in the Nineteenth Century* (Chapel Hill: University of North Carolina Press, 1999), 14–15.

16. Jill Lepore, *New York Burning: Liberty, Slavery, and Conspiracy in Eighteenth-Century Manhattan* (New York: Alfred A. Knopf, 2005), appendix A, "Sources and Methods: The People Data," 235–36.

17. Ibid., xii.

18. Ibid., 23–24.

19. Enculturation: "the process of learning about a culture through social interactions." David C. Leonard, *Learning Theories, A to Z* (Westport, CT: Greenwood Press, 2002), 65.

20. Epstein, *Sinful Tunes and Spirituals*, "Appendix II: Table of Sources for the Banjo, Chronologically Arranged," 359–62. Epstein's table does not include the 1736 *New-York Weekly Journal* reference to the "Banger."

21. Ibid., 52, 85. The term *Ebo* is an apparent reference to the Igbo (also Ibo), a large ethnic group in southern and southeastern Nigeria. It is ranked as one of three predominant ethnic-linguistic groups in Nigeria, the other two being the Hausa in the north and the Yoruba in the south. James S. Olson, *The Peoples of Africa: An Ethnohistorical Dictionary* (Westport, CT: Greenwood Press), 234.

22. Konin Aka, "Segesege," in *The Grove Dictionary of Musical Instruments: Second Edition, ed.* Laurence Libin, 5 vols. (Oxford: Oxford University Press, 2014), 4:459.

23. "Ichaka," in *The Grove Dictionary of Musical Instruments: Second Edition*, ed. Laurence Libin, 5 vols. (Oxford: Oxford University Press, 2014), 3:2.

24. The term *caxixi* may have been derived from *caki*, the generic Hausa designation for hand-held rattles. David W. Ames and Anthony V. King, *Glossary of Hausa Music and Its Social Contexts* (Evanston, IL: Northwestern University Press, 1971), 5–6.

25. See Gerhard Kubik, "Drum Patterns in the 'Batuque' of Benedito Caxias," *Latin American Music Review / Revista de Música Latinoamericana* 11, no. 2 (Autumn–Winter 1990): 152–53.

26. *Capoeira* is an Afro-Brazilian martial art that originated in Bahia.

27. The *caxixi* is held by the *berimbau* player in the same hand that holds the stick beater, typically the right, and shaken when the player strikes the berimbau's string with the beater.

28. See, for example, George Pinckard, *Notes on the West Indies*, 2nd ed., 3 vols. (London: Baldwin, Cradock and Joy, 1816), 2:84, quoted in Epstein's *Sinful Tunes and Spirituals*, 61–62.

29. Kirsten Olsen, *Daily Life in 18th-Century England* (Santa Barbara, CA: Greenwood Publishing Group, 1999), 167, 251. For a report of a cudgeling match at the 1721 Boughton Green Fair, see the June 5, 1721, edition of the *Northampton Mercury*, cited in John Styles's *The Dress of the People: Everyday Fashions in Eighteen Century England* (New Haven, CT: Yale University Press, 2007), 317, 400n47.

30. Richard P. Gildrie, "Defiance, Diversion, and the Exercise of Arms: The Several Meanings of Colonial Training Days in Colonial Massachusetts," *Military Affairs* 52, no. 2 (April 1988): 53–55.

31. Maureen Warner-Lewis, *Central Africa in the Caribbean: Transcending Time, Transforming Cultures* (Barbados: University of the West Indies Press, 2003), 199–214. For *calinda* as a designation for Afro-Creole dances accompanied by the early gourd banjo and drums, see Epstein's *Sinful Tunes and Spirituals*, 24, 28, 30–38, 82, 92, 94, 135.

32. Hodges, *Roots and Branch*, 88, 301n74.

33. See Shane White, "Pinkster: Afro-Dutch Syncretization in New York City and the Hudson Valley," *Journal of American Folklore* 102, no. 403 (January–March 1989): 68–75, and "'Proud Day,'" 13–50.

34. Ned Sublette, *Cuba and Its Music: From the First Drums to the Mambo* (Chicago: Chicago Review Press, 2004), 114–15.

35. White, "'Proud Day,'" 18.

36. *The New-York Weekly Journal*, March 7, 1736, 2.

37. Bonnie Blackburn and Leofranc Holford-Strevens, *The Oxford Companion to the Year* (Oxford: Oxford University Press, 1999), 631.

38. According to calculations created by Ronald W. Mallen, April 10 was Easter Sunday in 1735 and April 9 in 1730. Despite it occurring six years earlier, the latter actually would make more sense in the context of *The SPY*'s "letter" as the fair he describes could never have taken place on Easter Sunday proper. Rather, fairs and other popular public amusements traditionally occurred on the following day, Easter Monday, a traditional day off in the Mid-Atlantic colonies as it has been in Europe for centuries. For this reason, it seems more likely that *The SPY* had dated his "letter" on April 10—which was Easter Monday, 1730—as that could have been the only plausible calendar date for such a fair. See Ronald Mallen, "Easter Dating Method," Astronomical Society of South Australia (2002), http://www.assa.org.au/edm.html#List17, accessed October 25, 2017.

39. Dorothy Gladys Spicer, *Festivals of Western Europe* (New York: H. W. Wilson, 1958), 131. Tweede Paasdag traditions include *eierrapen* hunts for colored Easter eggs and *eiertikken* contests in which contestants in egg-knocking matches try to break their opponents' colored Easter eggs without damaging their own. In Brooklyn, the Dutch Easter egg

traditions of *eierrapen* and *eiertikken* were featured prominently in local observances of Paas Monday well into the nineteenth century. See Henry R. Stiles, *A History of Brooklyn* (Brooklyn, NY: "Published by subscription," 1869), 39–40.

40. "Paas Festival of The St. Nicholas Society," *The Knickerbocker or New-York Monthly Magazine* 51 (1858): 648. For African American observation of the Paas, see David Steven Cohen, *The Dutch American Farm* (New York: New York University Press, 1993), 160–61.

41. See Lepore's *New York Burning*, 158–59, for a discussion of slaves in early New York City celebrating Whitsuntide based on the court records from the trials of those accused of participating in the alleged 1741 New York Slave Conspiracy.

42. Olsen, *Daily Life in 18th-Century England*, 115.

43. White, "'Proud Day,'" 21.

44. Vincent Buranelli, "Peter Zenger's Editor," *American Quarterly* 7, no. 2 (Summer 1955): 175–76.

45. Ibid.

46. See Vincent Buranelli, *The Trial of Peter Zenger* (New York: New York University Press, 1957). Like Zenger, Bradford did not edit the newspaper he printed. Francis Harison was the shadow editor of *New-York Weekly Gazette* and Alexander's nemesis in the battle of invective that raged between the two papers from the first publication of *The New-York Weekly Journal* on November 5, 1733.

47. Buranelli, "Peter Zenger's Editor," 176; Patricia U. Bonomi, *A Factious People: Politics and Society in Colonial New York* (New York: Columbia University Press, 1971), 113–15; Lepore, *New York Burning*, xi, xiii, xv.

48. In his infamous 1735 trial, Zenger was charged with being "a frequent printer and publisher of false news and seditious libels," and not as the author of said material. At the time, it was no secret that Alexander was the main person behind *The New-York Weekly Journal*. Governor Cosby stated as much in his report to the Board of Trade on December 6, 1734: "Mr. James Alexander is the person whom I have too much occasion to mention. . . . A press supported by him and his party began to swarm with the most virulent libels. His open and implacable malice against me has appeared weekly in Zenger's *Journal*" (Buranelli, *The Trial of Peter Zenger*, 27).

49. Zenger was apprenticed to Bradford as a young teen shortly after emigrating from his native Germany with his family in 1710. Fifteen years later, he entered into a brief partnership with Bradford that lasted only a year. In 1726, Zenger opened his own print shop, "thus becoming the second printer in New York, and the first rival of his former master" (ibid., 4).

50. Buranelli, *The Trial of Peter Zenger*, 4; Bonomi, *A Factious People*, 113–15.

51. To the best of our research, we could find only one example of "Utopia" used as a place name prior to 1847. In 1625, John Utie (Uty) named his plantation on Hog Island, Virginia, "Utopia." Martha W. McCartney, *Virginia Immigrants and Adventurers: A Biographical Dictionary, 1607–1635* (Baltimore: Genealogical Publishing Company, 2007), 710.

52. See William Bailie, *Josiah Warren: The First American Anarchist* (Boston: Small, Maynard & Company, 1906), 50–57; Richard C. S. Trahair, *Utopias and Utopians: An Historical Dictionary* (Westport, CT: Greenwood Press, 1999), 421–22; John Humphrey Noyes, *History of American Socialisms* (New York: Hillary House, 1961), 94–101.

53. The term *utopia* first appeared in More's classic work, *Libellus . . . de optimo reipublicae statu, deque nova insula Utopia* (Concerning the highest state of the republic and the

new island Utopia; 1516; first published English translation, 1551). He combined the Greek words *ou* (no), and *topos* (place) to create *utopia* (no place). More framed his 1516 treatise as a fictitious anonymous letter in order to express his own social vision and juxtapose it to the current reality in a satirical commentary. See Thomas More, *Sir Thomas More's Utopia, Edited, with Introduction and Notes by J. Churton Collins* (Oxford: Clarendon Press, 1904); *Utopia, with Erasmus's The Sileni of Alcibiades, Edited and Translated, with an Introduction by David Wootton* (Indianapolis: Hackett Publishing Company, 1999).

54. *The New-York Weekly Journal*, March 14 and 21, 1736, 1–2.

55. Bonomi, *A Factious People*, 113.

56. By way of example, see the front pages of *The New-York Weekly Journal* editions of August 19, 1734, and February 14 and 28, 1736.

57. Buranelli, *The Trial of Peter Zenger*, 4.

58. Buranelli, "Peter Zenger's Editor," 176.

59. Lepore, *New York Burning*, 31.

60. Ibid., 33. Alexander placed an ad for "a Negroe Man named Yaff," who had "run away," in the June 23, 1729, edition of the *New-York Weekly Gazette*. In the ad, Alexander describes Yaff as follows: "He was born in this Country, and reads and writes. He is a sensible cunning Fellow, and probably has got a pass forged."

61. Shane White, *Somewhat More Independent: The End of Slavery in New York City, 1770–1810* (Athens: University of Georgia Press, 1991), 9.

62. See Kate Van Winkle Keller, "James Alexander's Collection of Country Dances, New York, 1730," in *Libraries, History, Diplomacy, and the Performing Arts: Essays in Honor of Carleton Sprague Smith: Festschrift Series, No 9* (Hillsdale, NY: Pendragon Press, 1991), 353–70.

63. The initials "F.C." here probably stood for "Faithful Correspondent."

64. "DOXIES. She beggars, Wenches, Whores." Nathan Bailey, *The Universal Etymological English Dictionary* (London, 1736), vol. 2.

65. "JADE. A term of reproach to women." Captain Francis Grose (1731–91), *The Dictionary Of The Vulgar Tongue* (London, 1811), 181.

66. *Mechanic*: skilled laborer; artisan.

67. *Pistole*: a gold coin.

68. *The SPY's* descriptor "*Kintekaying*" is probably a cognate of *Canticoy, Cantico*, and *Gekintekayt*, terms used to describe Amerindian dancing reported in the Dutch and English Mid-Atlantic colonies during the seventeenth and eighteenth centuries. See Kate Van Winkle Keller, *Dance and Its Music in America, 1528–1789* (Hillsdale, NY: Pendragon Press, 2007), 468–70.

CHAPTER 11

The Banjar Pictured
The Depiction of the African American Early Gourd Banjo in The Old Plantation, South Carolina, 1780s

Shlomo Pestcoe

Editor's Headnote

Shlomo Pestcoe sets out to contexualize and interpret The Old Plantation *painting dating from the late eighteenth century, noting that it is the earliest and most detailed portrayal of the early gourd banjo in North America. He essentially dissects the image and analyzes each element in depth, in the process correcting prior widely accepted faulty interpretations. He argues that the painting shows the confluence of various African, African American, and European American traditions. Pestcoe highlights the features that link the depicted instrument to its West African heritage, and also the features not found on West African traditional plucked spike lutes, that are European inspired. He also explains how the depicted dance shows West African precedents and influence, and how the image of the banjo player presents clues to early banjo playing technique.*

The Old Plantation is one of the most famous and iconic visual representations of traditional African American culture. It is, in fact, the oldest known period portrayal of early African American music and dance in North America. But the picture is also important from the standpoint of banjo history. The Old Plantation[1] offers the earliest depiction found thus far of the banjo on this continent (see figure N). It is also the second oldest known representation of the instrument in general—the first being the illustration of two Afro-Jamaican gourd-bodied "Strum Strumps" in plate III of Sir Hans Sloane's 1707 book on Jamaica (see figure H), stemming from his stay there twenty years earlier.[2] The type of banjo seen in both of these images is the *early gourd banjo*, my term for what Thomas Jefferson described as the "Banjar" in his *Notes on the State of Virginia* (1781):[3] the original gourd-bodied African American genus of the banjo[4] and the immediate forebear of the wood-rimmed five-string banjo, which first emerged in the United States around 1840.

Most likely painted sometime in the 1780s, the unsigned, undated watercolor from South Carolina shows twelve enslaved African Americans having a dance in the slave quarter of a plantation. In the center of the scene, a man grasps a wooden staff as he dances with two women. They hold what appear to be pieces of cloth. Upon closer inspection, however, these objects might also be possible music instruments—West African–type gourd vessel rattles, composed of a bottle gourd nested in long string netting affixed with clackers. Musical accompaniment is provided by two musicians sitting on a bench: one plays a four-string gourd-bodied banjo, while his partner drums on a small round object with two thin sticks.

Ever since 1935, when *The Old Plantation* was first put on public display in Colonial Williamsburg, which would become its permanent home, scholars have sought to determine who created the picture, as well as where and when it was painted. Seventy-four years later, those questions would finally be answered. In 2009, Susan P. Shames, the decorative arts librarian of the Colonial Williamsburg Foundation, using genealogical research techniques, conclusively identified the artist behind the seemingly anonymous picture as John Rose (1752 or 1753–1820) of Dorchester, South Carolina.[5]

Yet, while Shames's excellent detective work may have finally solved the mystery of *The Old Plantation*'s provenance, ongoing scholarly interpretation of what the historic artwork actually shows us remains open to further analyses and debate. In this chapter, I take up the challenge of contextualizing and interpreting this important historic image, so crucial to our better understanding of early African American music, dance, and material culture, as well as the history of the banjo.

At this point, I should clarify that I do not deal with *Plantation Scene*, an anonymous watercolor currently in the collection of the Mint Museum of Art (Charlotte, North Carolina), which was obviously inspired by *The Old Plantation*.[6] According to forensic analysis done in 1997, certain pigments used in the painting of the Mint Museum piece were not commercially available prior to 1919.[7] As *Plantation Scene* was clearly painted sometime in the twentieth century (most likely after *The Old Plantation* first went on public display in the fall of 1935), it offers no evidentiary value in interpreting the original painting.

In my analysis of *The Old Plantation*, I touch on what I call the "Turner-Herskovits Interpretation," which, until quite recently, was the most widely accepted interpretation of the picture. In 1954, the folk art expert Nina Fletcher Little (1903–93) was engaged by Colonial Williamsburg to catalogue for the first time the 424 pieces in its Abby Aldrich Rockefeller Folk Art Collection, which included *The Old Plantation*.[8] As part of this endeavor, a year later Little would write to Lorenzo Dow Turner (1890–1972) and Melville J. Herskovits (1895–1963)—then the leading authorities on African and African American cultures—to request "any information or comments" on the picture.[9] She combined the key points from Turner's and Herskovits's replies in her descriptive text for *The Old Plantation* (plate 66) in her work, *The Abby Aldrich Rockefeller Folk Art Collection: A Descriptive Catalogue* (1957), thanking and citing them as her sources.[10] Little's text was adopted by Colonial Williamsburg as the official description for *The Old Plantation* and it would become the conventional interpretation of the watercolor for nearly fifty years. Yet, over time, the fact that Turner's and Herskovits's readings of the image were the acknowledged sources of Little's writings on the picture was all but forgotten. This oversight is unfortunate as the "Turner-Herskovits Interpretation" was significant as the first attempt to connect the early African American scene portrayed in *The Old Plantation* to its West African roots. In acknowledging that fact, however, it is important to also recognize that Turner's and Herskovits's analyses were cursory and conjectural, with no basis in actual research of the painting. As such, several of their theories about *The Old Plantation* have not stood the test of time or the findings of more recent research, as I show throughout this chapter.

"Plantation Water Color"

In 1935, Holger Cahill (1887–1960)—the leading authority on American folk art at the time—purchased an anonymous "plantation water color" from the antique dealer Mary E. Lyles of Columbia, South Carolina, for inclusion in the portion of Abby Aldrich Rockefeller's folk art collection slated for permanent public display in Colonial Williamsburg.[11] For purposes of its exhibition, Cahill named the untitled work *The Old Plantation*. In his suggested descriptive text for the painting, he speculated that it dated to "probably about 1790"; the unknown painter was "probably a gentleman of the Carolina low country who painted for his own pleasure"; and the event depicted in the picture was "some sort of a dance, possibly a courting dance among the Gulla[12] of the Carolina Low Country."[13]

Cahill apparently guessed right in his conjectural character sketch of the mysterious artist: as Shames's research has revealed, John Rose was a slave-holding planter in South Carolina's Low Country who was also an amateur watercolorist.[14] Cahill's speculative dating of the painting to 1790 likewise correlates with Shames's other findings, which confirm those of previous research, that the picture was probably painted sometime between 1785 and 1790.[15]

Prior to Shames's investigation, the only known piece of documentary evidence pertaining to *The Old Plantation* was a handwritten inventory that had been first brought to the attention of Colonial Williamsburg's curatorial staff in 1976.[16] It was made by Henrietta "Nettie" Copes of Orangeburg, South Carolina, of the family heirlooms to be auctioned off in the subsequent estate sale following the death of her mother Rose Ellis Copes in 1927.[17] Shames's research would later reveal that Nettie Copes—through her mother's "Ellis" lineage—was John Rose's great-great-granddaughter.[18] Rose's watercolor sketch was included in Nettie's inventory as "Lot No. 35." In its listing, Nettie described what she knew of her unidentified ancestor's artwork from family lore:

> 35. One picture of a negro slave dance, done in water colors, on white drawing paper. . . . I have always been told that this was a drawing from actual life, my great grandfather having sketched his slaves as they were having a dance. All are barefooted. Their cabins are seen in the background. (12 in. x 18 in.)[19]

Early African American Culture in the Carolina Low Country

The dance scene that Rose depicted in *The Old Plantation* offers us a rare glimpse into the unique African American culture emerging in the Carolina Low Country during the eighteenth century. When he painted the picture, the overwhelming majority of the people living in the Low Country—the southern coastal region of South Carolina, which was its first locality of early colonial settlement (Charles Town, 1670) and its most populous area—were enslaved African Americans. These included both African-born survivors of the Middle Passage and Afro-Creoles (blacks of African descent born in the New World).[20] The 1720s saw the establishment of rice as the colony's principal staple commodity and large plantation farming as the mode of its production. As the scale of rice cultivation grew exponentially, so too did the demand for slave labor, thereby leading to the massive importation into the Low Country of enslaved captives from West Africa and West-Central Africa.[21] Up to that point, however, nearly all of Carolina's slaves had been mostly brought from the English West Indies incrementally. Still, many of those imported from the Caribbean were originally from Africa. Thus, by 1740, the majority of enslaved African Americans in South Carolina would be African-born.

The predominance of Africans within the Low Country's ever-growing black majority made for a volatile situation and the looming threat of an impending slave uprising weighed heavily on the region's dominant European American minority. That threat became a reality on September 9, 1739, when a slave revolt occurred on the banks of the Stono River, just twenty miles from the colony's capital Charles Town (renamed Charleston in 1783). It was led by Africans from Angola, the source of 8,045 slaves brought into the colony between 1735 and 1740, nearly 70 percent of a total of 11,562 African captives imported during that period.[22] The South Carolina Assembly responded by enacting two measures the following year: a prohibitively high duty on all further slave importation;[23] and a draconian Slave Act that imposed harsh regulations on the colony's enslaved blacks, ranging from prohibiting them from having or playing "drums, horns, or other loud instruments"[24] to dressing in clothing not made of "Negro cloth."[25]

The 1740 duty on slave imports had its desired effect: a total of only 1,562 African captives were brought into the colony between 1741 and 1750.[26] This drop-off in imports coincided with a dramatic increase in births in enslaved black families, leading to an African American "baby-boom" in South Carolina during the 1740s. As a result, by 1760, the majority of Afro-Carolinians were creoles, country-born in the colony, rather than Africans.[27] However, the large-scale importation of captive Africans resumed in 1751, with its peak years between 1770 and 1790, thereby raising the number of African-born slaves to more than one-third of all Afro-Carolinians.[28]

Taking this historical reality into consideration offers us a new perspective on *The Old Plantation*. Rose's highly detailed portrayal provides us with visual clues as to the folk process of cultural creolization at work. Here we see the confluence of various African, African American, and European American traditions, coming together in the uniquely syncretic cultural gumbo that was early Afro-Carolinian music-dance and material culture (e.g., the depicted music instruments, clothing, and kitchen vessels). Here we see the context in which Gullah (Geechee)—the Afro-Creole language and culture of the Sea Islands and coastal areas of South Carolina and Georgia—emerged.

To begin with, consider what the picture's central scene can tell us about the everyday reality and culture of the enslaved people portrayed. The participants in the depicted social dance gathering are clearly dressed in their own holiday clothes—typically either bartered for or purchased by the enslaved with what little they could earn through their limited sanctioned participation in the local market economy—rather than the rough everyday workwear supplied by their master.[29] Perhaps this event took place over a holiday like Christmas, when slaves were typically given three days off from work.[30] On plantations, such holiday celebrations were traditionally marked by the slaves having their own dances in their quarter. These were often attended by the planter and the planter's family.[31] Under these circumstances, Rose, as the plantation's owner-master, would have certainly had occasion to be present at a holiday dance party in the slave quarter on his plantation.

The Early Gourd Banjo and the Drum

In 1955, in his reply to Nina Fletcher Little's letter requesting his take on *The Old Plantation*, Lorenzo Dow Turner contended that the string instrument depicted in the picture "is called a *molo* and is found among the Hausa and Yoruba peoples of Northern and Southwestern Nigeria, British West Africa, respectively."[32] For his part, Melville Herskovits did recognize it as a "banjo," as did Little herself.[33] In attempting to reconcile these two divergent viewpoints in her descriptive text, Little described the depicted instrument "which resembles a banjo" as "an African *molo*."[34] And so, until quite recently, nearly everything written about *The*

Old Plantation has presented as a given fact this unfounded identification of the depicted banjo as an "African *molo*."

To be clear, *molo* is a generic designation for a plucked spike lute throughout West Africa and is used to describe a variety of different instruments. The Hausa and Yoruba instruments called *molo* (also called *tafashe* in Hausa and *duru* in Yoruba) are specifically semi-spike lutes (see figure B for an example) with narrow elliptical or canoe-shaped wooden bodies and, typically, two to three strings.[35] In sharp contrast, the depicted string instrument in *The Old Plantation* is evidently a full-spike lute (see figure A for an example) with a roundish gourd body and four strings.[36] Moreover, it has tuning pegs and a carved wooden neck with a flat fretless fingerboard (see figure P) rather than the sliding tuning rings and fretless round stick necks found on the Hausa-Yoruba *molo* and every other traditional West African plucked spike lute (see figure D for an example). Taking all of these factors into consideration, the plucked lute portrayed in *The Old Plantation* is clearly an African American early gourd banjo and not an "African *molo*."

As stated earlier, the early gourd banjo Rose depicted in *The Old Plantation* is of the four-string variety, the most prevalent form of the historic African American folk instrument ever since the four-string *banza* (as the early gourd banjo was known in the French Antilles) was first documented in the 1690s. The German physician-naturalist Dr. Johann David Schoepf (1753–1800) provides us with a valuable period account of the four-string early gourd banjo, in terms of both the instrument's construction and the context in which it was played. In 1784, when he set sail to the Bahamas from St. Augustine, Florida, Schoepf noted in his journal that "the negroes on board" the schooner entertained themselves by making music. He described several of their instruments, including the banjo of his day:

> Another musical instrument of the true negro is the *Banjah*. Over a hollow cala-bash (*Cucurb Lagenaria L.*) is stretched a sheepskin, the instrument lengthened with a neck, strung with 4 strings, and made accordant. It gives out a rude sound; usually there is some one besides to give an accompaniment with the drum, or an iron pan, or empty cask, whatever may be at hand. In America and on the islands they make use of this instrument greatly for the dance.[37]

Schoepf's description of the four-string *Banjah* and its playing context corresponds with the instrument's portrayal in *The Old Plantation*. Rose's watercolor offers us the earliest depiction yet found of the banjo in its original typical performance context of accompanying African American vernacular social dancing. Moreover, the picture shows us something even rarer: the banjo being played with its original musical partner—a drum or, as also described by Schoepf, a repurposed found-object used as a drum.[38]

In terms of the banjo's West African kin, in most ethnic traditions plucked spike lutes are traditionally played solo or in duos without the accompaniment of other types of instruments. That rule, however, has exceptions. For example, the three-string gourd-bodied *bunchundo* of the Manyago (also Manjak, Manjaco, etc.; Senegambia) is traditionally played in a duet with a found-object drum (typically, either a cooking pot or a glass palm wine bottle) that is beaten with two thin sticks (see figure E).[39] Another example would be the three-string gourd-bodied *gulom* of the Kotoko (Chad and northern Cameroon), which is accompanied by a drum made from a half of a gourd that is played by beating two sticks on its back wall.[40] These two examples are echoed in the African American duet of early gourd banjo and drum shown in *The Old Plantation* (see figure O).

The drummed object that Rose depicted has been the subject of some speculation. In his reply to Little, Turner categorically identified it as "a Yoruba instrument called *gudugudu*." "The body," he explained, "is a hollowed piece of wood over which animal skin is stretched to form the drum-head. . . . The drum-sticks are twisted pieces of leather and are attached to another strip of leather that encircles the drumhead."[41] Turner had firsthand knowledge of the *gudugudu*, having brought one back four years earlier from his Fulbright lectureship in Nigeria (1950–51).[42] He claimed that the *gudugudu* looked "exactly" like the depicted drum "in the picture."[43] Actually, upon closer inspection, the drum in *The Old Plantation* bears little resemblance to the small Yoruba kettle drum. The *gudugudu* (also *omole*)—traditionally played as part of a *dundun* drum ensemble—is distinguished by a large black dot of tuning paste on its soundtable, as well as a great deal of leather lacing all around to secure its animal hide soundtable.[44] Conversely, *The Old Plantation* drum is plain with no discernible features other than being small, tan, and round. Furthermore, Rose clearly shows the drummer playing his drum with straight wooden sticks rather than the "tightly twisted pieces of leather" used for playing the *gudugudu*, which are also invariably bent.

In his reply to Little, Herskovits suggested that the portrayed drummer "is perhaps playing a gourd," which seems closer to the mark.[45] The young Scotsman James Barclay had encountered just such a gourd drum in South Carolina's Low Country when he worked as an overseer on a plantation there in the early 1770s. Barclay reported that the local slaves' "instrument of musick is called a Bangier, made of Calabash."[46] He described it as being played "very artfully with two sticks, as we do on a drum," with the musician sitting on the ground and holding it between his legs.[47] Barclay's description of the "Bangier" gourd drum and how it was played matches what Rose depicted in *The Old Plantation*.

Rose's Depiction of the Early Gourd Banjo

Rose's highly detailed portrayal of the four-string version of the early gourd banjo offers us amazing views of the instrument's unique features, some never before depicted. The first of these features is the thumb-string, the defining element of the four-string version of the early gourd banjo and an indicator of the banjo's

West African heritage.[48] *The Old Plantation* is one of two period depictions of the four-string early gourd banjo that clearly show the short thumb-string. The other is the illustration of an early Afro-Surinamese version of the instrument (see figure L), the "Creole-Bania," no. 15 in plate 69, "Musical Instruments of the African Negroes [of Suriname]" in *Narrative of a Five Years Expedition against the Revolted Negroes of Surinam, from 1772 to 1777* (1796) by Captain John Gabriel Stedman (1744–97).[49]

Another critical feature that Rose shows us on the depicted early gourd banjo is a highly distinctive neck-through-body type of full-spike construction. This construction is also evident on the two late seventeenth-century Afro-Jamaican "Strum Strumps" illustrated in plate III in Sloane's 1707 book, *A Voyage to the Islands of Madera, Barbados, Nieves, S. Christophers and Jamaica*, as well as on Stedman's illustration of the Afro-Surinamese *creole bania* (see figures H and L). It is likewise seen on the three historic four-string early gourd banjos that are known to exist: the *creole bania* (Suriname, ca. 1773–77; Rijksmuseum voor Volkenkunde, Leiden, the Netherlands), which Stedman is thought to have brought back when he returned to Holland after his tour of duty in Suriname (see figure J); the *banza* (Haiti, 1840–41 [see figure K]; Musée de la Musique, Cité de la Musique, Paris, France); and the *panja* (*banja*) (Suriname, ca. 1850; Ethnologisches Museum, Staatliche Museen zu Berlin, Germany).[50]

On the gourd-bodied banjo depicted by Rose—as well as on both of Sloane's Afro-Jamaican "Strum Strumps" and the Afro-Haitian *banza*, all of which also have gourd bodies—the thick bottleneck of the hollowed-out bottle gourd used to make the instrument's body has been cut off, thereby leaving a hollow stub for the instrument's neck (see figure K). When the given instrument was assembled, its carved wooden neck was inserted into the sleeve of the gourd's neck stub. It was then pushed through the hollowed gourd body[51] until the narrow spike end of the neck protruded out of the bottom hole made in the body's tail end, hence the designation of early gourd banjos as "full-spike" instruments.

This full-spike characteristic links the early gourd banjo to a small but important subsection within the greater family of plucked spike lutes found throughout West Africa: full-spike lutes, all of which have non-wooden bodies made of gourd or, in some traditions, calabash. But the early gourd banjo's neck-through-body construction is only found on the few full-spike lutes from West Africa's Central Sudan[52] eastern subregion (e.g., the three-string calabash-bodied Kilba *gullum* [northern Nigeria] [see figure G], the two-string gourd-bodied Hausa *gurmi* [northern Nigeria], the two-string calabash-bodied Toubou *gurumi* [Niger], etc.). Conversely, the necks on all other West African plucked spike lutes (semi-spike and full-spike) do not pierce through the body but, rather, pass over the upper rim of the body. On the Central Sudanese full-spike lutes, however, the neck is not inserted through the sleeve of the open neck stub of the bottle gourd body. It appears, therefore, that the neck-through-sleeve insertion was a feature unique to early gourd banjos.

Another distinctive feature seen on *The Old Plantation* banjo that reflects the early gourd banjo's West African heritage are the decorative soundholes carved into the instrument's gourd body (see figure P). Throughout West Africa, the gourd or calabash bodies on full-spike lutes have soundholes cut into them. These holes may be round and/or in different shapes, such as triangles, diamonds, crescents, or *X*s. Carved soundholes are also found on the bodies of the *creole bania*, the *banza*, and the *panja* (for access to a photo of the *panja*, see note 50). Both of the Afro-Surinamese instruments have a single S-shaped soundhole in one side of the body. In addition, the *creole bania* has several small round holes on the back of its body, while the *panja* has but one there. Conversely, the Afro-Haitian *banza* has four holes in various shapes on its body's verso.

Yet another important feature shown on *The Old Plantation* banjo is its floating (movable) bipedal bridge (see figure P). It is the thin upright horizontal piece with two distinct legs resting on the instrument's animal-hide soundtable, over which the strings are lifted up as they pass from peghead to the body's tail end. Rose's depiction is the earliest and most detailed image of a banjo bridge in early banjo iconography. As noted above, the two Afro-Jamaican "Strum Strumps" seen in Sloane's plate III illustration are missing their bridges, as are all three of the extant historic early gourd banjos. While a bridge is clearly shown on the *creole bania* depicted in Stedman's *Narrative*, it appears only as a thick line since the image itself is too small to show any specific detail (see figure L). Still, the evidence of Stedman's illustration, as well as that of *The Old Plantation*, offers corroboration that the bridges on early gourd banjos were, indeed, floating bridges, akin to those used on the succeeding wood-rimmed five-string banjos from the 1840s on (see figure M). Furthermore, many early gourd banjo bridges might have been bipedal like the one seen in *The Old Plantation* as the configuration of two legs was also very common on early five-string banjo bridges.

The bipedal bridge on *The Old Plantation* banjo also links it to a specific subgroup within the West African family of plucked spike lutes, what I term the *Atlantic-Bak "folk lute"* cluster, found in the Greater Senegambian region of the Gambia, Casamance, and Cacheu Rivers along the Atlantic coast.[53] This cluster includes five nearly identical three-stringed full-spike folk lutes with gourd bodies: the Jola *ekonting* (see figure A), the Manyago *bunchundo* (see figure E), the Bujogo *ñopata* (see figure F), the Balanta *kusunde*, and the Papel *busunde*. A defining feature that they all share is a large upright floating bridge with two legs—a type of bridge not found on any other kind of West African plucked spike lute. It is, however, found on the banjo's North African cousins of West African heritage (all of which are three-stringed): the Gnawa *hajhuj* (also referred to as *gnbri*, *guinbri*, *guembri*, or *sintir*) of Morocco and Algeria, and the *gumbri*, the *gambara*, and the *fakrūn* of Tunisia.[54]

The early gourd banjo portrayed in *The Old Plantation* also reveals features not found on West African traditional plucked spike lutes, such as the banjo's flat-surfaced fingerboard and tuning pegs. In West African tradition, the strings are affixed to the lute's fretless round stick neck with sliding tuning rings (see figure D). In Rose's highly detailed depiction of the four-string early gourd banjo, we see something different: its strings are affixed to wooden tuning pegs (see figure P). The pegs for the three long strings are housed in a distinct peghead at the top of the neck, while the peg for the top fourth short thumb-string is inserted from behind into a hole in the upper portion of the fingerboard. Carved wooden necks fitted with a flat fingerboard and tuning pegs housed in a peghead are also found on Sloane's illustration of the Afro-Jamaican "Strum Strumps" and Stedman's of the Afro-Surinamese *creole bania*, as well as all three extant historic early gourd banjos. These features are European-inspired New World innovations that distinguish the African American early gourd banjo from its West African antecedents.

In his depiction of the early gourd banjo, Rose shows yet another non–West African feature clearly inspired by European lutes: a raised small piece at the top of the instrument's fingerboard called a nut (see figure P). Traditionally made of wood or bone, the nut's purpose is to raise the strings off the fingerboard and facilitate their passage to the tuning pegs. Raised nuts are found the world over on many kinds on plucked lutes and bowed lutes (fiddles)—as well as on other types of chordophones such as some zithers—which have tuning pegs, especially those housed in some sort of distinct peghead. It was a standard feature on early wood-rimmed five-string banjos and remains so on all subsequent modern banjo family instruments. Nuts, however, are conspicuously absent from two of the known historic early gourd banjos: the Afro-Surinamese *creole bania*[55] and the Afro-Haitian *banza*. However, a low-profile nut is found on the Afro-Surinamese *panja*.

Rose offers us one more first: the earliest depiction of a separate tailpiece on a banjo. As its name implies, the purpose of the tailpiece is to secure the tails at the ends of the strings to the tail end of the instrument's body (see figure R). Tailpieces have been used on both plucked lutes and bowed lutes (fiddles) the world over throughout history. Across Europe, tailpieces have historically been used primarily on fiddles, though they also have been used on some plucked lutes. Conversely, on most West African full-spike lutes, their strings' tails are tied onto the end of the neck where it protrudes past the body.[56] This type of attachment was apparently also used on the Afro-Surinamese *creole bania* and *panja*, and, perhaps, on the Afro-Haitian *banza*.[57] An interesting variation of this West African practice appears on both of the Afro-Jamaican "Strum Strumps": on the protruding stub of the neck's sawed-off spike are two small holes drilled into it apparently to receive the strings' tails. In any case, with the emergence of the wood-rimmed five-string banjo around 1840, tailpieces became standard on banjos.

In his painting, John Rose does not show the spike-end of the instrument's neck protruding through the body's tail end. Still, his depiction of a distinct tailpiece implies its presence. This tailpiece would not have been nailed or glued directly to the gourd body. The great amount of tension produced by the tuned strings would have made these types of attachment problematic at best and rendered the tailpiece very susceptible to being pulled off. That said, as shown by Rose, the depicted banjo player appears to have addressed this issue with an ingenious solution: fashioning the tailpiece from what was most likely a single piece of leather. Rather than being attached directly to the banjo's gourd body, the probable leather tailpiece in all likelihood had a hole cut out of its lower end to slip over the neck's spike-end. A discernable black dot in the center of the depicted tailpiece might have been the artist's way of indicating the hole for the spike-end of the neck and/or, possibly, the neck's spike-end itself.[58]

Aside from *The Old Plantation*, the earliest evidence of the use of a leather tailpiece on a gourd banjo is the Metropolitan Museum of Art's nineteenth-century gourd-bodied five-string banjo (89.4.598; attributed to William Esperance Boucher Jr. [1822–99] of Baltimore, Maryland, one of the earliest known commercial banjo manufacturers, ca. 1840–90),[59] accessioned into the Met's Crosby Brown Collection in 1889 (see figure 9.1 in chapter 9). Now missing, its original tailpiece was leather and slipped over the end of the neck's "perchpole" (dowel stick) that protrudes out of the tail end of its gourd body.[60]

The Old Plantation:
Clues to Early Banjo-Playing Technique

Rose's remarkably detailed depiction of the four-string early gourd banjo offers us not only rare visual evidence of how the instrument actually looked and was built, but also even rarer visual clues as to how it was played.

Looking at the banjo player's right hand—the one he uses for sounding the strings—it appears as if the thumb and index finger are coming together in a pinching action. This configuration would suggest that the player was perhaps plucking the strings employing a two-finger picking style, akin to those used in playing plucked spike lutes throughout West Africa, as well as in some regional traditions of old-time five-string banjo playing. Upon closer inspection of the banjoist's right hand in *The Old Plantation*, however, it is evident that the middle, ring, and pinky fingers of the player's right hand are curled in (see figure R). This position is in sharp contrast to what normally occurs with two-finger techniques, where the pinky—and sometimes the middle and ring fingers—rest on the instrument's head (soundtable) to brace the hand. The playing technique, however, in which those three fingers are generally curled in is down-picking (also referred to down-stroking), the earliest documented technique for playing the banjo. Forms of down-picking are also used to play several traditional plucked spike lutes (e.g., the Jola *ekonting* and the Bujogo *ñopata*) in West Africa, where it most likely originated, as well as the aforementioned North African plucked spike lutes of West African heritage.[61]

From the 1840s through the 1860s, down-picking was the popular "Banjo Style" for playing the five-string banjo. This playing technique consists of the player using the fingernail of one finger (either the index or middle finger) to pick out the melody by striking individual long melody strings (stopped and open) in a downward motion. The action of down-picking a long melody string is quickly followed up by the thumb catching the short thumb-string to create a rhythmic backbeat. As the striking finger and the thumb are the principal fingers used in down-picking, all of the other fingers are typically curled in alongside the striking finger. If the striker is the index finger, then all four fingers will appear clenched with the index finger jutting out slightly. However, if the middle finger is the striker, then the index finger will extend out—typically, as if pointing downward—so as to stay clear of the striking middle finger and the strings. Thus, it is possible to infer that the right hand of the banjo player depicted in *The Old Plantation* appears to be positioned in a down-picking playing action, as opposed to that of a two-finger playing technique.

Another depiction in early banjo iconography (see figure Q) in which the player's right hand is clearly shown to be engaged in down-picking is *The Banjo Player* (1856)[62] by the American genre painter William Sidney Mount (1807–68) of Long Island, New York, who was also an accomplished vernacular fiddler and flute player. In this painting, Mount portrays George Freeman, a local African American banjoist from Suffolk County, Long Island,[63] playing a period fretless five-string banjo of commercial manufacture, as were most banjos of that time. A noteworthy and exceedingly rare feature depicted on the "pot" (body) of Freeman's banjo is that it has two "heads" (top and back), akin to the double-headed Boucher banjo (ca. 1845–46) in the collections of the Smithsonian (094764).[64]

In *The Banjo Player*, Mount shows Freeman's right hand as it down-picks the strings, much like what we see in Rose's depiction of the banjoist's playing action in *The Old Plantation* (see figure R). Mount's portrayal of Freeman's right-hand position may be interpreted as a depiction of either the index finger or the middle finger as the striker. For the former, the fingernail of Freeman's index finger may be seen as striking the second string with his middle, ring, and pinky fingers curled in. For the latter, the index finger could be viewed as pointing away from the string to clear the way for the middle finger to strike it. In either case, however, Freeman's thumb rests on the short fifth thumb-string, poised to pluck it immediately after the sounding of the long melody string.

The Depicted Dance: West African Precedent and Influence

The early African American dance that Rose portrayed in *The Old Plantation* is a communal social dance gathering that is reminiscent of those seen throughout West Africa. West African dance gatherings typically involve the participants forming a ring wherein the dancers take turns in the center to express themselves through the medium of dance, as well as to perform a solo exhibition of their dancing skills. The dance ring formation came across the Atlantic with the millions of enslaved West Africans and has been a principal feature of communal social dancing throughout the African diaspora in the New World ever since.

Rose shows a male dancer taking his turn in the ring's center (see figure S). He brandishes a wooden staff. Sticks and wooden staffs are commonly used as props by male dancers in various different ethnic dance traditions throughout West Africa, such as those of the Jola (Diola) in Casamance (Southern Senegal) and the Fulbe (also Fula, Fulani, and Peul) and Songhai in Northern Mali. In his 1955 commentary on the painting, Melville Herskovits suggested that the staff held by the male dancer might indicate a slave wedding, referencing the custom known as jumping the broom in which the wedded couple leap over a broom handle or a stick.[65] Herskovits's speculation, however, has finally been laid to rest by Shames's uncovering of John Rose's will. It describes the painting as "the piece of drawing representing Negroes [dancing],"[66] with no mention of it being a wedding, let alone a jumping-the-broom ceremony. In fact, the findings of more recent research suggest that the tradition of jumping the broom might have actually started in the nineteenth century. Furthermore, as this custom is not found anywhere in Africa, but, rather, in some British and Western European folk cultures, it was probably introduced by slave owners—and, possibly, initially imposed on the enslaved by them—in the antebellum South.[67]

Another possibility to consider is that the depicted wooden staff may perhaps indicate a connection to stickfighting. During the eighteenth century, stickfighting was documented as an African American martial art in the Caribbean. It was also reported in the earliest known report of the early gourd banjo in North America, an account from 1736 of African Americans engaged in sports as well as dancing to the "Banger" at a holiday fair in New York City: "The Warriors were not idle, for I saw several Companies of the Blacks, some exercising the Cudgel, and some of them small Sticks in imitation of the short Pike."[68]

On some islands, stickfighting was called *calinda* (also *calenda*, *kalenda*, and *kalinda*), the same term used to denote Afro-Creole social dances that were typically accompanied by African-heritage drums as well as the early gourd banjo.[69] In his print, entitled, *A Cudgelling Match between English and French Negroes in the Island of Dominica* (1779), Agostino Brunias (1730–96) depicts two stickfighters holding short staffs akin to the one held by the dancer in *The Old Plantation*, much in the same manner that he grasps his with both hands.[70]

As for the two female dancers, they appear to be encouraging the male dancer, reflecting a practice that harkens back to West Africa. In West African social dance ring formations, some of those in the ring (especially women) move in closer to the dancer(s) in the center and offer encouragement. This may be done by gesturing with a piece of cloth or scarf held in both hands—which is also used as a prop, mostly by women dancers, throughout West Africa—or by providing rhythmic support by clapping and/or playing rattles and percussive clappers.

In considering Rose's depiction of both women holding what appears to be pieces of cloth, the anthropologist-historian Joseph A. Opala has argued that "scholars unaware of the Sierra Leone slave trade connection have interpreted the two female figures as performing a 'scarf' dance. Sierra Leoneans can easily recognize that they are playing the *shegureh*, a women's instrument (rattle) characteristic of the Mende and neighboring tribes."[71]

West African gourd vessel rattles, such as the Mende *shegureh* (also *segburreh*, *segbureh*) of Sierra Leone (see figure T) and the Vai *sasaa* and Lorma *kpolui* of Liberia, are traditionally played only by women as they sing to accompany dancing, ceremonies, and other occasions. These rattles are made of long string netting with a round bottle gourd housed in the netting's mesh tail end. Beads, shells, and/or buttons are laced into the netting's mesh-web nest to serve as clackers. To play the instrument, the player grasps the top of the netting with her raised left hand and the bottleneck of the gourd with her lowered right hand. She alternates between pulling the string netting taut and relaxing the tension, thereby causing the clackers in the mesh-web to strike against the gourd and produce a clacking sound.[72]

A textual description of what may have been West African-style gourd vessel rattles being used in the New World can be found in the German explorer Baron Albert von Sack's *A Narrative of a Voyage to Surinam* (1810). In a letter from Paramaribo, Suriname, dated January 1, 1806, von Sack describes the New Year's Day dance gathering of "the free negroes" in which "their dances vary according to the different negro tribes": "The musical instruments are chiefly pieces of hollow trees, the upper part covered with leather like a drum, and are beaten with sticks . . . the negro females who are not engaged in dancing, have strings with sounding nut shells, which are clapped to with hands, and sing a chorus to it."[73]

In the case of *The Old Plantation*, the two possible gourd vessel rattles are shown as having string tails at the bottom of the netting that the women grasp with their lowered right hands in the traditional West African playing position. In the foreground, the one held by the woman in the gray gown seems to show clackers laced into what may be a crossed netting nest at its base. Furthermore, the netting nests at the bottom of both women's possible gourd vessel rattles appear to be holding something spherical, perhaps Rose's way of indicating their round gourds.

These depicted cloth-like objects, however, may be just that—pieces of cloth. Period depictions of African American dancing in the Caribbean and Suriname during the eighteenth and early nineteenth centuries show female dancers (and sometimes male dancers) holding what are clearly pieces of cloth in both hands in attitudes similar to what we see in *The Old Plantation*. In his 1819 account of a black dance gathering in New Orleans' Common, Benjamin Latrobe (1764–1820), the architect famed for designing the United States Capitol, described African American women dancing with pieces of cloth in the same fashion: "In the first

[ring] were two women dancing. They held each a coarse handkerchief extended by the corners in their hands, & set to each other in a miserably dull & slow figure, hardly moving their feet or bodies."[74]

This manner of holding and using pieces of cloth as dance props by women is found in local vernacular dance traditions throughout West Africa. Herskovits—who did field research in the West African countries of Dahomey (present-day Benin), Gold Coast (Ghana), and Nigeria—also noted this resemblance in his analysis of *The Old Plantation*: "one also sees [West African women] dancing holding kerchiefs in the way in which two dancers in the picture hold them."[75]

Conclusion

In her 1957 descriptive text for *The Old Plantation*, Nina Fletcher Little asserted that "this unique watercolor is a valuable pictorial record of the survival of African cultural traditions in America as interpreted by a group of slaves on a South Carolina plantation."[76] Indeed, John Rose's wonderful picture is a rare period window into the African American culture emerging in the Low Country during the eighteenth century. Yet, *The Old Plantation* offers so much more. From the perspective of banjo history, Rose provides us with the earliest and most detailed portrayal of the instrument in North America. Here we can see in exquisite detail not only the features and construction of the four-string early gourd banjo, but also its original playing context: a folk instrument historically unique to black musicians used to accompany early African American social dancing. Moreover, the picture likewise shows us for the first time the banjo's original musical partner—a drum of African heritage—as well as rare visual evidence of how the banjo was played. That being said, it also makes clear the importance of period early banjo iconography as crucial historical evidence. All told, Rose's *The Old Plantation* is indisputably an invaluable cultural treasure on so many levels. As such, it certainly merits further serious study and discussion. Little put it best when she first wrote to Turner and Herskovits back in 1955: "the scene has considerable significance in the field of American folk art and is worthy of any investigation which we are able to make."[77]

Notes

This chapter is a version of a paper that I gave on May 17, 2012, at the joint meeting of the American Musical Instrument Society (AMIS) and the International Committee of Musical Instrument Museums and Collections (CIMCIM) at the Metropolitan Museum of Art (NYC). My thanks and appreciation to Barbara R. Luck, curator emeritus of paintings, drawings, and sculptures for the Colonial Williamsburg Foundation (CWF) for her cooperation and support, as well as for sharing archival materials, when I first approached CWF in the course of my initial research. I would also like to extend my grateful appreciation to John R. Watson, conservator of instruments and associate curator of musical instruments, CWF, for his assistance and support, as well as to other CWF staff: Marianne

Martin, visual resources librarian, John D. Rockefeller Jr. Library; Darnell Vennie, digital imaging technician-photographer; Laura Pass Barry, Juli Grainger Curator of Paintings, Drawings, and Sculpture and Manager for Curatorial Outreach; and Angelika R. Kuettner, associate registrar for imaging and assistant curator of ceramics.

1. *The Old Plantation*, watercolor on laid paper, 11 11/16 x 17 7/8 inches, Abbey Aldrich Rockefeller Folk Art Museum, CWF, Williamsburg, Virginia, gift of Mrs. John D. Rockefeller, 35.301.3.

2. Hans Sloane, MD, *A Voyage to the Islands of Madera, Barbados, Nieves, S. Christophers and Jamaica* (London, 1707), vol. 1, plate III, republished online by BHL Biodiversity Library: http://www.biodiversitylibrary.org/item/11242, accessed October 25, 2017. For more on plate III and the documentation of Afro-Jamaican early gourd banjos in Sloane's 1707 book, see in this volume my chapter "'Strum Strumps' and 'Sheepskin' Guitars: The Early Gourd Banjo and Clues to its West African Roots In the Seventeenth-Century Circum-Caribbean."

3. Thomas Jefferson, *Notes on the State of Virginia* (Philadelphia, 1781), query XIV, 266.

4. Dena J. Epstein (1916–2013)—the "mother" of modern empirical inquiry into the roots and early history of the banjo—referred to this kind of banjo as the "folk banjo." Epstein used this term to distinguish between the gourd-bodied "folk" (non-commodified) instrument of the early African Americans (enslaved and free) and its "commercial" (commodified) successor, the wood-rimmed five-string banjo. Dena J. Epstein, "The Folk Banjo: A Documentary History," *Ethnomusicology* 19 (September 1975): 347–71.

5. See Susan P. Shames, *The Old Plantation: The Artist Revealed* (Williamsburg, VA: The Colonial Williamsburg Foundation, 2010).

6. *Plantation Scene*, watercolor on laid paper, 11 3/8 x 16 3/8 inches, Mint Museum of Art, Charlotte, North Carolina. Gift of Mr. and Mrs. Donald Upchurch, 1985.83.1. Published in Leo G. Mazow's *Picturing the Banjo* (University Park: Palmer Museum of Art and Pennsylvania State University Press, 2005), figure 98, 110.

7. Jonathan Stuhlman, curator of American art, The Mint Museum, email correspondence, February 13, 16, and 17, 2009. One of the pigments cited in the 1997 lab report is titanium white (titanium dioxide), "the white of the 20th century." Invented in 1913, titanium white was first manufactured commercially three years later, but not available in artistic paints until 1921. Michael Douma, "Titanium White," *Pigments through the Ages* website, http://www.webexhibits.org/pigments/indiv/history/titaniumwhite.html, accessed October 25, 2017.

8. Russell J. Quandt, "Notes on Conservation," in Nina Fletcher Little's *The Abby Aldrich Rockefeller Folk Art Collection: A Descriptive Catalogue* (Williamsburg, VA: Colonial Williamsburg, Inc., 1957), 385.

9. Little to Professor Alonzo [sic] Turner and Dr. Melville Herskovits, August 5, 1955; CWF/AARFAM curatorial file 35-301-3. For more on Turner and Herskovits, see Margaret Wade-Lewis, *Lorenzo Dow Turner: Father of Gullah Studies* (Columbia: University of South Carolina Press, 2007), and Jerry Gershenhorn, *Melville J. Herskovits and the Racial Politics of Knowledge* (Lincoln: University of Nebraska Press, 2004).

10. Nina Fletcher Little, *The Abby Aldrich Rockefeller Folk Art Collection: A Descriptive Catalogue* (Williamsburg, VA: Colonial Williamsburg, Inc., 1957), plate 66, "The Old Plantation," 132–33.

11. Cahill to Mrs. Rockefeller, March 28, 1935, 4, Holger Cahill Papers, 1910–1993, bulk 1910–1960, Series 2: Correspondence Files, Correspondence, January–February 1935, Reel 5285, Frames 0792–0836, Frame 832, http://www.aaa.si.edu/collectionsonline/cahiholg/container183186.htm, accessed December 21, 2009.

12. Gullah (also Geechee; more recently, Sea Island Creole) is the Afro-English creole language historically spoken in the African American communities in the Sea Islands and coastal mainland regions of South Carolina and Georgia along their Atlantic coast. It is America's only known English-based creole language. Gullah-Geechee also refers to the unique traditional African American culture of this region. For more on Gullah-Geechee language, culture, and history, see Lorenzo Dow Turner, *Africanisms in the Gullah Dialect* (Chicago: University of Chicago Press, 1949; reprint Columbia: University of South Carolina Press, 2002); William S. Pollitzer, *The Gullah People and Their African Heritage* (Athens: University of Georgia Press, 1999); Lydia Parrish, *Slave Songs of the Georgia Sea Islands* (New York: Creative Age Press, 1942; reprint Athens: University of Georgia Press, 1992); and Bessie Jones, *For the Ancestors: Autobiographical Memories Collected and Edited by John Stewart* (Urbana: University of Illinois Press, 1983).

13. Cahill to James L. Cogar, October 20, 1935, with an attached list of new captions for the pictures from Mrs. Rockefeller's collection displayed in CW's Ludwell-Paradise House, item No. 10, "The Old Plantation," 5; Holger Cahill Papers, 1910–1993 bulk 1910–1960; Series 2: Correspondence Files, Correspondence, July–December 1935, Reel 5285, Frames 0884–0914, Frame 898, http://www.aaa.si.edu/collectionsonline/cahiholg/container183188 .htm, accessed December 21, 2009.

14. [Elizabeth Anne Poyas], *Our Forefathers: Their Homes and Their Churches* (Charleston, SC: Walker, Evans, 1860), 130, cited in Shames's *The Old Plantation*, 32.

15. Beatrix T. Rumford, ed., *American Folk Paintings: Paintings and Drawings Other Than Portraits from the Abby Rockefeller Folk Art Center* (Boston: Little, Brown and Company, Inc., New York Graphic Society in association with the Colonial Williamsburg Society, 1988), plate 82, "The Old Plantation," 122–23. An examination of *The Old Plantation* in 1968 revealed that the watercolor's paper bears the watermark of English papermaker James Whatman II (1741–98), who was active between 1777 and 1794. Linda Baumgarten, CWF's curator of textiles and costumes, argues that the depicted clothing styles—especially, the low waistlines on the women's gowns—narrows down the dating of the painting to a more probable timeframe of sometime between 1785 and 1790 (Abby Aldrich Rockefeller Folk Art Collection [AARFAC], curatorial notes on *The Old Plantation* [1935.301.5], September 22, 2008, 2–3) .

16. Rumford, *American Folk Paintings*, 123n4; Shames, *The Old Plantation*, 24.

17. Shames, *The Old Plantation*, 30.

18. Ibid., 30–32.

19. Rumford, *American Folk Paintings*, 123n4; Shames, *The Old Plantation*, 24.

20. *Creole* (Portuguese *crioulo*; Spanish *criollo*; French *créole*; and Dutch *creoolse*) describes someone or something of non-indigenous heritage that is native to a place. During the eighteenth century, the term was used to indicate both European Americans and African Americans "country born" in the Caribbean and the Americas in general. For the sake of clarity, here I use the designation *Afro-Creole* to specifically denote people, language, culture, music, and dance of African ancestry that originated in the New World.

21. For more on rice production and slavery in early South Carolina, see Peter H. Wood, *Black Majority: Negroes in Colonial South Carolina from 1670 through the Stono Rebellion* (New York: W. W. Norton & Company, 1974, 1996); Daniel C. Littlefield, *Rice and Slaves: Ethnicity and the Slave Trade in Colonial South Carolina* (Urbana: University of Illinois Press, 1981, 1991); S. Max Edelson, *Plantation Enterprise in Colonial South Carolina* (Cambridge, MA: Harvard University Press, 2006); and Philip D. Morgan, *Slave Counterpoint:*

Black Culture in the Eighteenth-Century Chesapeake and Lowcountry (Chapel Hill: University of North Carolina Press, 1998).

22. Wood, *Black Majority*, appendix C, table X, "Africans Arriving in Charlestown, South Carolina (March 1735–March 1740), by Year and by Origin of Shipment," 340–41. John K. Thornton and Mark M. Smith contend that the leaders of the revolt were most likely from the Kingdom of Kongo in northern Angola. See Thornton's "African Dimensions," 73–86, and Smith's "Time, Religion, Rebellion," 108–23, in Smith's anthology, *Stono: Documenting and Interpreting a Southern Slave Revolt* (Columbia: University of South Carolina Press, 2005).

23. Robert Olwell, *Masters, Slaves, and Subjects: The Culture of Power in the South Carolina Low Country, 1740–1790* (Ithaca, NY: Cornell University Press, 1998), 28.

24. Dena J. Epstein, *Sinful Tunes and Spirituals: Black Folk Music to the Civil War* (Urbana: University of Illinois Press, 1977, 2003), 59.

25. Olwell, *Masters, Slaves, and Subjects*, 63.

26. Littlefield, *Rice and Slaves*, 116.

27. Olwell, *Masters, Slaves, and Subjects*, 29.

28. Morgan, *Slave Counterpoint*, 61–62. The correlation between the predominance of slaves from Angola-Kongo in the Low Country and the Stono Rebellion of 1739 resulted in a dramatic shift in slave sourcing from West-Central Africa to West Africa when the massive importation of African captives into South Carolina resumed in 1751. From that year until 1801, South Carolina's principal sources for enslaved Africans were Greater Senegambia (present-day Senegal, The Gambia, Guinea-Bissau, Guinea, and Mali), and, to a lesser extent, Sierra Leone. Both areas were and are still noted for rice cultivation, a major factor in their appeal to the Low Country's rice-growing planters . See Gwendolyn Midlo Hall, *Slavery and African Ethnicities in the Americas* (Chapel Hill: University of North Carolina Press, 2005), 90–95. Greater Senegambia was an important area in the African heritage of the banjo, as discussed below.

29. Morgan, *Slave Counterpoint*, 601; Linda Baumgarten, *What Clothes Reveal: The Language of Clothing and Federal America, The Colonial Williamsburg Collection* (Williamsburg, VA: The Colonial Williamsburg Foundation in association with Yale University Press, 2002), chapter 4, "Common Dress: Clothing for Daily Life," 106–39.

30. Epstein, *Sinful Tunes and Spirituals*, 83–84.

31. Ibid., 159.

32. Turner to Little, AARFAC, August 15, 1955, CWF/AARFAM curatorial file 35-301-3.

33. Herskovits to Little, AARFAC, October 3, 1955, CWF/AARFAM curatorial file 35-301-3.

34. Little, *The Abby Aldrich Rockefeller Folk Art Collection*, plate 66, "The Old Plantation," 132–33.

35. See David W. Ames and Anthony V. King, *Glossary of Hausa Music and Its Social Context* (Evanston, IL: Northwestern University Press, 1971), for the Hausa form of the *molo*, 46–47; and Ulrich Wegner, *Afrikanische Saiteninstrumnete* (Berlin: Museum für Volkerkunde, 1984), for the Yoruban variant, 142.

36. Spike lutes are lutes that have their neck go through or over the wall of their body. A spike lute is categorized under one of two major divisions based on the span of its neck in relationship to its body: full-spike, the lute's neck extends the full length of its body to pass through or over the body's tail end; and semi-spike, the lute's neck extends about three-quarters the length of its body to end just short of the body's tail end. Most of the

known eighty members of the West African family of plucked spike lutes are semi-spike, but there is also a significant minority of full-spike lutes. Being a full-spike lute itself, the early gourd banjo was most closely related to West African full-spike lutes. For more on the relationship of West African plucked lutes to the early gourd banjo, see in this volume my chapter co-authored with Greg C. Adams, "Changing Perspectives on the Banjo's African American Origins and West African Heritage," as well as my chapter "Banjo Ancestors: West African Plucked Spike Lutes" and "List of West African Plucked Spike Lutes," which I co-authored with Adams.

37. Johann David Schoepf, *Travels in the Confederation, 1783–1784*, trans. and ed. Alfred J. Morrison (Philadelphia: W. J. Campbell, 1911), vol. 2, *Pennsylvania, Maryland, Virginia, the Carolinas, East Florida, the Bahamas*, 260–62.

38. For a fuller discussion of the relationship of the early gourd banjo to African-heritage drumming and dancing, see Epstein, *Sinful Tunes and Spirituals*, 30–61.

39. The Manyago *bunchundo* player Lawrence Abukwach Mendy, video interview by Chuck Levy and Greg C. Adams, Part 1, Banjul, The Gambia, July 23, 2008. My thanks to Levy and Adams for sharing this material.

40. Monique Brandily, "Gulom," in *The Grove Dictionary of Musical Instruments: Second Edition*, ed. Laurence Libin, 5 vols. (Oxford: Oxford University Press, 2014), 2:513.

41. Turner to Little, AARFAC, August 15, 1955, CWF/AARFAM curatorial file 35-301-3, p. 1.

42. See Wade-Lewis, *Lorenzo Dow Turner*, 165–85.

43. Turner to Little, AARFAC, August 15, 1955, CWF/AARFAM curatorial file 35-301-3, p. 1.

44. Ayodapo Ayansiji Oyelana, "Talking Drum: A Means of Communication in Yoruba Land," http://iyailu.wordpress.com/2011/03/23/talking-drum-presentation-3/, accessed October 25, 2017; Lágbájá, *Drums*, "Dundun Ensemble," http://www.lagbaja.com/drums/dundun.php, accessed October 25, 2017; and Bode Omojola, *Yorùbá Music in the Twentieth Century: Identity, Agency, and Performance Practice* (Rochester, NY: University of Rochester Press, 2012), 37, 50, 51–53, 56, 57–58.

45. Herskovits to Little, AARFAC, October 3, 1955, CWF/AARFAM curatorial file 35-301-3.

46. James Barclay, *The Voyages and Travels of James Barclay, Containing Many Surprising Adventures, and Interesting Narratives* (Dublin, 1777), 27; quoted in Morgan's *Slave Counterpoint*, 583. Morgan contends that "Barclay . . . seems to have witnessed drum playing and to have confused it with the most common slave instrument, the 'bangier' [banjo]" (ibid., 583). However, to the best of my research, I have yet to come across *bangier* in the historical record as a period name for the early gourd banjo. Earlier in his book, Morgan does provide us with what might have been a cognate term from colonial South Carolina, *bangio*, referenced in a 1749 report from the *South Carolina Council Journal* that describes enslaved African Americans "playing on the Bangio" (ibid., 474, 475n59). Regardless of whether or not *bangier* was actually a period designation for the early gourd banjo, it seems very unlikely that Barclay confused the drum he described so clearly with the African American plucked lute. *Bangier* appears to be a cognate of *bandiri* or *banga*, the names of two bowl-shaped drums of the Hausa of northern Nigeria. Ames and King, *Glossary of Hausa Music*, 13.

47. Barclay, *The Voyages and Travels of James Barclay*, 27; quoted in Morgan's *Slave Counterpoint*, 583.

48. For a more extensive discussion of the short thumb-string feature and its West African roots, see the "Changing Perspectives on the Banjo's African American Origins and West African Heritage" chapter in this volume.

49. John Gabriel Stedman, *Narrative of a Five Years Expedition against the Revolted Negroes of Surinam: Transcribed for the First Time the Original 1790 Manuscript*, ed. Richard Price and Sally Price (Baltimore: Johns Hopkins University Press, 1988; reprint New York: iUniverse, 2010), 539–40.

50. A photo of the *panja* may be accessed online at http://www.mimo-international .com/MIMO/doc/IFD/SPK_BERLIN_DE_EM_OBJID_169626, accessed October 25, 2017. For more on these instruments, see the "Changing Perspectives on the Banjo's African American Origins and West African Heritage" chapter in this volume. For more specifically on the *creole bania* and the *banza*, see in this volume Saskia Willaert's and Pete Ross's chapters.

51. In preparing a gourd for use as a lute body—be it a traditional West African plucked lute or a bowed lute (fiddle) or a New World gourd banjo—a side is sliced off to create a large opening. After the gourd's meat is scooped out, the inside area is cleaned and allowed to dry. An animal hide is then stretched over the opening and fastened to its rim to form the instrument's soundtable.

52. The Central Sudan (eastern West Africa) consists of present-day Burkina Faso, Chad, Côte d'Ivoire, Sierra Leone, Ghana, Togo, Benin, Nigeria, Niger, and Cameroon.

53. For more on the peoples and lutes of the Atlantic-Bak cluster, see my chapter "'Strum Strumps' and 'Sheepskin' Guitars: The Early Gourd Banjo and Clues to its West African Roots in the Seventeenth-Century Circum-Caribbean" in this volume.

54. For more on these North African instruments, see in this volume my chapter "Banjo Ancestors: West African Plucked Spike Lutes."

55. In the case of the actual *creole bania*, the absence of a nut may be explained by the fact that three parallel vertical grooves are deeply incised into the upper quarter of its fingerboard. This was done apparently to receive the four-string instrument's three long strings.

56. One notable exception is the method by which the string-tails on Manyago *bunchundos* are affixed to the spike end of the instrument's neck. On these lutes, the string-tails are tied to a large loop made of leather or twine, which goes over the neck's spike end to lodge against the body's lower end. This kind of loop fastening, which I characterize as a cord loop tailpiece, is similar to those seen on most West African single-string spike fiddles and harp-lutes.

57. As the Haitian *banza* is missing its bridge and strings (save for its top fourth thumbstring), it is clearly not set up in proper playing order. This being the case, it cannot be determined with any certainty whether or not the *banza* had a tailpiece.

58. My special thanks to gourd banjo builders Pete Ross and Bob Thornburg for their input and the benefit of their expertise on this issue.

59. My grateful appreciation to Robert B. Winans and Greg C. Adams for sharing the findings of their most recent research on Boucher.

60. *Catalogue of the Crosby Brown Collection of Musical Instruments of All Nations* (New York: The Metropolitan Museum of Art, 1913), 185; cited in the Met's curatorial notes on the banjo (89.4.598) and by Laurence Libin in his book *American Musical Instruments in The Metropolitan Museum of Art* (New York: The Metropolitan Museum of Art and W. W. Norton & Company, 1985), 108–9. My special thanks to Ken Moore for providing

me with the curatorial notes on 89.4.598 and to Laurence Libin for his insights on the instrument.

61. For more on the West African heritage of down-picking and two-finger picking, see in this volume the "Changing Perspectives on the Banjo's African American Origins and West African Heritage" chapter, and for *oo'teck*, the Jola form of down-picking, compared to that of early banjo technique, also see in this volume Greg C. Adams and Chuck Levy's chapter "The Down-Stroke Connection: Comparing Techniques Between the Jola *Ekonting* and the Five-String Banjo."

62. In the collections of the Long Island Museum of American Art, History, and Carriages (formerly known as The Museums at Stony Brook), gift of Mr. and Mrs. Ward Melville, 1955. Bartlett Cowdrey and Hermann Warner Williams Jr., *William Sidney Mount 1807–1868: An American Painter* (New York: Metropolitan Museum of Art, 1944), catalogue no. 99, 27; Janice Gray Armstrong, ed., *Catching the Tune: Music and William Sidney Mount* (Stony Brook, NY: The Museums at Stony Brook, 1984), 17. My special thanks to Robert B. Winans and Greg C. Adams for their input on the issues of period five-string banjo playing that I discuss here in the course of interpreting this painting.

63. Christopher J. Smith, *The Creolization of American Culture: William Sidney Mount and the Roots of Blackface Minstrelsy* (Urbana: University of Illinois Press, 2013), 123, 135–41, 274n36.

64. For the double-headed Boucher banjo in the Smithsonian, see Frances Densmore, *Smithsonian Institution, United States National Museum, Bulletin 136: Handbook of the Collection of Musical Instruments in the United States National Museum* (Washington, DC: Smithsonian Institution, 1927), 85, plate 37c; Greg C. Adams and George Wunderlich, *Banjo Sightings Database: Three Dimensional Sightings*, http://www.banjodatabase.org/browse3d.asp, accessed December 21, 2009.

65. Herskovits to Nina Fletcher Little, AARFAC, October 3, 1955, CWF/AARFAM curatorial file 35-301-3.

66. Shames, *The Old Plantation*, 52. In the handwritten will of John Rose, the transcribing clerk had inadvertently repeated the word *drawing* in place of *dancing* to describe what the "Negroes" in "the piece of drawing" were doing (Shames, *The Old Plantation*, 45).

67. Alan Dundes, "'Jumping the Broom': On the Origin and Meaning of an African American Wedding Custom," *The Journal of American Folklore* 109, no. 433 (Summer 1996): 324–29.

68. "*The SPY*," letter to the editor, dateline "UTOPIA, April 10," *The New-York Weekly Journal*, March 7, 1736, 1. See in this volume my chapter coauthored with Greg C. Adams: "Zenger's 'Banger': Contextualizing the Banjo in Early New York City, 1736."

69. Maureen Warner-Lewis, *Central Africa in the Caribbean: Transcending Time, Transforming Cultures* (Barbados: University of the West Indies Press, 2003), 199–214. For *calinda* as a designation for Afro-Creole dances accompanied by the early gourd banjo and drums, see Epstein's *Sinful Tunes and Spirituals*, 24, 28, 30–38, 82, 92, 94, 135.

70. *Stick Fighting, Dominica, West Indies, 1779*, Image Reference: NW0158. Image Source: Painted by Agostino Brunias; engraved print published London (1779). Copy in the John Carter Brown Library at Brown University. www.slaveryimages.org, accessed October 25, 2017, compiled by Jerome Handler and Michael Tuite, and sponsored by the Virginia Foundation for the Humanities and the University of Virginia Library. Charles Ford, Thomas Cummins, Rosalie Smith McCrea, and Helen Weston, chapter 6, "The Slave

Colonies," in *The Image of the Black in Western Art: From the "Age of Discovery" to the Age of Abolition: The Eighteenth Century, III Part 3*, ed. David Bindman and Henry Louis Gates Jr. (Cambridge, MA: The Belknap Press of Harvard University Press, 2011), 278–79.

71. Joseph A. Opala, *The Gullah: Rice, Slavery, and the Sierra Leone-American Connection* (Freetown, Sierra Leone: United States Information Service, n.d.), 9; published online by The Gilder Lehrman Center for the Study of Slavery, Resistance, and Abolition, "a part of the Whitney and Betty MacMillan Center for International and Area Studies at Yale," http://glc.yale.edu/gullah-rice-slavery-and-sierra-leone-american-connection, accessed October 25, 2017.

72. "Segbureh," in *The Grove Dictionary of Musical Instruments: Second Edition*, ed. Laurence Libin, 5 vols. (Oxford: Oxford University Press, 2014), 4:459.

73. Baron Albert von Sack, "Chamberlain to His Prussian Majesty," in *A Narrative of a Voyage to Surinam; of a Residence there during 1805, 1806, and 1807; and of the Author's return to Europe by way of NORTH AMERICA* (London: "Printed for G. and W. Nicol, Booksellers to His Majesty, Pall-Mall, by W. Bulmer and Co., Cleveland-Row, St. James, 1810"), letter VII, 62.

74. Benjamin Henry Latrobe, *The Journal of Latrobe: The Notes and Sketches of an Architect, Naturalist and Traveler in the United States from 1796 to 1820* (New York: D. Appleton and Company, 1905; reprint Carlisle, MA: Applewood Books, 2007), 180.

75. Herskovits to Little, AARFAC, October 3, 1955, CWF/AARFAM curatorial file 35-301-3.

76. Little, *The Abby Aldrich Rockefeller Folk Art Collection*, plate 66, "The Old Plantation," 132–33.

77. Little to Turner and Herskovits, August 5, 1955; CWF/AARFAM curatorial file 35-301-3.

CHAPTER 12

Black Musicians in Eighteenth-Century America
Evidence from Runaway Slave Advertisements
Robert B. Winans

Editor's Headnote

This chapter does not focus solely on the banjo. It presents data about the full range of musical instruments played by African American musicians in North America prior to 1800, providing a picture of the wider musical culture of enslaved African Americans to contextualize the banjo's role. The runaway slave advertisements identify not only the instruments the runaways played, but also frequently give information about their nonmusical occupations, their literacy, the circumstances and venues for their musical performances, and how proficient they were in playing their instrument. The chapter also analyzes the geographical distribution of the data.

Eileen Southern, Dena J. Epstein, and Richard Cullen Rath comment briefly on musicians cited in runaway slave advertisements in eighteenth-century American newspapers, but no systematic study of this source of information about African American musicians has been undertaken.[1] In 1983–85, I had occasion to peruse more than 300 eighteenth-century newspapers (more than 20,000 individual issues), gathering various kinds of data for a number of different projects. For this project on African American musicians, I systematically scanned all the runaway slave advertisements I encountered in these newspapers, a total of more than 12,000 advertisements, which have yielded information on 761 black musicians. If a runaway slave were a musician, he would be so described, because this would be a potential means of identifying him. In the aggregate, these data provide a kind of statistical picture of the instrumental side of African American musical culture in eighteenth-century America, at least as it came to the attention of white slave owners. This chapter summarizes that data and briefly discusses some implications. To leaven the statistical data, the chapter presents supplemental information about a sampling of individual musicians identified in the advertisements. Banjo players will receive particular attention since they will be of particular interest to the readers of this book (as they are to me), as well as fiddlers because they far outnumber the rest. But having a sense of the whole picture of instrumental traditions at the time is essential to understanding any one segment of that tradition.

Table 12.1 gives the number of runaway musicians from each state. Each runaway is located according to where he ran away from, not the location of the newspaper where he was advertised, since many runaways were advertised in papers far distant from their homes. We tend to think of black folk music as being a southern phenomenon, but the subtotal figures for the North and the South given in table 12.1 show that in the eighteenth-century there were nearly as many black runaway musicians in the North as in the South, with 370 in the North and 391 in the South. It is easy to forget that in the eighteenth century slavery was a northern as well as a southern institution, although the slave population was certainly much greater in the South than in the North.[2] But it appears that

Table 12.1   Number of Slave Musicians and Ratio to Total Number of Adult Male Runaways

State/Region	Number	Ratio	Regional Ratio
Maine	1	-	
New Hampshire	4	-	
Massachusetts	39	1/13	
Rhode Island	16	1/13	
Connecticut	64	1/8	
NEW ENGLAND			1/10
New York	89	1/13	
New Jersey	67	1/8	
Pennsylvania	90	1/12	
MID-ATLANTIC			1/12
NORTH	370 (48%)		
Delaware	23	-	
Maryland	138	1/20	
District of Columbia	7	1/21	
Virginia	132	1/21	
West Virginia	4	-	
Kentucky	6	-	
UPPER SOUTH			1/21
North Carolina	16	1/42	
MIDDLE SOUTH			1/42
South Carolina	54	1/61	
Georgia	11	1/73	
DEEP SOUTH			1/63
SOUTH	391 (52%)		
TOTAL	761		

although the South had more slaves, it did not have many more slave musicians (at least among those who ran away). In fact, the northern and southern figures might be even closer if the data were better from the New England states for the 1790s. By this time, although no state had fully outlawed slavery, the public sentiment for abolition (but not for equality) was fairly strong in the North, and many newspapers, especially in Connecticut and Massachusetts, refused to publish runaway slave advertisements. So this source of information about black musicians in New England essentially dries up in the 1790s. I return to the issue of the relative numbers of runaway musicians in different regions when I discuss the ratio figures from table 12.1.[3]

Table 12.2 lists the different instruments identified in the advertisements. Of the total of 761 musicians in the advertisements, 14 were identified as whistlers and 38 as singers; putting these 2 groups aside to concentrate on instrument-playing musicians, we are left with 709 individuals. These instrument-playing musicians were all adult males; a few of the runaways identified as singers were women, but not a single woman instrumentalist was identified. By far, in almost 90 percent of cases, the most common instrument was the fiddle, or violin, the latter term being used in a little more than one-third of the instances. Clearly, the fiddle was the almost universal black instrument in the eighteenth century, widely played in all regions of the country at the time. The earliest reference dates from 1711, when an advertisement in the *Boston News-Letter* described Jack, who had run away from his master[4] Robert Bunsey of Fairfield, Connecticut, as a very black man who "can play on a Violin, he hath carried his Fiddle with him."[5] All of the references up to the mid-1740s are to fiddle or violin players; after that time a sprinkling of other instruments begins to enter the advertisements (a total of eighteen advertisements for fiddle players before the first advertisement for a non-fiddle-playing musician appears in 1748). The advertisements frequently specify whether the runaway plays well or poorly on his instrument.

The distribution of fiddlers by colony-state is presented in table 12.3. In no way can I do justice to the totality of runaway fiddler advertisements in a chapter of this length, but some generalities can be offered, and those advertisements can be

Table 12.2   Eighteenth-Century Runaway Black Instrumental Musicians

Instrument	Number	Percentage
Fiddle/Violin	627	88.4
Fife	50	7.1
Drum	21	3.0
Flute	18	2.5
Banjo	18	2.5
French horn	8	1.1
Pipes	3	0.4
Guitar	1	0.1

mined for various kinds of more specific information. First of all, the majority of black fiddlers described in the advertisements were house servants or craftsmen of various sorts. A fair number of the runaways specifically are said to be house servants (sometimes, more precisely, a waiter or a dresser-shaver or a cook), but frequently it is the description of their clothing that leads to that conclusion. The most commonly noted craft occupations are carpenter and shoemaker-cobbler. Other occupations for fiddlers, in no particular order, are blacksmith, sawyer, hewer, joiner, wheelwright, carter, boatman, hostler, cooper, seaman, ship rigger, weaver, painter, tanner, forgeman, carriage driver, brickmaker, bricklayer, miller, hatter, basketmaker, distiller, carver, netmaker, butcher, and tinker. Few are described as field hands; in fact, that term is not used at all. But a number are described as "farmers," or "understands farming," which may mean more than field hand.

The advertisements convey other information as well. Advertisements for musicians also frequently note how well or badly the runaway speaks English and what other languages he speaks. On the issue of language, a surprising number of these runaways are described as being able to read, or read and write; some also can "cypher" or "do accounts." These abilities also suggest that those runaways are house servants. Very commonly, advertisements describe how light or dark in complexion the runaway is; sometimes complexion is implied using the terms *mulatto* or *mustee*. Sometimes the runaway's place of birth or where he is from is given; most often this information is given as "country born," that is, born in mainland North America, but some individuals are identified as being from Africa or the West Indies.

Table 12.3   Number of Runaway Fiddlers and Percentage of Total Runaway Musicians

COLONY/STATE	NUMBER	%
Virginia	120	90
Maryland	117	85
New York	67	75
Pennsylvania	62	69
Connecticut	59	92
New Jersey	55	82
South Carolina	44	81
Massachusetts	35	90
Rhode Island	16	100
Delaware	13	57
North Carolina	13	81
District of Columbia	7	100
Kentucky	5	83
West Virginia	4	100
Georgia	3	27
New Hampshire	3	75
Maine	1	100

More specifically related to fiddle playing, the majority of the advertisements merely state that the runaway plays the fiddle. Frequently this information is supplemented by noting that the runaway "carried" or "took" a fiddle with him, although many advertisements give no indication that the runaway had a fiddle with him. The phrasing here, especially in its "took" form, is ambiguous with regard to the ownership of the fiddle. The very first advertisement (in 1711) for a runaway fiddler, noted above, used the phrase "carried his Fiddle with him." Three other advertisements use this same "his fiddle" phrasing, implying that the fiddle was the runaway's own. About John, a "French negro" aged about 30, John Franklin of New York City states, "It is probable he may be found playing on his fiddle which he took with him."[6] Adam, also around 30, "took with him his fiddle, which he plays on with the bow in his left hand," according to John Craine of Middleburg, Loudon County, Virginia.[7] A surprising minority of runaway fiddlers are described as playing left-handed.

The third runaway in this group who apparently owned their fiddles is especially interesting, having been advertised twice in what appear to be two separate instances of his running away. Abraham Davenport of Stamford, Fairfield County, Connecticut, first advertised, in 1760, that Vanhall is a 31-year-old mulatto whose skills are in husbandry and farming, and that he "pretends to understand playing on the Violin."[8] Seven years later, Davenport advertised Vanhall again as a mulatto servant about 40 years of age, who "understands fiddling, and took his fiddle with him."[9] Vanhall has made real progress, from husbandry-farming to servant, and from pretending to understand fiddling to understanding it, though still inclined to run away.

For only one runaway fiddler are readers told that he was given his fiddle by his master. Thomas Pemble of Warwick Ferry on James River, Virginia, states that Jack "is fond of the violin, and has taken with him a new one, which his master lately gave him."[10] And for only two fiddlers are readers explicitly told that they stole the fiddle they took. Tite "can play the fiddle, and stole the one that he took with him," according to James Elliot of Philadelphia, Pennsylvania.[11] A 22-year-old runaway from the Albany area, Harr, is charged by Albert Van Der Zee, of Nisquetau, New York, with having stolen a fiddle.[12] For all of the rest, the advertisements provide no information on how they acquired the fiddles they took with them.

While the majority of the owners of runaway fiddlers did no more than state that their runaway played the violin or fiddle, a goodly number, like Vanhall's master, undertook to critique the runaway's playing ability. Of the four levels of skill assessment observable in the advertisements, the most common was the basic positive level, that the runaway fiddler "plays well," which appears more than four times as often as each of the other three levels (one negative and two increasingly positive). Descriptive language putting a runaway fiddler at the basic positive level, besides "plays well," includes "a good fiddler," and that he plays "tolerably well," "pretty well," or "middling well." On the negative side, the language includes that the fiddler plays "not well," "poorly," "badly," or "very badly," or that he "pretends to play the fiddle," or that his playing is "indifferent" or, at the lowest level, "miserable." Back on the positive side, the next level up from "plays well" is "plays very well," or his playing is "very good" or "excellent." A superior level is reserved for those that are "great" or "very expert" fiddlers, or those who play "extremely well," "remarkably well," "exceedingly well," and even "extraordinarily well." Among the more interesting of the advertisements rating a fiddler in the superior category is an early one describing an unnamed "boy," not a runaway but up for sale. His sale was advertised by an also unnamed party in Boston in 1734. The advertisement states that the boy "plays exceedingly well on the violin . . . none of his Colour can exceed him here."[13] Although one has no idea on what basis slave owners were making these judgments, it is reassuring to see that positive assessments outnumber negative ones by more than six to one.

Some slave owners also evaluated how committed to fiddling their runaways were, although not as often as they judged skill levels. The operative phrase in this endeavor was "fond of," with equal numbers of those who were merely "fond of" playing the fiddle and those who were "very fond of" it, and a select few who were "remarkably fond of" fiddling. Sometimes masters remarked on both fondness and skill level, although usually only when they saw a disjunction between them. Diamond, for instance, is described by W. Erskine of Boston as a very black man who "took with him a violin, of which he is very fond, tho' a miserable Performer."[14] And an unnamed runaway about 23 years old, according to Robert M'Malerton of Monckton Park, Bucks County, Pennsylvania, "is very fond of a fiddle, on which he plays very ill, [who] was seen . . . with a fiddle under his coat"; his skill level is perhaps understandable when one reads that he is somewhat deaf.[15] The "fondnesses" of some of the runaway fiddlers extend beyond the fiddle. For example, Philip, around 20 years old, "is fond of bad women, strong drink, fiddling and dancing," according to John Stevens, from near Bristol, Bucks County, Pennsylvania.[16] The data in the advertisements also yield some tidbits of minor interest. For instance, in seven instances, two fiddlers ran off together from the same slave owner, showing that, in some cases, at least, one owner's group of slaves included more than one fiddler. Twenty-three-year-old twin brothers, Bill and George, ran away from Michael Wallace in Little Elk, Cecil County, Maryland. Bill, a carpenter, turner, shoemaker, farmer, and miller, is described as "a good fiddler, fond of musick," while George, a farmer, miller, and driver, "is an indifferent performer and fond of the fiddle." They share not only a fondness for the fiddle but a penchant for drinking and an Indian grandmother.[17]

A few of the runaway fiddlers are said to have other music-related skills. Some are noted for their singing skills and some for their dancing. John, a 25-year-old shoemaker of a yellow complexion, ran away from Joseph Smith of Lunenburg Courthouse, Lunenburg County, Virginia, who stated that John "can play on the fiddle, but not well, and is the best negro dancer I ever saw."[18] Three of the runaway fiddlers are described as fiddle makers, and two apparently could read music. Sambo, 32 years old and a carpenter, born in Virginia, "makes fiddles, and can play upon the fiddle," according to Mark Johnson, of Amelia County, Virginia.[19] Jim, a mulatto about 20 years of age, is another maker; Isaac Holt of Elkton, Cecil County, Maryland, states that Jim "plays the violin, and took with him two of his own make."[20] The third fiddle maker only "pretends"; he is Ned, a 29-year-old who had also run away four years earlier, who Richard Gaines of Charlotte County, Virginia, says "plays on the violin, pretends sometimes to make fiddles."[21] The apparent music readers are, first, Michael Cox, about 30 years old; he "plays very well on a violin, which, with his music books, he took with him," according to John Lloyd, of Lloyd's Neck, Long Island, New York, who also notes that Michael can read and write.[22] The second apparent music reader, Moses, a 22- to 23-year-old literate shoemaker and woodworker, is described by Jacob Christman, of Rockingham County, Virginia, as "apt to be singing the new tunes by note [and] play the fiddle."[23] Although these two are the only ones whose advertisements suggest an ability to read music, certainly at least some others must also have had that ability.

A number of these runaway fiddlers are said to be quite well known in their time and place. The earliest of these is Dick, who ran away from Lewis Timothy in Charleston in 1736; Timothy states that Dick "can play on the fiddle" and "is well known about town."[24] Over the years, in fact, Charleston, a very music-conscious city in the eighteenth century, was well supplied with a series of well-known African American fiddlers. Runaway fiddlers designated as "well known" in Charleston and the surrounding area include Noah, who used to play for a dancing school;[25] Abraham, a "mustee";[26] Francis, a very black carpenter;[27] Davy, a 35- to 40-year-old carpenter;[28] Pompy, a netmaker and shoemaker who could read and write;[29] and Hardtimes, a house servant.[30] Also in South Carolina, Moon, a carpenter of yellow complexion, was a well-known fiddler in Pee Dee.[31] In New York City, an unnamed 40-year-old "Negro Indian Man Slave" who knows farming and brickmaking, is said by Cornelius Cozyn to be "well known in Town, being a Fidler."[32] In 1786, "Long Daniel the Fidler" ran away from J. Dunbar, of Charles City, Virginia, who notes that he "is famous for playing on the Violin, about Petersburg and Richmond."[33] In Wilmington, North Carolina, in 1797, Josh, a "mustee," was advertised as "well known in town as a fiddler," by James Carson, of Clarendon, west of Wilmington.[34]

Although the advertisements for runaway fiddlers do not provide information on what tunes were played by the fiddlers, they do give some sense of where or under what circumstances the fiddlers played. Certainly, some of them made money from their playing. Dan, about 24 years old, is described by Christian Wirtz, of Lancaster, Pennsylvania, as "fond of playing the fiddle, and has a good deal of money with him which he acquired that way."[35] Near Albany, New York, Harr, around 22 years old, ran away from Albert Van Der Zee, of Nisquetau, who notes that he "stole and carried off a fiddle, upon which he will probably play for a living."[36]

As to where a black fiddler might play to make money, a few of the advertisements offer some clues. For instance, Ishmael, described as a seaman by Alex Wylly, of Savannah, Georgia, can be found "often playing the fiddle at tippling houses."[37] Another advertisement offers data that hint at another playing venue. John Lardner, of Philadelphia, states that Jack "plays upon the fiddle, and is supposed to be harboured in some bad house about the city," presumably a reference to a brothel.[38] Of course, a fiddler might just play for tips on the street, as seems likely the case with Ned (although he also might have played at a "tippling house"), who ran away from John Dorsey, near Baltimore, but apparently did not go very far or make much effort to stay out of sight: he "took a fiddle with him" and "was seen, playing the fiddle, last night at Fell's Point," on the Baltimore waterfront.[39]

One assumes that many of these fiddlers must have played for other African Americans, for dances and other gatherings, although specific mention of that in the advertisements is rare. Jonathan Webster, of Wilkes County, Georgia, states that Ike or Isaac, a very black 20-year-old, "probably will be found playing at negro dances, being a tolerable good fidler."[40] Similarly, Tower "is good at playing on the Fiddle, and usually frequents Negro Dancing for that purpose," according to Henry Calder, of Edisto Island, Charleston County, South Carolina.[41] The final specific mention is an advertisement for Adam, who ran away from Cornelius Coningham, of Washington, DC, and who "has a fiddle with him, on which he is fond of scratching to negro Assemblies."[42]

Several runaway fiddlers had experience with teaching, connected either with dancing masters or with teaching instrumental music. Noah, mentioned above as well known in Charleston, used to play at a dancing school.[43] Noko, an old man with experience as a carpenter, waiting man, and boatman, "plays on the violin," according to Joseph Glover, of Ponpon, South Carolina, but "used to belong to a dancing-master, Mr. Brownell."[44] Of Cambridge, James Oliver of Boston, Massachusetts, states that he "plays well upon a Flute, and not so well on a Violin," and that he teaches apprentices and servants how to play.[45]

Finally, with regard to fiddlers, two more playing situations are mentioned. Tony, with a complexion "between black and yellow," is said by Goodin Elletson, of Mt. Pleasant, Baden County, North Carolina, to be "one of the fiddlers to the assemblies."[46] Since these "assemblies" are not labeled as "negro assemblies," one assumes that Tony was playing for whites. And the final fiddler to be mentioned here surely could not have been the only one whose primary function as a fiddler was to entertain his master. "Iverson's Sam," a waiter and house servant, "has for many years waited on me to play the fiddle," according to Loftin Newman, of King William County, Virginia.[47]

Richard Cullen Rath has an interesting discussion of why there was an "upsurge in runaway fiddlers" after the 1740s in South Carolina and Georgia. This upsurge coincided with the virtual disappearance of "mentions of drums being played by slaves," leading Rath to postulate that slave fiddle playing "was probably a re-invention of the drum music," in the sense of preserving the "encoding of a banned drum style" as a form of communication.[48]

The percentages on the right of table 12.2 add up to more than 100 because a few of these musicians played more than one instrument. A total of thirty-seven were multi-instrumentalists, with the most common combination being fiddle and fife, followed by fiddle and flute, and then fiddle and banjo.

All of the other instruments were played far less commonly than the fiddle, but the advertisements nonetheless yield interesting information about them. The next most popular instrument was the fife, played by only a little more than 7 percent of runaway black musicians. Half of these fifers also played another instrument, either fiddle, flute, or drum. Pennsylvania had the highest number of fifers with ten, followed by Connecticut and New York each with nine; the fife, in fact, was primarily played by northern blacks: more than two-thirds of the fifers were from northern states. But the fife was added relatively late to the repertoire of instruments played by blacks, and its initiation seems definitely related to the martial buildup just prior to the Revolutionary War; the earliest reference to a runaway black fifer occurs in July 1774.

That runaway was Caesar, a talkative young man, about 22 years old and born in Jamaica, who ran away from Philip Wilson in Philadelphia in 1774, who said he was "fond of playing scraps of tunes on the fife."[49] A later version of this advertisement notes that Caesar had several fifes.[50] A further sampling of runaway fifers includes Jordan, age 19, who "had a fife which it is likely he took with him." According to Reverend David Jewett of New London, Connecticut, he wanted to join the army.[51] Cato, age 18, "plays well on a fife," and is described by Colonel Jonathan Moulton of Hampton, Rockingham County, New Hampshire, as having been born in New York and having tried to enlist in the army at Lexington.[52] Bill, age about 29 and probably a house servant (judging from the clothing he is described as wearing), "plays well on the Flute and Fife, one of each he had with him," according to Jeremiah Platt of New Haven, Connecticut.[53] Tom, age 19, ran away from John Duffield of Philadelphia, who says he "is a tolerable good fifer" who wants to play in the army.[54] Jack, age 23 and a native of Guinea, with country marks, is described as a "sometime fifer to the company of Charleston volunteers" by Peter Zylstra of Charleston, South Carolina.[55] Solomon, described by Richard Johnson of Milton, Albemarle County, Virginia, as a 34- to 35-year-old sawyer and boatman, "carried . . . a new fife, which he is fond of playing, but not a professed hand at it."[56]

A few of the twenty-one advertisements for drummers also have a specifically military context, but here the earliest references are from the 1750s, at which time there was military activity during the French and Indian War. Pennsylvania had the highest number of drummers with eight, followed by South Carolina with seven; overall, the drummers were about equally divided between North and South. Several of the drummers also played the fife and a few the fiddle. The small number of drummers identified in the advertisements suggests that the colonial prohibitions against African drumming traditions as a dangerous form of communication among blacks was effective, or that the traditions survived mostly in secret.

James, who ran away from Joseph Chambers of York-Town, York County, Pennsylvania, in 1756, "can beat a drum, and has a great desire to be amongst soldiers" and he speaks good English.[57] Henry Middleton of Charleston, South Carolina, states that Prince was "formerly a drummer to one of companies of the regiment" and therefore well known in Charleston.[58] In 1779, Quash took with him when he ran away from John Postell of St. Bartholomews, Colleton County, South Carolina, a "drummer's suit of clothes which he formerly wore when a drummer to the Borough Company."[59] Cuff, a 33-year-old tinker, is "very ingenious at tinkering, and beating the drum and playing on the fife," according to Jesse Brown of New London, Connecticut.[60]

The flute seems to have been played by blacks earlier than the fife; the earliest references date from the 1740s. The earliest cited flute player, Cambridge, who ran away in 1743, "plays well upon a Flute, and not so well on a Violin," according to James Oliver of Boston, Massachusetts, who also notes that he teaches apprentices and servants how to play.[61] A majority of the eighteen black flute players identified in the advertisements also played another instrument; most of these also played the fife, and some the fiddle. Bill, as noted above, played both the flute and the fife in New Haven. An example of a flute-violin player would be Jack, about 25 years of age, of whom Michael Swoope of York-Town, York County, Pennsylvania, stated that he "plays on the violin and German flute."[62] Three of the advertisements specifically identified the flute as a German flute, and probably most of them were of this species since this was the instrument second in popularity to the fiddle among white musicians of the time.[63] Another German flute player was George, about age 30, who "plays the flute and fife, and took with him a neat German flute"; according to Charles Crismen of Knowlton, Sussex County, New Jersey, George is a farmer and blacksmith who speaks good English and Dutch.[64] The flute was primarily an instrument of northern blacks, two-thirds of the references being to runaways from northern colonies or states, half of these from Massachusetts and Connecticut, and the other half from the middle colonies or states of New York, Pennsylvania, and New Jersey.

The next instrument noted in table 12.2 is perhaps the most interesting instrument of all, the banjo. The fiddle, the fife, and the flute are instruments primarily identified with Western white musical culture, but the banjo is African in origin. Various African musical cultures, of course, made use of what might be called analogs of the fiddle, the fife, and the flute, but players of these African analog instruments who were enslaved and brought to this country seem to have fairly rapidly adopted the European instruments. However, enslaved and transported African players of the precursors to the banjo, West African instruments like the *xalam*, the *n'goni*, and, most especially, the *akonting*, did not find a preexisting, similar-enough European instrument to which to transfer their "allegiance." Granted, the cultures of European colonizers did have various kinds of plucked lutes, but they were constructed differently and none of them had the distinguishing feature of the West African plucked lutes (and of the banjo as it developed): a short drone string, the highest-pitched string, in the position where the European lutes would have their lowest-pitched string. The first place in the New World where slave instruments were modeled on West African plucked lutes was the Caribbean in the seventeenth century, and that is where the innovation of the flat fingerboard (borrowed from European instruments) was joined, in the African manner, with the African gourd body, before the instrument first appeared in North America.[65] For an image of what banjos referred to in the runaway advertisements looked like, see *The Old Plantation* watercolor (figures N, O, and P).

Not only was the banjo African in origin, but no evidence has yet been presented that it was played by whites before the nineteenth century.[66] Interestingly, the banjo seems not to have been widely played by eighteenth-century North-American blacks, with only 2.5 percent of the runaway black musicians in the newspaper advertisements identified as banjo players. The culture had apparently not yet decided how to spell the word; among the eighteen references to banjo players were eight different spellings of the word (*bonja, banjo, banger, bangeo, banjoe, bongo, banjeau,* and *banjeo*). But, importantly, users of those terms do not demonstrate any uncertainty about what the instrument was. That is, none of the ads in which the runaway's skill as a banjo player is used as an identifying feature show any concern about whether the newspaper reader will know what such a reference means; there was no felt need to explain the term, however it was spelled.

Only four of the banjo players (Toby, Prince, Sam, and Frank, discussed below) also played another instrument, and they all played the fiddle. Because the history of black banjo playing in the United States has many lacunae, and the total number of runaway banjo players is limited, the discussion includes all of the banjo players identified in the advertisements.

The earliest references to banjo players in runaway slave ads date from the late 1740s, and all three of the 1740s references come from Maryland. The earliest of these is Toby, described in 1748 by William Harris of Fairly, Kent County, Maryland, as a carpenter and sawyer, who "took with him . . . a new Fiddle, a Bonja, on both which he at times plays."[67] In the following year Scipio, "who plays on the Banjo and can sing," ran away from Captain Thomas Prather of Prince George's County, Maryland (figure 12.1).[68] Another Scipio eight years later ran away from Joseph Nicolson of Chester Town, Kent County, Maryland; this Scipio, a hatter who speaks broken English, "plays well on the Banjoe," and was formerly owned

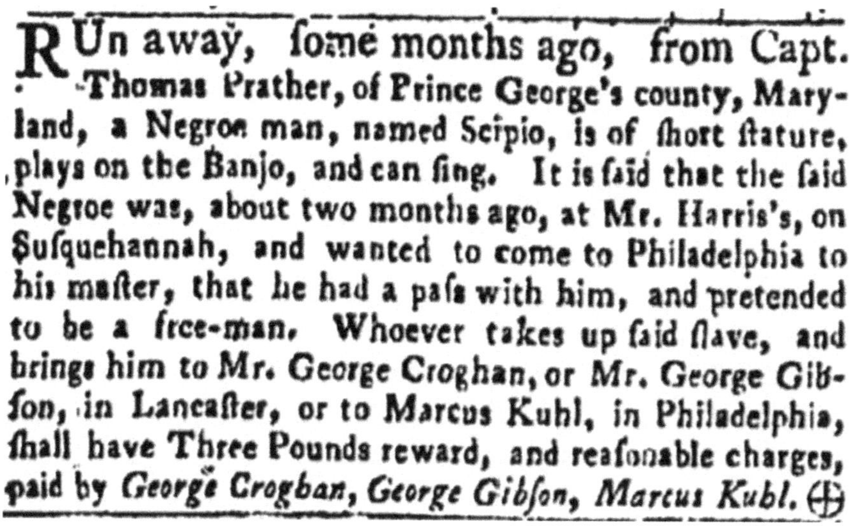

R Un away, fome months ago, from Capt.
Thomas Prather, of Prince George's county, Maryland, a Negro man, named Scipio, is of short stature,
plays on the Banjo, and can fing. It is faid that the faid
Negroe was, about two months ago, at Mr. Harris's, on
Sufquehannah, and wanted to come to Philadelphia to
his mafter, that he had a pafs with him, and pretended
to be a free-man. Whoever takes up faid flave, and
brings him to Mr. George Croghan, or Mr. George Gibfon, in Lancafter, or to Marcus Kuhl, in Philadelphia,
shall have Three Pounds reward, and reafonable charges,
paid by *George Crogban, George Gibfon, Marcus Kubl.* ⊕

Figure 12.1. Example of a typical advertisement for a runaway slave musician. It is also the earliest documented use of the modern spelling of "banjo." [Philadelphia] *Pennsylvania Gazette*, July 13, 1749, p. 3, col. 1.

by Marcus Kuhl of Philadelphia.[69] The third 1740s runaway banjoist is Prince, a 25-year-old mulatto; in 1749, he ran away from John Woolford of Cambridge, Dorchester County, Maryland, who stated that Prince took with him "an old Fiddle, and plays very well on the Banger."[70]

The banjo was primarily a southern instrument: all but three of the runaways identified as banjo players were from the South, six of them from Maryland, five from Virginia, two from Delaware, and one each from North Carolina and South Carolina. In addition to the four Maryland banjoists noted above, the other two Maryland banjoists identified were Will Wage and Charles. Will Wage "plays upon the banjoe," according to Richard Gambra of Port Tobacco, Charles County, Maryland, who also notes in 1778 that Will gambles and is "one of the Piccawaxon glebe slaves."[71] Charles "plays on the banjoe"; Richard Ellis of Head of Bohemia, Cecil County, Maryland, also describes him in 1785 as "pert," fond of liquor, and of a yellow complexion, and notes that he had previously lived near Dover, Kent County, Delaware; a similar advertisement in a different newspaper adds that Charles has several wives.[72]

The five Virginia banjoists identified as running away in Virginia between 1775 and 1799 are Charles, Humphrey, Will, Davie, and Adam. Charles, age 38 in 1775, ran away, perhaps multiple times, from John Giles from near Suffolk Town, Nansemond County, Virginia, who states that Charles, formerly living near Williamsburg, "plays exceedingly well on the Banger, and generally carries one with him."[73] Humphrey, age 26 and "born and bred up in Essex county," in 1784 ran away from Pitmon Kidd, from near New Bridges in lower Hanover County, Virginia, who notes that Humphrey is "fond of playing on the banjo."[74] Will, age 24 and of a yellow complexion, is said to be "fond of, and plays well on, an instrument called the banjo" by John Howard, from near Richmond, Virginia.[75] Davie, when in 1799 he ran away from John Arundell of Richmond, Virginia, is described as an "impertinent" but "remarkably neat and clean" carter who "plays on the Banjoe."[76] Adam's owner, Meredith Helm, of Winchester, Frederick County, Virginia, states that he "plays well on the banjeo."[77]

The four other southern runaway banjoists noted in the advertisements are Sam, Frank, Will, and Jack. Sam, about 30 years of age when he ran away in 1789, is described by Isaac Stouts of Thorofare-neck, New Castle County, Delaware, as a rough carpenter who "plays on the Banjoe and Fiddle, [and is] fond of dancing."[78] In 1796, Frank, no age given, ran away from John Clarke, of Broadkiln, Sussex County, Delaware, who states that he "plays on the violin and Banger, one of which he commonly carries with him."[79] Will, a 24- to 25-year-old shoemaker with a yellow complexion and "featured much like a white man," in 1796 ran away from Anthony Peele of Yadkin River, Rowan County, North Carolina, who notes that Will "plays on the banjo."[80] Jack, age 45 to 50 in 1797 and West India born, "plays very well on the banjeau," as described by an unnamed owner who resides in Edgefield County, South Carolina.[81]

Almost two-thirds of the banjo players were from Maryland and Virginia alone, with most of the earlier references (1748–57) from Maryland, suggesting that these two states were the crucible of black banjo playing in North America. In fact, one can be even more specific than that about the primary locus of black banjo players: twelve of the eighteen were from the Chesapeake Bay area (counting Delaware as part of the eastern shore), half on the eastern shore (Toby, Scipio #1, Prince, Charles [Maryland], Sam, and Frank) and half on the western (Scipio #2, Will Wage, Charles [Virginia], Humphrey, Will, and Davie).

Runaway black banjo players were identified in New York City in 1753, one in Hanover, Pennsylvania, in 1790, and another in Elizabeth, New Jersey, in 1794. Joe, age 38–40, in 1753, ran away from Captain Charles Ware of New York City, who states that Joe "can play on the bangeo" and speak good English; he is described as "lately from the Bay" and is dressed like a house servant.[82] In Hanover, York County, Pennsylvania, Abdiel M'Alister advertised in 1790 for runaway Nathan Butler, a mulatto house servant about 26 years old who can read and "plays well on the banjoe."[83] Antoine, according to Mr. Caradeux from near Elizabeth-Town, Union County, New Jersey, "plays very well upon the bongo" and speaks French well and a little English.[84] If the "Bay" the New York City player was described as being from was the Chesapeake Bay, then he too may have been from Maryland or Virginia. The New Jersey player was a French speaker with a master with a French name, suggesting that he was probably from the West Indies. In addition, one of the Maryland players advertised in 1757 (Scipio, as noted above) was said to have been formerly owned by a Philadelphia master. So, although the banjo was clearly a southern instrument, one can locate runaway black banjo players in both Philadelphia and New York City as early as the 1750s.[85]

But the fact remains that the banjo was apparently not widely played by blacks in eighteenth-century America. For every runaway black banjo player there were thirty-six runaway black fiddlers. This ratio is in decided contrast to the situation in the middle of the nineteenth century. Several years ago, I also gathered data from *Born in Slavery: Slave Narratives from the Federal Writers' Project, 1936–1938* (often referred to as the WPA [Works Progress Administration] Slave Narrative Collection) referring to the period roughly from the 1840s to the 1860s.[86] At that time the banjo was common among black musicians, still not as common as the fiddle, but outstripped by the fiddle by a ratio of only 2/1, instead of 36/1. This contrast in data from the eighteenth and mid-nineteenth centuries suggests a vast growth in banjo playing among blacks during the interim period. Although the banjo clearly was an African American instrument in the eighteenth century, as Thomas Jefferson acknowledged,[87] it became even more of one by the mid-nineteenth century.

The final instruments listed in table 12.2, noted in about 1 percent or less of the advertisements, are the French horn, the pipes, and the guitar. The French horn may seem like an odd instrument to be played by eighteenth-century blacks, but the instrument referred to in these advertisements was not the same as the modern French horn, now more appropriately just called a "horn." The eighteenth-century instrument of this name was what would now be called a "natural horn," that is, a coiled, conical bore, brass instrument without valves (which were not invented until the nineteenth century) developed as a hunting horn and "announcement" horn for royalty and the like. By the eighteenth century, however, it was used as an orchestral instrument in Europe, and apparently it was also a naval instrument at the time.[88] Several of the French horn players are identified as seamen, and of one in a 1772 advertisement it is said that in the last war he was "french-horn man on board . . . a privateer." The earliest reference to a French horn player is a 1770 advertisement. Three of the eight players were originally from the West Indies, and one was a native of Africa. Three of the eight also played the fiddle. Geographically, the French horn was more an instrument of southern blacks; three of the players were from South Carolina, two from Virginia, two from New Jersey, and one from Pennsylvania.

Another example of a French horn player is Mark, about age 25 in 1780, a speaker of Portuguese born on St. Jago (the largest of the Cape Verde Islands off the coast of Senegal), who "blows the French horn," also plays the fiddle, and "whistles many tunes well, and to be heard at a surprising distance, [and] is fond of marches and church musick, particularly that belonging to the Roman Catholic religion, which he professes," according to William Allason of Fauquier Courthouse, Fauquier County, Virginia.[89]

The three references to pipes indicated in table 12.2 are rather ambiguous. All three of these references are from Georgia, but writers of the advertisements were not really sure about the instrument they were describing. One runaway in 1780, the earliest reference, is said to be "very fond of making and blowing a pipe in imitation of a fife"; a 1792 ad speaks of a "Fife made of a reed"; and another 1792 advertisement makes reference to "a kind of flute or pipe." This latter player is especially interesting since he is described as newly from the Gold Coast.[90]

Only one runaway slave musician is described as playing guitar. A 1799 advertisement states that Breland, a French Negro, ran away from C. Grandmont, of Lamberton, Burlington County, New Jersey. Grandmont noted that Breland "is very fond of playing on a long guitar."[91] "A long guitar" may be a Spanish guitar rather than the shorter English guitar, which was more common earlier in the century; the Spanish guitar was gaining popularity late in the century.

In order to have an approximate measure of how large a proportion of the black population played a musical instrument, I kept track not only of the musicians themselves, but also of the total number of adult male runaways advertised in each state (although in several states with few musicians I did not collect the latter data). The right-hand columns in table 12.1 give the ratio of identified musicians to the total number of adult male runaways, first by state and then farther to the right by region: 1/10 in New England, 1/12 in the upper Mid-Atlantic, 1/21 in the Upper South, 1/42 in the Middle South, and 1/63 in the Deep South. These figures present a definite and most interesting pattern: the farther north, the higher the ratio, and the farther south, the lower the ratio. These figures are for runaway slaves; applying them to the whole black population may be questionable. It may be that musicians were more likely than non-musicians to run away, perhaps having more opportunity to do so, and of course free blacks as well as slaves lived in all of these areas. But these data are the best we have on this issue, and the idea that anything like one out of every eight adult male blacks in Connecticut and New Jersey was a musician, or one out of every twelve in Pennsylvania, is astonishing. It would seem that northern blacks in the eighteenth century were very musical.

This difference in proportion of black musicians between the North and the South is particularly fascinating. And even if these ratios might somewhat inaccurately reflect the actual proportions of musicians in the black populations in general, because musicians were more likely than non-musicians to run away, I can think of no reason why northern musicians were more likely to run than southern ones, so these regional differences are likely real, even if not as pronounced as my figures suggest. One possible explanation for the differences has to do with the musicians' occupations. From the information in the advertisements it appears that most slave musicians, in both the North and the South, were house servants or craftsmen rather than field hands, and the proportion of house servants-craftsmen to the total slave population was much higher in the

North than in the South. So it is logical that if the proportion of house servants-craftsmen was greater in the North, so would the proportion of musicians be greater.

Whatever the reasons, the fact of the regional differential has some interesting implications. It reiterates the point made at the beginning of this chapter, that, in the eighteenth century at least, black musicians are not to be thought of as primarily a southern phenomenon. The more important corollary of that is that northern whites had just as much chance of coming in contact with black musicians as southern whites had, and the potential for black influence on white music (and vice versa) was as great in the North as in the South.

This point brings up the general issue of acculturation and influence, the final topic I want to deal with here. The information on black musicians from the runaway slave advertisements makes clear that, even in the eighteenth century, these are not, except in a very few cases, African musicians; they are already African American musicians. If a runaway was African born, whether a musician or not, the advertisements almost always include that information because tribal features and tribal markings were means of identification, as was the degree to which the runaway could speak English. Of the 761 runaway black musicians reported on here, only 3 were described as African born. Overwhelmingly, these musicians were born in this country and spoke relatively good English (and sometimes other languages as well); at least one-eighth (and probably more) of them were of mixed blood. Most of them were house servants or craftsmen. About 6 percent of the runaway musicians were identified as being able to read and write, which is double the figure for all runaway slaves. In terms of instruments played, as noted above, the vast majority of eighteenth-century black musicians played the fiddle, which was also the central instrument of the prevailing Anglo-American tradition that surrounded these blacks, although of course bowed instruments similar to fiddles were also known in regions of Africa from which the forebears of these slaves originally came. All of these facts indicate that these were acculturated musicians. They probably played their music as much for whites as for other blacks; in the North they might have played more often for whites. The advertisements do not provide any information on what music they played, but Anglo fiddling and dance would likely have been at least a part of their repertory, along with specifically African American material.

But I do not want to suggest that these musicians just succumbed to the Anglo tradition. On the contrary, I believe strongly that they also maintained their own black musical identity. If they played for whites, the advertisements also make it clear that they played for all-black dances as well. One particularly interesting tidbit is the statement in one advertisement that there were "negro dancing cellars" in New York City by 1799 at which black musicians played.[92] We have little way of knowing at this point what was the specifically black repertory of eighteenth-century black fiddlers, but that may not even be the most important issue. In terms of black influence on white music, playing style may be much more important than repertory. Alan Jabbour had for some time been suggesting that it is in the realm of playing style that black fiddling most influenced white fiddling, and I agree with him.[93] The large number of black fiddlers I have discovered in eighteenth-century runaway slave advertisements suggests that cross-fertilization of the fiddle tradition must have begun very early. Certainly, the opportunity was there.

However, just as I am not suggesting that these black musicians simply succumbed to the Anglo tradition, I am not suggesting that their only importance is as influences on white musical traditions. These advertisements show that active black musical traditions were alive and well in eighteenth-century America in their own right, and they can be seen as the basis for future developments in African American music.

Notes

1. Eileen Southern, *The Music of Black Americans*, 3rd ed. (New York: W. W. Norton, 1997), 25–27; Dena J. Epstein, *Sinful Tunes and Spirituals; Black Folk Music to the Civil War* (Urbana: University of Illinois Press, 1977), 112–13; Richard Cullen Rath, "Drums and Power: Ways of Creolizing Music in Coastal South Carolina and Georgia, 1730–1790," in *Creolization in the Americas: Cultural Adaptations to the New World*, ed. Steven Reinhardt and David Buisseret (Arlington: Texas A&M Press, 2000), 99–130.

2. In 1790, the South had sixteen times more slaves than the North. US Bureau of the Census, *Historical Statistics of the United States, 1789–1945* (Washington, DC: US Government Printing Office, 1949), 27.

3. Locations by state in this table are based on modern boundaries, largely because, for some, boundaries changed during the eighteenth century. West Virginia, of course, was not created until much later, but using it helps to more specifically locate the runaways.

4. Rather than constantly repeating the descriptor "his master" throughout this chapter, I assume that readers will have no difficulty distinguishing between a slave's name and that of the slave owner who posted the advertisement.

5. *Boston News-Letter*, April 16, 1711, p. 2, col. 2.

6. *New-York Gazette or Weekly Post-Boy*, January 23, 1766, p. 1, col. 1; also advertised by a different master—Enoch Story from Philadelphia—in [Philadelphia] *Pennsylvania Gazette*, January 9, 1766, p. 3, col. 3.

7. *Lancaster* [PA] *Journal*, June 17, 1790, p. 3, col. 4.

8. *New-York Gazette or Weekly Post-Boy*, June 16, 1760, p. 2, col. 3; also *New-York Mercury*, June 16, 1760.

9. *New-York Mercury*, June 15, 1767, p. 4, col. 1.

10. [Williamsburg] *Virginia Gazette* (Rind), May 20, 1773, p. 2, col. 2.

11. [Hartford] *Connecticut Courant*, July 27, 1779, p. 3, col. 3.

12. *Albany Register*, June 29, 1798, p. 3, col. 4.

13. *Boston Gazette*, December 9, 1734, p. 4, col. 2.

14. [Boston] *Continental Journal*, October 30, 1777, p. 1, col. 3.

15. [Philadelphia] *Pennsylvania Journal*, November 13, 1782, p. 3, col. 1.

16. [Philadelphia] *Pennsylvania Journal*, April 2, 1783, p. 1, col. 1.

17. [Philadelphia] *Pennsylvania Gazette*, August 31, 1785, p. 3, col. 3.

18. [Richmond] *Virginia Gazette*, October 25, 1790, p. 3, col. 1.

19. [Williamsburg] *Virginia Gazette* (Purdy and Dixon), August 18, 1768, p. 3, col. 2.

20. [Philadelphia] *Porcupine's Gazette*, May 5, 1798, p. 3, col. 2.

21. [Williamsburg] *Virginia Gazette* (Purdy), May 23, 1777, p. 1, col. 3.

22. *New-York Daily Gazette*, December 10, 1790, p. 3, col. 1; also advertised in the [Danbury] *Farmer's Journal*, December 14, 1790, p. 3, col. 2, and in the [New Haven] *Connecticut Journal*, December 15, 1790, p. 3, col. 3.

23. [Fredericksburg] *Virginia Herald*, January 8, 1795, p. 3, col. 4.

24. [Charleston] *South-Carolina Gazette*, April 3, 1736, p. 4, col. 2.

25. [Charleston] *South-Carolina Gazette*, November 8, 1751, p. 2, col. 3.

26. [Charleston] *South-Carolina Gazette and Country Journal*, July 25, 1769, p. 4, col. 2.

27. [Charleston] *South-Carolina Gazette and Country Journal*, June 2, 1772, p. 3, col. 3.

28. [Charleston] *South Carolina Gazette and General Advertiser*, January 24, 1784, supplement, p. 1, col. 1.

29. [Charleston] *City Gazette*, November 13, 1793, p. 3, col. 1.

30. [Charleston] *City Gazette*, June 29, 1797, p. 2, col. 3.

31. [Charleston] *South Carolina Gazette and General Advertiser*, August 23, 1783, p. 3, col. 1. He was advertised as runaway again in 1785: [Charleston] State Gazette of South Carolina, May 5, 1785, p. 1, col. 2.

32. *New-York Gazette or Weekly Post-Boy*, September 3, 1761, p. 3, col. 3.

33. [Richmond] *Virginia Gazette and American Advertiser*, August 23, 1786, p. 3, col. 2.

34. *Hall's Wilmington Gazette*, August 24, 1797, p. 3, col. 4.

35. [Philadelphia] *Pennsylvania Packet*, June 6, 1779, p. 3, col. 3; also advertised in the [Philadelphia] *Pennsylvania Gazette*, June 30, 1779, p. 3, col. 3, and the [Philadelphia] *Pennsylvania Journal*, July 7, 1779, p. 4, col. 3.

36. *Albany Register*, June 29, 1798, p. 3, col. 4.

37. [Savannah] *Georgia Gazette*, October 25, 1775, p. 2, col. 1.

38. [Philadelphia] *Pennsylvania Evening Post*, May 29, 1777, p. 1, col. 1.

39. [Baltimore] *Maryland Journal*, June 5, 1792, p. 3, col. 2.

40. [Augusta] *Southern Centinel*, September 1, 1796, p. 4, col. 1.

41. [Charleston] *South-Carolina State-Gazette*, March 28, 1800, p. 3, col. 2; also in the [Charleston] *City Gazette*, March 29, 1800, p. 3, col. 3.

42. [George-Town] *Centinel of Liberty*, September 26, 1800, p. 2, col. 2.

43. [Charleston] *South-Carolina Gazette*, November 8, 1751, p. 2, col. 3.

44. [Charleston] *South-Carolina Gazette and Country Journal*, July 7, 1767, p. 3, col. 2.

45. *Boston Evening Post*, October 17, 1743, p. 2, col. 2.

46. *Wilmington Centinel*, June 18, 1788, p. 4, col. 2.

47. [Richmond] *Virginia Gazette*, November 25, 1780, p. 1, col. 3.

48. Rath, "Drums and Power," 112–16.

49. [Philadelphia] *Dunlap's Philadelphia Packet*, July 4, 1774, p. 3, col. 3.

50. [Philadelphia] *Pennsylvania Journal*, November 2, 1774, p. 3, col. 3.

51. [New London] *Connecticut Gazette*, October 13, 1775, p. 3, col. 2.

52. [Cambridge] *New-England Chronicle*, January 11, 1776, p. 2, col. 3.

53. [New Haven] *Connecticut Journal*, January 22, 1777, p. 3, col. 3.

54. [Philadelphia] *Dunlap's Philadelphia Packet*, June 3, 1777, p. 4, col. 3.

55. [Charleston] *City Gazette*, January 22, 1795, p. 3, col. 1.

56. [Richmond] *Virginia Gazette and General Advertiser*, February 21, 1798, p. 3, col. 4.

57. [Philadelphia] *Pennsylvania Gazette*, September 9, 1756, p. 3, col. 3.

58. [Charleston] *South-Carolina Gazette*, June 23, 1757, p. 4, col. 2.

59. [Charleston] *Gazette of the State of South Carolina*, March 31, 1779, p. 1, col. 2.

60. [New London] *Connecticut Gazette*, October 9, 1794, p. 3, col. 3.

61. *Boston Evening Post*, October 17, 1743, p. 2, col. 2.

62. [Philadelphia] *Pennsylvania Packet*, July 27, 1779, p. 1, col. 1.

63. David K. Hildebrand, "About Early American Music," published online by The Colonial Music Institute, http://www.colonialmusic.org/Resource/DHessay.htm, accessed November 8, 2013.

64. [Philadelphia] *Dunlap and Claypoole's American Daily Advertiser*, January 17, 1794, p. 3, col. 4.

65. For further discussion of African antecedents and Caribbean development of the banjo, see chapters in this book by Shlomo Pestcoe, Shlomo Pestcoe and Greg C. Adams, Greg C. Adams and Chuck Levy, Chuck Levy, Nick Bamber, Saskia Willaert, and Pete Ross.

66. See George R. Gibson's chapter in this book for some discussion of the possibility of white banjoists existing earlier than currently known documentation suggests.

67. [Annapolis] *Maryland Gazette*, June 8, 1748, p. 3, col. 2.

68. [Philadelphia] *Pennsylvania Gazette*, July 13, 1749, p. 3, col. 1.

69. [Philadelphia] *Pennsylvania Gazette*, November 17, 1757, p. 3, col. 2.

70. [Annapolis] *Maryland Gazette*, August 30, 1749, p. 3, col. 2; he was advertised as a runaway again five years later in the same newspaper.

71. [Baltimore] *Maryland Journal*, November 10, 1778, p. 1, col. 2.

72. [Philadelphia] *Pennsylvania Gazette*, September 21, 1785, p. 1, col. 1; [Philadelphia] *Pennsylvania Journal*, September 14, 1785, p. 3, col. 3.

73. [Williamsburg] *Virginia Gazette* (Dixon and Hunter), February 18, 1775, p. 3, col. 2; he was advertised as a runaway again five and then ten years later.

74. [Richmond] *Virginia Gazette and American Advertiser*, May 1, 1784, p. 3, col. 3.

75. [Richmond] *Virginia Gazette and General Advertiser*, June 6, 1792, p. 3, col. 4.

76. [Richmond] *Virginia Argus*, August 30, 1799, p. 1, col. 3.

77. *Winchester Gazette*, November 6, 1799, p. 3, col. 4.

78. [Philadelphia] *Pennsylvania Journal*, October 14, 1789, p. 3, col. 3.

79. [Wilmington] *Delaware Gazette*, November 12, 1796, p. 3, col. 4.

80. [Fayetteville] *North-Carolina Minerva*, July 23, 1796, p. 4, col. 3.

81. *Augusta* [Georgia] *Chronicle*, February 4, 1797, p. 3, col. 4.

82. *New-York Mercury*, November 5, 1753, p. 3, col. 2.

83. [York] *Pennsylvania Herald*, July 21, 1790, p. 3, col. 3; also in the *Carlisle Gazette*, August 4, 1790, p. 1, col. 2.

84. *New-York Daily Gazette*, June 13, 1794, p. 3, col. 2.

85. For evidence of a black banjo player in New York City as early as 1736, see "Zenger's 'Banger:' Contextualizing the Banjo in Early New York City, 1736," by Shlomo Pestcoe and Greg C. Adams, in this volume.

86. Robert B. Winans, "Black Instrumental Music Traditions in the Ex-Slave Narratives," *Black Music Research Newsletter*, Spring 1982, 2–5; reprinted in *Black Music Research Journal* (Spring 1990).

87. Thomas Jefferson, *Notes on the State of Virginia* (Philadelphia, 1785).

88. Horn information comes from Anthony Baines, *Brass Instruments: Their History and Development* (New York: Dover Publications, 1993).

89. [Richmond] *Virginia Gazette*, August 23, 1780, p. 4, col. 2.

90. [Savannah] *Royal Georgia Gazette*, September 28, 1780, p. 3, col. 2; *Augusta* [GA] *Chronicle*, September 1, 1792, p. 3, col. 2; *Augusta* [GA] *Chronicle*, November 2, 1792, p. 3, col. 2.

91. [Philadelphia] *Claypoole's American Daily Advertiser*, April 7, 1799, p. 3, col. 2.

92. [New York] *Daily Advertiser*, May 18, 1799, supplement, p. l, col. 1. For more on New York dancing cellars, see Shane White, "The Death of James Johnson," *American Quarterly* 51 (1999): 753–95.

93. See Alan Jabbour, "Fiddle Tunes of the Old Frontier," http://www.alanjabbour.com/Fiddle_Tunes_of_the_Old_Frontier_Schick.pdf, accessed November 11, 2013, and idem, "In Search of the Source of American Syncopation," *Strings* 16, no. 8 (May–June 2002): 46–56.

CHAPTER 13

Mapping Eighteenth- and Early Nineteenth-Century Citations of Banjo Playing, 1736–1840

Robert B. Winans

Editor's Headnote

Four of the prior chapters in this volume provide data about early banjo playing in North America. Other researchers, many of whom are referred to in these chapters, also present such data in their publications. Here, all of the data are brought together and presented in a graphical form, which allows us to visualize important features of early banjo tradition. This brief chapter functions as a kind of appendix to the banjo section of the preceding runaway slave musicians chapter.

The maps in this chapter display all of the known references (at the time of this publication) to banjo playing in North America up to 1840 that include enough information to geographically locate them and to provide them with a viable date.[1] The reason for using 1840 as a cut-off date is to look at the banjo scene before blackface minstrelsy became wildly popular. The data points are represented by black asterisks, located at least to county-level specificity. The map used for plotting the data is the 1814 "Map of the United States of America," by Mathew Carey, Philadelphia.

Mapping these data points reveals two important facts about the early history of the banjo in North America. The first of these is related to the four data point asterisks that have numbers next to them on the map; numbers 1 (dated 1830s, in central Virginia near the Appomattox River), 2 (dated 1830s, in southwestern Virginia), and 4 (dated ca. 1740s–1750s, in the eastern shore of Maryland) in the upper section of the map, and number 3 at the left margin of the lower section of the map (the arrow to the left of the asterisk denotes that the actual data point for this citation, dated 1828, is to the southwest, about 360 miles away in San Felipe, Austin County, slightly west of Houston, Texas). These four data points, numbers 6, 66, 75, and 76 in the list below, represent the only documented evidence of white persons playing the banjo before 1840. That other white persons played the banjo before 1840 is certainly plausible,[2] but direct, conclusive evidence is still to be found, and may well be found with further research. However, despite the possibility of some additional evidence of white banjo players in this period, the data are still very likely to show, as does the map, that the banjo was overwhelmingly an instrument of African American culture in this period.

The second major point to notice about the map is the degree to which the data points are concentrated in the area of the Chesapeake Bay watershed. The map graphically shows this concentration, as does a summary of the data.[3] Of the 85 data points on the 2 sections of the map, 47 (55 percent) are densely gathered in the Chesapeake states of Virginia, Maryland, and Delaware, while 38 (45 percent) are widely scattered (except for small clumps in and around New York City and New Orleans) in 15 other states. Dividing the data into eighteenth- and nineteenth-century segments, of the 43 data points for 1736–99, 26 (59 percent) are located in Virginia, Maryland, and Delaware, and only 18 (41 percent) are outside that Chesapeake area (in 8 states). For 1800–40, the 41 data points show a wider spread of banjo citations, with 20 (49 percent) outside the Chesapeake area (in 11 states) and 21 (51 percent) inside, where the distribution is still much denser than elsewhere.

DATE AND LOCATION FOR CITATIONS OF NORTH AMERICAN BANJO PLAYERS, 1736–1840

1. 1736, New York City
2. 1748, Fairly, Kent County, MD
3. 1749, Prince George's County, MD
4. 1749, Cambridge, Dorchester County, MD
5. 1749, along Cooper River, St. Thomas Parish, Berkeley County, SC
6. ca. 1740s–1750s, Talbot County and Queen Anne's County, MD (white player, James Hollyday, and banjoist among his mother's slaves)
7. 1753, New York City
8. ca. 1750, Philadelphia, PA
9. ca. 1750, Garrison, Baltimore County, MD
10. ca. 1750–ca. 1810, Nassau County and Westchester County, NY
11. 1750s, near Fredericksburg, Spotsylvania County, VA
12. 1754, Cambridge, Dorchester County, MD
13. Between 1755 and 1799, Newport, RI (arrow pointing northeast by asterisk in top right corner of map section 1 indicates actual data point is about 180 miles northeast of New York City)
14. 1757, Chester Town, Kent County, MD
15. 1759–75, Caroline-King George Counties, VA
16. ca. 1765, New York City (in or near)
17. 1766, Charleston, SC
18. ca. 1770, Surry-Isle of Wight-Suffolk Counties, VA
19. 1774, Nanjemoy, Charles County, MD
20. 1774, St. Mary's City, St. Mary's County, MD
21. 1774, Westmoreland County, VA
22. 1775, Suffolk Town, Nansemond County, VA
23. 1778, Port Tobacco, Charles County, MD
24. ca. 1780, New York City
25. 1781, Albemarle County, VA
26. 1781, Upper Spotsylvania County, VA

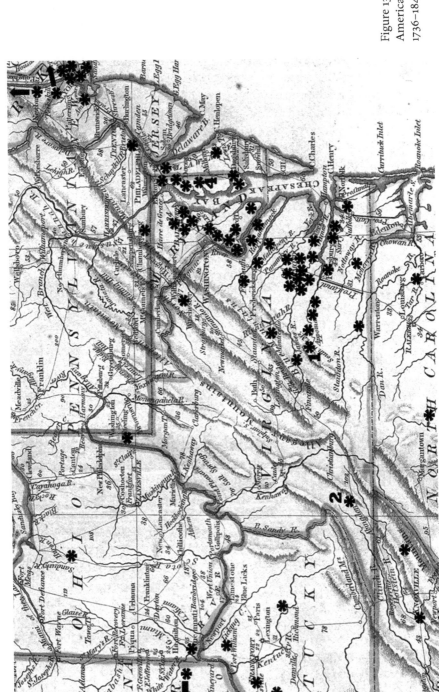

Figure 13.1. Map of North American banjo citations, 1736–1840, section 1.

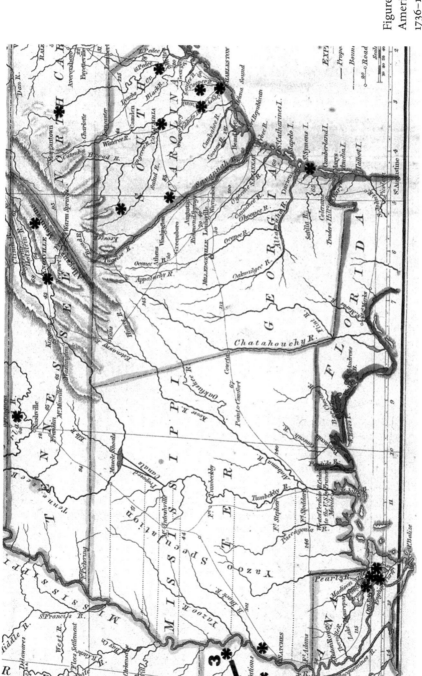

Figure 13.2. Map of North American banjo citations, 1736–1840, section 2.

27. 1781, Central Kentucky
28. 1784, New Bridges, lower Hanover County, VA
29. 1785–95, Dorchester, SC (*The Old Plantation* watercolor)
30. 1785, Head of Bohemia, Cecil County, MD
31. 1787, Tarborough, Edgecombe County, NC
32. 1780s (late), Greenville County, SC
33. 1789, Thorofare Neck, New Castle County, DE
34. 1790, Hanover, York County, PA
35. 1790s, Charles County, MD
36. 1792, Richmond, VA
37. 1794, Elizabeth Town, Union County, NJ
38. 1796, Broadkiln, Sussex County, DE
39. 1796, Yadkin River, Rowan County, NC
40. 1797, Edgefield County, SC
41. 1798, Knoxville, TN
42. 1799, Richmond, VA
43. 1799, Winchester, Frederick County, VA
44. 1799, Richmond, VA
45. ca. 1800, "The Carolinas," on route to Charleston from north, asterisk arbitrarily located in Georgetown County, SC
46. 1802, Prince George County, VA
47. 1802, South Virginia tobacco plantation, asterisk arbitrarily located in Amelia County, VA
48. 1803, Albany, NY (arrow pointing north by asterisk in top right corner of map section 1 indicates actual data point is about 150 miles north of New York City)
49. 1805, Richland County, SC
50. 1806, Wheeling, [W]VA
51. 1807, near Baltimore, MD
52. 1810s, Sumner County, TN
53. 1815, Richmond, VA
54. 1817, Richmond, VA
55. pre-1818, Richmond, VA
56. 1819, New Orleans, LA
57. 1820, Fairfax County, VA
58. 1820, Surry County, VA
59. 1820, Bardstown, Bullitt County, KY
60. 1820s, Chesapeake Watershed, VA (generalized comment about slave banjoists based on travels through ten Virginia counties, from Fredericksburg to Norfolk; asterisk arbitrarily located in James City County, VA)
61. ca. 1820s, Lynchburg, VA
62. 1820s, Appomattox County, VA (neighboring slaves who taught Joel Sweeney)
63. 1820s, Monroe County, IN (arrow by asterisk at left edge of map section 1 indicates actual data point is about 100 miles west, near Bloomington, IN)
64. 1825, New Orleans, LA

65. 1828, Prince George's County, MD
66. 1828, San Felipe, Austin County, TX (white player, Robert McAlpin Williamson) (arrow by asterisk at the left side of map section 2 indicates actual data point is about 360 miles to the southwest, slightly west of Houston)
67. 1829, near Baltimore, MD
68. ca. 1830, Shelby County, KY
69. 1832, Charles City County, VA
70. 1833, Tidewater Virginia—source traveled through several counties; asterisk arbitrarily located in Essex County, VA
71. 1833, New Orleans, LA
72. 1833, Greene County, TN
73. ca. 1833, Ouachita (Washita) River, LA
74. 1830s, Prince Edward County, VA
75. 1830s, Appomattox County, VA (white player, Joel Walker Sweeney)
76. 1830s, "Western Virginia" (white player, Archibald Ferguson; asterisk arbitrarily located in Washington County)
77. 1835, Grant County, KY
78. 1835, lower reaches of Mississippi River; asterisk arbitrarily located in Claiborne County, MS
79. 1835, New Orleans, LA
80. 1835, Cincinnati, OH
81. 1836, "Lower Virginia," probably Southampton County, where asterisk is located
82. 1838, St. Simon's Island, GA
83. 1839, Marion County, OH
84. 1840, near Baltimore, MD
85. 1840, Mecklenburg County, VA

Notes

1. Secondary sources where I found the data plotted on the map are here noted; each is followed by the numbers given in the data list below ("Date and Location for Citations of North American Banjo Players, 1736–1840") for items coming from that source. For some of the data, I have reinterpreted the dating given by the source and, in some cases, clarified the location. A few of the numbers are assigned to more than one source since I found them in more than one and because readers who want to track down these sources may find it easier to find some rather than others. Some of the data plotted here come from chapters in this volume: Robert B. Winans, "Black Musicians in Eighteenth-Century America: Evidence from Runaway Slave Advertisements" (##2, 3, 4, 7, 14, 22, 23, 28, 30, 33, 34, 36, 37, 38, 39, 40, 42, 43); Shlomo Pestcoe and Greg C. Adams, "Zenger's 'Banger': Contextualizing the Banjo in Early New York City, 1736" (##1, 10, 13, 48); Shlomo Pestcoe, "The Banjar Pictured: The Depiction of the African American Early Gourd Banjo in *The Old Plantation*, South Carolina, 1780s" (##5, 29); and George R. Gibson, "Black Banjo, Fiddle, and Dance in Kentucky and the Amalgamation of African American and Anglo-American Folk Music" (##26, 27, 32, 63, 66, 67, 68, 77). In addition, quite a bit of the data comes from both of the following publications: Dena J. Epstein, *Sinful Tunes and Spirituals: Black Folk Music to the Civil War* (Urbana: University of Illinois Press,

1977), 359–62, and idem, "The Folk Banjo: A Documentary History," *Ethnomusicology* 19, no. 3 (September 1975): 359–60 (##11, 12, 13, 18 [dated "pre-1775" in both sources], 19, 21, 25, 31, 44, 50, 54, 56, 60, 64, 69, 70, 73, 79, 82, 85 [the last in "Folk Banjo" only, p. 357, dated "about 1847," but that was a little later than Livermore (her source) was actually in Virginia]). Other publications also contributed data presented here: Philip D. Morgan, *Slave Counterpoint: Black Culture in the Eighteenth-Century Chesapeake and Lowcountry* (Chapel Hill: University of North Carolina Press, 1998), 583, 419, 587 (##5, 20, 45); Lowell H. Schreyer, *The Banjo Entertainers: Roots to Ragtime* (Mankato: Minnesota Heritage Printing, 2007), 3, 5–6, 21–25 (##10, 52, 61, 62, 75, 76); Bob Carlin, *The Birth of the Banjo: Joel Walker Sweeney and Early Minstrelsy* (Jefferson, NC: McFarland & Company, 2007), 3, 4, 5, 19–21, 58–59 (##61, 55, 62, 75, 76); Philip F. Gura and James F. Bollman, *America's Instrument: The Banjo in the Nineteenth Century* (Chapel Hill: University of North Carolina Press, 1999), 14–15 (##10, 17); Edward Baptist, *The Half Has Never Been Told: Slavery and the Making of American Capitalism* (New York: Basic Books, 2014), 161, 167 (##35, 49); Cecelia Conway, *African Banjo Echoes in Appalachia: A Study of Folk Traditions* (Knoxville: University of Tennessee Press, 1995), 57, 64, and 304 [misdated 1789], (##8, 41); Gilbert Chase, *America's Music: From the Pilgrims to the Present*, 3rd ed. (Urbana: University of Illinois Press, 1987), 272 (#59); Hans Nathan, *Dan Emmett and the Rise of Early Negro Minstrelsy* (Norman: University of Oklahoma Press, 1962), 190 (#72); Christopher J. Smith, *The Creolization of American Culture: William Sidney Mount and the Roots of Blackface Minstrelsy* (Urbana: University of Illinois Press, 2013), 251 (#83); Katonah Museum of Art, *The Birth of the Banjo* (Katonah, NY: Katonah Museum of Art, November 9, 2003–February 1, 2004), 20–21 (#53); Epstein, *Sinful Tunes and Spirituals*, xv (#6); Robert B. Winans, "The Black Banjo-Playing Tradition in Virginia and West Virginia," *Folklore and Folklife in Virginia* 1 (1979): 13 (#74). A few data points were shared with me through personal communication with banjo researchers Greg C. Adams (##16, 24, 46, 47, 51, 57, 58, 65, 71, 78, 80, 81, 84) and Robert Sayers (#65). One source that I did not use for gathering data is *Born in Slavery: Slave Narratives from the Federal Writers' Project, 1936–1938*, now available online at American Memory, Library of Congress (https://memory.loc.gov/ammem/snhtml/mesnbibVolumes1.html, accessed November 12, 2017), because nearly all of the ex-slaves talked about the immediate pre–Civil War years rather than a pre-1840 period. For a summary of data on musical instruments in those narratives, see my article "Black Instrumental Music Traditions in the Ex-Slave Narratives," *Black Music Research Journal* 10, no. 1 (Spring 1990): 43–53. In addition, although two of the data points here are based on period paintings (John Rose, *The Old Plantation*, ca. late 1780s, #29, and James Warrel, *The Banjo Man*, 1815, #53), three other period paintings (Samuel Jennings, *Liberty Displaying the Arts and Sciences*, 1792; unknown artist, *Banjo Man and Dancer*, ca. 1815–20; Nicolino Calyo, *Negro Dancer and Banjo Player*, 1834) are not included because, while dated, they cannot be assigned to a location. All three show African American banjo players, and all three can be found in the Katonah Museum of Art's *The Birth of the Banjo* noted above (pp. 38, 9, 24).

2. George R. Gibson, in his chapter in this book presents an argument for other whites learning to play the banjo before 1840.

3. See the text listing of the data below.

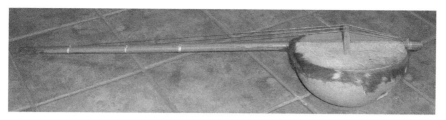

Figure A. Gambian *ekonting*, full-spike plucked lute; photo courtesy of editor.

Figure B. Malian *n'goni*, semi-spike plucked lute; photo courtesy of Greg C. Adams.

Figure C. *Ekonting* bipedal bridge; photo courtesy of editor.

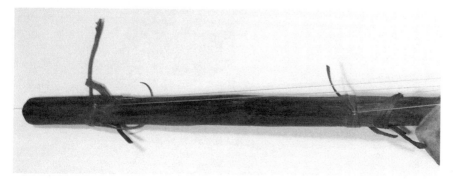

Figure D. Malian *n'goni*, showing leather thong tuning rings; photo courtesy of Greg C. Adams.

Figure E. Manjak-Manyago *bunchundo* and bottle drum; photo courtesy of Ulf Jägfors.

Figure F. Bujogo *ñopata*; photo courtesy of Nick Bamber.

Figure G. Kilba *gullum*, Nigeria, full-spike lute with cylindrical bridge; postcard from collection of Shlomo Pestcoe.

Figure H. Sloane 1707 "Strum Stumps" engraving; courtesy of the Smithsonian Institution.

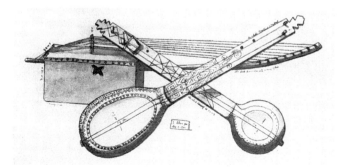

Figure I. Sloane 1701 "Strum Strump" master sketch; courtesy of the Royal Asiatic Society.

Figure J. Extant Stedman *creole bania*; courtesy of the Museum Volkenkunde, Leiden.

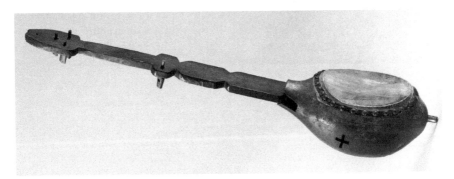

Figure K. Haitian *banza*; courtesy of Pete Ross.

Figure L. Stedman *creole bania* book engraving; courtesy of the Smithsonian Institution.

Figure M. Boucher banjos, 1840s–1850s, photo of 2014 exhibit at the Baltimore Museum of Industry; courtesy of editor, who was co-curator of the exhibit.

Figure N. *The Old Plantation,* watercolor by John Rose, 1780s; courtesy of The Colonial Williamsburg Foundation. Gift of Abby Aldrich Rockefeller.

Figure O. *The Old Plantation* detail of banjo and drum; courtesy of The Colonial Williamsburg Foundation. Gift of Abby Aldrich Rockefeller.

Figure P. *The Old Plantation* detail of banjo; courtesy of The Colonial Williamsburg Foundation. Gift of Abby Aldrich Rockefeller.

Figure Q. *The Banjo Player*, painting by Williams S. Mount, 1856; courtesy of The Long Island Museum of American Art, History & Carriages. Gift of Mr. and Mrs. Ward Melville, 1955.

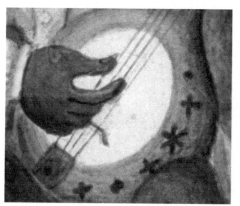

Figure R. *The Old Plantation* and *The Banjo Player* details of banjo player hand position; courtesy of The Colonial Williamsburg Foundation. Gift of Abby Aldrich Rockefeller and The Long Island Museum.

Figure S. *The Old Plantation* detail of male dancer; courtesy of The Colonial Williamsburg Foundation. Gift of Abby Aldrich Rockefeller.

Figure T. *The Old Plantation* detail of women dancers, courtesy of The Colonial Williamsburg Foundation. Gift of Abby Aldrich Rockefeller; and photo of Sierra Leone *segburreh* player, 1969, courtesy of photographer Chad Finer.

PART V

Inquiries into White and Black Banjo in Nineteenth- and Twentieth-Century America

Black Banjo, Fiddle, and Dance in Kentucky and the Amalgamation of African American and Anglo-American Folk Music

George R. Gibson

Editor's Headnote

George R. Gibson's historiographic chapter uncovers much new information about black banjo and fiddle players, and dance, in Kentucky, and their influence on white musicians, from the 1780s to the early twentieth century. He also makes use of corollary period data from other states to broaden his discussion. The deeply researched data are of great value in understanding the development of the folk musical culture of Kentucky. Gibson's central thesis is that the acknowledged richness of Kentucky's music traditions owe a great deal to African Americans. Beyond that, his interpretation of the data moves in two directions. The first of these is to argue that whites learned to play the banjo from blacks long before they are supposed to have taken up the banjo in the middle of the nineteenth century (due to the minstrel show). His second is to argue that creolization was responsible for both the New World banjo and southern traditional music, popularly known today as mountain music. His chapter gives voice to marginalized people, who provide new insight into this process. He also briefly notes that Luso-Africans provide a possible banjo connection between West Africa, the West Indies, and early colonial America.

The banjo and fiddle were intimately related through dance, and dance was the vehicle by which they traveled to remote frontiers. Viewing the three together is indispensable for exploring the synthesis of African American and Anglo-American folk music, and necessary for understanding the scope of African Americans' contribution to Kentucky music. The extent of this contribution was not known when rural whites and a few African Americans were recorded early in the twentieth century. Richard Nevins comments:

As the Mississippi delta is to the blues, Kentucky is to fiddle music, banjo playing and classic old ballads and songs, all mainstays of early American mountain music. No other state comes even close in both terms of fascinating diversity of styles and prodigious amounts of great performances. The explanations for this musical embarrassment of riches are lost to time, but thankfully this wonderful bounty is extremely well documented in both commercial and field recordings of the 1920's and 30's.[1]

The explanations for this "musical embarrassment of riches" are not lost to time. Evidence presented here will show that African Americans are largely responsible for the richness and diversity of Kentucky folk music.

The amalgamation of African American and Anglo-American music began in colonial America; however, there is a curious exception: the banjo tradition in white folk culture is popularly believed to have developed after the banjo was featured in minstrel shows beginning in the 1840s.[2] Those who support this argument do so by citing the well-documented history of the banjo in minstrelsy, and not by examining the history or folklife of common whites, defined by Bill Cecil-Fronsman as "white nonslaveholders and slaveholders who saw themselves as nonelite."[3]

Although the banjo became an instrument of professional northern musicians by the 1850s, the first known white banjo pickers were southern. Archibald Ferguson and Joel Walker Sweeney, common whites from the South, were the first documented minstrel banjoists; it is likely there would have been no record of their music had they not performed in blackface.[4] Robert McAlpin Williamson played banjo, sang, and patted juba to entertain friends in San Felipe de Austin, Texas, between 1828 and 1831.[5] Williamson, who became an associate justice of the Supreme Court of the Republic of Texas, was born in Georgia ca. 1804 and died in Texas in 1859.[6] He is remembered as a musician because he was a prominent member of pioneer society in Texas.

The African American banjo was adopted by rural white southerners; however, the continued existence of a mountain banjo tradition in the mid-twentieth century led many to believe the banjo was exclusively a mountain instrument. Some maintained there were not enough slaves in the mountains to have established an antebellum banjo tradition; this contributed to the popular beliefs that the banjo entered the mountains during and after the Civil War, and that the playing of the banjo and fiddle together originated on the minstrel stage. These popular beliefs are incorrect: evidence presented here will show that Appalachian Kentucky had a substantial African American population; that African Americans played banjo and fiddle together before minstrelsy; that the banjo was a rural instrument widespread in Kentucky before the Civil War, from the western flatlands to the Kentucky Mountains; and that the banjo was a part of white folk culture prior to 1840s minstrelsy.

African Americans in Colonial America and Kentucky

Most of the first enslaved African Americans in Kentucky came from Virginia and Maryland where common whites, including indentured servants, socialized with slaves. "It was common, for example, for servants and slaves to run away together, steal hogs together, get drunk together. It was not uncommon for them to make love together."[7] Slaves freed by the mid-seventeenth century established homes along the Chesapeake where some interacted on an equal basis with their white neighbors.[8] A genealogist documented the families of free African Americans in the 1790 federal census and found most were descendants of a white female indentured servant and a slave, who became free before racism fully developed: "Families like Gowen, Cumbo, and Driggers who were free in the mid-seventeenth century had several hundred members before the end of the colonial period. . . . The light skinned descendants of these families formed the tri-racial isolate communities of Virginia, North Carolina, South Carolina, Tennessee, Kentucky, Ohio and Louisiana."[9]

Tri-racial isolate is an academic term for mixed-race populations that remained somewhat separate through ca. 1900. Luso-Africans, creoles with Portuguese and African ancestry, were likely among the free slaves who formed unions with white female servants in the mid-seventeenth century; they provide a connection between the Gambia River in West Africa, the West Indies, and early colonial America. Luso-Africans were a large presence among Africans whom Ira Berlin describes as Atlantic creoles.[10]

In 1620, Richard Jobson found Luso-Africans along the Gambia River in West Africa; they claimed to be Portuguese, and although some were as dark as their African neighbors, they took offense at being classed as Negroes.[11] They lived in an area where several banjo-like folk instruments, including the *akonting*, have been found. Jobson described a banjo-like instrument and noted that Spaniards took enslaved Africans from the Gambia River to the West Indies.[12] It is likely that Luso-Africans were involved in the creation of the early gourd banjo, a creole instrument with both European and African features, and might have brought the instrument from the West Indies, where early descriptions of it have been found, to colonial America.[13] Many of the slaves imported into the colonies in the seventeenth century were from the West Indies.[14]

Those free of slavery and indenture moved west together on the early frontiers as slavery became institutionalized and access to land became prohibitive in the settled areas of Virginia and Maryland. Also, by 1728 runaway slaves were being sheltered by pioneers on the Virginia and Carolina frontiers.[15] The early frontier "was an open and fluid region" where "of necessity, convenience, and sheer pleasure, individuals appropriated cultural habits from others and in doing so altered their identity."[16]

Some descendants of free Luso-Africans blended into white society, some became enslaved, while others became members of mixed-race groups that remained somewhat separate; Melungeons, one of the better known groups, were early settlers in the southern mountains. Some Melungeons claimed to be Portuguese, and were likely descended from Luso-Africans.[17] Recent DNA testing of people with Melungeon ancestry has shown that some had a sub-Saharan African male in their direct paternal line.[18]

Mixed-race families had good reason to remain close as they migrated west: they did so for family cohesion and protection. There was an ever-present danger of them or their children being kidnapped and sold into slavery. This was the reason some lighter-skinned families later claimed Indian ancestry, and why some descendants of Luso-Africans held on to their Portuguese identity, although they had long since forgotten how their ancestors arrived in America.

By 1790, thousands of enslaved African Americans had been brought from Virginia and Maryland to the Kentucky frontier, which was a part of Virginia until 1792. The black population in Kentucky rose from 11,944 in 1790 to 236,167 in 1860. These African Americans, enslaved and free, were unevenly distributed in the different regions of Kentucky. During the antebellum period the highest concentration was in the central region, with a slightly lower concentration in the western region.[19] The Kentucky Mountains had the lowest concentration of African Americans; however, despite a lower concentration, the region had in excess of 75,000 African Americans in 1830.[20]

Recounting Kentucky history is complicated by frontiers separated by geography and time; however, I have merged all into two regions: central and western Kentucky, which include the more level lands that were settled beginning in the 1770s, and the Eastern Coal Field and Upper Cumberland, which include the more mountainous lands that were mostly settled after 1800. I use *Appalachia* to describe the forty counties in the Eastern Coal Field and Upper Cumberland.[21]

Central and Western Kentucky

African Americans who accompanied early immigrants to Kentucky were rarely documented. A notable exception, which includes the first known reference to the banjo in Kentucky, is a description of the migration of the Upper Spotsylvania Baptist Church from Virginia to central Kentucky:

> The moving train included with church members, their children, negro slaves and other emigrants . . . between five and six hundred souls and was the largest body of Virginians that ever set out for Kentucky at one time . . . they toiled over the Blue Ridge at Buford's Gap. . . . Some of the women were already in tears when Capt. Ellis spoke to one of his negro men whose willing hands began at once to make a well-worn banjo "talk." Like magic the signal passed along the dusky lines of chattering slaves who trudged beside the wagons with their bundles on their backs and soon one of the jolliest of the old plantation songs resounded from one end of the train to the other. The merry negroes sang as only the old time "darkies" could sing, the children screamed with delight and the emigrants descended the mountain road with lighter hearts.[22]

The immigrants arrived in Kentucky in the spring of 1781 via the Cumberland Gap.[23] Enslaved African Americans also accompanied Daniel Boone to Kentucky:

> In 1775 Shawnee Indians raided the camp of Daniel Boone's trail-blazing party. They killed three persons and seriously wounded another. Two of those killed were Negro slaves, the first to be brought to Kentucky. In time hundreds of others came over the Wilderness Road or were drifted down the Ohio with families fleeing the leached soils of Maryland and Virginia.[24]

Tobacco farming depletes soil very quickly; consequently, many planters in Virginia and Maryland relocated to Kentucky in search of better farmland.

The historian Marion B. Lucas concluded that "overall, there existed a strong interdependence among blacks and whites on the Kentucky frontier. The primitive living conditions in the forest and the ever-present Indian threat forced them to depend on each other for protection, though the white man was free and the black man usually a slave."[25] African Americans and common whites faced the same circumstances on the first frontiers in Virginia and the Carolinas. Racism, however, was not as prevalent on the early frontiers as it was after the Revolutionary War.

African American fiddlers were present early in pioneer Kentucky. Monk Estill, brought from Virginia in 1779, is the first known musician at Boonesborough.[26] He was possibly the first free black in Kentucky, and was one of four thousand African Americans estimated to reside in Kentucky in 1784.[27] A Boone biographer said Monk Estill "was a fiddler who played for all the parties and celebrations."[28] Several families accompanied Colonel George Rogers Clark's expedition to Kentucky, where they established a settlement at Corn Island, now Louisville.[29] A soldier described Clark leading off a frontier ball "with a jig" at the settlement in 1778.[30] The musician for Clark's ball was Cato Watts, an African American fiddler from Virginia.[31]

The fiddle tradition established by Cato Watts and Monk Estill in the eighteenth century persisted through the nineteenth. Owen Walker, born in Madison County in 1857, was a well-known African American fiddler who played for social events as far away as Louisville.[32] Doc Roberts, a white fiddler and recording artist born in 1898, acquired as much as 70 percent of his repertoire, directly or indirectly, from Walker.[33] The repertoire of Jim Booker Sr., an African American fiddler born in 1837 in Jessamine County, was passed on to his children and became widespread among white fiddlers in the surrounding area.[34] The senior Booker's eldest son, born in 1872, was "a brilliant square dance fiddler, as were many other black fiddlers in Kentucky going far back many generations into the early 1800's. Indeed, perhaps more than any other state, Kentucky had a long and strong tradition of black fiddlers playing the celtic derived dance music of the southern mountains."[35] The acquisition of African American fiddle tunes by white musicians began by the mid-nineteenth century. It would be logical to assume white banjoists were acquiring black banjo songs during this era.

It is popularly believed that the practice of playing fiddle and banjo together originated on the 1840s minstrel stage; however, African Americans played the banjo and fiddle together (sometimes with other instruments) in colonial America.[36] The former slave J. D. Green described a black dance in 1829 near Baltimore that had instruments featured later on the minstrel stage: "I then went to the dance, and told the fiddler to play me a jig. Che, che, che, went the fiddle, when the banjo responded with a thrum, thrum, thrum, with the loud cracking of the bone player."[37]

African Americans continued playing the banjo and fiddle together in Kentucky; an 1856 account from Nelson County describes an African American band playing banjo and fiddle for a white dance.[38] The banjo and fiddle were described as a part of the social life of Kentucky slaves in 1851: "They sometimes assemble for public worship; but, in general, deliver themselves up to visits, gossip, games, laughter, singing, *banjoing*, fiddling, and dancing."[39] Observers who describe the presence of a banjo and fiddle at dances in Kentucky never state they were played together, probably because something so common needed no comment. After all, African Americans had been playing the instruments together for more than one hundred years by 1860.

Former slaves provide information about several aspects of music prior to the Civil War. A description of music in Shelby County ca. 1830 by former slave Henry Bibb (b. 1815) notes that when slaveholders "wish to have a little sport of that kind, they go among the slaves and give them whiskey, to see them dance, 'pat juber,' sing and play on the banjo."[40] Dancing and patting juba to banjo picking was a part of white folk culture in Kentucky well into the twentieth century.[41]

Dan Bogie, a former slave from Garrard County, described banjo picking ca. 1860: "We would have camp fires and sing songs, and usually a big dance at the barn when the corn was shucked. Some of the slaves from other plantations would pick the banjo, then the dance."[42] Corn shuckings, from colonial days, were social occasions for neighbors to congregate for work and play. It was common for both blacks and whites to be present at these affairs, which usually featured a dance with fiddle or banjo.

Enslaved African Americans imported to Kentucky brought the practice of making gourd banjos with them. A description of music heard in African American cabins in central Kentucky ca. 1865 noted that the "banjo was played, but more commonly the fiddle. A home-made variety of the former consisted of a crook-necked, hard-shell gourd and a piece of sheep-skin."[43] A scene set in 1912 from a novel in Kentucky describes the banjo of an African American as "a cross between guitar and banjo, self-made of gut and a gourd."[44] Appalachian whites played gourd banjos until the mid-twentieth century.[45]

The folkways of a white pioneer in Kentucky included the banjo. Dr. Daniel Drake recounted scenes from his boyhood in 1790s Mason County, in which he described a neighbor, originally from frontier Virginia, making "fiddle strings for the Banjo," and commented, "What he [Mr. Rector] said about the Valley of Virginia indicated that it had, in the middle of the last Century [1750], rather a rude, vulgar and turbulent population."[46] The mixture of slaves, freed slaves, and white servants, both indentured and free, on the early frontier might have created a "rude, vulgar and turbulent population," but this mixture fostered the amalgamation of African American and Anglo-American music. Drake does not seem surprised that his neighbor made banjo strings; however, he goes to great length to describe Rector and his family as lower class; the banjo, from colonial days, was described as an instrument of the lower classes.[47] Rector could have been making banjo strings either for himself or an African American neighbor; however, the important fact here is that the banjo was a part of the folkways of a common white in the 1790s.

Tinie Force and Elvira Lewis, former slaves in western Kentucky, provided information about music ca. 1855 in Ballard County:

> Ring dancing was largely practiced during the slavery period . . . and was per-formed mostly by negro children. . . . The youngsters would congregate within the ring and dance to the rhythmic hand clapping and rhythm of the tambourine, which was performed by the white people of the community. . . . Another kind of entertainment . . . was the singing of negro folk songs and spirituals. . . . These singings . . . not only afforded a favorite pass time for the darkies; but also for the white people. Most always, the singings were attended by a large audience of white people, men, women and children. . . . Banjo and guitar playing were practiced by the many darkies of the slavery period also. . . . Melodious music might be heard at these old fashion contests, as most darkies, who acquired knowledge in the playing of these instruments were familiar with nearly all the melodies and folks songs that were common to the period.[48]

Clearly, the white community in Ballard County participated in the music of slaves, including the ring dance, which is thought to be an African retention. That blacks "were familiar with all the melodies and folks songs common to the period" indicates the repertoire of slaves included music commonly known in the community at large. The use of the guitar by slaves in this period, although earlier than might be expected, helps explain its later popularity in western Kentucky.

Based on interviews with people knowledgeable about pre–Civil War dances in Calloway County's white community, the folklorist Gordon Wilson (1888–1970) re-created a scene of such a dance in the 1850s, in which "the people have as-sembled at some cottage or cabin for an evening of enjoyment. The fiddler is there; the banjo picker is there; the boys are there with their best girls. . . . And the dance continues, warmed with cider and other drinks, until daylight comes."[49] This description confirms that a dance tradition with fiddle and banjo was established before the Civil War in western Kentucky's white folk culture. The presence of both a banjo and a fiddle in the scene suggests they were played together. The race of the musicians is not identified; however, if white musicians in this era commonly played the banjo and the fiddle, then there would have been no reason to specify race.

Square dances were described as "old fashioned" in Kentucky newspapers ca. 1900, indicating they were falling out of favor. Wilson commented on the demise of the square dance in Calloway County:

> Though the square dance was gone, except in the mountains when I was a small boy [ca. 1900], it was fortunate for me that my older sister had for her beau a genuine fiddler of the old tradition. His brother was equally good as a banjo-picker. Though neither sang, we were often entertained with evening concerts, all the way from *The Downfall of Paris* to *Old Man Garrison*.[50]

Wilson said antebellum traditions "rapidly vanished before education, travel, a new national life, and a supposedly higher culture."[51] These factors helped precipitate the demise of the square dance in both black and white communities that had early exposure to commercialization and new dances. Square dances gave the banjo public exposure; without square dances the banjo became less visible. A square dance tradition through the mid-twentieth century in the southern mountains helped advance the notion that the banjo was strictly a mountain instrument.

Accomplished African American musicians were often employed for dances and other community affairs, although there were many more white than black banjo and fiddle players by the early 1900s. John McCuiston was one such musician ca. 1900 in western Kentucky's Calloway County:

> But the prince of musicians was John McCuiston, an old negro who had absorbed from the life of his time the flavor and philosophy of breakdowns. He and his banjo were seldom separated, even though some of his religious brethren deplored his worldliness. John was in demand in the summers to play for merry-go-rounds,—then called "swings"—for barbecues, for Democratic rallies, for bran-dances.[52]

Breakdown was often used to describe the music played for Kentucky dances—the term was also sometimes used to describe the dance performed to breakdown music. The term *bran-dance*, commonly known as a barn dance today, was derived from the practice of scattering bran on the floor to aid dancing.

Some African American banjo pickers, after the Civil War, made a living from their music by employment in carnivals, circuses, and minstrel and medicine shows. Preston Hill, an African American in Graves County, made his living in 1902 "picking the banjo" for a carnival.[53] B. F. Saunders, a member of the Kentucky legislature, employed an African American banjo player ca. 1899: "Several Western Kentucky members, one of them from Warren County, said they had often seen Saunders on the streets with a negro and a banjo in the capacity of a street fakir, selling patent medicines."[54] Medicine shows were common in rural America in the nineteenth century, and continued in Appalachian Kentucky until the mid-twentieth century. Medicine shows usually employed local musicians or musicians from the general area.

To summarize, the presence in Kentucky of African American fiddlers by 1780 and of an African American banjo player by 1781 proves that enslaved African American musicians were brought to Kentucky by the first settlers. The nearly 12,000 African Americans who were in frontier Kentucky by 1790 likely included black musicians living in close contact with common whites; the interdependence fostered by frontier living conditions would have facilitated music exchange between the groups. That white fiddlers were adopting music from African American fiddlers by the mid-1800s implies a similar exchange was occurring between black and white banjo players.

The folkways of common whites in central and western Kentucky included music practices adopted from African Americans: the 1850s description of white dances with banjo and fiddle provides evidence this tradition was established before the Civil War, and the description of Rector making fiddle strings for a banjo in 1790s Mason County suggests that the African American banjo was a part of the folkways of common whites before 1800.

There was a change in music at upper-class balls from the colonial era to Nelson County in 1856: those in colonial America featured the fiddle and not the banjo; however, the ball in Nelson County featured both banjo and fiddle. This change likely occurred on the frontiers as settlers moved west from Virginia and Maryland.

Upper Cumberland and the Eastern Coal Field

Upper Cumberland includes counties, connected by the Cumberland River, in both Kentucky and Tennessee.[55] According to a former slave, frolics in Kentucky's Monroe County ca. 1850 included the banjo: "After their work in the fields was finished on Saturday, they would have parties and have a good time. Some old negro man would play the banjo while the young darkies would dance and sing. The white folks would set around and watch; and would sometimes join in and dance and sing."[56] The white community in Monroe County, as in western Kentucky's Ballard County, participated in the music and dance of slaves.

Another observer, also remembering the 1850s in the Upper Cumberland, put the banjo and fiddle together at white dances at Russell Springs in Kentucky: "On the occasion referred there was an all night dance, and there was a multitude of young people to 'trip the light fantastic toe' to the sound of the fiddle and the banjo."[57] The band playing for the dance could have been African American; however, the important point is that the banjo, fiddle, and dance were a part of the folkways of white settlers in Upper Cumberland by the 1850s.

Black musicians resided in the many enclaves of ex-slaves established after the Civil War in Upper Cumberland.[58] Black musicians in Kentucky in the early 1900s included Cal and John Coe, the Huddleston family, Claud and Osby Jones, and the Burchett brothers, while the Sadler family, the Farris brothers, the Bertram brothers, Martin Gore, and Marian Redmon were from Tennessee.[59] Cal and John Coe were mixed-race African Americans whose ancestors had been brought to Kentucky in 1811 by John Coe.[60] A neighbor said they carried the banjo with them and would pick and sing anything anybody asked them to play.[61] This comment suggests their repertoire included songs and tunes known in the community at large.

Both black and white musicians were numerous by the early 1900s:

> Fiddle and banjo players, both black and white, were plentiful across the Upper Cumberland, fiddlers more so. And because of the population inequity, white musicians were more common than blacks. . . . Black or white, these old time musicians were highly respected artists wherever they were heard. They played at barber shops, pie suppers, square dances, homecomings, and other informal gatherings.[62]

According to the memories of a white banjo player in this period, these black and white musicians interacted with one another:

> Burnett remembers blacks playing old time music when he was growing up: "Oh yeah. Yeah. Bled Coffee here in town, he was a fiddler during the Civil War and the Bertram boys here, Cooge Bertram was a good fiddler. He was raised in Corbin (Kentucky). Yes sir, there were a lot of black men playing old time music. Bled Coffee was the best fiddler in the county. Been dead for years. I played many a tune with him—used to play with me, oh, 60 years ago. He'd play any of the old songs that I did. The old fashioned tunes, like Cripple Creek, Sourwood Mountain, Soldiers Joy, Fire on the Mountain—them old fashioned tunes is about all he played."[63]

That Bled Coffee played tunes popular in the white community indicates the repertoires of black and white musicians were similar. A white musician playing with African Americans was not an anomaly in Kentucky. Virgil Anderson, an outstanding banjo and guitar player, learned tunes and songs from the black Bertram family.[64]

As in Upper Cumberland, enclaves of former slaves were established after the Civil War in the Eastern Coal Field. One such enclave, at Redfox in Knott County, had black musicians known to the folklorist Dr. Josiah Combs by 1900. Combs said white musicians adopted banjo songs brought in by enslaved African Americans before the Civil War:

The Highlander has adopted many banjo airs from the Negroes, although the Negro population of the Highlands has never been extensive. Such airs came into the Highlands prior to the Civil War, while the Negro railroad songs came in afterwards, largely during the past twenty-five years [1900–25]. The tunes of "Lynchburg Town," "Shortnin' Bread," "Raccoon," Shady Grove," "Hook and Line," "Houn' Dog," "Ida Red," "Little Gray Mule," "Big Stone Gap," and numerous others, are from the Negroes.[65]

Determining whether a banjo song is of black or white origin, however, is difficult. Many songs have verses that could have come from either the African American or Anglo-American community—or perhaps both. Combs commented further on songs adopted from African Americans:

The Highlanders have adopted a considerable number of songs belonging to or originating among the Negroes. Some of these songs have long been current in the Highlands, from the days prior to the Civil War, and include banjo—and nonsense—songs, besides some spirituals and songs of the British type. Since the Civil War a number of Negro occupational songs have crept in, notably such well-known ones as "John Hardy," "John Henry," the "Yew-Pine Mountain," "Frankie," "Lynchburg Town," "The Kicking Mule," "Turkey in the Straw," and others.[66]

Combs's comments affirm that African Americans played banjo in Appalachia before the Civil War; he also implies that white musicians were playing banjo before the war. Combs, born in 1886, likely knew musicians by 1900 who had learned their craft before the Civil War.

The Knott County attorney Hillard H. Smith (b. 1875), whose family came from Virginia in 1792, described the marriage celebrations attended by his grandparents in the 1850s: "And then that night what a party, and what dancing—the old kind—calling sets, square dance, Virginia Reel and hoe-downs with plenty of banjo picking and fiddling."[67] The banjo, fiddle, and dance tradition in the Eastern Coal Field, as in western Kentucky and the Upper Cumberland, was established before the Civil War. Smith does not comment on the race of the musicians; however, the important fact here is that by the 1850s a banjo, fiddle, and dance tradition had been established in white communities from the westernmost part of Kentucky to the Kentucky Mountains.

Quite a few African American musicians are remembered in Appalachia. The white Letcher County fiddler Manon Campbell (b. 1890), who first learned to play music on a homemade gourd banjo, learned fiddle tunes from Will Christian, an outstanding African American fiddler who played for dances in southeastern Kentucky ca. 1900.[68] Christian was living at Redfox in Knott County in 1920, where the black banjo player Cullie Williams also resided.[69] Dr. Josiah Combs said of Williams, "when I was a boy, 'Cull' stayed at our house and worked for us at Hindman, Knott County, about the turn of the century. He was a great 'banjer' picker."[70]

Addie Graham, born before 1900 in Wolfe County, remembered the black banjo player Grant Reed: "He'd go along the road pickin' the banjo and I'd stand and listen at him. I'd get out behind the house and here Grant come—and nobody on earth could pick it like Grant Reed—and I'd try to dance it."[71] A local reporter wrote in 1901 that "Grant Reed, the professional banjo picker, stopped and picked some beautiful tunes for ye scribe one day last week."[72] No mention is made that Reed was black, indicating he was well known in Wolfe County. Another newspaper reference described Reed's business in 1905: "Grant Reed, colored, who conducts a blind tiger saloon, about five miles east of Lee City had a picnic Sunday at which prizes were given to the best banjo picker, fiddler, dancer, etc. He had spread the news broadcast and a free dinner was a feature which attracted a large crowd."[73]

Grant Reed, however, was not the only African American banjo picker in Wolfe County in those years: "Hazel Green has perhaps the best banjo picker in Kentucky in the person of John Baker, a colored citizen who dropped in from the state of Virginia, his native place being Henry County. The remarkable feature of his playing is that he brings out every note as on a violin, whereas banjo performers as a general thing drop many of the minor notes."[74] John Baker is cited again as "'the best nigger in the state,' and his banjo playing is only one of his many accomplishments."[75]

Music was a part of court days and political affairs at county seats where people congregated to engage in commerce and to meet and greet friends and relatives from other sections of the county. The *Clay County Times* reported on a circuit court in 1903 that included banjo picking.[76] Coy Morton remembered an African American family playing guitar, banjo, and fiddle at the Letcher County court house in the late 1920s.[77] A banjo picker was described ca. 1945 at a political affair in McKee, the county seat of Jackson County: "Uncle Laney Gibson . . . held forth his banjo for me to admire. It was a square box made at home, with the bottom of a lard can tacked on for a head."[78] An acquaintance described Laney Gibson as an "Indian who lived on Indian Creek" in Jackson County.[79] Gibson was a common name among dark-skinned Melungeons, who described themselves as Portuguese, Indian, or white.[80]

It was common in east Kentucky for a musician to give up banjo playing when joining the church. Rufus Mitchell wrote a song about his repentance, in which he described playing banjo in the Civil War: "In the wars between the parties, / the gray coats and the blue, / I volunteered for freedom; / I picked my banjo too." Unfortunately, Mitchell also described burning his banjo: "I prayed and pled for mercy, / Christ filled my flowing cup; / I went home rejoicing / And burnt my banjo up."[81]

It was usual in Appalachia ca. 1900 for white girls in musical families to learn banjo, which led to many lady banjo players from Kentucky playing professionally in the 1930s and 1940s.[82] Young girls in African American families were also learning banjo: Mollie Combs (b. 1885), an African American from Perry County, "was an accomplished Banjo player and could 'play until the cows came home.'"[83]

Oral histories prove that the banjo was a part of white folk culture well before the Civil War. Tom Couch (b. ca. 1860) of Harlan County described the origin of banjo picking in his family: "One of his forbears started the tradition of picking and singing by making himself a banjo from an old gourd."[84] Reverend Buell Kazee (b. 1900), an outstanding Magoffin County musician, was playing banjo by the time he was 10 years old. Kazee dissented when asked if the banjo had entered the mountains after the Civil War; he said that as a boy he had learned tunes from a 90-year-old man who had learned banjo from his father.[85] This information implies the banjo-playing father was born ca. 1800. Phillip Collins spent much time with his banjo-playing grandfather, Neal Collins, born in 1891. Grandfather Neal said both his father Lewis (b. 1861) and his grandfather Conaway (b. 1831) made and played banjos. Lewis Collins migrated from Newman's Ridge in Tennessee to Pike County, Kentucky, ca. 1895.[86] Newman's Ridge was noted at one time for its mixed-race residents, now known as Melungeons, and Collins is one of the prominent Melungeon names.[87] Conaway Collins most likely learned his skill in making and playing banjos before 1850.

In summary, references to both the fiddle and banjo being present at dances before the Civil War justify Charles Wolfe's assertion that "the 'string band' of the 1800s was usually a fiddle and banjo."[88] As in western Kentucky, a banjo, fiddle, and dance tradition was established by the 1850s in white folk culture in both Upper Cumberland and the Eastern Coal Field. We can infer from this that the practice was widespread; however, we have no contemporary accounts; the accounts we have are by two people recalling events described by their grandparents and another individual reminiscing about his youth. The lack of contemporary accounts implies the practice was so common it was not noteworthy. The oral histories of Tom Couch, Reverend Buell Kazee, and Neal Collins provide evidence there were white banjo players in Kentucky prior to the Civil War, so it is quite possible that white banjoists and fiddlers played for antebellum dances. It is also likely that African Americans played for some dances: Josiah Combs provides evidence that African Americans were playing banjo in Appalachia before the Civil War, and that white musicians were adopting banjo songs from African Americans both before and after the war.

Mixed-race families were present early in southeast Kentucky. Both Uncle Laney Gibson, described as "Indian," and Conaway Collins might have had Melungeon ancestry; Conaway learned to play banjo before 1850 on Newman's Ridge in Tennessee, an area known for its Melungeon residents.

Dance

References to dances with banjo, or banjo and fiddle, are rare. This rarity is a reflection of the class of people who played the music: African Americans and common whites, people whose folkways were not recorded in traditional histories. References to the types of dance performed by African Americans are also rare in antebellum Kentucky; therefore, I cite references to the banjo, fiddle, and dance in both African American and Anglo-American communities outside Kentucky to provide a better understanding of those traditions in Kentucky, and to provide perspective for the early synthesis of African American and Anglo-American folk music in Kentucky and across the rural South.

Dance was a major factor for the banjo enduring in the folk culture of both African Americans and common whites, and was the vehicle by which the banjo and fiddle traveled west and south from Virginia and Maryland. After about 1800, a separate stream of emigrants entered Kentucky from North Carolina, where early settlers were mostly Virginians. Folkways established early in North Carolina, therefore, were likely transported to Kentucky. The first large group of settlers in southeast Kentucky's Letcher County (then Floyd County), for instance, were from the piedmont and mountains of North Carolina.[89]

In 1774, Nicholas Cresswell observed a dance in Maryland: "A great number of young people met together with a Fiddle and Banjo played by two Negroes. . . . I believe they have danced and drunk till there are few sober people amongst them. . . . I am sorry I was not able to join them."[90] That the dancers were white is evidenced by Cresswell's desire to join the party.

The banjo accompanied Virginians to the 1780s Carolina mountain frontier: "After the evening's labors were finished, they [young folks] would join in a regular old-fashioned Virginia reel, and keep time with flying feet to the delightful strains drawn from a gourd banjo."[91] The banjo and fiddle were used in South Carolina at white "socials, dances and weddings" during the Civil War.[92]

The early presence of the fiddle, banjo, and dance in the western Carolina mountains is supported by the historian John Preston Arthur (1851–1916): "The banjo and fiddle have been as constant companions of the pioneers of the mountains of North Carolina as the Bible and the Hymn Book."[93] A biographer quoted an acquaintance of Arthur, who said, "More so than any other local historian, he [Arthur] went to the original sources for facts. He sought out old diaries, journals, letters and even talked with old citizens, who shared their recollections with him."[94]

A mixed-race group, variously described as Indian, Portuguese, or Negro, migrated from Virginia to Robeson County, North Carolina, where they became known as the Lumbee Indians. A genealogist proved that most were descended from slaves free in Virginia in the mid-seventeenth century.[95] Members of a Lumbee family played banjo during the Civil War era: "The negro blood gave [Henry Berry] Lowery a 'love of rude music' and he had been spotted playing his banjo 'to the dancing of mulatto girls.'"[96] The Lowery family engaged in sectarian violence in Robeson County during the Civil War era; Steve Lowery was killed in 1873 as he "sat strumming his banjo."[97]

Free mixed-race families migrated to other counties in North Carolina. Paul Heinegg noted:

Whilst some North Carolina residents were complaining about the immigration of free African Americans, their white neighbors in Granville, Halifax, Herford and Northampton Counties welcomed them. Their neighbors may have been accustomed to living among free African Americans in Virginia; they may have moved from Virginia in company with them; or perhaps they were drawn together by the adversities of the frontier. Neighbor depended upon neighbor, and whites may have been more concerned with hostile Indians and harsh living conditions than they were with their neighbors' color.[98]

Mixed-race families in North Carolina later migrated west to southwestern Virginia, northeast Tennessee, and southeast Kentucky.

Baynard Rush Hall (1798–1863) described African Americans dancing to the banjo and fiddle in pioneer Indiana in the 1820s: "We feel tempted to give Uncle Tommy's 'murakalus' escape in fire-hunting! how he leveled his rifle at a 'beasts eyes,' and found it was light streaming through a negro hut, where, on Christmas eve, the merry rascals were dancing away to a cornstalk fiddle and a calabash banjo."[99] Historians believe Hall accurately portrayed pioneer life in Indiana.

The banjo and fiddle traveled with pioneers to the 1830s Arkansas frontier: "'Hoe-downs' and 'Virginia Reels' were tripped lightly to the tunes of 'Roaring River,' 'Fishers Hornpipe,' and 'Great Big Tree in the Sandy Lane,' which deft musicians drew from the horsehair strings and bow and the gourd banjo with its squirrel head and horsehairs."[100] That the banjo and fiddle were played together is implied; however, the race of the musicians is not specified. The majority of the pioneers in northwest Arkansas, which was settled after 1828, were from Kentucky and Tennessee.[101] It is logical, therefore, to assume settlers brought their banjo, fiddle, and dance traditions from those states to Arkansas. The Carolina and Arkansas descriptions are important because they place the banjo, fiddle, and dance tradition in white folk culture, from the 1770s to the early 1800s, in widely separated areas of the frontier.

Cecil Sharp's description of a white dance in Kentucky and John Allen Wyeth's description of a slave dance before the Civil War in northern Alabama prove that some dance practices of African Americans and Anglo-Americans were similar. Sharp observed a square dance without musical instruments at the Pine Mountain Settlement School in 1916:

> Throughout the dance the onlookers and the performers also, when not actually dancing, should enforce the rhythm of the music by "patting," i.e., alternately stamping and clapping. "Patting" is done in various ways, but the usual method is to stamp with the right foot on the strong accent and clap the hands on the weak one, the executant throwing his head back, inclining his body to the left and emphasizing the movement of feet and hands so that the rhythm may be seen as well as heard. In 6/8 time the hands are usually clapped on the third and sixth quavers, but the "patter" will often strike his thighs, right hand on right thigh on the second and fifth quavers, and left hand on left thigh on the third

and sixth, stamping, of course, on the first and fourth quavers. As an accompaniment to the dance, the "'patting" is almost as effective as music; so effective, indeed, that at Pine Mountain, where the dancers were wholly dependent on it, the absence of instrumental music was scarcely felt.[102]

The clapping and patting at Pine Mountain is "patting juba," which originated among African Americans. John Allen Wyeth described a similar practice at a slave dance ca. 1855 in northern Alabama:

> The banjo and the fiddle made up the orchestra, and there were accompanists who "patted" with the hands, keeping accurate time with the music. In patting, the position was usually a half-stoop or forward bend, with a slap of one hand on the left knee followed by the same stroke and noise on the right, and then a loud slap of two palms together. I should add that the left hand made two strokes in half-time to one for the right, something after the double stroke of the left drumstick in beating the kettle-drum.[103]

Wyeth's description of "patting" is virtually the same as the practice Sharp observed some sixty years later in a white community that had few African Americans.

Southern ex-slaves describe a variety of instruments providing music for dance, including the banjo and fiddle, played together (sometimes with other instruments) and separately. The dances described were those popular in the white community. Tom Mills of Texas said African Americans danced all of the old dances, including the Virginia reel and round dances like the schottische, polka, and waltzes.[104] Henry Childers of Texas said they danced the Virginia reel and other dances of the time, and that the caller was the most important person at the dance.[105] African American dances ca. 1850 included those practiced in the white community. It is evident, therefore, that African Americans had adopted popular dances of Anglo-Americans by the mid-nineteenth century.

African Americans both called and played music for white square dances. Ben Wall of Mississippi said he called square dances in the homes of white people, while Isaac Stier of Texas said that his band played for white dances while he called the figures.[106] Phil Jamieson makes a strong case that square dance calling originated with African Americans: "The written evidence suggests that dance calling was initiated in the African-American slave culture before it was adopted by the white culture."[107]

Some African American dances in southern states were also present in Kentucky. A former slave described a Louisiana square dance that included the bird in the cage figure: "One thing dey calls, 'Bird in de Cage.' Three joins hands round de gal in de middle, and dance round her, and den she git out and her pardner git in de center and dey dance dat way awhile."[108] Bird in the cage was a square dance figure popular in Appalachian Kentucky, where it was described in 1906: "First couple cage the bird with three arms around. Bird hop out and hoot owl in; three arms around and hootin' again."[109] Cecil Sharp observed bird in the cage in 1916 in Kentucky and thought the dance had English origins.[110] Jamieson, however, believes the dance originated with African Americans: "It is more likely that 'Bird in the Cage' developed from the earlier bird pantomime dances of the African-American dance traditions rather than being 'derived from ancient pagan ceremonials' in England as claimed by Sharp." Bird in the cage is a good example of the improvisation, spontaneity, and self-expression of African American ring dances with the structure of the European set dances.[111]

That bird in the cage was danced by common whites in Kentucky ca. 1900 and by African Americans in Louisiana before the Civil War is another indication that dances of common whites and African Americans were very similar. This similarity suggests an earlier integration of dance practices.

Philip Vickers Fithian, a tutor on Robert Carter's plantation in 1773–74, observed the Virginians' love of music and dance. Carter's children had a dancing master as well as a music teacher, and balls with formal dancing were highly regarded social events. Fithian, however, found his pupils Ben and Harry engaged in another type of dance on two different occasions:

> This Evening the Negroes collected themselves into the School-Room & began to play the *fiddle* and dance. . . . Ben and Harry were of the company—*Harry* was dancing with his coat off—I dispersed them however immediately. . . . This evening, in the School-Room several Negroes & *Ben* & *Harry* are playing on a *Banjo* and dancing![112]

Fithian was obviously not pleased; Ben and Harry may have been experimenting with banjo playing, and were likely performing African American dance steps to the fiddle and banjo. By the time Ben and Harry were engaging in African American dance, however, the practice had become a part of formal balls attended by Virginia elites.

Upper-class Virginians were adopting African American dance practices by the middle of the eighteenth century. One dance historian said that "the practice of imitating African and African-American dance on the American stage began before the Revolutionary War."[113] Another dance historian commented on Virginia dances in the latter part of the eighteenth century: "There are several descriptions of the 'Virginia Jig,' all danced by European Americans who were performing their own version of what they understood to be a traditional African dance type and a refreshing change from the usual structured ballroom dances."[114]

Andrew Burnaby, traveling through Virginia in 1759, described a Virginia dance borrowed from African Americans: "Towards the close of an evening, when the company are pretty well tired of country dances, it is usual to dance jigs; a practice originally borrowed, I am informed, from the Negroes. These dances are without any method or regularity."[115] The "lack of method or regularity" indicates the more spontaneous and improvisational dance movements associated with

African dancing. Nicholas Creswell saw a similar dance performed in Alexandria, Virginia, in 1775: "They have what I call everlasting jigs. A couple gets up and begins to dance a jig (to some Negro tune) others comes and cuts them out, and these dances last as long as the Fiddler can play. This is sociable, but I think it looks more like a Bacchanalian dance than one in a polite assembly."[116] It was the usual practice for a slave or servant to play for Virginia dances, so the "Negro tune" most likely refers to a fiddle tune with African American origins.[117] The "everlasting jigs" that resembled a Bacchanalian dance had steps adopted from African Americans, and were therefore new to Creswell, who was from England.

The balls attended by Burnaby and Creswell were upper-class events; the rigid class structure in colonial American mimicked that of England, and would have precluded common whites from attending these dances. One can infer, however, that if the upper classes were adopting African American dance practices, then common whites, who socialized with African Americans, were doing the same.

Jig, a general term for dancing, continued to be used in Kentucky; however, we do not know the term common whites used for the Virginia jig. Dr. Marion Mayo observed jig dancing in the 1880s in Floyd County: "Banjo picking and dancing were often seen at our elections. There would usually be one or two dancers on the floor, dancing something like a jig, 'classy' people did not engage in this diversion."[118] Kentucky jig dancing does not include the high steps typical of modern Irish dancing, but is characterized by steps in which the feet are usually kept low. This type of dancing has long been popular in Kentucky, and is known by a variety of terms, including *hoedown, breakdown,* and *double shuffle,* all terms still in use today. The hoedown was danced on the northwest Arkansas frontier in the 1830s and in Appalachian Kentucky in the 1850s. *Hoedown, breakdown,* and *double shuffle* were used by the former slave Isaac D. Williams (b. 1821) to describe African American dance ca. 1840 in Virginia:

> There are a great many white minstrel troupes traveling through our northern states, claiming to give exact delineations of negro character and plantation sketches and scenes, but they do not portray the real quintessence of ole Virginny, as I have seen it. It is like a counterfeit bill to a genuine one. I have many times seen both and ought to know. I've taken part myself over and over again in our southern dances and music, and danced the hoe down as well as the best of them . . . twenty-five cents was given to the best dancer of the regular break down. It would shake up the risables of the most solemn individual to see the double shuffle as we did it in the old slave days.[119]

In 1916, Cecil Sharp said that "the only other type of dancing other than the Running set that we have seen as yet in the mountains is a species of step- or clog-dance, locally known as the hoe-down," and further described hoedown steps as "a heel-and-toe, shuffle, or clog dance step."[120] The hoedown observed by Sharp is likely the same dance described by Williams. William Monroe Cockburn, describing pioneer life in Indiana, said: "Some of the people from Virginia understood dancing a reel that was called in old Virginia—'hoedown.'"[121] Lee Sexton described hoedown ca. 1940 in Letcher County, Kentucky: "We'd go to square dances . . . somebody'd have an old banjo or something, start playing banjo and we'd dance, and then from there why we'd hoedown then, the old hoedown dance, just flatfoot you know." It is therefore likely that *hoedown* is a term common whites used early on for the Virginia jig.[122]

The isolate communities that grew and spread throughout the South were descended from the unions of free slaves and white female servants; these unions created families that drew on the dance traditions of both African Americans and Anglo-Americans (including traditions brought to the colonies by Luso-Africans). It is reasonable to assume that dance with banjo and fiddle was a part of their folkways in the eighteenth century since slaves from the West Indies were present in the colonies before 1700. Although isolate groups remained somewhat separate, there was intermarriage with their common white neighbors on the frontier where music exchange was fostered by the leveling effect of harsh living conditions; these conditions are portrayed by Mrs. Phoebe Green, whose family emigrated from Virginia to the Carolina frontier in the 1780s; she said all her neighbors "were as one family":

> In those good old-fashioned times, when the high and the low, the rich and poor, were alike attired in *home-spun*, made by the industrious and ingenious hand of a busy housewife,—when split-bottom chairs, even, was a luxury never dreamed of, and a vehicle, other than a Jersey wagon, an ox-cart, or a sled never contemplated—the neighbors in the various settlements would meet alternately at each other's house to pick the seed out of the cotton and prepare it for the wheel.[123]

Common whites, slaves, and free slaves socialized well before the mid-1700s when upper-class Virginians were adopting the Virginia jig from African Americans. It is logical to assume, therefore, that common whites also adopted this dance. The close relationship of banjo to dance, in both African American and Anglo-American folk cultures, makes it likely that common whites were adopting the banjo at the time they were adopting African American dance practices.

Summary

The music of African American and Anglo-Americans was amalgamated to a remarkable degree during the two centuries prior to the Civil War. African Americans adopted the European fiddle, guitar, songs, and dance from Anglo-Americans, who in turn adopted from African Americans the banjo, banjo songs, the practice of playing the banjo and fiddle together, patting juba, the hoedown, and possibly square dance calling and the square dance figure bird in the cage. We know that white Virginians were adopting African American dance steps by the mid-1700s, so it is likely that African Americans were adopting white dance practices by the same time. The close relationship between the banjo, fiddle, and dance suggests that the early gourd banjo was part of this music exchange. This is supported by the widespread use of the African American gourd banjo in white folk culture, from the 1780s Carolina frontier to the 1830s Arkansas frontier, and in Appalachian Kentucky to the mid-twentieth century.

The oral histories of Buell Kazee, Tom Couch, and Neal Collins suggest that musicians playing for Kentucky dances in the 1850s could have been white. The distribution of white dances with banjo, and banjo and fiddle, from the 1770s in the Carolinas to the 1830s in Arkansas, and from western Kentucky to the Kentucky Mountains by the 1850s proves these folk traditions were established much earlier than previously thought. The Carolina and Arkansas dances with banjo and fiddle were certainly not influenced by minstrelsy, and it is highly unlikely that minstrel traditions originating in the 1840s influenced Kentucky square dances in the 1850s. The cumulative evidence supports the conclusion that a banjo, fiddle, and dance tradition was present in white folk culture before 1840, when minstrelsy was just beginning, and clearly shows that popular beliefs regarding the banjo are incorrect: these include the notion that there were not enough slaves in Appalachia to have established a folk banjo tradition; that the banjo was exclusively a mountain instrument; that the banjo entered the mountains during and after the Civil War; that the banjo was not in white folk culture prior to 1840s minstrelsy; and that the tradition of playing the fiddle and banjo together was initiated by stage minstrels.

The contributions of African Americans are the reason for Kentucky's "musical embarrassment of riches," which Richard Nevins thought was lost to time. By 1790, Kentucky had nearly 12,000 African Americans, mostly from Virginia and Maryland, states that had an early concentration of African American musicians. The melding of African American and Anglo-American folk music, which began in colonial America, continued in Kentucky. The African American banjo was adopted by common whites, and African Americans' use of the banjo and fiddle for dance was mirrored in Kentucky's white communities before the Civil War. The use of the banjo and fiddle continues today in both bluegrass and old-time music. The songs acquired from African Americans, before and after the Civil War, are still an important part of Kentucky's folk music. Kentuckians are indebted to African Americans for the richness and diversity of their traditional music.

Conclusion

The exchange of music between those of European and African descent has been continuous since Africans were first introduced into Virginia and Maryland. This exchange has been impeded at different times and different places by racism, separation, segregation, and class differences; however, these factors were least in play in colonial America and on the early frontier. It is apparent that the fiddle and dance were a part of the early music exchange; however, the banjo has been excluded, despite its close connection to both fiddle and dance. There is no logical reason for this exclusion; however, two factors are commonly cited: the first is the lack of citations prior to minstrelsy; the second is that colonials considered the banjo an instrument of no importance.

Two reasons are largely responsible for the lack of citations: first, the folkways of people who played the banjo were not recorded; and second, the banjo was nearly invisible in the eighteenth century. By the 1740s, the banjo was not described in any citation from extant newspapers in New York, Philadelphia, or Virginia—readers were assumed to be familiar with the instrument.[124] The only descriptions of the instrument, other than that of Thomas Jefferson, are from visitors from countries where the instrument was unknown. The commonality and wide distribution of banjos by the 1740s suggests they were in colonial America prior to 1700.[125]

The opinion of elites in colonial America, who regarded the banjo as an instrument of little value, has been conflated with that of all classes in a society that was as class-bound and stratified as that of England. The elites scorned the banjo because they considered it an instrument of the lower classes. Jonathon Boucher, an English tutor in colonial America, began a dictionary of American words after returning to England: "*Bandore, n.* A musical instrument . . . in use chiefly, if not entirely, among people of the lower classes. . . . I well remember that in Virginia and Maryland the favorite and almost only instrument in use among the slaves was a *bandore*; or, as they pronounced the word, *banjer*."[126] The first part of this definition, which states the banjo was chiefly used by the lower classes, has been ignored. The lower classes, of course, included common whites. The opinion that elites had of the banjo had not changed by the 1880s in Floyd County, Kentucky; Dr. Marion Mayo said "classy people" did not dance jigs to the banjo.[127] A relative by marriage, who learned to play banjo ca. 1930, told me that one of his neighbors referred to his banjo as an "ignorant stick," and told him he should be carrying a hoe instead.[128]

Religious groups that were gaining prominence by the Revolutionary War universally condemned the banjo and dance, which also helped obscure these practices. The several citations I have found are almost never from contemporary sources; they are usually from people recalling events of their youth or retelling events described by their grandparents.[129] The banjo was so common it was not noteworthy among those who played the instrument, and the upper classes did not deem it worthy of mention.

And finally, race is central to our perception of banjo history. The banjo, from its first sightings in the West Indies to minstrelsy in the nineteenth century, was described as an African instrument played by African Americans. By the mid-eighteenth century, racial mixing produced many common whites with some

African ancestry. Enumerators compiling early federal census forms used the label "free person of color (fpc)" to describe the race of some common whites. How would an eighteenth-century observer have described banjo-playing members of these families? The answer to this question, crucial to understanding banjo history, is that they would likely have been described as African American.

Knowledge of mountain culture led me to suspect the general consensus that minstrelsy is the source of the banjo in the mountain South. There has been no solid proof offered for this origin; instead, speculation has been based on two false premises: first, that there were few slaves in the mountains, and second, that whites adopted the banjo in the mid-nineteenth century (which ignores the two hundred years of American history prior to minstrelsy). That minstrelsy was responsible for popularizing the banjo is a trope used in support of the minstrel origin; this is vacuous at best and racist at worst, inferring that the many African Americans whose folkways included the banjo were unimportant or invisible. Dena J. Epstein, who has been lauded for her work regarding early black banjo traditions, wrote an article refuting this notion; however, this has been ignored by those who promote the minstrel origin of southern banjo traditions.[130]

The early banjo was a product of creolization, and the southern banjo tradition of song and dance was formed by the same process. By the seventeenth century, a tradition of banjo and dance was present among slaves in the New World; however, this tradition did not survive into the mid-twentieth century in places where there was not an early community of free biracial families: these include American colonies in the North, where banjo-playing slaves were present early, and the Caribbean Islands and South America, where banjo-playing slaves were documented beginning in the seventeenth century. These traditions, however, survived into the twentieth century in the rural South. Their roots were in Virginia and Maryland where free slaves established biracial families along the Chesapeake before slavery and racism became institutionalized. Among these families the banjo became integral to the dances and courting rituals of young people; these traditions were passed along to their neighbors as they moved west in the early frontier.

The rural southerners Archibald Ferguson and Joel Walker Sweeney introduced the banjo to minstrelsy; Sweeney is credited for planting the seeds of the banjo everywhere he played: the rural South, the North, and England. Although the banjo was wildly popular in England, a folk banjo tradition did not take root there; the music that survived was art music developed by professional northern musicians in the mid-nineteenth century.[131] A folk banjo tradition has not been found in New York, Pennsylvania, or New England, where Sweeney traveled and performed far more extensively than he did in the South; the remnants of banjo music that survived there is also art music developed by professional northern minstrels.[132] A previously existing folk banjo tradition—not minstrel art music—survived in the rural South.[133] Common whites from the mountain

South introduced the banjo to the circus and stage; by performing in blackface, however, they are somehow responsible for "minstrels" introducing the banjo into the folk culture from which it originated.

The transfer of the banjo from black folk culture to that of common whites developed over time and was likely more pronounced in some areas than others, depending on settlement patterns and social factors. It may be that in some pockets of the mountain South, where the banjo was scarce, minstrelsy inspired some to play banjo; however, the idea that this was universal over the entire region is grounded in a common stereotype: the notion that Appalachia is homogenous, and that what happens in one place is true for the entire region. A more likely scenario is that the appearance of the banjo in circuses and on stage encouraged southern musicians to play the banjo in more public settings, such as minstrel and medicine shows.

Southeast Kentucky, where a white as well as a black banjo tradition existed before the Civil War, had mixed-race settlers who originated in colonial America. The blending of music and genes did not cease after the colonial era, however, but was continuous; a musical family in Knott County, noted for banjo players and singers, had African American ancestry, confirmed by both census records and my grandmother. Their mother, from whom the children inherited their African genes, was a midwife who delivered many of the children in the area; this was one of the services that would have fostered interdependence on the frontier. Most of the children of this family were Indian in appearance; however, the best banjo player in the family had African American features, and was often recruited to play for square dances at a local school.[134]

I have searched for minstrel influence in the banjo music of southeast Kentucky but have not found any, other than the usual borrowing that transpires between the folk and stage. The folklorist Dr. Josiah H. Combs, who knew both black and white banjoists ca. 1900 in Knott County, Kentucky, classified southern mountain folk songs into twenty-one categories; he mentions minstrels in only one, humorous songs, some of which he said are "adaptions of vaudeville and minstrel show songs."[135] Many minstrel show songs, however, came originally from the folk tradition.

Combs was interested in song collecting as early as 1902 and would have known musicians who learned their craft before the Civil War. He makes no mention of the banjo being an instrument imported into Kentucky during or after the Civil War. In fact, I have not found a Kentucky folklorist or historian born in the nineteenth century who cites the banjo as an instrument imported into Kentucky after pioneer settlement.

Numerous banjo tunings were used throughout southeast Kentucky; however, the minstrel tuning with the lowered bass was not a part of the repertoire of my father, who used many tunings, or that of Reverend Buell Kazee, who used at least a dozen tunings; Kazee said he learned the lowered bass tuning later in life.[136] It is also not among the sixteen tunings Stuart Jamieson recorded from Blind Hobart Bailey of Hippo, Kentucky.[137]

Some folk songs contain history of the banjo's travel. One is "East Virginia," known throughout much of the mountain south: "I am from old east Virginia, / To North Carolina I did go, / There I met a fair young maiden, / Lord, her name and age I did not know. / Oh, her hair was black and curly, / And her cheeks a rosy red, / On her breast she wore white linen, / There I'd love to lay my head." I have found nothing in the music, diaries, histories, folklore, or oral history that suggests minstrelsy had much influence on the banjo in Kentucky. Perhaps this may still be found.

Notes

1. Richard Nevins, liner notes, *Kentucky Mountain Music*, Yazoo 2200 (a division of Shanachie Entertainment Corporation), 1. These recordings are a valuable resource for anyone who wishes to explore Kentucky folk music.

2. Robert B. Winans, "The Banjo: From Africa to Virginia and Beyond," in *Blue Ridge Folk Instruments and Their Makers* (Ferrum, VA: Blue Ridge Institute, 1993), 16. Winans maintained the following: "Before the advent of the minstrel show, the banjo was strictly a black instrument; once the show began exerting its influence, more and more whites started to play the banjo until, by the earliest twentieth century, the banjo was being seen as primarily a southern, rural, *white* instrument." Although Winans no longer supports this position, it is popularly believed today that minstrels were responsible for bringing the banjo to rural Southerners.

3. Bill Cecil-Fronsman, *Common Whites: Class and Culture in Antebellum North Carolina* (Lexington: University of Kentucky Press, 1992), 1. I chose to use Cecil-Fronsman's term, *common whites*, rather than such terms as *lower classes* or *poor whites*.

4. Lowell H. Schreyer, *The Banjo Entertainers* (Mankato: Minnesota Heritage Publishing, 2007), 5–12, 21–25. Schreyer provides short biographies of both Joel Walker Sweeney and Archibald Ferguson. Outlandish claims have been made about Sweeney, from his being the "inventor" of the banjo to his being the first white man to play the banjo. These claims are part of an effort, beginning in the nineteenth century, to divorce the banjo from its African American origins.

5. Noah Smithwick, *The Evolution of a State or Recollections of Old Texas Days* (Austin: University of Texas Press, 1984), 49. Patting juba is a rhythmic patting of hands and body parts borrowed from slaves. For information about patting juba, see Dena J. Epstein, *Sinful Tunes and Spirituals: Black Folk Music to the Civil War* (Urbana: University of Illinois Press, 1977), 141–44.

6. University of Texas School of Law, Tarlton Law Library, Jamail Center for Legal Research, http://tarlton.law.utexas.edu/justices/profile/view/116, accessed January 15, 2011.

7. Edmund S. Morgan, *American Slavery—American Freedom: The Ordeal of Colonial Virginia* (New York: W. W. Norton & Company, 1975), 327.

8. T. H. Breen and Stephen Innes, *Myne Owne Ground: Race and Freedom on Virginia's Eastern Shore, 1640–1676* (New York: Oxford University Press, 1980), 110–14.

9. Paul Heinegg, *Free African Americans of North Carolina and Virginia*, 3rd ed. (Baltimore: Genealogical Publishing Co., 1997), 1. For a description of isolate communities,

see Calvin L. Beale, "An Overview of the Phenomenon of Mixed Racial Isolates in the United States," *American Anthropology* 74, no. 3 (June 1972): 704–10, http://onlinelibrary .wiley.com/doi/10.1525/aa.1972.74.3.02a00340/pdf, accessed December 12, 2014.

10. For a description of Luso-Africans, see Peter Mark, "The Evolution of 'Portuguese' Identity: Luso-Africans on the Upper Guinea Coast from the Sixteenth Century to the Early Nineteenth Century," *Journal of African History* 40 (1999): 173–76.

For a description of Atlantic creoles, see Ira Berlin, *Many Thousands Gone: The First Two Centuries of Slavery in North America* (Cambridge, MA: Belknap Press of Harvard University Press, 1998), 17–28. Berlin describes Luso-Africans on page 9. See also Heinegg, *Free African Americans*, 1–28. Heinegg's award-winning genealogical study traces the families of early slaves that were defined by Berlin as Atlantic creoles, among whom were Luso-Africans. All recent studies trace isolate communities in the mountain south to colonial Virginia and Maryland.

11. Richard Jobson, *The Golden Trade* (London: Penguin Press, 1932), 36–41. Jobson was on the Gambia River in West Africa in the winter of 1620–21 and described the people who controlled most of the trade: "And these are, as they call themselves, *Portingales*, and some of them seem the same; others are *Molatoes*, betweene blacke and white, but the most part as blacke, as the naturall inhabitants . . . still reserving carefully, the use of the *Portingall* tongue, and with a kinde of affectionate zeale, the name of Christians, taking it in great disdaine, be they never so blacke, to be called a *Negro*: and these, for the most part, are the Portingalls."

12. Ibid., 38, 144–45. Jobson described the disposition of slaves from the Gambia River: "the blacke people are brought away by their owne nation, and by them either carried, or solde unto the Spaniard, for him to carry to the West Indies," and described a gourd instrument:

> They have little varietie of instruments, that which is most common in use, is made of a great gourd, and a necke thereunto fastned, resembling, in some sort, our Bandora; but they have no manner of fret, and the strings they are either such as the place yeeldes, or their invention can attaine to make, being very unapt to yeeld a sweete and musicall sound, notwithstanding with pinnes they winde and bring to agree in tunable notes, having not above six strings upon their greatest instrument.

This description implies that some of the gourd instruments had less than six strings and that they had tuning pegs.

The early gourd banjo may have developed among Luso-Africans. The Portuguese had been in Africa more than one hundred years by 1620. Stable mixed-race families had existed for several generations by then, allowing sufficient time for musicians to combine elements of African and Portuguese instruments. The West Indies, on the other hand, featured a brutish type of slavery that did not foster stable families; also, there is a problem in resolving how the early gourd banjo traveled between islands in the West Indies, where slaves had limited mobility.

13. Epstein, *Sinful Tunes and Spirituals*, 21–38.

14. See Berlin, *Many Thousands Gone*, 29, and Breen and Innes, *Myne Owne Ground*, 19, 70.

15. Louis B. Wright, ed., *The Prose Works of William Byrd of Westover* (Cambridge, MA: Belknap Press of Harvard University Press, 1966), 186.

16. William B. Hart, "Black 'Go-Betweens' and the Mutability of 'Race,' Status, and Identity on New York's Pre-Revolutionary Frontier," in *Contact Points: American Frontiers*

from the Mohawk Valley to the Mississippi, 1750–1830, ed. Andrew R. Cayton and Fredrika J. Teute (Chapel Hill: University of North Carolina Press, 1998), 90.

17. Swam M. Burnett, "A Note on the Melungeons," *American Anthropologist* 2, no. 4 (October 1889): 347–50, http://www.jstor.org/stable/658619?Search=yes&resultItemClick =true&searchText=melungeon&searchUri=%2Faction%2FdoBasicSearch%3FQuery% 3Dmelungeon%26amp%3Bacc%3Doff%26amp%3Bwc%3Don%26amp%3Bfc%3Doff%26 amp%3Bgroup%3Dnone&seq=1#page_scan_tab_contents, accessed December 12, 2014. Claiming Portuguese ancestry was not uncommon among mixed-race people. Several trials have been found in which people accused of being Negro have been described as Portuguese. See Heinegg, *Free African Americans*, 117–19.

18. Jack H. Goins, Penny Ferguson, and Janet Lewis Crain, "Melungeons, A Multi-Ethnic Population," *Journal of Genetic Genealogy* 7 (Fall 2011): 29–70, http://www.jogg.info/72/ files/Estes.htm, accessed December 13, 2014.

19. Marion B. Lucas, *A History of Blacks in Kentucky: From Slavery to Segregation, 1760–1891* (Frankfort: Kentucky Historical Society, 1992), xvi (figure 1), xx.

20. 1830 US Census, Doc. No. 238, http://www2.census.gov/prod2/decennial/documents/ 1830a-01.pdf/, accessed September 20, 2011.

21. John E. Kleber, ed., *The Kentucky Encyclopedia* (Lexington: University Press of Kentucky, 1992), 367–69.

22. George W. Ranck, *The Traveling Church, An Account of the Baptist Exodus from Virginia to Kentucky in 1781 Under the Leadership of Rev. Lewis Craig and Capt. William Ellis* (Louisville, KY: Press of the Baptist Book Concern, 1891), 6, 13, 15, Kentuckiana Digital Library, http://kdl.kyvl.org/cgi/t/text/text-idx?c=kyetexts;cc=kyetexts;type=simple;rgn=full%20 text;q1=ranck;cite1=ranck;cite1restrict=author;view=reslist;subview=detail;sort=occur; start=1;size=25;didno=b92-88-27380652, accessed January 15, 2005.

23. Thomas D. Clark, *Kentucky: Land of Contrast* (New York: Harper & Row, 1968), 40–51. Cumberland Gap connects Claiborne County in Tennessee with Bell County, Kentucky.

24. Ibid., 109.

25. Lucas, *A History of Blacks in Kentucky*, 1:xii, xiii.

26. Ted Franklin Belue, *The Hunters of Kentucky: A Narrative History of America's First Far West, 1750–1792* (Mechanicsburg, PA: Stackpole Books, 2003), 164–79. Boonesborough is in Madison County.

27. Robert Morgan, *Boone: A Biography* (Chapel Hill, NC: Algonquin Books of Chapel Hill, 2007), 306.

28. Ibid., 224.

29. Lowell H. Harrison and James C. Klotter, *A New History of Kentucky* (Lexington: University Press of Kentucky, 1997), 101. Louisville is in Jefferson County.

30. Harriette Simpson Arnow, *Flowering of the Cumberland* (Lexington: University Press of Kentucky, 1984), 403.

31. Lucas, *A History of Blacks in Kentucky*, 1:35.

32. Guthrie Meade, liner notes, *Old Time Fiddle Band Music from Kentucky* (Morning Star Records, 1980), 1.

33. Ibid.

34. Ibid.

35. Nevins, liner notes, 3. The fiddling of the junior Jim Booker can be heard on CD 1 track 19, CD 3 track 18, and CD 4 track 9.

36. For documentation of the early joint playing of fiddle and banjo by African Americans in Rhode Island in 1756, and in Maryland in 1774, see Orville Platt, "Negro Governors," *New Haven Historical Quarterly* 6 (1900): 324, cited in Eileen Southern, *Music of Black Americans* (New York: W. W. Norton Co., 1982), 54, and Nicholas Creswell, *Journal of Nicholas Creswell, 1774–1777* (New York: Dial Press, 1924), 30, cited in Epstein, *Sinful Tunes and Spirituals*, 115.

37. J. D. Green, *Narrative of the Life of J. D. Green: a Runaway Slave from Kentucky; Containing an Account of His Three Escapes in 1839, 1846, and 1848* (Huddersfield, UK: Henry Fielding, 1864), 12.

38. Anna Blanche McGill, *The Sisters of Charity of Nazareth Kentucky* (New York: Encyclopedia Press, 1917), 125, Kentuckiana Digital Library, http://kdl.kyvl.org/cgi/t/text/text-idx?c=kyetexts;cc=kyetexts;view=toc;idno=B92–138–29329037, accessed November 13, 2008.

39. Dr. Daniel Drake, *Dr. Daniel Drake's Letters on Slavery to Dr. John C. Warren of Boston, from The National Intelligencer (Washington, April 3, 5, and 7, 1851)* (New York: Schuman's, 1940), 16.

40. Henry Bibb, *Narrative of the Life and Adventures of Henry Bibb: An American Slave* (Mineola, NY: Dover Publications, 2005), 6.

41. Lossus Slone, interview by author, Knott County, June 2000. Slone had a grocery store in the mid-1970s. He often picked the banjo as Junior Jacobs patted juba while dancing.

42. The Federal Writers' Project for the States of Kansas and Kentucky during 1936–38, *Slave Narratives: A Folk History of Slavery in the United States From Interviews with Former slaves*, 17 vols. (Washington, DC: Works Progress Administration, 1941), 7:15.

43. James Lane Allen, "The Blue-Grass Region of Kentucky," *Harper Magazine*, 189–279, Kentuckiana Digital Library, http://kdl.kyvl.org/cgi/t/text/text- idx?c=kyetexts;cc=kyetexts;view=toc;idno=B92–121–28575457, accessed November 7, 2008. The gourd banjo was observed in Fayette County.

44. Everett MacDonald, *The Red Debt: Echoes from Kentucky* (New York: G. W. Dillingham Co, 1916), 15, Kentuckiana Digital Library, http://kdl.kyvl.org/cgi/t/text/text-idx?c=kyetexts;cc=kyetexts;view=toc;idno=B92–232–31280811, accessed November 7, 2008.

45. George R. Gibson, "The Banjo in Appalachia," *The Appalachian Quarterly* (December 2001): 41.

46. Dr. Daniel Drake, *Pioneer Life in Kentucky* (Mount Vernon: The Golden Eagle Press, 1948), 214–17.

47. Jonathan Boucher, *Boucher's Glossary of Archaic and Provincial Words. A Supplement to the Dictionaries of the English Language, Particularly those of Dr. Johnson and Dr. Webster* . . . (London: Printed for Black, Young and Young, 1832), Bandore: p. xlix, BAN., cited in Epstein, *Sinful Tunes and Spirituals*, 34.

48. The Federal Writers' Project, *Slave Narratives*, 7:66–67.

49. Gordon Wilson, "Breakdowns," *Mountain Life and Work* 1, no. 3 (October 1925): 20, Kentuckiana Digital Library, http://kdl.kyvl.org/cgi/t/text/text-idx?page=home;c=journals;cc=journals, accessed January 5, 2009.

50. Ibid., 24.

51. Ibid., 20.

52. Ibid., 24.

53. Local News, *Paducah Sun*, Kentucky, May 15 and 26, 1902, 1, Kentuckiana Digital Library, http://kdl.kyvl.org/cgi/t/text/text-idx?xg=0;page=simple;g=news, accessed January 12, 2009.

54. *Earlington Bee*, Kentucky, January 19, 1899, 2, Kentuckiana Digital Library, http://kdl.kyvl.org/cgi/t/text/text-idx?xg=0;page=simple;g=news, accessed January 12, 2009.

55. William Lynwood Montell, *Upper Cumberland Country* (Jackson: University Press of Mississippi, 1993), xiii–xix.

56. The Federal Writers' Project, *Slave Narratives*, 7:53–54.

57. Local News, Russell Springs, *Adair Newspaper*, June 19, 1901, 3, Kentuckiana Digital Library, http://kdl.kyvl.org/cgi/t/text/text-idx?xg=0;page=simple;g=news, accessed January 12, 2009. Russell Springs is in Russell County.

58. Montell, *Upper Cumberland Country*, 18.

59. Ibid., 68.

60. William Lynwood, *The Saga of Coe Ridge: A Study in Oral History* (Knoxville: University of Tennessee Press, 1970), 28, 39.

61. Ibid., 126.

62. Montell, *Upper Cumberland Country*, 68.

63. Kip Lornell, "Pre-Blues Banjo & Fiddle," *Living Blues* 18 (Fall 1974): 25. Richard Burnett grew up near Monticello in Wayne County. Corbin is located at the junction of Whitley, Knox, and Laurel Counties.

64. Bobby Fulcher, liner notes, *Virgil Anderson, on the Tennessee Line*, 33 rpm (County Records, Floyd, VA, 1980).

65. Josiah H. Combs and D. K. Wilgus, eds., *Folk-Songs of the Southern United States* (Austin: University of Texas Press, 1969), 92.

66. Ibid., 79.

67. Hillard H. Smith and Albert F. Stewart, eds., "Letter from Hillard H. Smith to Ann Raleigh Eastham," *Appalachian Heritage* 2, no. 4 and 3, no. 1 (Fall–Winter 1974–75): 19, 22.

68. Jeff Todd Titon, *Old-Time Kentucky Fiddle Tunes* (Louisville: University of Kentucky Press, 2001), 22, 200–201.

69. *Knott County Kentucky 1920 Census* (Whitesburg Letcher Co. Historical and Genealogical Society), 148, 153.

70. Combs and Wilgus, *Folk-Songs of the Southern United States*, 223–26.

71. Barbara Edwards and Rich Kirby, liner notes, *Addie Graham: Been A Long Time Traveling* (Whitesburg, KY: June Appal Recordings, 1978, 2008), JA020, www.appalshop.org/juneappal, 1, accessed January 20, 2009.

72. *Hazel Green Herald*, Wolfe County, Kentucky, July 25, 1901, 3, Kentuckiana Digital Library, http://kdl.kyvl.org/cgi/t/text/text-idx?xg=0;page=simple;g=news, accessed January 13, 2009. Hazel Green is in Wolfe County.

73. *Hazel Green Herald*, June 8, 1905, 1. Lee City is in Wolfe County. Blind tigers, common in Appalachian Kentucky ca. 1900, were buildings from which illegal whiskey was dispensed.

74. *Hazel Green Herald*, April 10, 1902, 1.

75. *Hazel Green Herald*, May 1, 1902, 1.

76. *Clay County Times*, Clay City, Kentucky, July 2, 1903, 1.

77. Coy Morton, interview by author, Whitesburg, Kentucky, June 2002.

78. Allan M. Trout, *Greetings from Old Kentucky* (Louisville: The Courier-Journal, 1947), 63.

79. Interview by author, April 2010. Edward Davidson, a banjo player from Jackson County, knew Uncle Laney Gibson.

80. Pat Spurlock Elder, *Melungeons: Examining an Appalachian Legend* (Blountville: The Continuity Press, 1999), 212–28, and Heinegg, *Free African Americans*, 318–327. Elder clings to the notion that Melungeons were primarily descended from Indians (because some claimed Indian ancestry), while Heinegg proves most descended from free slaves.

For a contemporary description of mixed-race people with several family names, including Gibson, in Knott and Letcher Counties in southeast Kentucky, see Benjamin F. Luntz, *Forgotten Turmoil: The Southeastern Kentucky Ku Klux Klan* (Xlibris Corporation, 2006), 50–53.

81. Jean Thomas, *Ballad Makin' in the Mountains of Kentucky* (New York: Henry Holt and Company, 1939), 175–77. Thomas, unfortunately, has been dismissed by some academics because of her preoccupation with Elizabethan and Anglo-Saxon origins of mountain folk life. She describes accurately many aspects of music in Appalachian Kentucky, including gourd banjos; see 9, 29.

82. I have had numerous people in Appalachian Kentucky describe an aunt, grandmother, or some other female relative playing banjo in the first half of the nineteenth century. It is likely most extended families in that era had a female playing banjo. Nora Carpenter, Molly O'Day, Cousin Emmy, Mabel Damron, Blanche Coldiron, Dora Mae Wagers, Lily May Ledford, and the Amburgey sisters are some Kentucky women who played banjo professionally.

83. Renee Hagans, Karen Clayton, and Newton McCravy III, eds., *Williams, Hagans, Higgins and Combs Reunion: Family Genealogy of 1999* (Lexington, July 10, 2000), 1.

84. Leonard Roberts, *Sang Branch Settlers: Folksongs and Tales of a Kentucky Mountain Family* (Austin: University of Texas Press, 1974), 41.

85. Larry Bare, interview by author by email and telephone, December 2001.

86. Letter from Phillip Collins, January 29, 2001, along with Collins genealogy.

87. Elder, *Melungeons*, 174–75, 202–12, and Heinegg, *Free African Americans*, 215–18.

88. Charles K. Wolfe, *Kentucky Country* (Louisville: University of Kentucky Press, 1982), 12.

89. Henry P. Scalf, *Kentucky's Last Frontier* (Johnson City: The Overmountain Press, 2000), 153–59. I became aware of this group through genealogical research; some members of the group were among my ancestors.

90. Cresswell, *The Journal of Nicholas Cresswell*, 30, cited in Epstein, *Sinful Tunes and Spirituals*, 115.

91. George Stueckrath, "Art. VII—Upper Country of South Carolina," *Debow's Review* 27, no. 6 (December 1859): 692–93, University of Michigan Digital Library Text Collections, Making of America Journal Articles, http://name.umdl.umich.edu/acg1336.1-27.006, accessed January 5, 2009.

92. Library of Congress, Manuscript Division, WPA Federal Writers' Project Collection. "I Was Born in Barnwell County," 3, http://www.loc.gov/resource/wpalh3.31131003/?sp=3, accessed January 5, 2009.

93. John Preston Arthur, *Western North Carolina, A History: From 1730 to 1913* (Raleigh: Edwards & Broughton, 1914; reprint Johnson City: The Overmountain Press, 1996), 268.

94. Reverend O. L. Brown, "John Preston Arthur Biographical," 12 http://toto.lib.unca.edu/findingaids/mss/moore/john_preston_arthur.htm, accessed December 14, 2013.

95. Heinegg, *Free African Americans*, 22–25.

96. Anna Bailey, "How Scuffletown became Indian Country: Political Change and Transformation in Robeson County, North Carolina, 1865–1956" (PhD diss., University

of Washington, 2008), 65. Bailey was quoting George Alford Townsend, who wrote sensational articles about the "The Swamp Outlaws" for the *New York Herald* beginning in 1872. https://books.google.com/books?id=cMt4XAn2shoC&pg=PP5&lpg=PP5&dq=anna +bailey+scuffletown&source=bl&ots=HJDonAamoj&sig=b6Qwitc8nW6Io8Yoncxlug BBDyc&hl=en&sa=X&ei=NwDZVMDWEbfLsAT2kIGADQ&ved=0CDgQ6AEwBg#v =onepage&q=banjo&f=false, accessed December 17, 2014.

97. Robert C. Lawrence, *The State of Robeson* (New York: J. J. Little and Ives Company, 1939), 120.

98. Heinegg, *Free African Americans*, 7.

99. Robert Carleton [Baynard Rush Hall], *The new purchase; or, seven and a half years in the far West* (New York: G. S. Appleton and D. Appleton & Co., 1843), 200, https://books .google.com/books?id=mV4eAAAAMAAJ&pg=PR5&dq=robert+carlton,+the+new +purchase+or+seven+and+a+half+years+in+the+west&hl=en&sa=X&ei=dQ7ZVLb SK42wsAT2woEw&ved=0CCYQ6AEwAA#v=onepage&q=robert%20carlton%2C%20 the%20new%20purchase%20or%20seven%20and%20a%20half%20years%20in%20the%20 west&f=false, accessed December 17, 2014.

100. *Goodspeed's 1889 History of Northwest Arkansas* (Chicago: Goodspeed Publishing Co, 1889), 148–49, http://www.hearthstonelegacy.com/arkansas products.htm, CD-ROM, accessed December 18, 2014.

101. Ibid., 142.

102. Cecil J. Sharp, *The Country Dance Book: Part V* (London: Novello and Company, 1918), 17. The Pine Mountain Settlement School is in Harlan County.

103. John Allan Wyeth, *With Sabre and Scalpel* (New York: Harper & Brothers Publishers, 1914), 59, University of North Carolina, Documenting the American South, http:// docsouth.unc.edu/fpn/wyeth/tyeth.html, accessed November 16, 2008.

104. Federal Writers' Project, *Slave Narratives*, http://Ancestry.com, under heading of Stories, Memories & Histories, click on Slave Narratives, Enter the name: Tom Mills in the first and last name box, accessed May 12, 2009.

105. Ibid., Henry Childers.

106. Ibid., Ben Wall and Isaac Stier.

107. Phil Jamieson, "From Plantation to Puncheon Floor: The African-American Roots of Dance Calling," *The Old-Time Herald* 8, no. 6 (Winter 2002–3): 51.

108. Federal Writers' Project, *Slave Narratives*, http://Ancestry.com, under heading of Stories, Memories & Histories, click on Slave Narratives, Enter the name: Chris Franklin in the first and last name box, accessed May 13, 2009.

109. William Henry Haney, *The Mountain People of Kentucky* (Cincinnati: The Robert Clarke Co., 1906), 52. Dr. Josiah Combs collected the calls for bird in the cage from Dan Gibson in Knott County, Kentucky, ca. 1915.

110. Sharp, *Country Dance Book*, 11–12.

111. Phil Jamieson, "Bird in the Cage," *The Old-Time Herald* 11, no. 1 (October–November 2007): 14.

112. Philip Vickers Fithian, *Journal and Letters of 1773-1774: A Plantation Tutor of the Old Dominion* (Charlottesville: Dominion Books of the University Press of Virginia, 1968), 61–62.

113. Mark Knowles, *Tap Roots: The Early History of Tap Dancing* (Jefferson, NC: McFarland & Company, Inc., 2002), 73.

114. Kate Van Winkle Keller, *Dance and Its Music in America, 1528-1789* (Hillsdale, NY: Pendragon Press), 180.

115. Andrew Burnaby, *Travels through the Middle Settlements of North America in the Years 1759 and 1760* (London, 1775; reprint Ithaca: Great Seal Books, 1960), 26, cited in Keller, *Dance and Its Music in America*, 180–81.

116. Creswell, *The Journal of Nicholas Creswell*, 53, cited in Keller, *Dance and Its Music in America*, 181.

117. Keller, *Dance and Its Music in America*, 181–83.

118. Dr. Marion Mayo, liner notes, *Rufus Crisp CD* (New York: Folkways Records, Album No. FA2342, 1972), 2.

119. Isaac D Williams, *Sunshine and Shadow of a Slave Life: Reminiscences as told By Isaac D. Williams to "Tege"* (East Saginaw, MI: Evening News Printing and Binding House, 1885), 60–61, http://docsouth.unc.edu/neh/iwilliams/menu.html, accessed October 20, 2009.

120. Sharp, *Country Dance Book*, 8, 16.

121. William Monroe Cockburn, *Pioneer History of Indiana: Including Stories, Incidents, and Early Customs of the Early Settlers* (Oakland City: Press of Oakland City Journal, 1907), 186.

122. Rich Kirby and Nina Dryer, liner notes, *Whoa Mule CD* (Whitesburg: June Appal Recordings, 2001), 2–3.

123. Stueckrath, "Art. VII—Upper Country of South Carolina," 692–93.

124. The first known mention of the banjo in a newspaper (New York, 1936; *Zenger's Banjo*) does not describe the banjo. Robert B. Winans did not find a description of the banjo in eighteenth-century runaway slave advertisements ("Black Musicians in Eighteenth Century America: Evidence from Runaway Slave Advertisements," in this volume). I found an interesting runaway slave advertisement on the website www.afrolumens.org, but the citation has since disappeared. The advertisement appeared in *The Pennsylvania Gazette*, July 12, 27, 1749, and describes Scipio, a banjo player and singer, but does not describe his banjo.

125. Thomas Jefferson, *Notes on the State of Virginia* (Philadelphia, 1781), 257, cited in Epstein, *Sinful Tunes and Spirituals*, 34.

126. Boucher, *Boucher's Glossary of Archaic and Provincial Words*, xlix, cited in Epstein, *Sinful Tunes and Spirituals*, 34.

127. Dr. Marion Mayo, liner notes, *Rufus Crisp CD*, 2.

128. I had numerous conversations with Coy Morton regarding banjo traditions in Knott and Letcher Counties. Coy played banjo all his life; his brother Cullen, who was said to have been an excellent banjo player, singer, and dancer, married my father's only sister, who was also reputed to be a good banjo player and singer.

129. I did not use all the citations I have because some did not fit within the framework of this chapter. The most interesting first-person account of banjo playing I have found, however, is in the Library of Virginia, accession number 38743. Charles Doe wrote a letter dated February 22, 1850, from Danville, Virginia, where he was visiting a brother:

> The black have almost universally good voices, quick ears, & great love for music. Not one of them knows a note. Their national instrument is the Banjo; some of them play on a violin. The whites play the banjo a great deal, at least as much as northerners do on the flute.

The late Tim Thompson of Richmond, Virginia, transcribed the letter for me after I located the citation.

130. Dena J. Epstein, "The Folk Banjo: A Documentary History," *Ethnomusicology* 19, no. 3 (September 1975): 359.

131. Robert B. Winans and Elias J. Kaufman, "Minstrel and Classic Banjo: English Connections," *American Music* 12, no. 1 (Spring 1994): 1. Winans and Kaufman noted that "in England . . . blackface minstrelsy, though popular, spawned no lasting *folk* tradition of banjo playing. The most likely explanation of this phenomenon is that while the American folk tradition was already an amalgam of Anglo-American and African American music, into which the banjo fit musically, mid-nineteenth century British folk music was *not* such an amalgam. English traditions have existed primarily at the professional and parlor levels with which this article is mainly concerned."

The professional and parlor levels of banjo playing developed from art music written by northern minstrels in the mid-nineteenth century, when they standardized and reduced an older style of minstrel playing to European music notation, and developed music notation for the "parlor level," a finger-picking style of playing banjo.

132. Bob Carlin, *The Birth of the Banjo: Joel Walker Sweeney and Early Minstrelsy* (Jefferson, NC: McFarland & Company, Inc., 2007), 163–66. Carlin provides a chronology of Sweeney's performances; Sweeney traveled and performed far more often in the North, where transportation was better and the population more concentrated. The classic banjo style (parlor level), an art music developed in minstrelsy and popularized mostly in the North and in England in the late 1800s, survives primarily because The American Banjo Fraternity (www.banjofraternity.org), which has a few dozen active members, meets twice yearly in Pennsylvania to play the music.

133. Gene Bluestein, "America's Folk Instrument: Notes of the Five-String Banjo," *Western Folklore* 23, no. 4 (October 1964): 245, 246. Bluestein, who played old-time banjo and recorded Reverend Buell Kazee, a mountain master of the banjo, said: "Because it was increasingly removed from the folk community in which it developed, the music of the minstrel banjoists soon lost the flavor of folk song and became a vehicle for the virtuoso instrumentalist." He commented on the playing of Appalachian white banjoists: "And since their manner of playing is not closely related to the minstrel tradition, it may be that it represents a closer approximation of earlier Negro styles."

Bluestein is likely correct on both observations; however, since we cannot know how early minstrels played banjo we can only judge by comparing modern banjoists' interpretation of the music written in the minstrel tutors with folk banjoists, black and white, recorded in the twentieth century. The *Minstrel Banjo Style* recording from Rounder Records (CD 0321) has several accomplished musicians re-creating music from the tutors; compare this with the recordings of any mountain master, such as Bill Cornett, Reverend Buell Kazee, Dink Roberts, John Snipes, or others. The formulaic and stilted art music from the minstrel tutors is quite unlike the recorded music of any folk banjoist I have heard. The art music in the minstrel tutors, however, has been revived and is promoted as the "authentic" music of the Civil War.

Stuart Jamieson, email, November 12, 2002. Jamieson, who recorded Rufus Crisp and other southern musicians, commented regarding Robert B. Winans's tracks on *The Minstrel Banjo Style* CD: "The dynamics are limited compared to Rufus' playing."

134. This musical family and a few other neighbors were descended from Stuffley Moore (b. ca. 1828), who is listed as a mulatto in the 1850 federal census for Letcher County, Kentucky. My grandmother Cordelia Pugh Hammons told my mother that Stuffley was African American. Stuffley's descendants were all accepted members of the white community. I do not intend to name this family because this is still, unfortunately, a sensitive subject for some people. Race was anomalous on the frontier and in southeast Kentucky.

See T. R. C. Hutton, *Bloody Breathitt: Politics and Violence in the Appalachian South* (Lexington: University Press of Kentucky, 2013), 31–33, 57, 58.

135. Combs and Wilgus, *Folk-Songs of the Southern United States*, 54–56.

136. The modern equivalent of the minstrel tuning with the lowered bass is g—CGBD; which is pitched higher than the tunings used in minstrelsy. Some of the older banjo players in Knott County, including my father, did tune their banjos to a lower pitch; however, none that I heard used the lowered bass tuning. I learned this tuning from a bluegrass banjo player who was using the tuning to play Earl Scruggs's version of "Farewell Blues."

Reverend Buell Kazee said he learned the standard C tuning later in life. He does so on Yazoo 516 Video: *Traditional Music Classics Featuring Doc Watson, Roscoe Holcomb, Buell Kazee and Kilby Snow* and also on YouTube, https://www.youtube.com/watch?v=AgBgfn9S3gw, accessed December 16, 2014.

My father and Buell Kazee were born in 1900; both were playing banjo ca. 1910.

137. I acquired Blind Hobart Bailey's tunings from Stuart Jamieson ca. 2005; Stuart was with Hedy West when she recorded Bailey in 1966.

CHAPTER 15

The Changing Intonational Practice
of Mid-Nineteenth-Century Banjo

Jim Dalton

Editor's Headnote

This musicological chapter deals with concepts that may seem esoteric, but it indicates that many methodologies can, and should, be applied to the study of the banjo. Dalton presents a rigorous technical analysis of the acoustics of the early banjo, using as his data the instructions found in early banjo tutors. All the acoustic theory employed helps to explain a major change in the construction of banjos. Early banjos had unfretted fingerboards until the final third of the nineteenth century, when fretted fingerboards became the norm. Dalton makes the case that the changes in intonational methods (simplistically, how instruments are tuned) partly account for this shift.

The earliest published banjo tutors (ca. 1851–68) have long been recognized as an excellent source of information about mid-nineteenth-century technique, repertoire, and performance practice. Careful examination of these sources reveals details of intonational practices that deserve more attention. In our efforts to more fully understand earlier practices and rediscover the sounds of the era, something as fundamental as the precise tuning of intervals should be explored. I believe this evidence sheds light on larger issues such as the rapid growth and development of the instrument, as well as changes in technique, repertoire, and the physical nature of the instrument itself.

Players of fretted and keyboard instruments are often blissfully unaware of the nature of the compromised tuning that their instruments require. However, since ancient times, the cognoscenti have wrestled with issues of tuning and temperament[1] and have proposed, used, and discarded a variety of compromise solutions to the historical problems of tuning. The mid-nineteenth-century banjo represents a special case.

The earliest banjos were fretless and able to play pure, untempered intervals. Before long, however, the addition of fret markers (later actual raised frets) and more harmonically diverse repertoire made temperament necessary (or, at least, desirable) and quite quickly rendered the banjo an equal-tempered instrument like the guitar and modern piano.

Some authors of early banjo tutors (and significantly, performers) describe a practice of playing pure intervals in a form of just intonation. This practice and subsequent changes are documented in the tutors. The evidence from these sources takes several forms: tuning directions, fretting patterns, pedagogy, and repertoire. This evidence offers interesting insights into the practice of certain performers, the way those performers taught their students, and why the instrument and its repertoire developed as they did.

To facilitate this discussion, an introduction to some basic tuning theory is necessary.

Just intonation has been defined as "any system of tuning in which all of the intervals can be represented by whole-number frequency ratios, with a strongly implied preference for the simplest ratios compatible with a given musical purpose."[2] As accurate as this definition is, it may be a bit daunting to the uninitiated. For our purposes here, we can informally say that just intonation is what most people consider to be purely "in tune." Idealized pure, or "just," intervals can be represented by small-integer ratios representing either vibrating string lengths and/or the vibrations themselves.

For example, if the pitch A is an open string, half the length of that string will produce an A one octave higher than that of the whole string; these proportions give a ratio of 2/1.[3] At a constant tension, half the string length will vibrate at two times the rate of the full string. So, A = 110 hz (hertz = vibration cycles per second) and an A one octave higher is 220 hz; 220/110 = 2/1.[4] Table 15.1 presents the vibrational ratios of some other important intervals.

Purely tuned intervals, though acoustically ideal, are problematic both musically and mathematically. If we generate the pitches of the chromatic scale (musical example 15.1) by tuning successive perfect fifths (P5s), the final note misses being a pure octave by nearly an eighth of a tone. This audible discrepancy is termed the *Pythagorean comma*.

Another important tuning anomaly rises from a comparison of P5s and major thirds (M3s); see musical example 15.2. The M3 produced by tuning successive just P5s does not coincide with the just M3 (5/4). The difference here is approximately one-ninth of a tone, a very slightly smaller amount than the Pythagorean comma, but still very audible. This particular discrepancy is called the *syntonic comma* or the *comma of Didymus*.

One can see by the traditional names of the commas that these issues have been known and documented as far back as classical Greece.[5] Other similar

Table 15.1   Vibrational Ratios

Unison	Perfect Fifth	Perfect Fourth	Major Third	Minor Third	Major Second
1/1	3/2	4/3	5/4	6/5	9/8

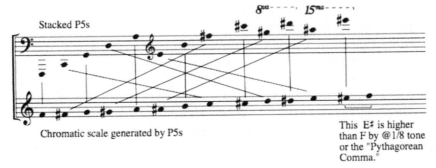

Musical Example 15.1. Chromatic scale pitches generated by perfect fifths.

discrepancies can be discovered by comparing the intervals produced by other pairs of prime numbers, most notably the great diesis (128/125), just less than an equal-tempered quarter tone, which is the difference between three major thirds and an octave. However, the limited harmonic palette of the early banjo repertoire makes this and others less significant than the first two to the discussion at hand. Collectively, these issues have been called the "historical tuning problem."[6]

Just intonation requires either a very large number of pitches or some constraints on the number of pure intervals. Many solutions to the problem have been proposed over the centuries. Some have had a period of popularity before being superseded and falling into disuse. Others have had their proponents but have never become common. The currently popular solution is 12-tone equal temperament (more properly called 12-part equal division of the octave, or 12EDO). In this tuning, the octave is divided into twelve equal semitones. For convenience, each semitone is said to consist of 100 parts called cents; therefore, an octave contains 1,200 cents.[7] This measure enables us to compare intervals between tuning systems in a clear and understandable way.

In 12EDO, all intervals except the octaves (and, of course, unisons) are compromised, or "tempered," to a greater or lesser extent. Tempered perfect fifths are around 2 cents narrower than just and their inversions, the perfect fourths, are approximately 2 cents wider. Tempering by 2 cents is usually considered to be negligible since most people are unable to distinguish the difference.

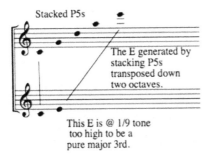

Musical Example 15.2. Comparison of perfect fifths and major thirds.

12EDO major thirds, on the other hand, are around 14 cents wider than just. This is substantial and quite audible. Many musicians are unaware of this because they have become accustomed to hearing these oversized thirds. The usual explanation is that their ears accept a greater deviation in thirds than in fifths.

Accurate equal temperament for keyboards has only been possible since 1917, but workable 12EDO has been with the fretted instrument world much longer. It has arguably been the most common pattern for fretted instruments since the sixteenth century.[8] But, of course, the earliest banjos had no frets and therefore were not constrained to the 12EDO of fretted instruments, or to the keyboard temperaments such as the various meantones and circulating or well temperaments still being used at the time. For a discussion of the banjo tutors that were published before 1870, a basic understanding of just intonation and equal temperament (12EDO) will suffice.

Several types of information in the tutors bear witness to intonational issues: tuning directions, fretting directions (or lack thereof), playing instructions for the left hand, and the repertoire itself. Period tutors include those of Chaff,[9] Briggs,[10] Rice,[11] Buckley,[12] Winner,[13] and Converse.[14]

The Tuning Directions

The primary tuning indicated by each of the tutors has the same interval structure (table 15.2). The pitch varies somewhat and several of the tutors include scordaturas (usually raising the fourth or bass string by a whole step). Briggs alone offers a different tuning for minor key pieces but, unfortunately, does not include any tunes arranged in that tuning.

We will return to this information later. For now, we focus on the directions for putting the instrument "in tune." The tutors contain two different types of tuning instructions seemingly linked to the presence or absence of frets or fret markers.[15] Each gives a very different result.

When frets are described, these are incorporated into the tuning rubric. The player is instructed to tune a unison between a fretted note and an open string. I refer to this as the "open/fretted unison" method. Of the tutors, Converse's *Method* gives the clearest description of this tuning procedure.[16]

MANNER OF TUNING THE BANJO

Tune 4th string to A. (Tuning Fork or Piano.) Place a finger on the 4th string at the 7th fret, which makes E, tune the third string in unison. Then place a finger on the 3d string at the 4th fret, making G♯, tune the second string in unison. Then place a finger on the 2d string at the 3d fret, tune the first string in unison. Tune the 5th string an octave above the 3d string.

The two Buckley books and the Rice have identical though somewhat garbled versions of the same general method of tuning.

Table 15.2   Tunings Represented in Published Banjo Tutors, 1851–68

Book	Year	Primary Tuning	Tuning at Other Pitches	Raised Bass Tuning	Other Tunings	Comments
Chaff	1851	cFCEG	dGDF♯A Other pitches likely but not explicit.	No		
Briggs	1855	dGDF♯A	cFCEG * d♭G♭D♭FA♭ e♭A♭E♭GB♭ eAEG♯B fB♭FAC f♯BF♯A♯C♯ g♭C♭G♭B♭D♭ [for the major keys of the fourth and third strings]	Yes	dGDFA * All the other major key tunings can be made into this minor key tuning by lowering the second string.	Calls for banjo to be tuned to different pitches for better vocal range. ------------------ Only tutor that describes a minor key tuning.
Rice	1858	eAEG♯B	dGDF♯A	No		
Buckley New Banjo Book	1860	eAEG♯B	dGDF♯A "If necessary tune Banjo one step lower."	Yes		"Capo d'Astros are used when it is requisite to put the banjo higher, and tune the 5th string accordingly."
Winner	1864	dGDF♯A	"When the performer wishes to play in other keys, the pitch of the instrument should be changed."	No		Calls for banjo to be tuned to different pitches for better vocal range.
Converse Instructor	1865	eAEG♯B		No		
Converse Method	1865	eAEG♯B		Yes		Contains the largest number of different keys despite the single tuning.
Buckley Banjo Guide	1868	eAEG♯B	dGDF♯A*	Yes	d♯BEG♯B A misprint. G natural is in the text.	

* These tunings are mentioned, but no pieces using them are included in the book.

When frets are not described, the player is instructed to tune just intervals. These directions vary from implied to explicit. Briggs, for example, says simply:

> The 3d string is tuned first, then the 2d string is tuned a third above the third string, then the 1st string is tuned a fifth above the 3d string, then the 5th string is tuned an octave above the 3d string, then the 4th or Bass string is tuned a fifth below the third string.[17]

Since no frets are described here and, we assume, none are on the instrument, tuning is accomplished by tuning just intervals from one open string to another.

Briggs, of course, presumes that the student already knows intervals. A similar method is described in the Winner and Chaff books.

Because Converse, the most adept pedagogue of the early banjo book authors, does not use frets in his *Instructor*,[18] he is careful to adequately describe a method for tuning that will give accurate results. Here, Converse explicitly describes just intervals, a method that will prove to be even more significant as we examine other aspects of his approach in this tutor:

4th String.

Commence with this string, which tune to A (tuning fork or pitch pipe)

3rd String.

Measure the distance from the nut to the bridge, and at one third the distance (measuring from the nut) stop the 4th string with the second finger of the left hand, making E. Tune the 3rd string in unison with it.

2nd String.

At one fifth of the distance, measuring as before, stop the 3rd string with the second finger, making G♯. Tune the 2nd string in unison with it.

1st String.

At one third the distance, measuring as before, stop the 3rd string with the second finger, making B. Tune the 1st string in unison with it.

5th String.

Tune the 5th string in unison[19] with the 3rd string sounded open.

Unison.

When two strings are in unison, by sounding one, it will cause the other to vibrate.[20]

Already, the lines are drawn, so to speak. The authors who do not use frets tune just intervals while those who use frets tune tempered intervals. Though the fifths and fourths are tempered almost imperceptibly, the tempering will, of course, be more obvious on the major third between the second and third strings and the minor third between the second and first strings. To state it simply, the second string will be 14 cents lower on the just-tuned banjo than on the tempered one.

The Directions for Adding Frets

Converse, in his *Method*, provides a fingerboard diagram "being the exact size and properly proportioned" for a banjo with a scale length (nut-to-bridge distance) of 27 1/2 inches. Rice's book gives a fretboard diagram and instructions to make the scale length 28 inches. In both of these books equal tempered (12EDO) fretting is used.

The two Buckley books make use of the so-called rule of 18 first described by Vincenzo Galilei (ca. 1520–91), composer, lutenist, theorist, and father of the astronomer Galileo.[21]

HOW TO FRET THE BANJO

Great care must be used in doing this. The distance between the nut and bridge must be divided into 18 equal parts. After putting your first fret on, then again divide the space between this and the bridge into 18 parts; putting your second fret on, then again divide from the second to the bridge into 18 parts, and so on until you have as many frets as you require. The bridge, of course, must always be kept stationary.[22]

This method gives a very good approximation of 12EDO.[23] The error is negligible and is offset (or, for that matter, exacerbated—but usually by still tiny amounts) by the other variables that always come into play on fretted string instruments: variation in string quality, displacement of the string by finger pressure, position of the bridge, humidity, and the like.[24] Any of these factors could alter the physical position of an "in-tune" equal tempered pitch, potentially making the fretting more or, just as likely, less accurate.

The logic of pairing the "open/fretted unison" method and 12EDO fretting should be apparent, as should that of tuning open strings to just intervals in the absence of frets. Table 15.3 provides information regarding fretting and tuning in the early banjo tutors.

Of all the authors of the period, including those of the next few decades, only Buckley gives us an exception to the rule of 18 fretting:

The frets are all to be put the entire width of the finger-board, with the exception of the 2nd, which only crosses the 2nd, 3rd and 4th strings. On the 1st string you must have a small fret an 1/8th of an inch nearer the first fret.[25]

See figures 15.1 and 15.2 showing the split fret.

Table 15.3   Fretting and Tuning Directions in Published Banjo Tutors, 1851–68

Book	Year	Frets	How Described	Tuning Instruction	Special
Chaff	1851	No	NA	Just interval	
Briggs	1855	No	NA	Just interval	
Rice	1858	Yes	Diagram	Open/fretted unison*	
Buckley New Banjo Book	1860	Yes	Rule of 18	Open/fretted unison*	Partial second fret for first string
Winner	1864	No	NA	Just interval	
Converse Instructor	1865	No	NA	Just interval	
Converse Method	1865	Yes	Diagram	Open/fretted unison	
Buckley Guide	1868	Yes	Rule of 18	Open/fretted unison*	Partial second fret for first string

* These tuning instructions are literally the same.

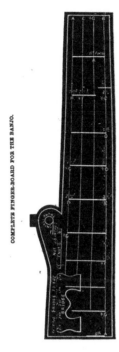

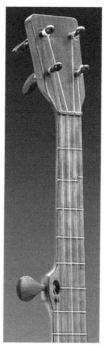

Figure 15.1. Buckley 1860 fretboard diagram, with split second fret; photo courtesy of Greg C. Adams.

Figure 15.2. Ashborn split fret. Photograph © Museum of Fine Arts, Boston, accession number 2007.975.

Evidence from the Pedagogy of Converse's *Instructor*

The most intriguing intonational evidence is found in Converse's 1865 *Instructor*. As a way of analyzing the intonational system taught in this book, I use just-intonation lattice diagrams. The purpose of these diagrams is to clearly show the relationships between pitches especially where the intonation would vary. They are a representation of pure P5s (3/2) horizontally and just M3s (5/4) vertically. They should be understood to represent a portion of a theoretical lattice that extends to infinity.[26] To understand the full implications of this diagram, remember that the pure thirds are approximately 14 cents lower than in equal temperament and the pure fifths are approximately 2 cents higher. For example, starting from the middle row C, the E above it is approximately 14 cents lower than in equal temperament but the E in the middle row is approximately 8 cents higher (2 cents for each P5 C-G, G-D, D-A, A-E). Therefore, the E in the top row is about 22 cents lower than the E in the middle row and the E in the bottom row is still 22 cents higher. The same applies to any other pitch names.

A SEGMENT OF THE FIVE-LIMIT JUST INTONATION LATTICE:

```
  |   |   |   |   |   |   |   |   |   |   |   |
 -A – E  – B – F#– C#– G#– D#– A#–E#– B# – F×–C×–
  |   |   |   |   |   |   |   |   |   |   |   |
 -F – C – G – D – A – E – B  – F#–C#– G#– D#– A#–
  |   |   |   |   |   |   |   |   |   |   |   |
 -Db–Ab– Eb– Bb– F –  C – G – D – A – E – B – F#–
  |   |   |   |   |   |   |   |   |   |   |   |
```

As I have already noted, Converse, in his *Instructor,* gave very explicit just intonation tuning directions. These tuning instructions result in just P5s and a just M3. The fifth string E is tuned an octave higher than the third string. This tuning, with A tuned to a fork or pipe, can be represented by a portion of the just intonation lattice:

```
    G#
    |
A – E – B
```

Both E strings, being an octave apart, are represented by the same lattice position. The G♯ is shown as a pure M3 above E.

Page 15 of the *Instructor* has a diagram called "The Five Principal Positions" that deserves close examination (musical example 15.3). Since he references a banjo with-

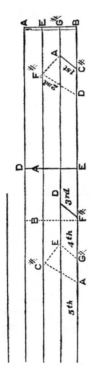

Musical Example 15.3. Converse's "Five Principal Positions" diagram.

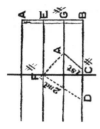

Musical Example 15.4. First close-up of Converse's "Principal Positions" diagram.

out frets, Converse uses these positions ostensibly as a way of teaching the location of the pitches, but certain features reveal attention to the details of intonation.

Musical Example 15.4 presents a close-up of a portion of the diagram, on which I have drawn a line parallel to the nut through F♯ for the sake of clarity. Notice that although the first and third strings are tuned a pure P5 apart, the interval F♯—C♯ is not represented as a straight line parallel to the nut. In other words, Converse is not presenting this interval as pure fifth—the C♯ is tuned as a pure M3 above A. This positioning means, among other things, that the whole tone E—F♯ is larger than the whole tone B—C♯. If we were to tune the F♯—C♯ fifth purely, we would end up with an A—C♯ major 3rd that is 22 cents too wide. Melodically, this interval could work well but the purity of the tonic major triad would be sacrificed. This pure M3 is an easy interval for a beginner to learn—following Converse's tuning instruction, one would have already tuned a pure major third between strings 2 and 3.

"Juba" and "Calabash Dance," the first two pieces in the book, are based on Converse's "first position" with neighbor tones above and below the C♯. Though not explicit, the assumption is that D (in the diagram above and as used in these tunes) is 4/3 (a just P4) above the A.

The lattice diagram below and those following will demonstrate the growth of the required gamut of pitches throughout the *Instructor*.

```
C# – G#
 |    |
D – A – E – B
```

"Cane Break Reel" enables the banjoist to contextualize the tuning of D by making it the 7th of an E7 chord. It also adds a low B (4th string) that differs in distance from the nut as compared to the first string C♯. This configuration is the first practical demonstration that two different size whole steps are required. The use of different size whole steps will be discussed in more detail later, but for now it would at least be of value to mention their ubiquity through most of the history of music well into the twentieth century as documented in recordings of the piano from the 1920s, ostensibly a period of equal temperament.[27] The octaves on A are a proven way to practice and refine intonation.

"Original Essence of Old Virginny" adds second position, which contains F#. According to Converse's diagram, the F# seems to be part of a chain of fifths rather than a just M3 above D. This interpretation places the third of a D major chord 22 cents (a syntonic comma) higher than just.

```
    C# – G#
    |    |
D – A – E – B – F#
```

Referring again to the "principal positions" diagram (another close-up, musical example 15.5), one sees that even the higher position D major chord does not have a low or pure M3 (F#). Contrast this with the higher position E chord, which does. I have added the line parallel to the nut through C# for clarity.

The next two pieces, "Oh Susannah" and "Yankee Doodle," are melodic studies on the pitches already learned. Converse teaches accuracy in intonation harmonically and then applies it to familiar melodies. This sequence is important because the ear will often accept a wider variation in intonation melodically than harmonically. Interestingly, though these two tunes are in different keys ("Yankee Doodle" in A and "Oh Susannah" in E, the first piece in the book that is not in A), this hexatonic version of "Oh Susannah" has no leading tone (D# in this case)—hence, no new pitch to tune.

The first tune to include the D# in a full scale of E major is "Boston Jig," the eighteenth piece in the book.

```
    C# – G#– D#
    |    |   |
D – A – E – B – F#
```

At this point, let's compare the two scales (table 15.4). Notice that the whole steps are of two different sizes: 9/8 and the slightly smaller 10/9. The 9/8 is only 4 cents larger than the familiar equal-tempered whole step and will sound very similar. The 10/9 is 22 cents smaller than the 9/8 whole step.

The difference between the two scales is subtle but noticeable and both are quite viable. The A scale has a 9/8 between the fifth and sixth degrees and a 10/9

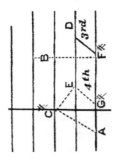

Musical Example 15.5. Second close-up of Converse's "Principal Positions" diagram.

Table 15.4   Pitch Intervals for A Major and E Major Scales

		A Major Scale						
Intervals between pitches		9/8	10/9	16/15	9/8	9/8	10/9	16/15
	A	**B**	**C♯**	**D**	**E**	**F♯**	**G♯**	**A**
Intervals from tonic	1/1	9/8	5/4	4/3	3/2	27/16	15/8	2/1

		E Major Scale						
Intervals between pitches		9/8	10/9	16/15	9/8	10/9	9/8	16/15
	E	**F♯**	**G♯**	**A**	**B**	**C♯**	**D♯**	**E**
Intervals from tonic	1/1	9/8	5/4	4/3	3/2	5/3	15/8	2/1

between the sixth and seventh. The positions are reversed in the E scale. This kind of difference is typical of some of the eighteenth- and nineteenth-century well-temperaments (also called circulating temperaments). In these, it was considered a virtue for the tuning to have a slightly different character to each key.

I have already mentioned the intonation of the sixth degree (F♯) in the key of A—at 27/16 it will be a bit less consonant than the 5/3 sixth degree in the key of E. It is not really harsh enough to be considered dissonant to most ears but may be "more active" or "less restful" than the more consonant intervals in that key. Since the book contains no pieces in the key of D major, a less-than-pure D major triad is not a liability especially in its position as IV in the key of A.

Of course, this discussion of the tuning is idealized. With no frets, it is likely that some players would shift their fingers slightly to bring that scale degree into the same intonation in both keys.

Evidence from the Repertoire: Expansion
of the Pitch Palette in the Repertoire and Its Effect

Of the banjo tutors between 1850 and 1870, only three provided a significant increase in the number of pitches used (per tuning) and the harmonic significance of these pitches. These are the two Buckley books and Converse's *Method*.

We will take these chronologically. The first Buckley book contains a fair amount of essential chromaticism (the use of chromatic pitches that change the nature of a chord rather than being decorative), most of which can be described as secondary dominants or middle sections that modulate to the dominant or relative keys. It also contains a bit of simple mode mixture (shifting between major and parallel minor); this occurs only in the key of A.

The Converse *Method* contains very little of this type of essential chromaticism. The expanded pitch resources here are a result of an increased number of keys used. In fact, this book has the most numerous and diverse key choices of all the tutors of the period (table 15.5). "Whack Row de Dow," on page 25, represents the first time in any of the tutors that a third major key is introduced without

Table 15.5 Correlation of Keys and Tunings in Published Banjo Tutors, 1851–68

Book	Year	Primary Tuning	Primary Keys Used	Secondary Tuning	Secondary Keys Used	Notes
Chaff	1851	cFCEG	See note*	dGDF♯A	See note*	
Briggs	1855	dGDF♯A	G (44) D (20) D mixolyd. (3)			
Rice	1858	eAEG♯B	A (32), E (20) A minor (1) B dorian (1) E mixolyd. (8)	dGDF♯A	D (1), G (1)	
Buckley New Banjo Book	1860	eAEG♯B	A (80), E (22) A minor (2) E mixolyd. (1) A mixolyd. (1) B dorian (1)	dGDF♯A	D (19), G (6)	
Winner	1864	dGDF♯A	G (22) D (14) D mixolyd. (2) A dorian (1)			
Converse Instructor	1865	eAEG♯B	A (21), E (6) B minor (1) B dorian (1) E mixolyd. (1)			First two E major pieces are hexatonic without leading tone.
Converse Method	1865	eAEG♯B	A (34), E (19) D (6), G (5) A minor (8) F♯ minor (3) E minor (3) E dorian (2) B minor (2) E mixolyd. (1)			First tutor to have more than two major keys per tuning. Most variety of keys in general.
Buckley Guide	1868	eAEG♯B	A (61), E (36) D (1) A minor (4) F♯ minor (3) E mixolyd. (1)	d♯BEG♯B Tuning listed with a misprint G natural.	One piece in E with a number of mistakes in the text.	

* The Chaff book is not really a method per se but a collection of tunes. The relationship between keys and tuning is unclear.

retuning the instrument. The first Buckley book and the earlier Rice book have pieces in D and G major, but the player is instructed to play these in the lower dGDF♯A tuning.

In the second Buckley book, the repertoire presented has a more significant structural use of keys. The increased pitch requirements here stem from the modulation to dominant, subdominant, relative, and parallel minor keys for the middle sections of ternary forms and the trios of marches and similar pieces.

It is ironic that Converse and Buckley, the two authors who paid the most attention to non-12EDO intonational issues in their earlier books, probably contributed most to the seeming need for a shift to 12EDO and fretting. Though the pieces in these books need an expanded number of nominal pitches, the number of actual pitches would have been even greater in just intonation. For example, the B required as a major 3rd above G in just intonation would be 22 cents (syntonic comma) lower than that required as a perfect 5th above E.

```
B  –  F#– C#  – G#
|     |    |     |
G – D – A – E – B – F#
```

The same is true for the major 3rd D-F♯ and perfect 5th B-F♯. This intonational problem would arise again with each new key presented.

Of course, intelligent players with good ears could accommodate this kind of intonation on a fretless instrument; after all, it is common in the playing of bowed string instruments. The situation is exacerbated on the banjo because of the harmonic nature of the pieces. Since the earliest tutors, and, we might presume, in the performances of the earliest stage banjoists, the pieces played on the instrument relied heavily on chord arpeggiations and, somewhat less, on strummed chords. As this chordal vocabulary expanded, intonational issues increased as well.

This evidence points to a quickly evolving intonational practice in the 1850s and 1860s. The limited pitch palette and key choices of the first collections were easily learned, taught, and played in just intonation. The increasing complexity of the repertoire, requiring more essential chromaticism as well as the authors' intentions to teach more keys without changing the tuning made twelve-tone equal temperament a more desirable choice. This choice was made even more urgent by the strictures of teaching through print method books rather than in person. It is likely that, among at least some banjo teachers, a practice of teaching just intonation might have lingered until raised frets became ubiquitous.

In fact, quite possibly the nature of the pedagogy in the print tutors as well as the changes in the musical features of the repertoire they presented (presumably played on stage and in the parlor) contributed in no small part to the change from the banjo as an unfretted instrument to one that was virtually always fretted—at least in its commercially available form.

We should also keep in mind that many of the early banjoists were also fiddlers and this experience would shape their approach to the banjo. They would be undaunted when faced with a fretless neck. As time passed and the "guitar style" technique of picking the strings rather than striking as in the "banjo" or "stroke" style became more prevalent, more players probably came to the banjo from the guitar and would have felt more at ease with a fretted neck.

Recent research into tuning practice has shown that although equal temperament was considered to be the lingua franca of keyboard tuning from the nineteenth century forward, it has only been accurately executed by tuners since 1917. Meantones and well-temperaments were still used for many decades longer than most have supposed. The practice of intonation on other instruments, especially the bowed strings, has not been monolithic either. Examining these sources should lead us to a deeper understanding of the performance practices of banjo, insight into those of other instruments, and a richer intonational palette from which to draw in both contemporary and historically informed performances.

Notes

1. Mark Lindley defines temperaments: "Tunings of the scale in which some or all of the concords are made slightly impure in order that few or none will be left distastefully so." See Mark Lindley, "Temperaments" *Grove Music Online*, http://catalog.berklee.edu:2057/subscriber/article/grove/music/27643, accessed October 21, 2017.

2. David Doty, *The Just Intonation Primer: An Introduction to the Theory and Practice of Just Intonation* (San Francisco: Other Music, 1993), 1.

3. Sometimes written as 2:1.

4. In discussing intervals, it is customary to put the larger number in the numerator.

5. There is evidence that earlier cultures have had this knowledge as well.

6. Larry Polansky, Dan Rockmore, Douglas Repetto, Kimo Johnson, and Wei Pan, "A Mathematical Model for Optimal Tuning Systems," *Perspectives of New Music* 47, no. 1 (Winter 2009): 74.

7. Hermann von Helmholtz and Alexander John Ellis, *On the Sensations of Tone as a Physiological Basis for the Theory of Music*, 2nd English ed. (New York: Dover Publications, 1954), 41.

8. Mark Lindley, *Lutes, Viols and Temperaments* (Cambridge: Cambridge University Press, 1984).

9. Gumbo Chaff, *The Complete Preceptor for the Banjo* (Boston: Oliver Ditson & Co., 1851).

10. Thomas F. Briggs, *Briggs' Banjo Instructor* (Boston: Oliver Ditson, 1855).

11. Phil. Rice, *Phil. Rice's Correct Method for the Banjo: With or Without a Master* (Boston: Oliver Ditson & Co., 1858).

12. James Buckley, *Buckley's New Banjo Book* (Boston: Ditson & Company, 1860), and James Buckley, *Buckley's Banjo Guide* (Boston: Oliver Ditson & Co., 1868).

13. Septimus Winner, *Winner's New Primer for the Banjo* (New York: Wm. A. Pond, 1864).

14. Frank B. Converse, *Frank B. Converse's Banjo Instructor Without a Master* (New York: Dick & Fitzgerald, 1865), and idem, *Frank B. Converse's New and Complete Method for the Banjo With or Without Master* (New York: S. T. Gordon, 1865).

15. For brevity's sake, I use the word *fret* to refer to both raised frets and flush fret markers since the differences are moot for the present discussion.

16. Commonly known to the early banjo revival community as "the green book."

17. Briggs, *Banjo Instructor*, 8.

18. Commonly referred to as "the yellow book."

19. More properly, "octave."

20. Converse, *Instructor*, 11–12.

21. Lindley, *Lutes, Viols and Temperaments*, 21.

22. Buckley, *New Banjo Book*, 6.

23. A better approximation would be 17.817 used by modern luthiers instead of 18 for the logarithmic progression.

24. For other historical approaches to fretting, see Lindley, *Lutes, Viols and Temperaments*.

25. Buckley, *Banjo Guide*, 6.

26. Doty, *Just Intonation Primer*, 36–45.

27. Ross W. Duffin, *How Equal Temperament Ruined Harmony (and Why You Should Care)* (New York: W. W. Norton, 2007), 109.

CHAPTER 16

Gus Cannon—"The Colored Champion Banjo Pugilist of the World" and the Big World of the Banjo

Tony Thomas

Editor's Headnote

Gus Cannon's banjo playing might be thought of as arising from the long history of black banjo playing, much of which is presented, from new perspectives, in earlier chapters in this book. Although, to a limited extent, that thought is true, it leads to placing Cannon in the category of "folk musician," where previous commentators on his life and career have placed him, in line with studies of other African American banjoists who were folk musicians. Tony Thomas presents Cannon's life and recordings as offering a different perspective on African American banjo playing in the late nineteenth and early twentieth centuries. He demonstrates that Cannon, and African American musicians like him, were "nested" in what he aptly calls "the big world of the banjo" in that period. Cannon was an up-to-date professional musician, and the chapter focuses on his 1927–30 recordings, dealing with his repertory, his recording partners, and, especially, the details of his banjo playing style, including the tunings he used.

The August 2, 1919, *Indianapolis Freeman* described "Show No 1" of the Min-Hal-Erb Strutters, a black medicine show then touring "Old Kentucky." It reported that "Mr. Guss Cannon," "the colored champion banjo pugilist of the world," playing with "Prof. H. W. Woods and his Little Jazz Band," was "offering $1,000 for his equal" on the five-string banjo.[1]

Cannon's billing as the "colored champion banjo pugilist" surely references what the nineteenth-century banjoist Frank B. Converse called "the day of 'musical sparing bouts,' 'the banjo pugilistic age.'" In the middle and late nineteenth century, European American banjoists took off the minstrel mask and established themselves as soloists and virtuoso musicians through celebrated banjo contests and one-on-one challenges like the one Cannon offered. The editors of *S.S. Stew-*

art's Banjo and Guitar Journal, the banjo world's preeminent publication, judged the "'pugilistic' banjo age" "a thing of the past" in 1890, but in 1919 that age lived on with Gus Cannon's thousand-dollar challenge. Yet, the "colored champion" also echoes the African American banjo star Horace Weston (1825–90), whom the *S.S. Stewart's Banjo and Guitar Journal* advertised as "The Champion Banjoist of the World."[2] Both allusions represent the degree to which Cannon represented not only an African American folk continuity in banjo playing, but the larger world of banjo playing that emerged in the nineteenth century involving African American, European American, and European banjoists playing folk, show business, and parlor music.

Gus Cannon's thirty-four recordings from 1927 to 1930 for Paramount, Victor, and Brunswick records are unique in black banjo history.[3] No other early twentieth-century African American five-string banjoist was recorded so extensively. When "the colored champion banjo pugilist of the world" first recorded in 1927, he had played the banjo thirty-two years and had toured for thirteen years in medicine shows as "Banjo Joe," the name on his first records.[4]

These recordings suggest how African American five-string banjoists might have played blues and ragtime-influenced popular music in the late nineteenth and early twentieth centuries. Cannon's 1927–30 recordings link him to the nineteenth- and early twentieth-century's big world of banjo, a world of intensive international interaction between folk, show business, popular music, and parlor banjoists, promoted by banjo manufacturers, professional banjo teachers, venders of banjo publications and sheet music, and international star banjo entertainers. This banjo world is commonly associated with middle-class white parlor banjoists, white banjo capitalists like S. S. Stewart, and white banjo recording stars like Vess L. Ossman and Fred Van Eps. Yet, Cannon's life leading to his 1927–30 recordings and the recordings themselves suggest that African Americans like him were also nested in this big world of the banjo.

As such, Cannon's life and recordings offer a different perspective on African American banjo playing than offered by previous studies of African American banjo playing. Those studies concentrated on late twentieth-century Upper South African American banjo survivors' playing as a folk tradition, on exchange between white and black folk banjoists, and on their links with West African tradition. Most of these Upper South black banjoists used the down-picking and the thumb and index finger picking banjo techniques.[5] Cannon's recordings illustrate his mastery of the guitar banjo style, the dominant international banjo technique of the late nineteenth century.[6] Folklorists and banjo enthusiasts captured the music of the Upper South banjoists after it passed out of black vernacular use. Yet, from 1927 until 1930, the Paramount, Brunswick, and Victor record companies considered Gus Cannon's music as commercial "product" for African American record buyers. While the Upper South folk banjoists played a rich repertoire of old-time folk tunes, Cannon's 1927–30 recordings included only one old-time banjo song, "Feather Bed." Surveying the repertoire of late twentieth-century Virginia and West Virginia black traditional banjoists, Robert B. Winans found that blues were "a minor portion" of their repertoire.[7] Yet, twenty blues dominated Cannon's thirty-four recordings, and he called two other recordings blues.[8] He also recorded five ragtime-influenced popular songs.

A Life of Motion as a Worker and an Entertainer

Cannon's early life of constant motion brought him to sites of intense convergence and exchange between folk, blues, ragtime, and black and white show business music. He was born on Henderson Newell's plantation, north of Red Banks, in Marshall County, Mississippi, on September 12, 1883.[9] During his childhood, the family moved from plantation to plantation in the Red Banks-Victoria area, a typical pattern in Mississippi. In Red Banks, Cannon "grew up with banjo and fiddle songs—'John Henry and all that mess'—all around him." While his parents did not play instruments, his brothers played: Louis played guitar, Elmore played bowed bass, and Houston played "good banjo." His older brother Tom, a Spanish American war veteran, taught Gus "the rudiments of fiddle" in Red Banks.[10]

In 1895, 12-year-old Gus left to help his brother Tom sharecrop cotton in Hushpuckena in the Mississippi Delta Southwest of Clarksdale. Cannon said he learned his first down-picking banjo tune, "Old Johnny Booker, Call That Gone," at the age of 12 from "Old Man Saul Russell," an African American, in Hushpuckena.[11] Cannon told Hurley that he learned the thumb and index finger picking banjo playing style a few months later from another black banjoist, Bud Jackson, originally from Alabama, but living in Clarksdale.[12] At 14 in 1897, he began playing banjo and fiddle for black country dances.[13] At 15, when his brother gave him $10.00 and told him to make his own way, Gus Cannon joined the masses of African Americans walking the roads and riding the rails seeking work. He sharecropped, worked on railroads, dug ditches, built levees, and was a roustabout on riverboats. In his late teens and early twenties, he lived and worked up and down the Mississippi valley and elsewhere across the South wherever work could be found. In addition to playing banjo, Cannon had become "a proficient fiddler, an adequate guitarist, and could find his way around a piano."[14]

A Hotbed of Musical Innovation

Until Memphis replaced it around 1908–10, the Mississippi Delta remained the center of Gus Cannon's musical life. Though he sometimes worked out of the Delta and Mississippi, "Gus kept returning to Hushpuckena and Clarksdale to see friends, help in the fields, and play for dances."[15] The Mississippi Delta, with its concentrated black population, intense economic development, and unique rewards for black musicians, was a hotbed of musical innovation. In 1895, when Cannon arrived, the Delta resembled a frontier. Much of the land had been recently cleared and settled. Plantation owners paid premium wages to lure black laborers from across the South into the Delta. David Evans explains that the Delta's "highly intensified plantation and sharecropping system made the region somewhat like a rural factory, sharing to a certain degree some of the characteristics of an urban environment." The Mississippi River and the railroads that crisscrossed the Delta delivered new musicians from across the South and beyond. Elijah Wald explains that the Delta's black population, characterized by "youth and mobility," was "in flux, ready to cast off the old ways and receptive to new musical fashions," and its distinctive blues style "was as much of a sign of modernity as any links to the African past."[16]

Money in black hands there offered musicians like Cannon financial opportunities. He made "$2.50 a night" playing Saturday night "balls" at age 14 in 1897, compared to $6.00 he made working an entire week in a levee camp around 1900.[17] Charlie Patton, the best-paid Delta blues performer, made between $50.00 and $100.00 a week. These opportunities intensified competition between musicians, favoring those with the most modern and developed styles,[18] making the Delta not only a center for the newly emerging blues, but also for ragtime and the bluesy, raggy country dance music represented by Cannon's recordings of "The Cairo Rag" and "The Pig Ankle Strut."

Ragtime pervaded the Mississippi Delta in Cannon's formative years.[19] The Harvard archeologist Charles Peabody surveyed the music of black laborers who excavated Indian Mounds for him in 1901 and 1902 in Coahoma County where Clarksdale is located. While these African Americans sang hymns and blues, they favored ragtime tunes like "Molly Brown" and "Goo-Goo Eyes," and called most other secular music, including early blues, "ragtimes." Peabody thought their tunes were more suited to May Irwin, a Canadian American Broadway star, than his rural African Americans.[20] Yet, the popularity of "Goo Goo Eyes" and the likening of the laborers' music to that of May Irwin illustrate a more profound interchange than Peabody understood.[21] Such ragtime popular music resonated with black Mississippians because it reflected black music. These years saw "the emergence of black music, especially ragtime, as a favorite form of popular music" in the whole country.[22] May Irwin, who became a star by singing songs by black composers and by "portraying the black male characters of her coon songs," exemplified this interest.[23]

What Peabody calls "Goo Goo Eyes" is "Just Because She Made Dem Goo Goo Eyes," a 1900 coon song hit by the white songwriters John Queen and Hughie Cannon (the author of "Bill Bailey, Won't You Please Come Home"). Significantly, Peter Muir points out that "Goo Goo Eyes" was Hughie Cannon's "first proto blues." Muir defines such songs as "compositions published before the 1912 start-up of the blues industry that show a clear musical and/or textual relationship to blues."[24] Cannon's song with its opening line "Can You Blame the Colored Man (for making those Goo Goo Eyes)" is a parody of "Goo Goo Eyes" focusing on Booker T. Washington's 1901 visit to Theodore Roosevelt at the White House. It shares the same melody as Queen and Cannon's song.[25] The January 11, 1902, *Indianapolis Freeman* suggests a black show business origin for "Can You Blame the Colored Man." It reported, on December 23, 1901, that James J. Helton, a black comedian, opened at the Mascotte Theater of Tampa, Florida, and "made an instantaneous hit with his clever monologue and a parody on 'Goo Goo Eyes,' relative to the Roosevelt-Washington episode."[26] Cannon learned "Can You Blame the Colored Man" in the early 1900s in Coahoma County from Alec Lee, a Clarksdale slide blues guitarist.[27]

Being pulled to the Delta was decisive for Gus Cannon. If he had stayed in Red Banks, he might never have learned banjo from Old Man Saul Russell or met Bud Jackson[28] who taught him the two-finger style.[29] He might never have run into Alec Lee, the Clarksdale slide guitar player who taught him two songs Cannon recorded in his first recording session, "Poor Boy" and "Can You Blame the Colored Man."[30] Indeed, Cannon and Lee may have been among the Coahoma County laborers Peabody described. Certainly, Cannon and Lee crafted their music for black folk like Peabody's laborers. In Clarksdale, Cannon first came to admire Jim Turner, the Alabama-born master fiddler of both black traditional fiddling and the newer ragtime and show music. He also came to admire W. C. Handy, who from 1903 to 1905 led a twenty-piece brass band for the Knights of Pythias that played on Clarksdale's main street every Saturday. Handy also led a ten-piece dance orchestra that was known throughout the Delta. By 1904, Handy's dance orchestra had added blues-influenced tunes like "Make Me a Pallet Floor" to its marches, waltzes, and ragtime.[31]

After 1908, Gus Cannon sharecropped on Dillehunt's plantation in Ashport, Tennessee, where he joined a band that included Jim Guffin, a fiddler and guitarist who introduced him to jug playing.[32] Around 1910, Cannon began to play with the guitarist and blues singer Ashley Thompson from Ripley, Tennessee, and the harmonica virtuoso Noah Lewis from Hennings, Tennessee. Cannon worked dances, juke joints, and country suppers ranging north into Missouri and south into Mississippi. He began visiting Memphis, sometimes with Lewis and/or Thompson. After sharecropping on Macon Road east of Memphis, in Chatfield, Arkansas, and near Cairo, Illinois, he permanently relocated to Memphis in 1918.[33]

In Memphis, Cannon maintained contact with Thompson and Lewis. When not touring with medicine shows, he "seems to have divided his time between doing odd jobs on farms and going back and forth to Ripley to see friends and play for dances." In the middle and late 1920s, when jug bands became popular in Memphis, he organized a jug band that worked weekend dances in Arkansas and Mississippi. Cannon also became "a common sight" in Memphis's Church

Park on weekends where "the country people would come to town" for a good time.[34]

Over these years Cannon learned to play the music of the new dances that arose in the black South in the early twentieth century. Some like the slow drag were danced to the blues.[35] Other dances, "a crazy-quilt blend of folk material such as shuffles, struts, hops, twists, and grind, with a touch of flat-footed Buck,"[36] required the swinging, raggy music Cannon played in his recordings of "Jazz Gypsy Blues." Black country people new to the towns like those who heard Cannon at Church Park might have created these dances. Marshall Winslow and Jean Stearns explain that in this period "the strongest component of Afro-American dance occurred in less-well-to-do urban surroundings, where the Negro folk, in the course of adjusting to city life, were less inhibited and more footloose."[37]

This music was not separate from the show business music of the African American medicine shows, minstrel and tent shows, and traveling musicals that spread over the South in the early twentieth century. Gus Cannon was part of that world. From 1914 to 1930, from spring until fall, he toured the South and Midwest as a medicine show entertainer. He worked shows headquartered in Clarksdale, Mississippi; Memphis, Tennessee; Indianapolis, Indiana; Nashville, Tennessee; and Louisville, Kentucky, that traveled to Tennessee, North Carolina, Virginia, Louisiana, Arkansas, Tennessee, Kentucky, Alabama, Illinois, Missouri, and the Midwest, "all the way to Chicago."[38] Touring entertainers like Cannon spread dances like "the snake hips, cakewalk, Texas Tommy, Virginny breakdown, black bottom, Charleston, and Georgia hutch."[39] The shows reached into the most remote areas. For example, the Texas songster Mance Lipscomb said black folk around Navasota where he lived in East Texas learned the slow drag from black dancers from the Barnum and Bailey Circus.[40]

How Cannon Played the Five-String Banjo in His 1927–30 Recordings

Cannon's banjo technique is not an arcane detail of interest only to banjoists. It marks the exchange between African American banjo playing and the late nineteenth century and early twentieth century's big international world of popular music and parlor banjo. Speculations about Cannon's banjo playing on recordings have focused on "folk" styles such as the idea he used the traditional two-finger style he learned from Bud Jackson on these recordings miss the mark.[41] The belief that I advanced before this study that Cannon used a flat pick is equally wrong.[42] Some of these misunderstandings reflect the way Cannon played the banjo in the 1960s and 1970s when age, problems with his hands, and alcoholism limited him physically and when he attempted to cater to paternalistic notions white audiences had of an aged black "folk" banjoist, rather than the needs of black dancers.[43]

Most importantly, such misunderstandings ignore the world of banjo exchange Gus Cannon inhabited. Cecelia Conway, for example, calls the banjo style associated with Cannon's jug band recordings "unorthodox."[44] On the contrary, Cannon used the guitar banjo style, the international banjo world's orthodox style at the time he learned the banjo. Then, internationally famous African American performers and African American parlor banjoists played guitar banjo, a style closely linked to the ragtime popular music Cannon absorbed in the Mississippi Delta and played on his recordings.

As "Banjo Joe," "the colored champion banjo pugilist of the world," Gus Cannon had mastered several banjo techniques, not only guitar banjo. In his 1967 interview with University of Memphis Professor F. Jack Hurley, Cannon demonstrated five different banjo styles: clawhammer, which he called "banjo"; strumming the banjo's four top strings, which he called "tenor"; strumming all five strings, which he called "five-string"; and two-finger picking, while he attempted tunes like the waltz "Daisy Bell" (often called "Bicycle Built for Two") and "Beale Street Blues" in the guitar banjo style. He also played down-picking banjo songs like "Johnnie Booker" and a down-picked version of "Old Blue" that resembled the one the North Carolina black banjoist Dink Roberts played.[45]

Yet, on at least eighteen of his recordings Cannon plays an articulate version of the guitar banjo style.[46] The Paramount recording of "Jonestown Blues," his introductions to "Springdale Blues" and "Hollywood Rag," and his two recordings of "Money Never Runs Out" illustrate this style clearly. His lead playing combines single-string playing with two-, and three-, and, possibly, four-string pinches.[47] Especially accompanying himself or his bandmates, Cannon often alternated pinches with picking the lowest available note in the chord. Only pinched-chord accompaniment can be heard on the Jug Stompers' "Ripley Blues," "Pig Ankle Strut," "Noah's Blues," "Cairo Rag," "Bugle Call Rag," and "Viola Lee Blues." On other tunes, pinched chords prevail once Cannon plays the jug. In these recordings, he made good use of his fifth string and rarely down-picks.

Gus Cannon's consistent use of pinched chords strongly suggests that he fingerpicked with three or four fingers. The poor recording quality makes it impossible to rule out that on some tunes he played two-finger style or even used a flat pick. However, banjoists playing with a flat pick or with two fingers cannot pinch with the speed and precision he displayed. On rapid-fire tunes like "Pig Ankle Strut," "Hollywood Rag," "Cairo Rag," and "Bugle Call Rag," Cannon pinched chords so precisely that his banjo and Elijah Avery's guitar and six-string banjo-guitar sound like one instrument.[48] Obviously, two-finger style banjoists cannot pinch three-note chords. Flat-pick banjoists pinch with their middle and fourth fingers while holding the pick held by the thumb and index finger. They must often pinch in a direction opposite to the motion of the thumb and index finger. Consequently, they reserve this technique for slow tunes, not the fast music where Cannon's pinching excelled.

The Memphis banjoist and guitarist Bob Bostick met Cannon in the 1950s and asked Cannon to teach him how he played banjo. What Cannon showed Bostick over the years is the guitar banjo style. Bostick likened Cannon's finger style to classical guitar technique, itself the origin of guitar banjo style. Bostick said Cannon finger-picked using his thumb on the fifth and fourth strings, the index finger on the third string, the middle finger on the second string, and the ring finger on the first string. Cannon added his fifth finger for tremolos. Bostick said Cannon felt using four fingers was better than the two-finger style because it added more fingers.[49]

Cannon played most of his tunes in C, G, or F, keys easily played in the gCGBD tuning, the standard tuning of the guitar banjo style.[50] Most of the 1927–30 recordings sound as if the banjo is tuned in the gCGBD tuning. Bostick noted that in later years Cannon usually tuned his banjo gCGBD even for tunes played in the key of G for which folk banjoists usually retune their banjo to the gDGBD tuning.[51] However, in the Hurley interview, Cannon can be heard retuning his banjo from the G tuning to the C tuning after playing and singing "Old Blue." His 1927–30 recordings included fifteen songs in C, eight in G, three in F, three in D, two in E, two in D♯, and one in B♭. Most of the non-C tunes were in G, F, and D, keys that are not difficult to play in the drop C tuning. Cannon's two recordings in E—the slide blues "Poor Boy" in an open E tuning and the banjo song "Feather Bed" whose tuning cannot be determined due to the poor recording—are exceptions.

On the tunes in B♭ and in D♯ Cannon might have altered the pitch of his banjo. At the same 1927 Paramount session Cannon recorded the "Madison Street Rag," played in D♯ and B♭ (the song has sections in different keys), and he played the next song, "Jazz Gypsy Blues" in B♭. On both songs, the banjo sounds as if it is tuned down a whole step from gCGBD to fB♭FAC, so the same fingering needed to play in C or F in the gCGBD tuning produces tunes in B♭ and D♯. In 1928, Cannon recorded "Madison Street Rag" with the Jug Stompers in F and C, not D♯ and B♭. Similarly, the two Beale Street Boys recordings appear to have the banjo either tuned to a higher pitch or capoed so that playing as one would to play in C came out in D♯ on "Last Chance Blues."

Most of Cannon's recording in keys other than C featured his band mates. All eight songs in G featured Ashley Thompson or Noah Lewis, his two band mates from the Ripley-Henning area in Tennessee.[52] Thompson or Lewis sang six of these songs, and the other two, the instrumentals "Ripley Blues" and "Noah's Blues," featured Lewis's harmonica. Cannon played all his other instrumentals except the Paramount recordings of "Madison Street Rag" and "Jazz Gypsy Blues," discussed above, in C. His musical partner Hosea Woods preferred to sing in D, D♯, and F. Cannon recorded his Beale Street Boys blues duets with Woods in D♯ and in F. Woods recorded "Last Chance Blues" with the Jug Stompers and his duet with Cannon on "Mule Get up in the Alley" in D. Similarly, Woods sings "Prison Wall Blues" in F.

The guitar banjo technique dominated the banjo world when Cannon became "the colored champion banjo pugilist of the world." After the Civil War, this style spread rapidly throughout the United States, England, and other English-speaking countries, through the travels of banjo entertainers; the popularity of banjo tutors; the flood of banjo magazines, books, and contests; and schools championing it. Guitar banjo arrangements of popular music, particularly rags, marches, cake wakes, and even some classical pieces, became a major business. The arrangements were bought not only by entertainers, but by parlor banjoists in middle-class homes, many of whom belonged to the banjo clubs, banjo orchestras, and banjo, mandolin, and guitar clubs promoted by banjo manufacturers and teachers. Masters of this style like Vess L. Ossman, Alfred A. Farland, Fred Van Eps, and Fred Bacon became national stars through their concerts and recordings.[53]

Certainly, Cannon played differently from white parlor banjoists or Van Eps and Ossman. Classic banjo pieces "often consist of several contrasting sections in different keys and use up-the-neck chords."[54] However, all of Cannon's recordings except "The Madison Street Rag" are in one key. Cannon did not play "up-the-neck chords." Aiming to play loudly he chiefly stayed below the fifth fret where more volume and greater sustain can be produced. In the Hurley interview, he explained he once tried using finger picks, but he played so hard that he knocked the picks off his fingers. Musically illiterate, Cannon did not participate in the standard notation discourse of guitar banjo's banjo tutors, banjo magazines, and sheet music.[55]

Cannon was not the only African American to play guitar banjo. Horace Weston and the Bohee Brothers, internationally prominent black banjo entertainers of the nineteenth and early twentieth centuries, played both guitar banjo and the stroke style of down-picking.[56] In 1884, Charles. P. Stinson (1854–1911) gained national notoriety as the first African American banjoist permitted in a major banjo contest. He gained even more notoriety when he won a gold medal as best player in a contest in Kansas City in 1887. He toured the United States, the Netherlands, Germany, Great Britain, France, Italy, Scotland, Ireland, and Belgium with minstrel companies and as a soloist. He also manufactured banjos in the 1880s; taught banjo, mandolin, and guitar in Youngstown, Ohio; and later managed theaters in Pittsburgh. In 1911, just before his death, Stinson teamed up with the comedian and banjoist Vance Lowry, in what the *Indianapolis Freeman* expected would be "a strong vaudeville attraction."[57] Hosea Easton (1854–199), born in Hartford, Connecticut, who toured the world as "America's Great Banjo King," arrived in Australia in 1877 with a black show business troupe and remained there the rest of his life. As both teacher and entertainer he became a seminal figure in spreading the guitar banjo style in Australia and New Zealand. Two thousand admirers attended his Sydney Australia funeral.[58]

The late nineteenth- and early twentieth-century parlor banjo movement that centered on the guitar banjo technique to an extent that it is often called parlor banjo is often thought of as exclusively white. Yet, African Americans participated in this movement's banjo, guitar, and mandolin societies. In the 1890s, an African American, William A. Heathman, was "elected to the leadership of the University Banjo, Mandolin, and Guitar Club" in his second year at Boston University, and retained the position until he graduated. The photographer Frances Benjamin Johnston's 1898 photos of Hampton Institute include one of eleven uniformed students including two banjoists, configured as a standard banjo, mandolin, and guitar society. Some of the black societies held large public concerts. More than five hundred attended the August 8, 1901, concert of Atlantic City's Crescent Banjo, Mandolin, and Guitar Club, an African American group. In March 1902, Washington, DC's Aeolian Mandolin, Guitar and Banjo Club, "the largest colored club of its kind," had thirty members and scheduled performances in Washington, Baltimore, and Philadelphia that April. In April 1903, more than two thousand people filled the Zion Baptist Church in Washington for a musical and literary program featuring the Aeolians and others.[59]

Ragtime and Guitar Banjo

Cannon learned the banjo and much of his repertoire in the heyday of ragtime, and the five-string banjo and the guitar banjo style were closely associated with ragtime. Cannon plays some of his most developed guitar banjo on the rag "The Madison Street Rag" and on "Can You Blame the Colored Man" and "My Money Never Runs Out," his refashioning of two coon songs, a ragtime genre. His most famous song, "Walk Right In," alludes to another coon song. Indeed, Robert Cantwell suggests that ragtime may have originated in black adaptation of guitar banjo.[60] No less a figure in African American ragtime than Scott Joplin learned the banjo at age 7; used banjo-originated figures in pieces like the "Maple Leaf Rag"; dedicated his "Cascades" to the white banjo entertainers Kimball and Donovan; and hung out his shingle as a piano, banjo, and mandolin teacher in Sedalia, Missouri, in 1896.[61]

After 1897 saw the publication of banjo arrangements of Krell's "Mississippi Rag" and the composition of the "Alabama Rag," the first piece titled a "rag" written for the five-string banjo, music publishers produced a flood of banjo ragtime arrangements and banjo ragtime compositions in the guitar banjo style. The top cylinder recording guitar banjoist, Vess Ossman, began recording ragtime in 1897 and continued with ragtime recordings of his own ragtime compositions and adaptations of piano rags. The banjo's "percussive punch" and ragtime's popularity among banjoists made the five-string banjo "the most popular solo instrument for recording ragtime" in the days of acoustic recording.[62]

The prominence of coon songs in Cannon's repertoire reflects his connection with the ragtime-influenced popular music of the 1890s. "In the late 1890s, ragtime sung and performed by black musicians reached the mainstream popular stage" through coon songs.[63] Six hundred coon songs were published in the 1890s with some selling millions of copies. They were popular with black dancers because they first appeared in the popular dance forms like two-steps, cakewalks, and marches with "foot-tapping, time-clapping rhythms accompanying the ostensibly funny descriptive lyrics." Their syncopated beats and attractive rhythm, earlier associated with minstrel banjo and African American folk music, gave a new impetus to social dancing among African Americans as well as whites.[64] Cannon's recordings of "My Money Never Runs Out," "Can You Blame the Colored Man," and "Walk Right In" that he wrote with his band mate Hosea Woods, reflect how Cannon's repertoire was shaped by coon songs written by black ragtime show business song writers.

African American performers like Cannon often deleted racially offensive lyrics and turned coon songs into assertions of humor, bravado, and joy, as Cannon did in his recording "Can You Blame the Colored Man." In this song Washington's visit is transformed into a fantasy of wine, fine food, and luxury with Washington both "in his car" and renting a carriage to "take the whole town in."[65] Cannon's version of "My Money Never Runs Out" celebrates the revels of an opium addict ("I love my 'hop' says he") with "a money tree," who does not care if he ever wakes up. In black voices, these songs became dreams of high life with what black vernacular English now calls "swagger," creating the type of escape found in black bad man ballads like "Stagolee." Cannon's version of "My Money Never Gives Out" combines two popular coon songs, "I Don't Care if I Never Wake Up" and "My Money Never Gives Out," written by Irving Jones, one of the most outstanding black writers of ragtime coon songs in 1900.[66] Cannon removed the term *coon* from both of his recordings.[67]

Cannon's most famous tune, "Walk Right In," which the Rooftop Singers took to the top of the Billboard charts in 1962, also flowed from this world of ragtime popular music. Paul Oliver links the words "sit right down, and honey, let your mind roll on" in "Walk Right In" to "La Pas Ma La," published in 1895 by Ernest Hogan (1865–1909), a major performer in black show business, with its line "put your hand on your head and let your mind roll on."[68] Hogan's hit illustrated the tight connection between such ragtime songs and the guitar banjo world. The September 1895 *Cadenza*, a Kansas City, Missouri, music journal that eventually rivaled *S.S. Stewart's Banjo and Guitar Journal* as the major publication of the fretted instrument world, announced, "All the local bands and orchestras are playing" an arrangement of Hogan's "La Pas Ma La" for banjo, mandolin, and guitar by the Kansas City publisher J. R. Bell.[69] This article probably refers to the banjo arrangement of the song by Mrs. C. L. Partee, wife and musical partner of Clarence L. Partee. As editor of the *Cadenza* and founder of the American Guild of Mandolinists, Banjoists, and Guitarists, Clarence L. Partee was a major figure in the world of parlor banjo.[70] Cannon's playing of "Walk Right In" was not an example of the polite parlor banjo the Partees promoted. Yet, the Partees and "the colored champion banjo pugilist of the world" shared the same big world of banjo exchange.

Cannon's use of the guitar banjo style in his 1927–30 recordings, his repertoire from the days when the five-string banjo was vital to ragtime popular music, and his title "The Colored Champion Banjo Pugilist of the World" express how he was an active participant in the big world of banjo exchange of the late nineteenth and early twentieth centuries. In this world African American folk banjoists, show business banjo entertainers, parlor banjoists, banjo teachers, and, banjo makers were in permanent exchange not only with their white American counterparts, but also their counterparts in Europe and other continents. To understand banjoists like Cannon, the study of African American banjo playing must go beyond the banjo as African American folk tradition and its links with white folk banjoists to examine the intense interaction between black banjoists and this big world of the banjo.

Notes

The author is indebted to David Evans, Samuel Charters, and Robert B. Winans for their support and advice.

1. Clyde Richardson, "Notes from Min-Hal-Erb Strutters," *Indianapolis Freeman*, August 2, 1919. From the research of Lynn Abbott and Doug Seroff supplied by David Evans of the University of Memphis. The *Freeman* regularly published messages from traveling black entertainers.

2. Frank B. Converse, *A History of the Banjo: Frank Converse's Banjo Reminiscences*, ed. Paul Heller (Create Space, 2011), 30; "First Banjo Tournament in America," *S.S. Stewart's Banjo and Guitar Journal* 7, no. 2 (June–July 1890), reproduced in *Tuckahoe Review* (April 1997): 15; "Horace Weston, 'The Champion Banjoist of the World,'" *S.S. Stewart's Banjo and Guitar Journal* 2, no. 11 (August–September 1884): 10. I am indebted to the banjo scholar Joel Hooks for the observation that the contests represented an attempt by minstrel banjoists to establish themselves as independent musicians (Hooks, email to the author, October 20, 2013).

3. Cannon played five-string banjo on all his 1927–30 recordings. He recorded six songs as "Banjo Joe" in Chicago for Paramount Records in November 1927. All except the "Jonestown Blues," Cannon's only solo banjo and vocal recording, featured Blind Blake (Arthur Blake) on guitar. During the same session, Cannon's banjo accompanied Blind Blake's guitar and vocal recording of "He's in the Jailhouse Now." Cannon recorded four songs in Memphis for Victor Records on January 30, 1928, with Ashley Thompson on guitar and vocals and Noah Lewis on harmonica as Cannon's Jug Stompers. The Jug Stompers recorded ten songs for Victor in Memphis on September 5, 9, and 20, 1928, with Elijah Avery replacing Thompson on guitar and banjo guitar. Cannon continued on vocals, jug, and banjo. Lewis continued on vocals and harmonica. Hosea Woods on kazoo joined Cannon, Lewis, and Avery on the September 20 recording. Cannon, banjo and vocals, and Woods, guitar and vocals, made two recordings in Chicago for Brunswick Records as the Beale Street Boys on September 12, 1929. The Jug Stompers, composed of Cannon on banjo, jug, and vocals, Lewis on harmonica

and vocals, and Woods on guitar, guitar banjo, jug, vocals, and possibly banjo mandolin, recorded another twelve songs for Victor in Memphis on October 1 and 3, 1929, and on September 24 and 28, 1930. Two Document Records CDs contain all these recordings, and recordings Noah Lewis made apart from Cannon: *Gus Cannon: Complete Recorded Works in Chronological Order, Volume 1 (November 1927 to 20 September 1928)*, DOCD-5032, 1990, and *Gus Cannon: Complete Recorded Works in Chronological Order, Volume 2 (12 September 1929 to 28 November 1930)*, DOCD-5033, 1990. I follow the liner notes for these CDs by Chris Smith that coincide with the listings in Robert M. W. Dixon and John Godrich's *Blues and Gospel Records, 1890–1943* (Harrow, UK: Steve Lane Musical Publicity Services, 1963), 109–10. Corrections to both Smith and Dixon and Godrich are that Woods, not Cannon, sings lead vocal on the Beale Street Boys' recording of "Last Chance Blues." Also, Cannon plays banjo and Woods plays guitar on both Beale Street Boys recordings. Cannon does not play jug on all Jug Stompers recordings. Woods plays the jug while Cannon sings at least on the September 1930 recordings of "Wolf River Blues" and "My Money Never Runs Out," if not other recordings. Woods's jug playing is higher-pitched, faster, and more sputtery than Cannon's.

4. Once blues and folk music enthusiasts, starting with Samuel Charters in the 1950s, "rediscovered" him, Cannon made other recordings including a 1963 Stax Album, *Walk Right In*. Yet, these recordings reflect limitations on his playing imposed by age and health problems as well as catering to what he thought these white enthusiasts wanted of him.

5. For a definition of down-picking, see discussion on pages 94 and 95 of Chapter 6. The thumb and index finger style is fairly self-explanatory; while the thumb strikes with a downward motion, the index finger strikes with an upward motion.

6. Elias J. Kaufman and Robert B. Winans describe the guitar banjo technique: "the right hand stays more or less stationary over the strings, using two or three fingers to pluck upward on strings while the thumb plucks downward (similar to the finger style of guitar playing, hence its earliest name)." Robert B. Winans and Elias J. Kaufman, "Minstrel and Classic Banjo: American and English Connections," *American Music* 12 (1994): 25n18. This is not to be confused with six-string banjos configured like guitars called guitar banjos.

7. Robert B. Winans, "The Black Banjo-Playing Tradition in Virginia and West Virginia," *Journal of the Virginia Folklore Society* 1 (1979): 23.

8. Cannon's blues recordings are the Paramount recording of "Jonestown Blues"; the Victor recordings of "Poor Boy," "Minglewood Blues," "Big Railroad Blues," "Springdale Blues," "Ripley Blues," "Noah's Blues," "Heart Breakin' Blues," "Viola Lee Blues," "Riley's Wagon," "Last Chance Blues," "Tired Chicken Blues," "Going to Germany," "Rooster Crowing Blues," "Jonestown Blues," "Pretty Mama Blues," and "Wolf River Blues"; and, the Brunswick recordings of "Last Chance Blues" and "Fourth and Beale." Cannon's country rag, "Jazz Gypsy Blues," bears "blues" as a title but is not a blues, while "Prison Wall Blues" is a "popular blues," a genre of popular song alluding to "blues" but not a blues. Peter C. Muir discusses this genre in *Long Lost Blues: Popular Blues in America, 1850–1920* (Urbana: University of Illinois Press, 2010).

9. Bengt Olsson, "Biography," liner notes, *Cannon's Jug Stompers: The Complete Works in Chronological Order 1927–1930 including Gus Cannon as Banjo Joe*, Herwin 208, 1975, 33 1/3 rpm. "Biography" concludes with the dates "August–September 1973." Unless otherwise noted, biographical information about Cannon comes from this essay. Olsson gives as 1883 Cannon's birth year; 1884 and 1885 appear as Cannon's birth year in other sources.

10. Ibid.

11. In his 1967 interview with the University of Memphis professor F. Jack Hurley, Cannon first said he learned banjo in Hushpuckena at age 12. Then Cannon said he began playing the banjo at "8 years old." He told Olsson, "I made my first banjo from a guitar neck and a bread pan mama used to bake biscuits in" when he lived in Hushpuckena ("Biography"). Cannon told Samuel Charters that "his mother gave him the bread pan, and he put holes through the sides of it to hold the guitar neck" (Samuel Charters, *Sweet as Showers of Rain* [New York: Oak Publications, 1975], 29). But Cannon did not move to Hushpuckena until he was 12 when his mother's baking pans were back in Red Banks. Perhaps Cannon built his bread pan banjo in Red Banks before he moved to Hushpuckena. Perhaps this is a charming story Cannon made up to entertain folk music enthusiasts. See Gus Cannon, "Interview by F. Jack Hurley," February 7, 1967, Memphis State University Oral History Research Office Project Documenting Jazz and Blues in the Memphis Area. Tape recording transcribed by the author. Henceforth, this is referred to as the Hurley interview.

12. Hurley interview.

13. Olsson, "Biography."

14. Ibid.

15. Ibid.

16. David Evans, "Mississippi Blues Today and its Future," in *The Voice of the Delta: Charley Patton and the Mississippi Blues Traditions, Influences, and Comparisons: An International Symposium*, ed. Robert Sacre (Liège, Belgium: Presses Universitaires de Liège, 1987), 317; Alan Lomax, *The Land Where the Blues Began* (New York: Pantheon Books, 1993), xv; David Evans, "Charley Patton, the Conscience of the Delta," in *The Voice of the Delta: Charley Patton and the Mississippi Blues Traditions, Influences, and Comparisons: An International Symposium*, ed. Robert Sacre (Liège, Belgium: Presses Universitaires de Liège, 1987), 148; Elijah Wald, *Escaping the Delta: Robert Johnson and the Invention of the Blues* (New York: Amistad, 2004), 85.

17. Olsson, "Biography."

18. Evans, "Charley Patton," 144, 144, 149.

19. The author initially suspected Cannon's familiarity with ragtime popular songs reflected the links of the medicine shows he worked in with show business, but this music was in the air of the Delta where he first came into musical life.

20. Charles Peabody, "Notes on Negro Music," *The Journal of American Folklore* 16 (1903): 148–52, quotes on 148, 151, and 151.

21. Karl Hagstrom Miller, *Segregating Sound: Inventing Folk and Pop Music in the Age of Jim Crow* (Durham, NC: Duke University Press, 2010), 23–24.

22. Thomas Laurence Riis, *Just Before Jazz: Black Musical Theater in New York, 1890–1915* (Washington, DC: Smithsonian Institution Press, 1989), xxi.

23. Ibid., 34, 36, 42; Miller, *Segregating Sound*, 127.

24. Muir, *Long Lost Blues*, quotes on 189, 189, 181.

25. Dom Flemons, "Can You Blame Gus Cannon," *Oxford American* 83 (December 16, 2013), http://www.oxfordamerican.org/articles/2013/dec/16/oa83-can-you-blame-gus-cannon/, accessed January 15, 2014.

26. Lynn Abbott and Doug Seroff, *Out of Sight: The Rise of African American Popular Music, 1889–1895* (Jackson: University Press of Mississippi, 2002), 468n479. Cannon never claimed he wrote it or any other song except "Walk Right In."

27. Paul Oliver, *Songsters and Saints: Vocal Traditions on Race Records* (Cambridge: Cambridge University Press, 1984), 125.

28. That Cannon's brother in Red Banks played banjo does not ensure Gus would have learned the banjo. Traditional African American banjoists often talk of fathers or brothers who played the banjo who tried to prevent them from playing. Gus's role in family music making in Red Banks seemed to have been as a fiddler, not a banjoist.

29. This is contrary to Dom Flemons's unsupported assertion that Cannon learned to play banjo in "neighboring communities" to Red Banks (Flemons, "Can You Blame Gus Cannon").

30. Olsson, "Biography"; Oliver, *Songsters and Saints*, 125.

31. Hurley interview; David Robertson, *W.C. Handy: The Life and Times of the Man Who Made the Blues* (New York: Alfred A. Knopf, 2009), 38, 88, 93, 94, 98.

32. Olsson, "Biography." Like many other things, in his later years, Cannon made other claims about where he first played the jug.

33. Olsson, "Biography."

34. Ibid.

35. Lynne Fauley Emery, *Black Dance: From 1619 to Today* (Princeton, NJ: Princeton Book Co., 1988), 221; Jacqui, Malone, *Steppin' on the Blues: The Visible Rhythms of African American Dance* (Urbana: University of Illinois Press, 1996), 85.

36. Malone, *Steppin' on the Blues*, 65.

37. Marshall Winslow and Jean Stearns, *Jazz Dance: The Story of American Vernacular Dance* (New York: Macmillan, 1968), 24.

38. Olsson, "Biography."

39. Katrina Hazzard-Donald, *Jookin': The Rise of Social Dance Formations in African-American Culture* (Philadelphia: Temple University Press, 1990), 67.

40. Mance Lipscomb, *I Say Me for a Parable: The Oral Autobiography of Mance Lipscomb, Texas Bluesman, As Told to and Compiled by Glen Alyn* (New York: Da Capo Press, 1994), 247.

41. In the Hurley interview, Cannon clearly differentiates the two-finger style he learned from Jackson from his three- and four-finger popular music, blues, and ragtime style.

42. Tony Thomas, "Did Banjo Joe use a flat pick?" H-Southern-Music Discussion, http://h-net.msu.edu/cgi-bin/logbrowse.pl?trx=vx&list=H-Southern-Music&month=0902&week=b&msg=oi77tJoVaV8ECfcjDBC8tw&user=&pw=, accessed February 11, 2009.

43. This analysis of Cannon in his final years is based on the Bostick interview discussed below, and my discussions with David Evans, Robert B. Winans, Samuel Charters, and others who knew or visited Cannon during those years.

44. Cecelia Conway, *African Banjo Echoes in Appalachia: A Study of Folk Traditions* (Knoxville: University of Tennessee Press, 1995), 125.

45. Cannon's version is in the Hurley interview. For Dink's version, see Dink Roberts, "Old Blue," *Black Banjo Songsters of North Carolina and Virginia*, Smithsonian Folkways SFW40079, 1998, CD.

46. This banjo style is best exemplified by Cannon's playing on "Jonestown Blues," "Jazz Gypsy Blues," "Can You Blame the Colored Man," and "My Money Never Runs Out" in the Paramount Recordings; "Last Chance Blues" and "Fourth and Beale" in the Brunswick recordings; and "Springdale Blues," "Heart Breakin' Blues," "Riley's Wagon," "Last Chance Blues," "Tired Chicken Blues," "Walk Right In," "Mule Get up in the Alley," "Jonestown Blues," "Bring it with You When You Come," "Wolf River Blues," "Money Never Runs Out," and "Prison Wall Blues" in the Victor recordings. Cannon plays this style on parts of both recordings of "The Madison Street Rag" and on "Minglewood Blues," "Big Railroad Blues," "Rooster Crowing Blues," and "Pretty Mamma Blues."

47. In a pinch, the banjoist presses down on a string with the thumb and pulls up with the other fingers at the same time, producing a chord sound by playing all these strings at once. In contemporary bluegrass and two-finger style old time banjo, this term often applies to pinching only the first and fifth strings for emphasis.

48. Cannon and Avery had worked together in medicine shows since 1914. Their tight playing reflects their professionalism and long experience playing together. Olsson, "Biography."

49. Bob Bostick, telephone interview with the author, May 24, 2009; Bob Bostick, interview with the author, November 9, 2010, at Bostick's home, Memphis, Tennessee, digital video in possession of the author.

50. Cannon's 1927–30 recordings as reproduced in the Document recordings are in concert pitch except "Heart Breaking Blues," which is between B and C due to recording problems. While the pitch of the string instruments and voices on the recording can vary, harmonicas like the one played by Noah Lewis are set to a standard pitch.

51. Bostick interview, November 9, 2010.

52. The songs in G are all Victor recordings: "Minglewood Blues," "Ripley Blues," "Noah's Blues," "Viola Lee Blues," "Going to Germany," "Rooster Crowing Blues," "Pretty Mama Blues," and "Big Railroad Blues."

53. Patrick Huber, *Linthead Stomp: The Creation of Country Music in the Piedmont South* (Chapel Hill: University of North Carolina Press, 2008), quotes on 113, 114, and 114. See also Karen Linn's survey of this cultural movement in "The 'Elevation' of the Banjo in the Late Nineteenth Century," in *That Half-Barbaric Twang: The Banjo in American Popular Culture* (Urbana: University of Illinois Press, 1994), 5–39.

54. Bill Evans, *Banjo for Dummies* (Hoboken, NJ: Wiley Publishing, 2007), 153.

55. Samuel Barclay Charters, *The Country Blues* (New York: Da Capo Press, 1975), 118.

56. Lowell H. Schreyer, *The Banjo Entertainers: Roots to Ragtime, A Banjo History* (Mankato: Minnesota Heritage Press, 2008), 157; Hal Allert, email to the author, August 8, 2010.

57. Converse, *A History of the Banjo*, 52–53; "Musical," *Pittsburgh Press*, December 9, 1894, 9; *American Musical Times* (Youngstown, Ohio), December 1891, 4; "Gossip of the Stage," *Indianapolis Freeman* (Indianapolis), July 29, 1911, 6, NewsBank/Readex, Database: America's Historical Newspapers, SQN: 12CC9D2105DAA458. The Lowry-Stinson collaboration may be a link between five-string and tenor banjoists since Lowry went on to become a leading tenor banjo performer in New York and in Europe.

58. "Hosea Easton," *Australian Variety Theatre Archive Popular Culture Entertainment: 1850–1930*, http://ozvta.com/practitioners-e/, accessed February 19, 2013; Gary Le Gallant, "Bessie Campbell and the Fisk Jubilee Singers," http://www.nugrape.net/bessie.htm, accessed March 7, 2013; Bessie Campbell, "Miss Bessie Campbell," *S.S. Stewart's Banjo and Guitar Journal* 13, no. 6 (February–March 1897): 4; Walter J. Stent, letter to the editor, *S.S. Stewart's Banjo and Guitar Journal* 16, no. 5 (December 1899–January 1900): 10. For more on Easton, see Matthew W. Wittmann, "Empire of Culture: U.S. Entertainers and the Making of the Pacific Circuit, 1850–1890" (PhD diss., University of Michigan, 2010), 231–87.

59. "The Only Colored Barrister Mr. Wm. A. Heathman Who Alone Represents the Afro-Americans in Providence," *Colored American* (Washington, DC), July 20, 1901, NewsBank/Readex, Database: America's Historical Newspapers, SQN: 12C5FB6B729DF260; Frances Benjamin Johnston, "Hampton Institute, Hampton, Va., ca. 1898—11 students in uniform playing guitars, banjos, mandolins, and cello," Prints and Photographs Online Catalog,

Library of Congress, http://www.loc.gov/pictures/item/2001703821/, accessed February 27, 2012; "The Sea's De News. A Sensation in Salons Circles—the City Still Wide Open—the Elite Dramatic Club on the Bills," *Colored American* (Washington, DC), August 17, 1901, NewsBank/Readex . . ., SQN: 12C5FB723827BB80; "Musical Melange," *Colored American* (Washington, DC), March 1, 1902, NewsBank/Readex . . ., SQN: 12CCE594216ACF40; "Echoes Pro The Complimentary: Musical and Literary Entertainment at Zion Baptist Church," *The Washington Bee* (Washington, DC), April 11, 1903, NewsBank/Readex . . ., SQN: 12CCED9DD26EC7D0.

60. Robert Cantwell, *Bluegrass Breakdown: The Making of the Old Southern Sound* (Urbana: University of Illinois Press, 1984), 104.

61. Ray Argyle, *Scott Joplin and the Age of Ragtime* (Jefferson, NC: McFarland & Company, 2009), 27; Lowell H. Schreyer, "The Banjo in Ragtime," in *Ragtime: Its History, Composers, and Music*, ed. John Edward Hasse (New York: Schirmer Books, 1985), 58; Henry L. Gates and Evelyn B. Higginbotham, *African American Lives* (New York: Oxford University Press, 2004), 461.

62. Cantwell, *Bluegrass Breakdown*, 66; and Schreyer, "The Banjo in Ragtime," 61–66.

63. Lynn Abbott and Doug Seroff, *Ragged but Right: Black Traveling Shows, "Coon Songs," and the Dark Pathway to Blues and Jazz* (Jackson: University Press of Mississippi, 2007), 11.

64. James H. Dormon, "Shaping the Popular Image of Post-Reconstruction American Blacks: The 'Coon Song' Phenomenon of the Gilded Age," *American Quarterly* 40 (1988): 450–71, quote on 453.

65. The dinner's significance was not only in the white racist opposition to the alleged social equality involved, but "progressive" Republican support for Washington who favored complete submission to southern segregationists and opposed those who fought for political or social equality for black people in the North and the South. It cemented Washington's Tuskegee Machine's control over black federal employment. See Jeffrey B. Perry's *Hubert Harrison: The Voice of Harlem Radicalism, 1883–1918* (New York: Columbia University Press, 2009), 126–35, for how Washington had the New York City educator Hubert Harrison, who coined the term *New Negro*, fired from the Post Office for criticizing Washington and exposing housing segregation.

66. Abbott and Seroff, *Ragged But Right*, quotes on 31, 31–32, 33, 30, and 39.

67. This contrasts with the white Grand Ole Opry star Uncle Dave Macon, who introduced his September 1926 Vocalion recording of "I Don't Care if I Never Wake Up" (Vocalion—15446) by explaining the song is about "a certain yellow coon." Tony Russell and Bob Pinson, *Country Music Records: A Discography, 1921–1942* (New York: Oxford University Press, 2004), 575.

68. Oliver, *Songsters and Saints*, 34.

69. Abbott and Seroff, *Out of Sight*, 445.

70. "La Pas Ma La," Ernest Hogan, "Arr. By Mrs. C. L. Partee," Abbott and Seroff, *Ragged But Right*, 446; all references I have found are to "Mrs. C. L. Partee" or "Mrs. Clarence Partee," rather than to her first name. "History," *American Guild of Music*, http://www.americanguild.org/images/about_history.html, accessed September 28, 2011; Jeffrey Noonan, *The Guitar in America: Victorian Era to Jazz Age* (Jackson: University Press of Mississippi, 2008), 32–33.

CHAPTER 17

Defining a Regional Banjo Style
"Old Country Style" Banjo or Piedmont Two-Finger Picking

Robert B. Winans

Editor's Headnote

This oral history-ethnographical chapter, like all the other chapters in this volume, delves into a previously unexplored corner of banjo history, the existence of a fairly unique style of playing the banjo found in the Piedmont areas of North Carolina and southern Virginia. It is based on fieldwork in these areas, areas in which Charlie Poole, an important banjoist of the early twentieth century, grew up and learned to play the banjo. A dozen informants are discussed, three of them in great detail, giving information about their playing styles, their repertoires, and their performance contexts. A number of the informants, originally guitar players, mentioned being influenced by black two-finger guitar picking, which had an impact on their banjo playing. The chapter is also a good companion piece to Tony Thomas's preceding essay on Gus Cannon since in both cases the "big world of the banjo" of the late nineteenth and early twentieth centuries, in which the classic finger style of banjo playing came into prominence, influenced both black and white banjoists.

A distinctive style of banjo playing developed in the Piedmont sections of northern and central North Carolina and southern Virginia (from south of Asheboro to Appomattox); in North Carolina it is generally called "old country style" to distinguish it from both the older frailing-clawhammer style and modern bluegrass. This style came into prominence in the area in the late 1920s and 1930s and was still widely played there in the early 1980s by older banjo players. In general, in the Piedmont in the early twentieth century, although the older down-stroking frailing style had not disappeared, it had largely been replaced by up-picking styles, either two-finger or three-finger. This chapter focuses on a particular two-finger picking style, glancing only occasionally at three-finger pickers. As Bob Carlin noted, "legions of two- and three-finger banjoists [were] living in the Piedmont of North Carolina" by the 1920s.[1]

The defining features of this Piedmont "old country style" include picking with thumb and index finger; playing almost exclusively in a band context, sometimes taking the lead but frequently in an accompaniment role, using syncopated, arpeggiated chords and bass runs; lead playing, which fills out melodies with a kind of ragtimey, syncopated shuffle out of chord positions; using the classic C-tuning (gCGBD) but pitched up a whole step to D (aDAC♯E); playing in many different keys without the use of a capo or retuning, out of moveable chord positions up the neck; and most striking of all, little or no use of the fifth string.

Glenn Davis (Luther Glenn Davis, 1909–86) was a prime exponent of this "old country style" banjo playing. He was a 72-year-old retired hosiery mill knitter when I met him in 1981 (figure 17.1).[2] He was raised southeast of Asheboro, his home in the latter part of his life, and began playing banjo in 1923. He had an uncle to the east in Chatham County who played in some form of frailing style, but Davis wanted to learn what he saw as a more up-to-date style. That was thumb-index finger picking, using picks. Like nearly all of the other players I am going to mention, he played on a Gibson Mastertone banjo (a much prized top-tension model, in his case, that he bought new in the 1930s); the passion for Mastertones was fierce among players of this style.

I describe his playing in some detail because the description establishes the features of the style. He played most often, and felt most comfortable, in the context

Figure 17.1. Glenn Davis; photo courtesy of author.

of a string band, rather than solo. In this context he most often played backup, but he also had a repertoire of pieces on which he played lead. His backup playing consisted of arpeggiated chords, rather syncopated, plucked two- and three-note chords, and bass runs. When he played lead, he played the melody and filled in around that with a kind of syncopated shuffle out of chord positions. It was neither strictly thumb lead nor finger lead but both, as needed. He tuned in the standard C-tuning (gCGBD), but with the strings pitched up one step (aDAC♯E) so that the basic key was D. However, out of this tuning he could play in virtually any key and did not use a capo to do this. He rarely used the fifth string, and in some pieces not at all.[3]

Davis's repertoire was a combination of traditional and popular songs, heavily weighted toward the latter. At his home, he demonstrated for me his solo or lead style, accompanied by his wife on piano. They played a lot of sacred songs, which they sang together. These included "Too Near My Heavenly Home," "As Pretty as Flowers," "I Want My Lord to Be Satisfied with Me," and "Private in the Army of the Lord." He played most of these in the key of B♭, without capoing his banjo. When asked why he used that key, he said that many good songs were in this key, especially ones he used to sing in a quartet, and that the key suited his voice. Secular pieces included "When You and I Were Young, Maggie," "Little Log Cabin in the Lane" (on which he used the fifth string more often than on other pieces), "Chicken Reel," "Whispering," "A Shanty in Old Shanty Town," "My Blue Ridge Mountain Home," "Back to My Old Smoky Mountain Home," "Sweet Bunch of Daisies," "Flop-Eared Mule," "Love Letters in the Sand," "In the Mood," "Under the Weeping Willow," "Alexander's Ragtime Band," and "Old 97." A lot of these pieces, since he played them with a subtle syncopation, had a nice "ragtimey" feel.[4]

On these pieces, Davis played the melody notes sometimes with his finger and sometimes with his thumb, and filled in between melody notes with plucked two- and three-note chords. In describing his playing, he said it was "more by chords, like a guitar." Like many of the other banjo players I will mention, Davis's first instrument was the guitar, which he played with thumb and index finger in a style similar to his banjo playing, suggesting a fairly direct transfer or at least strong influence. His guitar playing, in turn, was much influenced by a local black player, from whom he learned pieces like "Cincinnati Buck" and "The Titanic." Davis did not know of any black banjo players active at the time I visited, but did remember a left-handed black fiddler from near Siler City named Mayron (or Marion) Jordan.

Over the years, Davis regularly played in contests and festivals, and with lots of other area musicians in bands.[5] Except for playing at home accompanied by his wife (and it was clear that he felt a strong need for accompaniment), he felt most comfortable playing in a band. His band at the time I visited him was the Buffalo Ford String Band. The repertoire of this band was typical of older string bands in the region: a wide-ranging mixture of traditional dance tunes, pop tunes of the 1930s and 1940s, religious songs, and country and western songs, all done in a style that I would call sort of ragtimey (syncopated) and reminiscent of Charlie Poole and the North Carolina Ramblers.[6] This connection should not be too surprising since Poole grew up in the same region at a slightly earlier time than these men. The band members were Davis, Dwight Reece (fiddle), Lee Hemric (amplified mandolin), Maynard Perry (amplified rhythm guitar), and his brother Raymond Perry (electric bass), all in their sixties and seventies. Davis said the band played for fish fries and civic organization events, and not so much for dances anymore.

At the practice session I recorded, the band's pieces included "Pennsylvania Polka," "Carolina Darlin'," "Put Your Arms Around Me," "Lost Indian," "Spring Street Waltz" (learned directly from Arthur Smith), a very ragtimey "Evening Star," "There'll Be Some Changes Made," "Your Cheatin' Heart," "Any Time You're Feeling Lonely," "Five Foot Two," "Walking in My Sleep," "Pole Cat Rag," "Under the Double Eagle" (a favorite tune in the area), "Just Because," "The Old Rugged Cross," "What a Friend We Have in Jesus," "Down Yonder," and "Orange Blossom Special." This list indicates that their repertoire leaned more heavily toward popular songs than toward traditional dance tunes.[7]

In the band context, Davis played occasional lead, but mostly backup. As noted above, his backup style was mostly syncopated arpeggiated chords, in positions up and down the neck, varied at times with plucked two- and three-note chords, and bass runs. He largely ignored the fifth string in his backup mode.

Another practitioner of the style whom I visited in 1981 was Kelly Sears (1907–84),[8] born of a musical family in Chatham County near Siler City, where he lived at the time of my visit and where he was the proprietor of a fabric store (figure 17.2). His father bought Sears his first banjo when he was 9, and his mother, who sang and played the piano and some banjo, taught him to play "Catfish." His mother's brother played banjo in a two-finger style.[9] But he said that his most important mentor was a legendary banjoist from Randolph County, Daner Johnson (1879–1955). Sears took some lessons from him from 1919 to 1922, and he told me that "Johnson and my father were friends; they used to do a minstrel show or two together. And he wouldn't show anybody his technique on a banjo, but my dad got after him and he finally decided that he would show me few licks on it. He was the best I've ever heard. He'd play them old overtures. . . . and so I learned what I know by him."[10] What Sears learned apparently did not include using three fingers (i.e., thumb and two fingers), as did Johnson, rather than the two fingers (thumb and index) that Sears had started out with.

As Bob Carlin states: "At the turn of the century, Daner was the preeminent Piedmont banjoist using the new three-finger picking technique. Local musicians held him in the highest regard and often chose not to compete rather than to face him in local banjo contests. However, since Daner never recorded, his fame stayed within the Piedmont and one can only imagine how he sounded."[11]

Figure 17.2. Kelly Sears; photo courtesy of author.

Johnson not only competed in local contests but also, at least once, in a national contest. According to Sears, Johnson won the banjo contest at the 1904 Louisiana Purchase Exposition in St. Louis, playing the tune "Little Old Log Cabin in the Lane." Sears played this tune for me, in what he claimed was Johnson's style. This performance may be heard on *The North Carolina Banjo Collection* CD,[12] which may give one an idea of what Johnson sounded like, even though Sears played with two fingers what Johnson played with three.

Johnson's relatives had a somewhat different version of the St. Louis story. They told Kinney Rorrer that Johnson had beaten Fred Van Eps (not mentioned by Sears) in the contest and that the tune he played was "Dixie." Others in the area had also heard this version:

> Norman Woodlieff, guitarist on Charlie Poole's first records, reports seeing Daner Johnson play banjo at Poole's sister's house in Spray in the mid-'20s. Woodlieff had already heard Charlie rave about Johnson, a great banjo player who had defeated Van Eps at the St Louis banjo contest in 1904. According to Woodlieff, Johnson was a "real professional" who played *Dixie* on the five-string banjo unlike anyone he ever heard before or since.[13]

Johnson appears to have exerted a major influence on early twentieth-century banjoists in the North Carolina Piedmont. Rorrer presents some evidence to suggest that Daner Johnson may have been Charlie Poole's "major source of inspiration."[14] He points out that Johnson's three-finger picking style "evolved into a classical style of banjo which was popular by the 1890s." He goes on to say

that "on circumstantial evidence it seems quite probable that Poole learned from
Daner Johnson. . . . if Johnson was Poole's source of musical instruction, it would
certainly help explain Poole's use of a classical approach to his picking. Although
he could play the older clawhammer style, Charlie rarely used it in public, pre-
ferring the three-finger picking technique."[15] Carlin notes that "many Randolph
County musicians cite his influence, including Glenn Davis from Coleridge and
Kelly Sears of Siler City."[16]

This discussion of Daner Johnson serves to introduce the topic of the influence
of classic finger-style banjo (a three-finger style) on both two-finger and three-
finger banjoists in the Piedmont. The classic style was a popular stage, parlor,
and recording style whose peak popularity coincided with Johnson's heyday, that
is, the 1890s to the 1920s (which also coincides with the birth of the recording
industry).[17] That, taken with all of the remarks collected about his playing, particularly Kelly Sears's comment that "he'd play them old overtures" (which were a
part of the classic repertory, but not of the preexisting local banjo tradition), and
that his protégé Charlie Poole in fact recorded a number of classic finger-style
pieces, tells me that we should consider Johnson a classic finger-style banjoist.
And through his reputation and influence, together with the availability of recordings of the style, the "new" method of banjo playing that young musicians
wanted to emulate, the classic style fed into the development of both two-finger
and three-finger picking in the Piedmont. That progression would seem most
obvious with regard to the three-finger pickers, but it also makes sense for the
two-finger pickers as well. Johnson was chary about demonstrating his technique,
and with recordings musicians had only their ears to go on. So it is not surprising
that some musicians, inspired to learn the "new" style from hearing it, would work
out a simplified two-finger version of it. And this version, "old country style," has
a definite ragtime tinge since the classic finger-style repertory not only included
overtures (and marches, etc.), but was also heavily influenced by ragtime, whose
heyday was also the 1890s to 1920s period. In addition, the rare use of the fifth
string among players of the "old country style" correlates with classic banjo, where
the fifth string is generally used only when it is needed as a melody note.

Bringing up ragtime leads me back to Kelly Sears. His playing shared nearly
all of the elements found in the playing of Glenn Davis, including picking with
just thumb and index finger, using syncopated rhythms, playing out-of-chord
positions up the neck, playing in various keys without using a capo, using the
classic finger-style C-tuning (although with a difference since Sears did not tune
up a pitch), and almost no use of the fifth string. In fact, Sears carried that latter
feature to its logical conclusion: he eliminated the fifth string by playing on a plectrum banjo, with the exception of a few pieces that seemed to require occasional
use of the fifth string, for which he brought out a Stewart five-string banjo. His
explanation for using the plectrum banjo as his primary instrument was that the
fifth string was not very useful in the keys he most often played in (E♭ and A♭).

But Sears's playing is not exactly "old country style" as the others play it. His was truly a "ragtime" style, more than that of other area players, and Sears was also a little different because of playing solo or with piano accompaniment rather than with a band, at least at the point in his life at which I met him. He first performed professionally at around age 18 in medicine and other tent shows, and then had an act, called "The Musical Fools," with his brother Howard and Ray Lamb.[18] These early performances were followed by about fifteen years of more professional playing with others in vaudeville, on local radio, and sometimes in nightclubs. After this early professional music career, he went to work in his father's furniture-making business, followed by work for RCA in Camden, New Jersey, as a tool and die maker, before returning to North Carolina. In 1981, he was trying to get back into music on a more full-time basis. At that time he was playing with a piano accompanist for various local gigs, especially at shopping malls.

Sears highlighted the ragtime element in his playing by calling his style "ragtime piano style." He demonstrated this on several tunes—"Old 97," "When You and I Were Young, Maggie"—by first playing them straight and then "ragging" them, at which he was quite effective. By "ragging," I mean playing a note slightly ahead or behind where it would come in a "straight" version of a tune, and using other forms of presenting the melodic structure of the tune within "off-beat" rhythms. Other pieces he played during our session included "Downhome Rag," "Alexander's Ragtime Band" (another tune he learned from Daner Johnson), "St. Louis Blues," "Down Yonder," "Walking Up that Pathway to Heaven" (his own composition), "My Little Girl You Know I Love You" (comic song), "Old Piano Roll Blues" (part of his Liberace impression), "Margie," "Sweet Georgia Brown," and "Swanee River." Before going out with medicine shows, Sears had played locally for parties and square dances, pointing out that he would not have played ragtime for square dances. Square dance tunes he played for me included "Old Joe Clark" and "Redwing."

Sears had a few interesting things to say about past black musicians in the area. He talked about southern black guitar playing and, in particular, about what he called the "boogie lick" using thumb and index finger, suggesting once again that black two-finger guitar picking exerted an influence on the two-finger banjo picking of the region. He also said that he had very seldom encountered black banjo players, whom he in general associated with the "thumping," that is, frailing, style, and commented that he would rather have a black piano player to dance to (without specifying what kind of dancing).

Kelly Sears was clearly the most sophisticated banjo player in the region. But it seems likely that the less complicated and less sophisticated style of the others is a representation or reflection of this Daner Johnson-Kelly Sears-ragtime style.

Moving farther south, another area banjoist in this style who also had some early professional experience was Price Saunders (Sterling Price Saunders, 1916–83) (figure 17.3).[19] He was a 65-year-old housepainter living in Biscoe, North Carolina, south of Asheboro, when we met. He had played banjo since the late 1920s, when he consciously set out to learn a new style, different from frailing. That turned out to be a thumb and index-finger picking style similar to Glenn Davis's, but with some features of his own, especially a neat technique of playing runs on the bass string with a rapid back-and-forth movement of thumb and index finger, creating an effect similar to plectrum playing. Much of his picking was back and forth between the thumb on the second string and index finger on the first string. He said he never used the fifth string. His playing also included another feature sometimes found in the regional style, though Saunders used it much more regularly than the others: an occasional downward brush, as in frailing, of the index finger after it has picked up on a string, filling in after a sustained melody note. He used the same tuning as Glenn Davis (aDAC♯E), and also played out-of-chord positions much of the time and did not use a capo for different keys. And, again like Davis, when playing lead he alternated between thumb-lead and finger-lead as needed. He most often played with other people, and then more often played backup than lead, although he had a good repertoire of songs he could play lead on. Saunders played in this style as a professional musician for a number of years, first with J. E. Mainer, in 1939–40, taking Snuffy Jenkins's place, and then for a couple of years with Gurney Thomas and the Hillbilly Pals.[20]

Before working with Mainer, Saunders played for dances in people's homes in winter, and at picnics and ice cream socials the rest of the year. He said that his

Figure 17.3. Price Saunders; photo courtesy of author.

style (without his signature bass runs) was generally used in the area in his youth, in the 1930s and 1940s, before bluegrass. At one point, he described his style as being "between" frailing and bluegrass. Saunders said he did not learn his style from anyone in particular; he had just heard some people playing in the "new way" and set out to learn that style. He had some help from an uncle in Randleman who was a good guitar player and, even though he did not play the banjo, could show Saunders chords on the banjo. Another influence was Uncle Dave Macon, whose playing Saunders heard on recordings and on radio's Grand Ole Opry, although he wanted to play something more modern than what he considered Macon's older style, "the real old country style." Refining the description noted above, he suggested that his own style was between Macon's and bluegrass. In a further triangulation of where he saw his style fitting in, Saunders discussed Don Reno (not from the area) as an early bluegrass player who did some things similar to what Saunders did. "He [Reno] sort of worked the old-time country style and the bluegrass together for a while." And he agreed that his style was similar to Glenn Davis's. He also said that he picked up some of his tunes—that is, "Spanish Fandango"—from a banjo player in Star, North Carolina, Val Green, who played in the same style.

In my solo session with Saunders, he played the following tunes in his lead style: "Under the Double Eagle," "Long Journey Home," "Sweet Bunch of Daisies," "Kentucky," "Fly Around My Pretty Little Miss," "Listen to the Mocking Bird," "John Henry," "Grandfather's Clock," "Silver Bells," "The Old Country Church," "Spring Street Waltz," "Bells of St Mary's," "Chicken Reel" (for buck dancing), "Whistling Rufus" (a standard in the classic finger-style repertory), and "Wildwood Flower."

Price Saunders and his wife Orrie were both anxious for me to hear him play with Lauchlin Shaw (1912–2000),[21] a well-known area fiddler with whom Saunders most often played at the time, since playing solo was not what he usually did. So about three weeks later, I met with Saunders and Shaw, and a bunch of other musicians (as well as Bill Mansfield and a couple of other folklorists from Chapel Hill), at Shaw's "music house" in Spring Lake, North Carolina. Besides Shaw and Saunders, the other area musicians were Bill Green (Star), guitar; Wade Drye (Biscoe), guitar; and Walter (Mac) Mackenzie (Jackson Springs), string bass. This group played great old-time music for an hour, giving me a good opportunity to hear Saunders in his usual setting, a band. His two-finger style complemented Shaw's fiddle very nicely. He played lead on a few of his "signature" pieces, but for the most part he played backup, a combination of pinched and arpeggiated chords, with, as usual, no capo (or retuning) for key changes and no fifth string. The group's repertoire for the evening included "Ragtime Annie," "Eighth of January," "Little Old Log Cabin in the Lane," "Little Log Cabin for Sale" (a waltz, with nice guitar bass runs, on which Saunders took a lead, to which Shaw played a really nice harmony part), "Under the Double Eagle" (a real showpiece as a band number, especially Saunders's bass solo at the end), "Bells of St Mary's," "Honeysuckle Rose," "Bonny Eloise," "Liberty," "Mississippi Sawyer," "Soldier's Joy," "Flop-Ear Mule," "Peacock Rag," "Sugarfoot Rag," "Orange Blossom Special," and three apparently very local tunes that the guitarists were not familiar with, "Dancing Lady," "Song of the Birds," and "A Duck's Eyeball." As with Glenn Davis, the repertory presented in this and the previous paragraph shows a combination of popular tunes (with some age) and traditional tunes, with the former clearly outweighing the latter.

The banjoists discussed above define the central parameters of the "old country style"; other practitioners of the style can be presented in less detail. Somewhat younger musicians in the area also play in the "old country style." These include the Britts, whom I met at the old Britt family place in Star, North Carolina, near Biscoe. J. G. Britt (John Gainey Britt Jr., b. 1925) and his cousin Jerry Wayne Britt (b. 1944) played banjos in the style already described when I visited them, accompanied by Jerry's brother Ira Eugene (b. 1937) on guitar (figure 17.4). J. G., 56 at the time, was a chicken farmer in Star, and Jerry, then 37, and Gene, then 44, were in the timber business in Candor, North Carolina.[22]

Jerry and Gene's father, Ira Britt (1909–65, making him of the same generation as Glenn Davis and Kelly Sears), played banjo, also in the "old country" two-finger style, and his playing also included the use of an index-finger tremolo technique. J. G. learned to play from both his uncle Ira and Price Saunders, and also cited Earl Scruggs as an influence. Obviously, they were aware of bluegrass, but they

Figure 17.4. J. G. Britt, Gene Britt, and Jerry Britt; photo courtesy of author.

all agreed that bluegrass banjo runs notes together too much and does not play the melody as clearly as does the "old country style." Both J. G. and Jerry played guitar before taking up the banjo as teenagers, and both are still excellent guitar players. All the Britts are also excellent singers and have sung for many years in local gospel quartets.

A most interesting aspect of their family tradition is the duets they play in the "old country style," where, instead of one playing lead and the other playing a chordal back-up accompaniment, one banjo plays a real harmony part to the other's lead. J. G. attributed their inspiration for these duets to Don Reno's twin banjo recordings. They tuned their banjos to aDAC♯E, as did Glenn Davis and Price Saunders, whom they knew (they also knew all the musicians I had recorded at Lauchlin Shaw's place). The twin banjo pieces they played for me included "Evening Waltz," "Missouri Waltz,"[23] "Silver Bells," "Roll Out the Barrel," "Under the Double Eagle," "Listen to the Mocking Bird," "San Antonio Rose," and "Down Yonder" (learned from Ira Britt). When I asked if they played the old fiddle tunes, they said they did at times, but not as duets, and that Ira Britt had played all those old tunes. The rest of the pieces they chose to play, mostly songs sung by Gene accompanied by Jerry on banjo and J. G. on guitar, show that the old fiddle tunes are not prominent in their repertory: "John Henry," "I'll Be All Smiles Tonight," "There's a Bluebird Singing," "The Great Speckled Bird," "Go Home," and " What a Day That Will Be." After Gene and his family left, J. G. (guitar) and Jerry (banjo) played a few more tunes, one, "Dear Old Dixie," learned from an Earl Scruggs record, and the rest learned from Ira Britt: "Chinese Breakdown," "Coal Creek" (bass string tuned octave below third string), and "Down Under the Coconut Tree" (ditto).

Another banjo-playing family in the area was more distant from the core "old country style" but was connected to it through the family patriarch. The Morris family, from Ophir, North Carolina, southwest of Asheboro, had at least five generations of banjo pickers, three of which I met with: W. A. "Walt" Morris, the patriarch, born 1898, then 83; his son Claude, born 1929, then 52; and great-grandson Greg Corbett, born 1973, then 8. Grandson Robert also played the banjo, but was not around when I visited. Their playing is related to but not the same as "old country style." They all play with two fingers and a thumb and call themselves bluegrass players, though none plays in a standard bluegrass style.

Walt Morris's father played in a "framming" style, which Walt described as "like Uncle Dave Macon."[24] Walt did not want to learn that style and started out with the newer two-finger "old country style." He said that thirty to forty years earlier there had been many players of what he called "the Glenn Davis" style. To that style, Walt then added the extra finger in late middle age. The result, rather than bluegrass, sounds like the old style with extra notes thrown in because of the extra finger, and much more use of the fifth string. Either his thumb or his index finger may have the melody lead at any point, with the non-lead digits filling in with an arpeggiated chord in what seemed like a somewhat haphazard manner, not the patterned "rolls" of bluegrass. One of the clues that the genesis of Walt's playing traces back to the "old country style" is that, although he occasionally tuned up his bass string to D to be in the standard bluegrass G-tuning (gDGBD), he most often played in the standard classic C-tuning (gCGBD). He put in lots of notes, but the melody was clear and simple. His style was somewhat related to George Pegram's (whom both Walt and Claude knew), but not the same. Walt won the Star Fiddler's Convention banjo contest many times, and played for years, with groups, for dances, something he was still doing in 1981. In this band context, Walt's playing was pretty much limited to backup—just arpeggiated chords. I am sure that there must have been other players in the region who, like Walt Morris, learned the "old country style" and then added the middle finger and approached bluegrass picking. Walt was somewhat ashamed of his playing because it was not exactly bluegrass—but that, of course, is what makes it interesting.

Claude Morris learned to play when he was about 15, first in the two-finger style and later adding another finger, so that his playing is similar to, but less hectic than, his father's. At the time of my visit, he was playing regularly with a bluegrass band.

The style young Greg Corbett was learning from a local music teacher is really George Pegram style, also not bluegrass. Pegram was born, raised, and learned to play the banjo near Oak Ridge, North Carolina, northwest of Greensboro, but lived the final five years of his life in Asheboro; but his three-finger style and the "old country style" Piedmont two-finger picking indigenous to the area are quite different.[25] Pegram's style has been described as "a three-finger movement employing single notes; the melody is picked with the thumb and the drone is alternated between the first and second strings, using the index and the middle fingers."[26]

One more North Carolina player is worth mentioning briefly. Ed Allred, a 68-year-old retired mill worker when I interviewed him in 1981, was from Central Falls, North Carolina, near Asheboro. His first instrument, in his teens, was the guitar that he played in a two-finger style; he talked about black guitar players in the area in the past whose two-finger picking had influenced white guitar players. After several years of playing the guitar, he learned to play the banjo from an uncle. This uncle played with thumb and index finger; therefore, so did Allred at first. Like Walt and Claude Morris, he later added the middle finger to become a three-finger player. His playing does not involve any melody lead; it is strictly an accompaniment style, just arpeggiated and pinched chords with lots of bass runs, which is what ties it to the "old country style."

While the North Carolina Piedmont around Asheboro is the primary locus of the style, a related branch of it extends up into the Virginia Piedmont. Closest in style to the North Carolina players was George Abbitt, a 74-year-old semi-retired judge when I visited him in 1981 in Appomattox, Virginia, who plays fiddle and guitar as well as banjo, and was a member of a local string band, the Appomattox String Band. His thumb and index-finger playing exhibited all the features of the North Carolina "old country style" already noted. He named a number of other deceased Appomattox area banjo players of his vintage who had all played in the same style, including a cousin of his from whom he had learned in his teens. His actual picking technique was more regimented than that of, say, Glenn Davis or Price Saunders. His index finger only picked the first string; his thumb played melody notes on strings four through one, plus the fifth string, although he did not use the fifth string much. He knew lead parts for only a small number of tunes; largely his playing was backup to the fiddle in a band context, out of which he felt uncomfortable. He also had a technique, like Saunders, of a rapid back-and-forth picking with thumb and finger he sometimes used, sounding rather like he was using a flat pick.

The other Virginia players I want to comment on, all from a wide area around Danville, played in a somewhat different but related style. The tradition in this area was a Charlie Poole–style three-finger picking, that is, thumb, index, and middle finger. What this style shares with the "old country style" is the C tuning pitched up to D (though there is some switching to G tuning, pitched to A), playing in many keys out of moveable chord positions up the neck without using a capo, the band context in which the banjo much more often plays backup than melody lead, and a kind of ragtimey feel using syncopated, arpeggiated chords, plucked chords, and bass runs. What is different is the extra picking finger, and therefore the actual pattern of picking, and greater use of the fifth string, though some pieces, depending on the key, still do not make use of it.

This area had produced a number of banjoists contemporaneous with Charlie Poole and who had played in a style much like his, and who also recorded around the time Poole did. Among these were Red Patterson and his Piedmont Log Rollers and Arthur Wells, who recorded with the fiddler Charlie LaPrade and the Blue Ridge Highballers.[27]

Among those banjoists I visited in the Danville area were Herman Owen, then 74, of Halifax, Virginia, northeast of Danville; and Lewis McDaniel, also 74, of Ridgeway, Virginia, west of Danville. Neither of these men played banjo much anymore at the time I visited. Owen's father had played banjo, in the clawhammer style, and fiddle. But when he decided to play the banjo as a boy, he learned to pick rather than frail it because that was the new thing; he had first seen a neighbor doing it. He played with three fingers rather than two, but, in the common "old country style" mode, he mostly played in the aDAC♯E tuning (occasionally raising the bass); did not use a capo; played in a number of different keys using movable chords up the neck; and was most comfortable in a band context where he almost always played backup to the fiddle, using a combination of plucked and arpeggiated chords. He said that he did not normally play lead, and had some difficulty the few times he tried. He did step out of the "old country style" paradigm by making regular use of the fifth string. Owen remembered a black fiddler his father had played with, and a black banjo player in South Boston known as "Bully Woody," but whom he had never heard play.

Lewis McDaniel had been primarily a guitar player, having played guitar and recorded with the Blue Ridge Highballers in the late 1920s and early 1930s, and then with Posey Rorer and the Carolina Buddies, a group that Rorer started after the breakup of the North Carolina Ramblers.[28] He was raised in the mountains, near Rocky Knob in Floyd County, where his father played banjo, in a drop-thumb clawhammer style, and fiddle. He first learned the clawhammer style (and apparently a bit of two-finger picking), but, after the family moved to Danville around 1924, so his father could work in the mills (which McDaniel also did), he learned to play guitar and then learned a new banjo style. His guitar playing got him a job playing with Charlie LaPrade and the Blue Ridge Highballers. The band's banjo player was Arthur Wells, from whom McDaniel learned to pick the banjo with three fingers. He also had played frequently with Charlie Poole. McDaniel's three-finger style, however, is actually thumb and index-finger picking with the middle finger thrown in occasionally, and only in particular situations: when he pinches a chord and when a melody note falls on the first string. He moved away from the "old country style" model by using the fifth string regularly and playing mostly in the gDGBD tuning, although he sometimes lowered the bass string. After playing the banjo for a while, he got out his guitar, and I noted that his guitar and banjo playing styles were very similar thumb and index-finger picking.

A final Virginia banjoist to note is Posie Roach (in his early to mid-seventies in 1981), another contemporary of Charlie Poole, from Axton, Virginia, west of Danville. He had played with many bands in his musical career; in 1981, he was playing with The Four Virginians. I met with and recorded the band at a practice session. Besides Roach on banjo, the other band members, all from Danville, were Richard Bigger, fiddle, and George Gover and James Greer, guitars.[29] Without reciting the list again, I will just state that Roach's playing exhibited all the features of the "old country style," except that he played with three fingers instead of two. His playing sounds very much like Charlie Poole's, with whom he had played a lot and from whom he had learned much. Before I knew this, the band played a Poole classic, "Don't Let Your Deal Go Down." His playing sounded so much like Poole's that I made the faux pas of asking him if he had learned to play it that way from the Poole recording. No, he replied, he had learned it directly from Poole himself.

Two-finger banjo pickers were common in many areas in the early 1900s, but "old country style" two-finger picking, with all the features described here, has been found only in the Piedmont of North Carolina and Virginia. One might ask, why the Piedmont? I do not really have an answer to the "why" question, but portions of this chapter do address the question of "how." Due to the influx of textile mills, the Piedmont was undergoing rapid social and cultural change, bringing it into greater contact with American popular music. One segment of that music Piedmont musicians would have been aware of was classic finger-style banjo, and the origins of "old country style" banjo bear some relationship to that style, especially in its ragtime phase, popular at the beginning of the twentieth century. In that regard, these Piedmont banjoists at that time were participating in the same "big world of the banjo" in which Tony Thomas places Gus Cannon, in his chapter in this volume. The classic finger-style was also performed by one well-known local player, Daner Johnson. Granted, the classic finger-style and Johnson's playing were three-finger picking, but even Kelly Sears, who learned partially from Johnson, converted it to two-finger picking. One must also consider the black contribution to the "old country style" since many of its practitioners first played the guitar and were especially influenced by the two-finger picking of black guitar players, itself likely to have been carried over from two-finger picking of black banjo players. And the "old country style," in its turn, likely contributed to the development of bluegrass, which largely occurred in the North Carolina Piedmont, on its western fringes. As well, it was part of the musical matrix out of which Charlie Poole's style came. In its own right, it was still being played in Piedmont North Carolina and Virginia in the 1980s, and is a lively style worthy of wider knowledge and preservation.

Notes

1. Bob Carlin, *String Bands in the North Carolina Piedmont* (Jefferson, NC: McFarland & Company, 2004), 150.

2. Full name and dates from ibid., 224.

3. Kirk McGee, longtime performer on the Grand Ole Opry, frequently playing with Uncle Dave Macon and/or with Sam McGee, his brother, played banjo in a two-finger style with features similar to the "old country style" described here, even though he was born and raised in Franklin, Tennessee, well west of the Piedmont. Stephen Wade, liner notes, *Banjo Diary: Lessons from Tradition*, Smithsonian Folkways SFW 40208, 2012; and personal email from Stephen, March 19, 2015.

4. Davis may be heard, playing "Blue Ridge Mountain Home" with a band in 1973, on *The North Carolina Banjo Collection*, produced by Bob Carlin, Rounder Records CD 0439/40, 1998.

5. See Carlin, *String Bands*, 66, 125, 139, 165, 224, 225, 226.

6. Patrick Huber mentions the "ragtime-inflected music" of Charlie Poole and the North Carolina Ramblers, stating that it "emerged from a southern cotton mill culture that, already by the time of his birth, was engulfed in swift social and cultural transformation." More specifically, he comments on "Piedmont millhands' increasing contact with American popular music and mass culture during the 1910s and 1920s." *Linthead Stomp: The Creation of Country Music in the Piedmont South* (Chapel Hill: University of North Carolina Press, 2008), 110, 107.

7. Huber points out that the North Carolina Ramblers' repertoire was similarly weighted toward popular music (ibid., 107). Treating the songs-tunes listed here for Glenn Davis and his band as a representative sample of his repertoire, only a couple would qualify as

traditional. Beyond that, dating them by first publication or earliest recording, four are pre-1900 and all but two of the rest date from 1900 to 1940, with one-quarter of the whole list coming from the 1920s.

8. Dates from Carlin, *String Bands*, 148.

9. Ibid.

10. Also cited in ibid.

11. Ibid., 147. As Carlin well knows, three-finger banjo picking technique was not all that new at the turn of the century. It first made its appearance in a banjo tutor in 1865 and became increasingly dominant among professional banjoists (and music-reading banjoists in general) in the later nineteenth century. However, it is true that this technique received a great deal more exposure at the turn of the century via the popular recordings of virtuoso banjoists such as Vess Ossman and Fred Van Eps, and therefore might be considered somewhat "new" at that time.

12. See note 4.

13. Kinney Rorrer, *Rambling Blues: The Life and Songs of Charlie Poole* (Danville, VA: McCain Printing, 1982), 17–18. Carlin (*String Bands*, 147) has shown that Poole and Johnson were distant cousins. To my knowledge, no one has yet found documentary evidence to support either version of the story.

14. Huber reiterates this point (*Linthead Stomp*, 115–16), citing Rorrer, *Rambling Blues*, 17–18.

15. Rorrer, *Rambling Blues*, 17–18.

16. *String Bands*, 147. I did not think to ask Davis about Daner Johnson, but Sears knew Davis well and said that Davis had known and been influenced by Johnson.

17. Huber also comments on the "classic banjo style, which had filtered down from concert stage and phonograph recordings, exerted a particularly strong musical influence on the Carolina Piedmont's banjoists well into the 1920s and beyond" (*Linthead Stomp*, 114).

18. For a photo of this group, see the liner notes to *The North Carolina Banjo Collection* CD.

19. Full name and dates from Carlin, *String Bands*, 220.

20. For further discussion of these bands, see ibid.

21. Dates from ibid., 28.

22. Dates and J. G.'s full name from liner notes, *North Carolina Banjo Collection*.

23. This performance can be heard on *The North Carolina Banjo Collection* CD.

24. This comment is potentially confusing since Macon played in many styles. But one of his main ones was a down-stroking style based on the minstrel stroke style, that is, frailing, for which "framming" was another folk term. I take Morris to mean that his father's down-stroking style was like Macon's down-stroking style.

25. Bob Carlin, liner notes, *George Pegram*, Rounder Records CD 0001 (1995), a reissue of Rounder Records first release in 1971.

26. Robert Black, liner notes, LP *Pickin' and Blowin'; Banjo and Mouth-Harp Songs* (New York: Riverside Records, 1959), Riverside 12–650. Cited in Carlin, *String Bands*, 165.

27. Rorrer, *Rambling Blues*, 39–40; Huber, *Linthead Stomp*, 125–26, 135.

28. Rorrer, *Rambling Blues*, 50–51; Huber, *Linthead Stomp*, 125.

29. Bigger had been a member of the original Four Virginians in the 1920s. Carlin, *String Bands*, 152.

CONTRIBUTORS

GREG C. ADAMS is an archivist (MLS), ethnomusicologist (MA), and musician. For more than twenty years, he has been collaborating with scholars, collectors, musicians, and instrument builders to foreground the banjo's multicultural history. Grounded in critical heritage research and programming, his efforts include fieldwork in West Africa (2006, 2008), developing a work plan for maintaining data about banjo-related material culture through an NEH Digital Humanities Start-Up Grant (2009), and serving as an apprentice to the Malian *n'goni* player Cheick Hamala Diabate through a Maryland State Arts Council Apprenticeship Award (2009–10). In 2014, Adams worked with the banjo scholars Robert B. Winans and Pete Ross as guest curators for the Baltimore Museum of Industry exhibit *Making Music: The Banjo in Baltimore and Beyond.* He currently works in Washington, DC, as assistant archivist with the Smithsonian Center for Folklife and Cultural Heritage. He regularly lectures about banjo history at universities, museums, festivals, camps, and historical sites.

NICK BAMBER was born in Blackpool, United Kingdom, in 1959 and raised in Manchester. He learned to play the five-string banjo as a teenager and modeled his playing on the English Edwardian-era banjoist Olly Oakley. Having studied both chemistry at Oxford University and composition at the Royal Academy of Music, Bamber thereafter divided his time between school teaching and composing. In 1992, he moved to Finland, where he worked as a teacher and translator. In the 2000s, he relocated to Tallinn, Estonia, and began to retrain as a piano technician. His interest in the banjo was revived following the death of his father in 2001. This led to the first of six visits to the Casamance area of Senegal, West Africa, where he made extensive field recordings of folk musicians playing gourd lutes, especially the Jola *akonting (ekonting)*. Bamber now runs a piano business in Brunei, Borneo.

JIM DALTON, a multi-instrumentalist and composer, is a professor of music theory at the Boston Conservatory. He and his wife, the soprano-guitarist Maggi Smith-Dalton, specialize in performing nineteenth- and twentieth-century American music in historically informed style. An active freelancer on banjo, guitar, mandolin, and other plucked string instruments, he is equally at home playing traditional music as he is in performing with symphony orchestras and in theater-opera pits. His compositions are performed throughout the United States, Canada, and Europe. Dalton has presented his research on intonation and microtonality to groups of composers and theorists in the United States and abroad.

GEORGE R. GIBSON is a banjoist, researcher, and instrument collector, who began playing the banjo in the 1950s. Outside his early career as an educator and later work as an insurance executive and business owner, Gibson has dedicated his life to studying banjo history, learning Kentucky-based banjo songs, and becoming a tradition bearer of regional oral histories and traditional music. He attended Caney Junior College (now Alice Lloyd College) and graduated from the University of Kentucky. Gibson first appeared on stage in 1994 as the guest of honor at the Florida Old Time Music Championships and has since performed at festivals in various states. His recordings include *Banjer Days*, a compilation featuring five of his banjo songs, and *Last Possum up the Tree*, which includes twenty-four songs and tales.

CHUCK LEVY is a musician, educator, scholar, and doctor of medicine located in Gainesville, Florida. Levy is a state champion banjoist and fiddler and recording artist. Levy directs the Stephen Foster Old-Time Music Weekend, and has taught banjo and fiddle at the Suwannee Banjo Camp, Banjoseed at the Florida Folk Festival, and other music camps and gatherings. He is the founder and past president of the Florida Banjo Society and a past president of the Florida State Fiddlers Association. In 2007 and 2008, Levy traveled to The Gambia and Southern Senegal to study the *akonting* (*ekonting*). He is also the chief of the Physical Medicine and Rehabilitation Service, the medical director of the VA Center of Innovation on Disability and Rehabilitation Research at the North Florida-South Georgia Veterans Health System, and an adjunct associate professor at the Center for Arts in Medicine, and in the Department of Occupational Therapy at the University of Florida. His current work includes the delivery of creative arts therapy via telehealth directly to veterans in their homes.

SHLOMO PESTCOE was an independent ethno-organologist and banjologist, an acclaimed banjoist and multi-instrumentalist, and a multi-instrument teacher (private). His research interests included the origins, history, development, and globalization of the banjo, as well as the family of eighty known plucked spike lute traditions found throughout West Africa. In 2008, Pestcoe and Greg C. Adams formed Banjo Roots Research Initiatives (BRRI), a scholarly partnership to further the study of the banjo's early history and West African heritage. Pestcoe was the first banjo scholar to present the findings of banjo-focused research to the international organologist community when he was invited to give a paper at the joint meeting of the American Musical Instrument Society (AMIS) and the International Committee of Musical Instrument Museums and Collections (CIMCIM) at the Metropolitan Museum of Art (New York City) in May 2012.

PETE ROSS is a banjo maker, researcher, and musician based in Baltimore, Maryland. His reconstructions of eighteenth- and early nineteenth-century banjos have been featured internationally in museums, art galleries, movies, documentaries, and live performances. In the late 1980s, Ross studied fine art at the School of Visual Arts in New York City and later became an apprentice to the luthier Scott Didlake of Jackson, Mississippi, in the early 1990s. From these experiences, he began his exploration of early banjo history through early images, descriptions, and extant instruments. Ross is one of the earliest contemporary makers of gourd banjos, ranging from those of his own design to exact replicas of historic instruments. In addition to being an accomplished old-time banjo player and a bass player in the punk music scene, he also builds open-back banjos in collaboration with the luthier Kevin Enoch.

TONY THOMAS is an author, scholar, and musician living in West Palm Beach, Florida. His work includes organizing the 2005 Black Banjo Gathering, which launched the current Black Banjo revival. Thomas's published research includes the essay "Why African Americans Put the Banjo Down" in *Hidden in the Mix: The African American Presence in Country Music* (Duke University Press, 2013); the online publication of "The Banjo and African American Musical Culture" with the Oxford African American Studies Center; and contributing to the *African American National Biography*, a joint project of the W. E. B. Du Bois Institute for African and African American Research at Harvard University and Oxford University Press. He both advised and was featured in the PBS documentary *Give Me the Banjo* and the film *The Librarian and the Banjo*. Thomas has presented at black history and banjo history gatherings and has performed at old-time music, folk, and blues festivals across the United States and in Germany, England, and Sweden. Thomas holds a master's of fine art in creative writing from Florida International University, has published literary fiction and poetry, and during the 1960s and 1970s published on issues of black liberation in the socialist press and in journals of African American opinion like *The Black Scholar*.

SASKIA WILLAERT has an MA in musicology from the Katholieke Universiteit Leuven, Belgium, and a PhD in historical musicology and ethnomusicology from King's College London. She was a research assistant at KU Leuven for seven years and is currently curator of the African Collections of the Musical Instrument Museum in Brussels. She has a deep knowledge of African musical instruments and considerable experience mounting exhibitions of them.

ROBERT B. WINANS is a banjo historian, musician, collector, and professor emeritus of American literature and folklore, Gettysburg College. Throughout his academic career at Wayne State University (1970–87) and Gettysburg College (1987–2004), Winans integrated his interest in folklore with more than forty years of studying banjo history, music, and performance, along with related topics. He has published numerous journal articles, book chapters, and encyclopedia entries on banjo history and topics associated with blackface minstrelsy, presented twenty-five papers about the banjo at various academic meetings, and consulted on a variety of documentaries. Winans has performed extensive fieldwork with traditional banjo players (some of it as a Smithsonian Fellow), especially African American banjo players in the late 1970s and early 1980s. As a musician, he has mastered nineteenth-century minstrel-era banjo techniques, old-time clawhammer banjo, and classic finger-style banjo and has performed on three studio recordings, one of which he directed and produced for New World Records, *The Early Minstrel Show* (1985).

INDEX

MUSIC IN AMERICAN LIFE

That Old-Time Rock & Roll: A Chronicle of an Era, 1954–63   *Richard Aquila*
Labor's Troubadour   *Joe Glazer*
American Opera   *Elise K. Kirk*
Don't Get above Your Raisin': Country Music and the Southern Working Class
   Bill C. Malone
John Alden Carpenter: A Chicago Composer   *Howard Pollack*
Heartbeat of the People: Music and Dance of the Northern Pow-wow   *Tara Browner*
My Lord, What a Morning: An Autobiography   *Marian Anderson*
Marian Anderson: A Singer's Journey   *Allan Keiler*
Charles Ives Remembered: An Oral History   *Vivian Perlis*
Henry Cowell, Bohemian   *Michael Hicks*
Rap Music and Street Consciousness   *Cheryl L. Keyes*
Louis Prima   *Garry Boulard*
Marian McPartland's Jazz World: All in Good Time   *Marian McPartland*
Robert Johnson: Lost and Found   *Barry Lee Pearson and Bill McCulloch*
Bound for America: Three British Composers   *Nicholas Temperley*
Lost Sounds: Blacks and the Birth of the Recording Industry, 1890–1919   *Tim Brooks*
Burn, Baby! BURN! The Autobiography of Magnificent Montague
   Magnificent Montague with Bob Baker
Way Up North in Dixie: A Black Family's Claim to the Confederate Anthem
   Howard L. Sacks and Judith Rose Sacks
The Bluegrass Reader   *Edited by Thomas Goldsmith*
Colin McPhee: Composer in Two Worlds   *Carol J. Oja*
Robert Johnson, Mythmaking, and Contemporary American Culture
   Patricia R. Schroeder
Composing a World: Lou Harrison, Musical Wayfarer   *Leta E. Miller
   and Fredric Lieberman*
Fritz Reiner, Maestro and Martinet   *Kenneth Morgan*
That Toddlin' Town: Chicago's White Dance Bands and Orchestras,
   1900–1950   *Charles A. Sengstock Jr.*
Dewey and Elvis: The Life and Times of a Rock 'n' Roll Deejay   *Louis Cantor*
Come Hither to Go Yonder: Playing Bluegrass with Bill Monroe   *Bob Black*
Chicago Blues: Portraits and Stories   *David Whiteis*
The Incredible Band of John Philip Sousa   *Paul E. Bierley*
"Maximum Clarity" and Other Writings on Music   *Ben Johnston,
   edited by Bob Gilmore*
Staging Tradition: John Lair and Sarah Gertrude Knott   *Michael Ann Williams*
Homegrown Music: Discovering Bluegrass   *Stephanie P. Ledgin*
Tales of a Theatrical Guru   *Danny Newman*
The Music of Bill Monroe   *Neil V. Rosenberg and Charles K. Wolfe*
Pressing On: The Roni Stoneman Story   *Roni Stoneman, as told to Ellen Wright*
Together Let Us Sweetly Live   *Jonathan C. David,
   with photographs by Richard Holloway*
Live Fast, Love Hard: The Faron Young Story   *Diane Diekman*
Air Castle of the South: WSM Radio and the Making of Music City
   Craig P. Havighurst
Traveling Home: Sacred Harp Singing and American Pluralism   *Kiri Miller*

Charles Ives's *Concord*: Essays after a Sonata   *Kyle Gann*
Don't Give Your Heart to a Rambler: My Life with Jimmy Martin, the King
    of Bluegrass   *Barbara Martin Stephens*
Libby Larsen: Composing an American Life   *Denise Von Glahn*
George Szell's Reign: Behind the Scenes with the Cleveland Orchestra
    Marcia Hansen Kraus
Just One of the Boys: Female-to-Male Cross-Dressing on the American Variety
    Stage   *Gillian M. Rodger*
Spirituals and the Birth of a Black Entertainment Industry   *Sandra Jean Graham*
Right to the Juke Joint: A Personal History of American Music   *Patrick B. Mullen*
Bluegrass Generation: A Memoir   *Neil V. Rosenberg*
Pioneers of the Blues Revival, Expanded Second Edition   *Steve Cushing*
Banjo Roots and Branches   *Edited by Robert Winans*

The University of Illinois Press
is a founding member of the
Association of American University Presses.

_____

University of Illinois Press
1325 South Oak Street
Champaign, IL 61820-6903
www.press.uillinois.edu

Printed by Printforce, United Kingdom